Holy Things and Profane

Holy Things and Profane

Anglican Parish Churches in Colonial Virginia

Dell Upton

Yale University Press

New Haven and London

First published in 1986 by the Architectural History Foundation
and the Massachusetts Institute of Technology.
Paperback edition published in 1997 by Yale University Press.

Printed in the United States of America.

Library of Congress Cataloging in Publication Number 96–61611
ISBN 0–300–06565–5 (pbk.)

A catalogue record for this book is available from the
British Library.

The paper in this book meets the guidelines for permanence and
durability of the Committee on Production Guidelines for Book
Longevity of the Council on Library Resources.

Contents

Preface *vii*
Abbreviations of Parish Records *x*
Abbreviations Used in the Captions and Notes *xii*
Introduction *xiii*

|I| Power|

Chapter 1   An Established Church *3*
Chapter 2   Building *11*
Chapter 3   Builder and Designer *23*
Chapter 4   Structure *35*
Chapter 5   Churches *47*

|II| Hospitality|

Chapter 6   Holy Things and Profane *101*
Chapter 7   The House of God *163*
Chapter 8   Hearers *175*

|III| Dancing|

Chapter 9   Spaces *199*
Chapter 10   Dancing *219*

|Appendix|

Agreement for Spring Swamp Chapel,
Albemarle Parish, 1747   *233*

Notes *235*
Glossary *261*
Index *265*

Preface

Holy Things and Profane is a study of architecture — of the thirty-seven extant colonial Anglican churches of Virginia and of their vanished neighbors whose existence is recorded in contemporary records, particularly the forty-six vestry books and registers that have survived in whole or in part. My thirty-seven churches differ from the forty-two parish churches in the canonical list included in James Scott Rawlings's *Virginia's Colonial Churches* in that I have omitted six churches — Buck Mountain, Cattail, Grace at Yorktown, Hickory Neck, Hungar's, and Pungoteague — that have been altered too extensively to have anything architectural to offer. (Neither have I considered a forty-third structure, the chapel of the College of William and Mary, which was never a parish church and which was at any rate entirely reconstructed inside the walls during the restoration of Colonial Williamsburg.) I have included one church — the Tillotson Parish church, now Buckingham Baptist church, in Buckingham County — that has never before been published. The surviving buildings and the surviving vestry books are from eastern Virginia, and so my study concentrates on the Anglican church in the Piedmont and Tidewater regions.

Many of the surviving churches received new saints' names during the nineteenth-century revival of the Episcopal church. The best-known example is the alteration of the name of Newport Parish church to St. Luke's church. Although, strictly speaking, these names are anachronisms, in many cases they are the most familiar names of the buildings, and I have felt free to use them where it seemed appropriate.

It has not been possible to be absolutely consistent in dating the churches. My preference has been to give the dates a building was begun and received, or accepted, by the parish as completed. Single-year dates without either of these designations were taken from builders' inscriptions on the churches. Dates designated *ca.* are derived from architectural estimates or indirect documentary evidence.

In quoting from the vestry books, I have not altered the original spelling except to change the thorn (y) to *th* and to drop superscripts. Until 1752, Anglo-Americans clung to the Julian calendar, which used March 25 as its New Year's Day, and wrote dates between the Julian New Year and the Gregorian New Year (January 1) using both years. I have reduced all such dates to the Gregorian year reference, e.g., January 19, 1748/9, becomes January 19, 1749.

In the plan drawings, I have indicated original construction using close hatching for brick and solid walls for wood; pre-Civil War additions are signaled by sparser hatching and hollow walls, respectively. Stippling indicates post-Civil War work, with no attempt to differentiate wooden or masonry construction. Dot-and-dash lines are used for reflected elements (usually galleries) and dashes for missing original features. In the reconstruction drawings, I have shown only those features specifically mentioned in the primary documents.

As this project has grown, I have incurred many pleasant debts to friends, colleagues, and sponsoring institutions. The greatest is to The Henry Francis du Pont Winterthur Museum, which awarded me a National Endowment for the Humanities (NEH) Research Fellowship for 1981–82. It would be difficult to think of a pleasanter or more stimulating place to work. Conversations with members of the Winterthur community, especially Robert L. Alexander, Kenneth L. Ames, and Harriette Hawkins, whose work on South Carolina churches was an early incentive for my own work, stimulated my thinking. The library staff was always helpful; among them, I relied particularly on Neville Thompson's expertise. Not least, the magnificent decorative arts collection enticed me to extend my thinking beyond buildings to their contents. Michael Zuckerman commented on oral presentations on three occasions and gave me an early opportunity to present my ideas to the colonial historians' discussion group he has organized; I am grateful to him in particular and to members of the group as a whole for their suggestions.

Since I left Winterthur, other institutions have helped me along. Case Western Reserve University released me from part of my teaching load for a semester while I was employed there. The University of California at Berkeley, my present home, has been generous with Committee on Research funds, and my chairman in the Department of Architecture, Jean-Pierre Protzen, encouraged me with much-appreciated summer research and mentor-program grants as well. Trips to Virginia to speak at Colonial Williamsburg and at the NEH Summer Institute at the Flowerdew Hundred Foundation helped me to complete my fieldwork.

Every researcher is the object of incidental kindnesses that are difficult to categorize but that speed the project immeasurably. I am particularly grateful for information and assistance supplied by Abbott Lowell Cummings, Margaret T. Peters, Robert F. Trent, and Mark R. Wenger; by photographic librarians Mary Moore Jacoby of the Virginia Museum of Fine Arts, Kathryn McKenney of Winterthur, and Donna Quaresima of Colonial Williamsburg, as well as research librarian Mary Keeling of Colonial Williamsburg; and by E. Holcombe Palmer, secretary-treasurer of the Diocese of Virginia, and J. R. McDowell, assistant to the bishop of the Diocese of Southern Virginia. Orlando Ridout V, Paul Touart, and Johanna Mennucci of the Maryland Historical Trust measured and drew two Maryland churches for me.

Intellectual debts are harder to assess. My oldest and greatest are to my two teachers, James Deetz and Henry Glassie, whom I first encountered when I was still an American Studies graduate student with an amateur interest in old houses, and who showed me that it was possible to understand artifacts in endlessly fascinating ways. With the passage of time, I realize increasingly how much I owe them. While I was working on domestic architecture in Virginia, and after I had turned to the churches, Rhys Isaac helped me through his publications, in several conversations with him in Virginia, and during my Winterthur stay. On several occasions Carl Lounsbury shared his knowledge of Virginia builders with me, and he very kindly vetted the section on courthouses, saving me from several misinterpretations. My colleagues at Berkeley have contributed to my thinking more than they suspect through the example of their own broad and passionate approach to the history of architecture.

My work has been expedited and cheered by the patient assistance of many pastors, members, and administrators of Virginia churches. They include the Reverend Dennis J. J. Schmidt and Colonel B. B. Manchester at Abingdon church; Nancy E. Gates and the Reverend William D. Boyd, Aquia church; Grace McCracken of the Department of Tourism, City of Petersburg, Blandford church; the Reverend Cotesworth P. Lewis, Bruton Parish church; the Reverend Richard Long, Buckingham Baptist church; Louise R. DeNegre, Henrietta Goodwin, and Jane A. Sheeran, Christ church, Lancaster County; the Very Reverend Jere Bunting, Jr., Christ church, Middlesex County; Judy Thompson and Lee Briggs, Falls church; the Reverend Sam Catlin, Fork church; the Reverend Claude S. Turner, Grace Episcopal church; the Reverend William H. Brake, Jr., and the Reverend Christopher T. Hayes III, Little Fork church; Sidney Lee, Mangohick church; Francis A. Garnett, Mattapony Baptist church; George R. Gilliam, Merchant's Hope church; the Reverend Charles Bartholomew, Old Church United Methodist church; the Reverend William L. Russell, Old Donation church; Kenneth M. Hart and Mr. and Mrs. Louis P. Atkinson, Providence Presbyterian church; the Reverend Wayne P. Wright, St. John's church, Chuckatuck, and Glebe church; Beverly F. Gundry, St. John's church, Hampton; the Reverend Charles E. B. Gill, St. John's church, King William County; Mrs. Polly Eustace and Wilson B. Ramsey III, St. John's church, Richmond; Cecil Gwaltney, St. Luke's church; the Reverend Lewis M. Cobb, Peggy C. Pollard, and Thomas H. Forsyth, Jr., St. Mary's White Chapel church; the Reverend Hugh C. White III, St. Paul's church, Norfolk; the Reverend Norman C. Siefferman, St. Paul's church, Stafford County, and Lamb's Creek church; the Reverend E. Allen Coffey and R. Allan Fabritz, St. Peter's church; the Reverend Robert L. Bohannon, Slash Christian church; Warren Grinde, Vauter's church; the Reverend Michael H. Murray, Ware church; the Reverend Marian K. Windel, Westover church; the Reverend Richard R. Baker III, Wicomico Episcopal church; and the Reverend James S. Guy, Yeocomico church.

Many friends and colleagues came along to look, to hold tapes, and to help me see. Cary Carson, Edward

Chappell, Marlene Heck, Martha Hill, Carl Lounsbury, Bob Machin, Fraser Neiman, Jeff O'Dell, Orlando Ridout V, John Vlach, and Camille Wells all made the Virginia climate seem less miserable and the work worthwhile.

Cary Carson, Edward Chappell, and Spiro Kostof kindly read the manuscript, and John Hemphill examined the early chapters. Their comments improved the book substantially.

Karen Kevorkian contributed her professional literary and editorial expertise to honing the manuscript at several stages; and her love and wit, on which I depend, sustained me through the worst bouts of mental and emotional exhaustion created by this project.

The core of a project like this is the fieldwork, which I began at the very end of my residence in Virginia and completed after I had left. This fieldwork has a personal as well as an intellectual significance for me. Over the decade I lived in Virginia I was privileged to collect a group of cherished friends who are inseparable from my idea of what it means to be an architectural historian. Together with them I have learned most of what I know about buildings, and in my discussions with them I have developed many of my ideas. At leisure with them I have been relaxed and entertained. This book is for them. And for my father, Wentney B. Upton, who died the day I completed it.

Abbreviations of Parish Records

Albemarle Reg. *Register of Albemarle Parish, Surry and Sussex Counties, 1739–1778.* Edited by Gertrude R. B. Richards. N.p.: National Society of Colonial Dames of America in the Commonwealth of Virginia, 1958.

Albemarle VB Albemarle Parish, Sussex and Surry Counties, Vestry Book, 1742–1786. 2 vols. MS., Virginia State Library [VSL].

Antrim VB Antrim Parish, Halifax County, Vestry Book, 1752–1818. MS., VSL.

Augusta VB Augusta Parish, Augusta County, Vestry Book, 1747–1787. 2 vols. MS., VSL.

Blisland VB *The Vestry Book of Blisland Parish, New Kent and James City Counties, Virginia, 1721–1786.* Edited by Churchill G. Chamberlayne. Richmond: Library Board, 1935.

Bristol VB Bristol Parish, Prince George and Dinwiddie Counties, Vestry Book, 1720–1789. MS., VSL.

Bristol VB* *The Vestry Book and Register of Bristol Parish, Virginia, 1720–1789.* Edited by Churchill G. Chamberlayne. Richmond: privately printed, 1898.

Bruton Recs. W.A.R. Goodwin. *Historical Sketch of Bruton Church, Williamsburg, Virginia.* Petersburg: Franklin Press, 1903.

Camden VB Camden Parish, Pittsylvania County, Vestry Book, 1767–1785. MS., VSL.

Christ, Lancaster VB Christ Church Parish, Lancaster County, Vestry Book, 1739–1786. MS., VSL. Begins as St. Mary's White Chapel Parish Vestry Book.

Christ, Lancaster VB, 2 Christ Church Parish, Lancaster County, Vestry Book, 1832–1869. MS., VSL.

Christ, Middlesex VB *The Vestry Book of Christ Church Parish, Middlesex County, Virginia, 1663–1767.* Edited by Churchill G. Chamberlayne. Richmond: Old Dominion Press, 1927.

Christ Reg. *The Parish Register of Christ Church, Middlesex County, Va., from 1653 to 1812.* Baltimore: Genealogical Publishing Co., 1964.

Cumberland VB *Cumberland Parish, Lunenburg County, 1746–1816. Vestry Book, 1746–1816.* Edited by Landon C. Bell. Richmond: William Byrd Press, 1930.

Cunningham Recs. Cunningham Chapel Parish, Clarke County. Christ Church Records, 1738–1883, 1910, 1914. MS., VSL.

Dettingen VB Dettingen Parish, Prince William County, Vestry Book, 1745–1785. 2 vols. MS., VSL.

Elizabeth City VB Elizabeth City Parish, Elizabeth City County, Vestry Book, 1751–1784, 1806–1883. MS., VSL.

Elizabeth River VB *Vestry Book of Elizabeth River Parish, 1749–1761.* Edited by Alice Granbery Walter. New York: editor, 1967.

Fairfax VB Fairfax Parish, Christ Church, Alexandria, Vestry Book and Records, 1765–1928. Miscellaneous microfilm reel 137, VSL.

Frederick VB Frederick Parish, Frederick County, Vestry Book, 1764–1780. MS., VSL.

Fredericksville VB *Fredericksville Parish Vestry Book, 1742–1787.* Edited by Rosalie Edith Davis. Manchester, Mo.: Rosalie E. Davis Books, 1978.

Hanover VB Hanover Parish, King George County, Vestry Book, 1779–1796. MS., VSL.

Henrico VB Henrico Parish, Henrico County, Virginia, Vestry Book, 1730–1860. MS., VSL.

Henrico VB* *The Vestry Book of Henrico Parish, Virginia, 1730–1773.* Edited by R. A. Brock. Richmond: St. John's Church, 1904.

Hungar's VB Hungar's Parish, Northampton County, Vestry Book, 1758–1782. MS., VSL.

Kingston VB *The Vestry Book of Kingston Parish, Mathews County, Virginia, 1676–1796.* Edited by Churchill G. Chamberlayne. Richmond: Old Dominion Press, 1929.

King William VB *Vestry Book of King William Parish, Virginia, 1707–1750.* Edited by R. H. Fife. Midlothian: Manakin Episcopal Church, 1966.

Lexington VB Lexington Parish, Amherst County, Vestry Book, 1779–1880. MS., VSL.

Lynnhaven VB *The Colonial Vestry Book of Lynnhaven Parish, Princess Anne County, Virginia, 1723–1786.* Edited by George Carrington Mason. Newport News: editor, 1949.

Newport VB Newport Parish, Isle of Wight County, Virginia, Vestry Book, 1724–1772. MS., VSL.

Petsworth VB *The Vestry Book of Petsworth Parish, Gloucester County, Virginia, 1677–1793.* Edited by Churchill G. Chamberlayne. Richmond: Library Board, 1933.

St. Andrew's VB St. Andrew's Parish, Brunswick County, Vestry Book, 1732–1797. MS., VSL.

St. Anne's, Alb. VB St. Anne's Parish, Albemarle County, Vestry Book, 1772–1785. MS., VSL.

St. Anne's, Essex VB St. Anne's Parish, Essex County, Vestry Book, 1787–1857. MS., VSL.

St. George's, Acc. VB St. George's Parish, Accomack County, Vestry Book, 1763–1786. MS., VSL.

St. George's, Spots. VB St. George's Parish, Spotsylvania County, Vestry Book, 1727–1843. 2 vols. MS., VSL.

St. James VB St. James–Northam Parish, Goochland County, Vestry Book, 1744–1850. MS., VSL.

St. Mark's VB St. Mark's Parish, Culpeper County, Vestry Book, 1730–1843. MS., VSL.

St. Patrick's VB St. Patrick's Parish, Prince Edward County, Vestry Book, 1755–1774. MS., VSL.

St. Paul's VB *The Vestry Book of St. Paul's Parish, Hanover County, Virginia, 1706–1786.* Edited by Churchill G. Chamberlayne. Richmond: Library Board, 1940.

St. Peter's VB *The Vestry Book and Register of St. Peter's Parish, New Kent and James City Counties, Virginia, 1684–1786.* Edited by Churchill G. Chamberlayne. Richmond: Library Board, 1937.

Shelburne VB Shelburne Parish, Loudoun County, Vestry Book, 1771–1805. MS., VSL.

Southam VB Southam Parish, Powhatan County, Vestry Book, 1745–1791. MS., VSL.

Stratton Major VB *The Vestry Book of Stratton Major Parish, King and Queen County, Virginia, 1729–1783.* Edited by Churchill G. Chamberlayne. Richmond: Library Board, 1931.

Suffolk VB Suffolk Parish, Nansemond County, Vestry Book, 1749–1784, 1825–1856. MS., VSL.

Tillotson Recs. 1 Tillotson Parish, Buckingham County, Records, 1771–1796. MS., VSL.

Tillotson Recs. 2 Tillotson Parish, Buckingham County, Records, 1773–1796. Photostat, VSL.

Truro VB *Minutes of the Vestry. Truro Parish, Virginia. 1732–1785.* Lorton: Pohick Church, 1974.

Upper VB *The Vestry Book of the Upper Parish, Nansemond County, Virginia, 1743–1793.* Edited by Wilmer E. Hall. Richmond: Library Board, 1949.

Wicomico VB Wicomico Parish, Northumberland County, Vestry Book, 1703–1795. MS., VSL.

YCM Association for the Preservation of Yeocomico Church in Cople Parish, Westmoreland County, Minutes, 1906–1973. MS., VSL.

Abbreviations Used in the Captions and Notes

Addleshaw and Etchells G.W.O. Addleshaw and Frederick Etchells. *The Architectural Setting of Anglican Worship: An Inquiry into the Arrangements for Public Worship in the Church of England from the Reformation to the Present Day.* London: Faber and Faber, 1948.

Brydon G. MacLaren Brydon. *Virginia's Mother Church, and The Political Conditions Under Which It Grew.* 2 vols. Richmond: Virginia Historical Society, 1947–1951.

Cal. State Pap. *Calendar of Virginia State Papers and Other Manuscripts,* 1, 1652–1781. Edited by William P. Palmer. Richmond: Superintendent of Public Printing, 1875.

Carter Landon Carter, *The Diary of Colonel Landon Carter of Sabine Hall,* 1752–1778. Edited by Jack P. Greene. Charlottesville: University Press of Virginia, 1965.

Fithian Philip Vickers Fithian. *Journal and Letters of Philip Vickers Fithian, A Plantation Tutor of the Old Dominion,* 1773–1774. Edited by Hunter Dickinson Farish. Charlottesville: Dominion Books, 1968.

Hening William Waller Hening, ed. *The Statutes at Large* (1819–23). 10 vols. Reprint. Charlottesville: University Press of Virginia, 1969.

HMPEC *Historical Magazine of the Protestant Episcopal Church*

JSAH *Journal of the Society of Architectural Historians*

Latrobe Benjamin Henry Latrobe. *The Virginia Journals of Benjamin Henry Latrobe,* 1795–1798. Edited by Edward C. Carter III and Angeline Polites. New Haven: Yale University Press for the Maryland Historical Society, 1977.

Mason George Carrington Mason. *Colonial Churches of Tidewater Virginia.* Richmond: Whittet and Shepperson, 1945.

Meade William Meade. *Old Churches, Ministers and Families of Virginia* (1857). 2 vols. Reprint. Baltimore: Genealogical Publishing Co., 1966.

Perry William Stevens Perry, ed., *Historical Collections Relating to the American Colonial Church,* 1, *Virginia* (1870). Reprint. New York: AMS Press, 1970.

Rawlings James Scott Rawlings. *Virginia's Colonial Churches: An Architectural Guide.* Richmond: Dietz Press, 1963.

VG *Virginia Gazette*

VHLC Virginia Historic Landmarks Commission, Richmond

VHS Virginia Historical Society, Richmond

VMHB *Virginia Magazine of History and Biography*

VSL Virginia State Library, Richmond

WMQ *William and Mary Quarterly*

WP *Winterthur Portfolio*

Introduction

Virginia's Anglican churches were central to a lively and powerfully symbolic pre-Revolutionary landscape that altered so rapidly and so thoroughly in the last quarter of the eighteenth century that its meaning was inaccessible even to sympathetic observers in the early republic. One night in 1814, when Virginia militiaman Samuel Mordecai camped with his unit in the ruins of the upper church of Blisland Parish in James City County, he wrote to his sister:

Our first business here was to clear out a corner in this old church, of which the walls and a part of the roof only remain—the floors, doors, windows and all the timber having been put to other uses by the pious parishioners. An inscription over one of the doors informs that this is Blisland parish and that the church was built in 1703. The walls are still very good and the few pieces of timber remaining in them perfectly sound. Two ancient tombstones show where the ancient churchyard was. How many reflections does it excite to consider what a change from its former to its present state and uses—the tombstones serve to cut up our beef on—the church vault resounds with martial musick, loud laughter and some blasphemy. Our first business was to kindle a large fire in the center of the building and then to clear a space of the great heap of rubbish it contained. We picked up loose bricks eno' to pave it and six of us stowed ourselves in a space just large eno' to contain our bodies.[1]

Mordecai's letter went on to place the ruined church in the context of an eastern Virginia landscape that masked significant changes behind superficial similarities. Forty years after the Revolution, many Virginians continued to live in small, widely scattered and poorly constructed one-room houses. Mordecai observed that the country lying between the James and York rivers from New Kent Court House east to the Blisland Parish church was "miserably poor. Here and there a hovel and the inhabitants of them looked half starved." A quarter century earlier, George Washington, traveling south of the James River, had noted that "there is not within view of the whole road I travelled from Petersburgh . . . a single house which has anythg. of an elegant appearance—they are altogether of Wood and chiefly of logs—some indd. have brick chimneys but generally the chimneys are of split sticks filled with dirt

between them." Similarly, some large plantation houses continued to be built and the great mansions of pre-Revolutionary Virginia were still conspicuous and important elements of the Virginia landscape. Yet these apparent continuities masked more important changes. Many parts of eastern Virginia had only recently changed from an agriculture based on tobacco to one in which tobacco was one, but not the most important, of several crops grown commercially. In some localities a reorganization of landholding accompanied this economic transformation. The majority of planters in those counties owned less land in 1810 than they had in 1780. For those few whose holdings remained stable or had been enlarged, the economic prospects were more hopeful, and many of these planters responded to their improved condition by building new houses. In the Blackwater River region between the James River and the North Carolina border, among other places, these new houses comprise the earliest surviving houses available to the present-day observer. Though larger than their owners had been accustomed to, they were much more modest than the colonial grandees' mansions. What stylish houses were being built in 1800 rose in the burgeoning towns that had developed from the new agricultural system.[2]

Just as the private landscape changed in the late eighteenth century, so did the public landscape. Courthouses continued to be central meeting places, though the attractions of court day, that monthly gathering of great and small at the county seat, diminished. The parish church suffered an even greater loss of importance. Many were abandoned and some were ruinous. At best, the late eighteenth-century visitor to a former Anglican church could expect to find a shabby building, sparsely attended, as Benjamin Henry Latrobe did in 1796 when he visited the old church at Jamestown, in the colony's original parish. It was "a plain brick building well fitted with pews, but in bad repair. The congregation consisted of only four Gentlemen, and half a dozen Negroes. The Bishop of this State Dr. Maddison read prayers. We were too few to deserve a

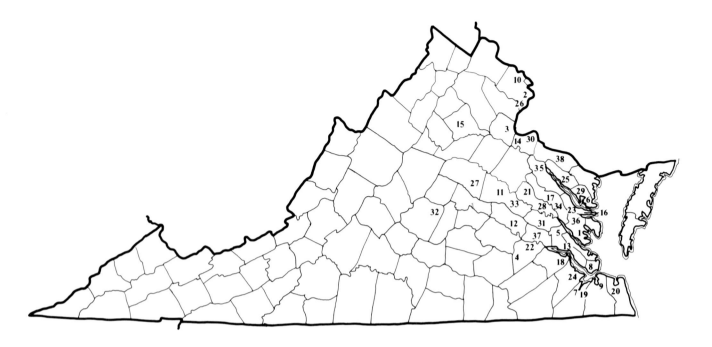

sermon, though Christ had promised to grant his presence to *two* or *three*." [3]

It would be difficult to guess from Mordecai's and Latrobe's accounts, or from the handful of surviving churches (Fig. 1), the importance of the Anglican (now Episcopal) Church just a few years before. As the state Church, it had enjoyed the benefit of official protection and tax support, and in turn it had provided a variety of social and spiritual services. It had also enjoyed a considerable following among white Virginians. The Church's strength and significance were evident in its institutional expansion and ambitious building programs. As new sections of the back country were opened up and as the older settled regions grew and prospered, the Anglican Church extended its dominion and constantly upgraded its properties. At the beginning of the eighteenth century, there were twenty-five counties and fifty parishes in Virginia. In 1774, in Tidewater Virginia alone, there were thirty-four counties and fifty-nine parishes, and in the entire colony there were ninety-five Anglican parishes (Figs. 2, 3). The parishes built and enlarged churches at a brisk rate. Direct documentary evidence (contracts in vestry books and advertisements in

the *Virginia Gazette*) and standing structures account for 166 churches built between 1700 and the Revolution, and for forty-six additions to existing churches (see Tab. 2). This evidence underrepresents the scale of construction. The church historian George MacLaren Brydon estimated that there were 250 churches standing in Virginia in 1776, but many of these were the second, third, or even fourth buildings on their sites. In Spotsylvania and Caroline counties, for instance, a total of at least fifteen churches were built during the colonial era, yet only a handful existed at any one time. [4]

The Revolution marked a change in this flourishing state of affairs. The "difficulty of the times in making of the [tax] Collection" that was noted by the vestry of St. Anne's Parish in Albemarle County made it hard to meet routine expenses and to pay the minister's salary, much less to undertake major building projects. Many churches were abandoned while under construction or were completed much later in a makeshift manner. Building craftsmen were often equally pressed to meet their obligations during the Revolutionary years, and simply absconded from their jobs. The construction of the St. Asaph's Parish church in 1780

Fig. 1. Extant and partly extant churches in Virginia examined in the field and discussed in the text. Familiar or modern names are given in brackets. (Drawing, Dell Upton.)

1. Abingdon Parish church (ca. 1751–55), Gloucester County

2. Alexandria [Christ] church (1767–73; James Wren, designer; James Parsons, undertaker), Fairfax Parish, Alexandria

3. Aquia church (1754–57; Mourning Richards, undertaker), Overwharton Parish, Stafford County

4. Bristol Parish [Blandford] church (1734–37; Col. Thomas Ravenscroft, undertaker; enlarged 1752–70; Col. Richard Bland, undertaker), Petersburg

5. Bruton Parish church (1711–15; James Morris, undertaker; enlarged 1752–54; steeple 1769–70; Benjamin Powell, undertaker), Williamsburg

6. Christ church (ca. 1732–35), Christ Church Parish, Lancaster County

7. Chuckatuck [St. John's] church (1753–55; Moses Allman, undertaker), Suffolk Parish, Suffolk

8. Elizabeth City Parish [St. John's] church (begun 1728; Henry Cary, Jr., undertaker; tower 1761; Charles Cooper, bricklayer; Thomas Craghead, carpenter), Hampton

9. Elizabeth River Parish [St. Paul's] church (1739), Norfolk

10. Falls church (1767–70; James Wren, designer and undertaker), Fairfax Parish, Falls Church

11. Fork church (begun ca. 1737), St. Martin's Parish, Hanover County

12. Henrico Parish [St. John's] church (1739–41; Richard Randolph, Gent., undertaker; enlarged beginning 1773; enlarged 1830–34, 1905), Richmond

13. James City Parish church (ca. 1680; tower ca. 1699), Jamestown, James City County

14. Lamb's Creek church (ca. 1770), Brunswick Parish, King George County

15. Little Fork church (1773–76; William Phillips, undertaker), St. Mark's Parish, Culpeper County

16. Lower chapel (begun 1714; Capt. Henry Armstead and Maj. Edmond Berkley, undertakers), Christ Church Parish, Middlesex County

17. Lower [Mattaponi Baptist] church (ca. 1730–34), St. Stephen's Parish, King and Queen County

18. Lower church (begun ca. 1751), Southwark Parish, Surry County

19. Lower [Glebe] church (ca. 1737; enlarged beginning 1759), Suffolk Parish, Suffolk

20. Lynnhaven Parish [Old Donation] church (1733–34; Peter Malbone, undertaker), Virginia Beach

21. Mangohick [Mangohick Baptist] church (1731), St. Margaret's Parish/St. David's Parish, King William County

22. Merchant's Hope church (ca. 1725), Martin's Brandon Parish, Prince George County

23. Middle [Christ] church (begun 1712; Alexander Graves, bricklayer; John Hipkins, Sr., carpenter), Christ Church Parish, Middlesex County

24. Newport Parish [St. Luke's] church (ca. 1685), Isle of Wight County

25. North Farnham Parish [Farnham] church (begun ca. 1734), Richmond County

26. Pohick church (1769–74; Daniel French, undertaker), Truro Parish, Fairfax County

27. Providence Presbyterian church (ca. 1750), Louisa County

28. St. John's Parish church (ca. 1731–34; enlarged mid-18th century), King William County

29. St. Mary's White Chapel Parish church (1739–41; James Jones, undertaker), Lancaster County

30. St. Paul's Parish church (begun ca. 1766), King George (formerly Stafford) County

31. St. Peter's Parish church (1701–3; Will Hughes, carpenter; Cornelius Hall, bricklayer; tower 1739–40; William Walker, undertaker), New Kent County

32. Tillotson Parish [Buckingham Baptist] church (ca. 1760), Buckingham County

33. Upper [Slash Christian] church (1730–32; Thomas Pinchback and Edward Chambers, Jr., undertakers), St. Paul's Parish, Hanover County

34. Upper [Old Church United Methodist] church (before 1725), Stratton Major Parish, King and Queen County

35. Vauter's church (ca. 1719; enlarged 1731), St. Anne's Parish, Essex County

36. Ware Parish church (mid-18th century), Gloucester County

37. Westover Parish church (ca. 1731), Charles City County

38. Yeocomico church (1706; enlarged second quarter 18th century), Cople Parish, Westmoreland County

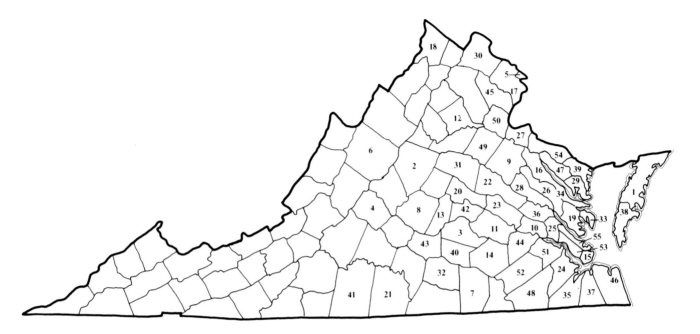

Fɪɢ. 2. Counties mentioned in the text. (Drawing, Dell Upton.)

1. Accomack
2. Albemarle
3. Amelia
4. Amherst
5. Arlington (part of Fairfax County in the 18th century)
6. Augusta (much larger in the 18th century)
7. Brunswick
8. Buckingham
9. Caroline
10. Charles City
11. Chesterfield
12. Culpeper
13. Cumberland
14. Dinwiddie
15. Elizabeth City (now City of Hampton)
16. Essex
17. Fairfax
18. Frederick
19. Gloucester

20. Goochland
21. Halifax
22. Hanover
23. Henrico
24. Isle of Wight
25. James City
26. King and Queen
27. King George
28. King William
29. Lancaster
30. Loudoun
31. Louisa
32. Lunenburg
33. Mathews (part of Gloucester County until 1790)
34. Middlesex
35. Nansemond (now City of Suffolk)
36. New Kent
37. Norfolk (now cities of Norfolk, Portsmouth, and Chesapeake)
38. Northampton

39. Northumberland
40. Nottoway
41. Pittsylvania
42. Powhatan
43. Prince Edward
44. Prince George
45. Prince William
46. Princess Anne (now City of Virginia Beach)
47. Richmond
48. Southampton
49. Spotsylvania
50. Stafford
51. Surry
52. Sussex
53. Warwick (now City of Newport News)
54. Westmoreland
55. York

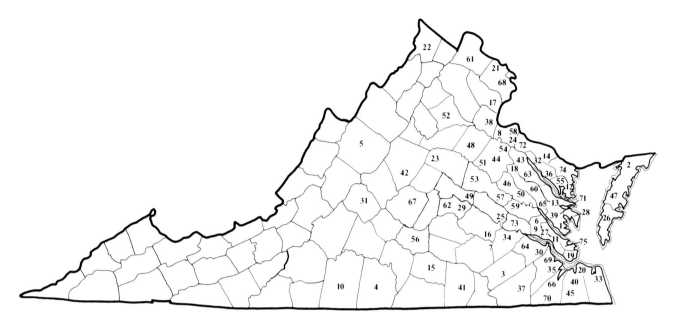

FIG. 3. Eighteenth-century parishes mentioned in the text. Since parish boundaries often shifted in the 18th century and have changed since, only the relative locations of parishes are indicated. Seventeenth-century parishes extinguished early in the colony's history are not included. (Drawing, Dell Upton.)

1. Abingdon, Gloucester County
2. Accomack, Accomack County
3. Albemarle, Sussex County
4. Antrim, Halifax County
5. Augusta, Augusta County
6. Blisland, James City County
7. Bristol, Prince George, and Dinwiddie counties
8. Brunswick, King George County
9. Bruton, James City County
10. Camden, Pittsylvania County
11. Charles, York County
12. Christ Church, Lancaster County
13. Christ Church, Middlesex County
14. Cople, Westmoreland County
15. Cumberland, Lunenburg County
16. Dale, Chesterfield County
17. Dettingen, Prince William County
18. Drysdale, King and Queen County
19. Elizabeth City, Elizabeth City County
20. Elizabeth River, Norfolk County
21. Fairfax, Fairfax County
22. Frederick, Frederick County
23. Fredericksville, Louisa, and Albemarle counties
24. Hanover, King George County
25. Henrico, Henrico County
26. Hungar's, Northampton County

27. James City, James City County
28. Kingston, Gloucester (now Mathews) County
29. King William, Powhatan County
30. Lawnes Creek, Surry County
31. Lexington, Amherst County
32. Lunenburg, Richmond County
33. Lynnhaven, Princess Anne County
34. Martin's Brandon, Prince George County
35. Newport, Isle of Wight County
36. North Farnham, Richmond County
37. Nottoway, Southampton County
38. Overwharton, Stafford County
39. Petsworth, Gloucester County
40. Portsmouth, Norfolk County
41. St. Andrew's, Brunswick County
42. St. Anne's, Albemarle County
43. St. Anne's, Essex County
44. St. Asaph's, Caroline County
45. St. Bride's, Norfolk County
46. St. David's, King William County
47. St. George's, Accomack County
48. St. George's, Spotsylvania County
49. St. James-Northam, Goochland County
50. St. John's, King William County
51. St. Margaret's, Caroline County
52. St. Mark's, Culpeper County

53. St. Martin's, Hanover County
54. St. Mary's, Caroline County
55. St. Mary's White Chapel, Lancaster County
56. St. Patrick's, Prince Edward County
57. St. Paul's, Hanover County
58. St. Paul's, Stafford (now King George) County
59. St. Peter's, New Kent County
60. St. Stephen's, King and Queen County
61. Shelburne, Loudoun County
62. [St. James-] Southam, Powhatan County
63. South Farnham, Essex County
64. Southwark, Surry County
65. Stratton Major, King and Queen County
66. Suffolk, Nansemond County
67. Tillotson, Buckingham County
68. Truro, Fairfax County
69. Upper, Isle of Wight County
70. Upper, Nansemond County
71. Ware, Gloucester County
72. Washington, Westmoreland County
73. Westover, Charles City County
74. Wicomico (officially Lee), Northumberland County
75. York/Yorkhampton, York County

marked the end of a 170-year building tradition in the Old Dominion.

However, the Anglican Church did not disappear from Virginia after the Revolution, as is often supposed. Some congregations, particularly in northern Virginia, managed to continue without interruption. Yet the Church came perilously close to expiring. The organization of an annual convention after the Disestablishment in 1784 and the 1790 appointment as first bishop of Virginia of the diffident James Madison, a cousin of the fourth president of the United States, were efforts to keep the Church going on a voluntary footing. Unfortunately Madison, who was also a professor at, and later president of, the College of William and Mary, was overworked and physically and temperamentally unsuited to his desperate assignment. Many parishes ceased to function during the years of his incumbency, and the annual convention failed to meet after 1805. By the second decade of the nineteenth century, when Samuel Mordecai visited the Blisland Parish church, the social role and many of the buildings of the Anglican parishes had been taken over by the vigorous evangelical congregations that had begun in the last decades before the Revolution to challenge the legitimacy and the mores of the gentry-dominated Anglican Establishment.[5]

As the social role and institutional structure of the Anglican/Episcopal Church had changed in the post-Revolutionary years, so had Virginians' understanding of its character. The evangelical outlook introduced by the colonial dissenters came to dominate early nineteenth-century Virginia. It emphasized emotional, heartfelt religion, ascetic self-discipline, and individual moral responsibility in ways that eighteenth-century Anglicans found repellent. The man most responsible for reviving the fortunes of the Church in the nineteenth century, Bishop William Meade, was an evangelical Christian, though one of a more restrained variety than his Methodist and Baptist colleagues. The first historian of the eighteenth-century Virginia Church, Meade has shaped our own understanding of the colonial institution. Throughout his ministry, he was a tireless collector of information about the Church. His *Old Churches, Ministers and Families of Virginia* was a parish-by-parish account of the Establishment in its heyday, and it included descriptions of the surviving colonial buildings, along with lists of vestrymen and accounts of the great families in each parish. Meade's purpose was to remind mid-nineteenth-century Episcopalians of the critical role that their Church had played in Virginia's history. He wished to hold up to the state's elite their forebears' services to the Church, and to inspire them to make similar efforts. His accounts are full of the names and actions of pre-Revolutionary vestrymen, and even more pointed tales of some post-Revolutionary Virginians' efforts to defend the prerogatives and the property of the Church against legal and popular attacks. In one story, Meade reported of Vauter's church in Essex County that "So soon as Mrs. Muscoe Garnett [of Elmwood, a large Virginia mansion near the church] heard that persons had commenced carrying away the paving-stones of the aisles, and perhaps some of the bricks, she claimed the church as her own, and threatened prosecution to the next offender. The ground on which she placed her claim was that the church stood on her land, or that of her family."[6]

If Meade recalled to Virginians the Church's former glory, he judged its leaders by the standards of the colonial Church's enemies. Meade had little understanding of what the Church meant to its eighteenth-century adherents. He explained the progress of the Baptists and other evangelical groups in the mid-eighteenth-century as a result of the unsuitability of eighteenth-century Anglican churches for proper — evangelical! — forms of worship. His description of the standard arrangement of Virginia parish churches reveals his concern with effective preaching. He emphasized that the

location and form of their pulpits were . . . such as to show that [the ministers] did not care to look at the congregation. The pulpits in the old churches were either on the side of the church, if oblong, or on one of the angles, if cruciform. The aisles were wide, and a cross aisle and door nearly opposite the pulpit, so that only a small portion of the congregation could be seen by the minister. It was also so deep, that unless he were a very tall man his head only could be seen. In the earlier part of my ministry I have often been much at a loss how to elevate myself in many of these old churches which I visited, and have sometimes hurried to church before the congregation assembled, in order to gather up stones, bricks, and pieces of plank to raise a little platform under me, and which was not always very steady. . . . All of these old pulpits have been lowered and their location changed

at his own direction.[7]

Though he offered up the eighteenth-century gentry as models for their descendants, Meade was unable to understand their mores, and his approval was therefore a limited one. Their self-absorbed love of display shocked him. In his description of Rosewell, the largest and one of the most elaborate of the eighteenth-century Virginia mansions, Meade condemned

the great folly of erecting such immense and costly houses . . . , even in monarchical and aristocratic days. . . . It may be said that, as [the builder's] mother was the rich heiress of Timberneck Bay, he had a right to do it, and could afford it, as he was the first-born son and chief heir. We do not admit that any one has a right thus to misspend the talent given to him by God to be used for his glory, and God often punishes such misconduct by sending poverty on the persons thus acting, and on their posterity. A most remarkable exemplification of this appears in the case of Mr. Page, who began to build Rosewell, and which was finished by his widow and son,

who had to sell large portions of the family land to do so. "How much," Meade concluded, "of that now needlessly expended in building and furnishing large houses might be more rationally and charitably devoted to the improvement of the dwellings of the labourers, whether on the plantations of the South or the neighbourhoods of the North!" [8]

Meade's rejection of gentry conduct extended to their relationship to the Church. He condemned vestrymen for accepting compensation for their services to the parish. The attachment of great families to their private pews and galleries was sketched in humorous terms. At Grubhill church in Amelia County, "such was the old family feeling of attachment to [the private galleries] on the part of the descendants of those who built and first occupied them, that even after it became somewhat unsafe to sit in them, being propped up with large poles and in other ways, they could not be induced to abandon them." Meade's principal objection to this absurd assertion of inherited privilege was that it "presented an obstacle for some time to remodeling and improving other parts of the church; and the attachment to the whole building, such as it was, though decaying and very uncomely and uncomfortable, for a long time stood in the way of a new and better one." [9]

The bishop was equally hard on the colonial clergy. He took at face value the complaints about the low quality and occasional moral dereliction of the Establishment's ministers, and set the tone for historians' treatment of the colonial clergy since. For Meade, the pre-Revolutionary era was a dissolute and often shocking period that was salvaged

by the efforts of a handful of dedicated clerics and gentlemen. [10]

Meade was fond of the old buildings for didactic and spiritual reasons. He valued them, as he valued the old gentry, for the lessons they could give to nineteenth-century Virginians. He revered them as consecrated places. But, as with the gentry, his affection was not unreserved. While he saved many colonial churches from destruction, he was ready to alter them to suit his purposes, and to demolish them where they seemed to hinder spiritual progress. Indeed, because he was fundamentally unsympathetic to the Anglicanism of his predecessors, he was unable to understand the buildings that he knew so well, or the people who used them.

The bishop's antebellum evangelical outlook did not allow him to see the parish churches of eighteenth-century Virginia as elements of a specific social landscape. In their context of courthouses, large plantations, small planters' houses, and slave quarters, they were important aspects of a unified, though not monolithic physical structure through which the dominant culture was made tangible. The culture and its landscape were inseparable. Thus, the dissolution of the colonial culture in the late eighteenth century *included*, rather than caused, the disintegration of the landscape, and it occasioned the desecrations that shocked Bishop Meade.

Meade's befuddlement complements that of Samuel Mordecai. The reaction of Mordecai, a young Jew born in Philadelphia a few years after the Revolution and raised in Richmond, a city that hardly existed when the upheaval began, is emblematic of the speed and the extent of the dissolution of the landscape and its social content. Encountering the remains of one of its most conspicuous landmarks, Mordecai was made vaguely uneasy at its current state, but he could formulate his discomfort only in the sentimentalized terms of the nineteenth-century concept of a church. It was purely an abstract notion for him; his attitude toward the ruined building was divorced from all sense of the specific, living culture in which Blisland Parish church had flourished. As a clergyman working for the revival of Episcopal fortunes in antebellum Virginia, Meade subjected the colonial church builders to the same unsympathetic scrutiny. The colonial Church's merit sprang from its ordination as a divine institution; it was worthy in spite of most of its leaders, rather than because of them. In his eyes, churches were instrumental things, useful for their associative value, perhaps usable if they were altered. Neither man could really empathize with the churches' builders and users. For Samuel Mordecai, the first historian of Richmond, and for William Meade, the first historian of Virginia Anglicanism, the eighteenth-century churches were already antiquities.

Though Meade was not an architectural historian, church buildings were an important part of his text, and the interest in colonial Anglicanism that he generated has been expressed repeatedly in the century and a quarter since he wrote in an affection for the surviving buildings. Previous students of the churches — the ministers and laymen and -women in the 1907 *Southern Churchman* volume *Colonial Churches in the Original Colony of Virginia*, George Carrington Mason in the 1930s through the 1950s, and James Scott Rawlings and Vernon Perdue Davis since the 1960s — have written as committed Episcopalians. I have learned from all of them, but my tasks are different.

Buildings for me are powerful artifacts whose effects extend beyond mere aesthetics; I try here to define and to understand those effects. As *Holy Things and Profane* should make clear, the construction and use of churches was an absorbing activity for colonial Virginians. The planning of churches might take half a year, or longer if there was a dispute over the size and location of a new building. Specifications were carefully drawn up, then altered piece by piece. A new church was meticulously examined before its vestry accepted it from the builder. The act of construction of these largest and most numerous of Virginia public buildings was thus a major event in the life of a parish. Once completed, the church became the scene of weekly gatherings, the most frequent public events in Virginians' lives. Most reports of eighteenth-century Virginia suggest that churchgoing was widespread. Churches were filled on Sundays, and in a colony where population was dispersed and transportation primitive, where parishes might extend for thirty or forty miles, about half of the adult whites attended the state Church. What attracted them to the churches? Some sense of piety and perhaps of legal duty may have helped, but by all reports the parish churches of colonial Virginia were rarely edifying places. The daily morning and evening services enjoined by Church law had been reduced by the eighteenth century to a single Sunday morning service. The service itself, so carefully thought out in the sixteenth and seventeenth centuries and ordered by the rubrics to be performed in its

entirety, was routinely cut to its bare bones. Most accounts suggest that even the read portion was presented in a perfunctory way.[11]

Traditionally in the Church of England, the repetitiousness of the prayer-book service was relieved by the sermon. Anglican clergy were required to present sermons only a few times a year, but capable preachers held forth regularly and attracted crowds. In Virginia, sermons varied in quality. St. Peter's Parish asked its church wardens and vestry to inform the Reverend Mr. [Alexander] Forbess that they were unwilling to have him preach again, "his Voice being so Low that the [   ] people cannot Edifie." Landon Carter, the diarist and master of Sabine Hall, as was his wont, tended to dwell on the bad ones, noting of the Reverend Mathews of St. Anne's Parish, Essex County, that "he drawls his words so; but in this the Clerk imitated him, and is so distinguishable for it in his Psalmody, that all time with him was common." Yet Carter concluded that while he had heard better preachers, he had heard many who were worse. The low-key style that Carter alluded to was a legacy from the late seventeenth-century Latitudinarian preachers. Its presence can be detected as the antithesis of the "new and striking Manner" in which William Dunlap delivered a marriage sermon "in his usual Animated Manner," and in the pejorative comments of evangelically minded observers. For the New Jersey Presbyterian Philip Fithian, a Virginia Anglican sermon was a "cool, spiritless harangue," most striking for its brevity. David Mossom, a Cambridge University alumnus, served St. Peter's Parish for forty years, and when he died in 1767 his monument in the parish church noted that "he was second to few in letters." Though by the eighteenth century the Latitudinarians' learned discourse had been downgraded to what Horton Davies has called an essay, the controlled preaching style of men like Mossom entailed the reading of a text from the pulpit. According to the Methodist preacher Devereux Jarratt, who grew up in Mossom's parish, the cleric was "very unapt to teach or even to gain the attention of an audience. Being very near-sighted, and preaching wholly by a written copy, he kept his eyes continually fixed on the paper, and so near, that what he said seemed rather addrest to the cushion than to the congregation. Except at a time, when he might have a quarrel with any body — then he would straiten up, and speak lustily, that all might distinctly hear." Yet Jarratt admitted that "a great many people" attended Mossom's church.[12]

I will argue that while pious impulses and a desire for religious edification moved many Virginians to attend church, these are not sufficient to explain churchgoing in the colony, for the churches were inseparable from the secular life of the parish community. Holy things *and* profane, fused in an eloquent manner, animated the Church and gathered the parishioners, in a process in which the church building and its contents were catalysts. The construction and use of the church were symbolic acts. To build a church was to build the world — not a model of the world or an image of it. The church was one way for eighteenth-century Virginians to explore and ultimately to describe their environment. It provided a meaningful context within which to comprehend and digest change.

One aim of *Holy Things and Profane*, then, is to understand what the colonial Anglican churches meant to their builders and users. The task must begin with a description of the mundane processes of planning and constructing the building, move on to consider its physical appearance, and conclude with a consideration of the less tangible meanings that the church acquired in the social and architectural context of colonial Virginia. A complementary aim of the book is methodological: to ask how we might understand artifacts — buildings and their contexts — in ways that do justice to as many aspects of these artifacts as possible.

This is a study of a specific group of churches and furnishings. The traditions for the study of buildings and artifacts in pre-Revolutionary America are very old and fairly narrow ones. In his *Domestic Architecture of the American Colonies and of the Early Republic* of 1922, Fiske Kimball compared eighteenth-century American houses with English architectural books, and concluded that the history of early American domestic architecture was one of growth from traditional to aesthetically advanced forms guided by published treatises. This form of source search and the assumptions behind it have dominated the study of colonial American architectural history since. Thomas Tileston Waterman carried the premise a step further in his *The Mansions of Virginia, 1706-1776*, first published in 1944. Waterman looked for specific English buildings that might be identified as sources for Virginia's great eighteenth-century mansions. As a result, he gave his attention only to those Virginia houses that followed English precedents relatively closely, and relegated those with unusual or unidentifiable plans to his appendix. Waterman's premise

was that Virginians were led to aesthetic maturity by English-trained individuals as much as by published sources. Historians of the arts have always assumed a closer connection with English ideas in Virginia than in the other colonies. Hence in recent years, furniture scholars have begun to argue for the similarities between Virginian and English furniture along the lines established by Kimball and Waterman for architecture half a century ago.[13]

It may be that working methods govern one's approach to these questions. Kimball was an art historian who surveyed the sweep of colonial domestic architecture by means of photographs, the use of libraries, and brief visits to sites. The presentation of his material confirms this: there are few plans or measured drawings. Those he did use were derived from other publications. Waterman worked for the Colonial Williamsburg restoration in the early days. That prodigious effort was based on copious and very intensive fieldwork, but anyone who reads the museum's early publications or who looks at the lovingly drawn and meticulous field notes left by the early Williamsburg architects will immediately see that their eye was for surface detail and visual accuracy — for the building's skin. This is as it should have been, given the task these architects were assigned — of restoring the eighteenth-century appearance of Williamsburg. For them the buildings were art objects, and they wanted to find in Virginia's eighteenth-century buildings the qualities of order and reason they admired.

My way of working is different by necessity and by training. It is possible from the surviving physical and documentary evidence to depict a fairly complete physical image of Virginia's parish churches and their furnishings. There are written descriptions of every element of the buildings and fittings, and actual examples survive of everything except textiles and Royal Arms. But the picture must be pieced together. Even the most apparently complete of the churches — Christ church in Lancaster County — lacks vestry books, textiles, Bible and prayer books, chest, Royal Arms, and several other incidental items that commonly furnished colonial churches. Consequently the extended description of outstanding individual examples has not been an appropriate method to follow in discussing the Virginia churches. Simply to collect the information has required the detailed physical examination of individual structures, drawing what was there, searching in attics and crawl spaces for clues to what was missing, in a manner not so different from the Colonial Williamsburg approach. This has been supplemented with the juxtaposition of visual and documentary evidence that Fiske Kimball did so well, particularly in his chapter on the seventeenth century.

At the same time, many years of working with vernacular architecture has shown me that the surface appearance is often the least informative part of a building; its plan, structure, and method of construction are more useful. Moreover, I have been taught by my teachers that buildings are really only as interesting as the people who made them and used them, and I have been taught by my times to distrust explanations that credit single authorities for accomplishments that many people carried out. For these reasons, I am unable to grant as much importance to outside sources of architectural ideas as my predecessors did. When I examine a church, I cannot believe that the parts of it that are common, that are Virginian, are merely lapses in the builders' attempt to reproduce European forms. They are as noteworthy as that which is English and fashionable. I assume the users' alterations to the church are as significant as the builders' intentions. The Anglican church is not just Wren and the Renaissance, it is *The Builder's Dictionary*, and the Reformation, and the gentry, and slave and indentured labor, and the taxation system. It is the vestries, and the builders, and the parishioners, and Virginia and England.

I wish, then, to avoid the narrowness that most architectural historians have brought to their studies of colonial buildings. If we compare Virginia churches to Wren's churches, we can only be disappointed — not because those in Virginia are worse, but because the standard of comparison comes from a different context. If Virginia churches are our standard, then Wren's churches must seem equally wanting.

At the same time, I do not want to fall into the trap that has caught many historians of vernacular architecture. Having limited the importance of the search for external design sources, I would not deny that Virginia's church builders knew about such "high-style" architecture or were affected by it. Too often vernacular building has been treated as a phenomenon isolated from outside ideas. Vernacular builders have been portrayed as members of self-contained, even idyllic, communities uncontaminated by corrupt stylish design. Revolutionary-era Virginians would have found this an appealing image, but it does not apply to them. Neither do I impute any superior wisdom to Virginia church builders. My intention is simply to see them as people living in a particular place at a particular time, striving to construct a physical world with all the means at their disposal. By starting from the local context and working out, rather than beginning outside the local and working in, or beginning with the local and staying there, I think that it is possible to eliminate the artificial distinctions that scholars have created between vernacular and high-style design. More important, I believe that it is possible to treat these or any other objects on their own terms, without either denigrating them or creating a special category to defend them from comparison with the canonical monuments of architectural history.

Like Bishop Meade, I find it hard as a twentieth-century person not to disapprove of eighteenth-century Virginia's gentry. They were a proud and unlovely people. On the whole, they made life miserable for most of their neighbors, white as well as black. But I hope that I have described them fairly, and that I offer some insights into a material world that remains for me fascinating and exciting after more than a decade of study.

| I | Power |

1 | An Established Church |

Zachariah Sneed, a young married man, was not wealthy, but he was getting by. The year's tobacco crop had just been harvested. Using his own and his wife, Rebecca's, labor and that of their slave, they were able to produce thirty-five hundred pounds of tobacco. So on an October Sunday in 1725, the Sneeds set off in good cheer, walking to the parish church five miles away. Their route took them across the glebe farm, and they admired the handsome new house the parish had just built to encourage its minister to stay. The glebe house rooms were spacious—the Sneeds' only room would fit easily inside the smaller of the minister's two main rooms. The parson had a cellar, a finished attic, a freestanding kitchen (itself as big as the Sneeds' house), a smokehouse, a milkhouse, and a slave house besides. The glebe house's glazed bricks looked beautiful in the sun, and they kept the parson's family a lot warmer in the winter than the Sneeds' flimsy wooden house with its wooden chimney and dirt floor. The new glebe cost the parish fifty thousand pounds of tobacco, and the parish tax increase that paid for it pinched the Sneeds' small budget the last couple of years.

As Zachariah and Rebecca approached the church, they came out of the fields onto a broad road lined with cedar trees that connected the church with the house of James James, the county's richest man. His duties as a member of the royal council seemed to take up a lot of his time these days: he had missed several meetings of the county court, even though he was the head magistrate, and he hardly ever came to the vestry meetings anymore, but there he was, surrounded by the other justices, in the churchyard.

It was still early, and the Sneeds had time to catch up with friends' doings. The work of a tobacco plantation was a lonely one; the Sneeds saw no one but immediate neighbors during the week, so Sunday presented a welcome chance to catch up on events throughout this end of the county. Some of their friends sat on benches under the trees, some drank from the churchyard well, others leaned against the little house where the vestry met. It was a small, square

wooden building with a wooden chimney, not too different in appearance from the church itself, except much smaller. The church, like most in Virginia, was a rectangular wooden building, set with its gables east-west. The walls and roof had a drab appearance created by their protective coating of tar and relieved only by the white paint on the doors and trim. There was a door in the west end, and one in the south side near the east end for the minister and the people who sat in the prestigious seats at that end of the building.

The parish clerk called—it was time for the service. The Sneeds did not have far to go. Ordinary folks like them found seats on the public benches just inside the west door, with the men on one side of the aisle and the women on the other, for the parish separated the sexes in the old way.

At the far end of the church, surrounded by a low rail, was a velvet-draped table that served as an altar. On either side of it were two great pews, enclosed, like the others in the church, with paneling. On the left sat the family of James James. On the right sat the county justices. The pew was empty since the magistrates were still outside talking and laughing. Scattered through the other large pews near the east were a handful of women and children, but all the front pews on the men's side were vacant. Suddenly there was a commotion—Crazy Jacob had tried to sit in the vestry's pew again! Every year the vestry gave him an allowance from the parish treasury to live on, and he thought of them as his friends. However, the church warden dragged him out of the pew and shoved him toward the benches at the back. Many people laughed, but some called to the warden not to be so rough.

A little more than halfway down the church, at the lowest desk in the towering pulpit, sat the lay reader, a great leather-bound prayer book on the ledge before him. A couple of feet above, at the middle desk, sat the minister. He had another big prayer book, and a large Bible bound in matching leather. The cleric wore his ordinary coat and minister's bands. It had always been a matter of annoyance to him that the parish provided no surplice, but the vestrymen were afraid the robe would offend those members of the congregation who retained the ancestral suspicion of "popery" in the Anglican Church.

The minister began to read a passage from his prayer book. Then came a responsive reading. Only the few people who owned prayer books joined in; otherwise it was a vocal duet between the two desks. The minister moved from the desk to the altar rail, and knelt to recite a prayer he had memorized from the book. As he returned to the desk, the reader called out the number of a psalm and led the congregation in singing it in unison. A few moments later, the minister climbed to the pulpit, under the great canopy, to deliver his sermon. While the reader went out to summon the gentlemen, the clergyman took from his pocket a sheaf of papers and laid them on the velvet cushion in front of him. When the gentlemen had found their pews, he began reading in a quiet, uninflected voice, sometimes losing his place. It was hard to hear from the back, and Sneed's mind wandered. He stared at the vestrymen and wondered whether it was really true, as his neighbor said, that they planned to let a contract for a big new church when they met the next week. Sneed could not see anything wrong with this one, and a new church would mean three more years of doubled taxes to pay for it! He might be hired to carry the timbers on his ox cart, at least.

Above the vestrymen Sneed could see the tablets of the altarpiece. He could not read them, but he knew the Ten Commandments were up there—his father had told him all churches had them. The gold letters were handsome against the black, and Marmaduke Hornsbee had done a fine job painting them and the king's coat of arms that hung above them. Over the parishioners rose a great arched ceiling, painted blue with clouds on the cornice. Sneed's eye fell on the parish chest—his uncle had made it fifty years before— and it reminded him of his and Rebecca's child. She had died last winter, and the parish clerk had written down the date on the register book inside it. The bench on which Sneed sat was hard, and he wondered whether he would ever be accounted important enough for his family to be given seats in the pews.

Suddenly Sneed realized the benediction was being read. Was it true that the Calvinists in New England spent all day in church? This was bad enough, but at least on Sundays Virginians had time to talk, and time to rest at home as well. Before Zachariah and Rebecca Sneed had spoken to everyone they wanted to see, the church warden was bolting the doors, and the vestrymen had ridden off with the councillor to dinner. The Sneeds struck out for home.

Our imaginary Virginians of 1725 shared an experience that was familiar to most of their white neighbors. English and Virginian lawmakers accepted the traditional belief that the state's security depended on this Sunday ceremony, but Virginia circumstances transformed the occasion into an essential ritual of local social bonding that transcended legislation and theology. Nevertheless, the laws of Church and state helped shape customary practices. The roles of local parish leaders were defined by law, and the lack of a strong, legally established hierarchy left them free to operate nearly unimpeded by outsiders. Laws established the liturgy, and laws specified the architectural setting and the liturgical implements that each parish must provide. It is thus appropriate to begin to understand the Anglican parish church through its legal underpinnings.

Three days after landing at the mouth of the Chesapeake Bay, on April 26, 1607, the Virginia Company's settlers set up a cross and named the site Cape Henry. Two weeks later, on May 13, they arrived at the swampy near-island their scouts had selected as the site of a settlement. In his memoirs, the adventurer Captain John Smith, one of the English contingent, wrote, "I well remember wee did hang an awning (which is an old saile) to three or foure trees to shadow us from the Sunne, our walles were rales of wood, our seats unhewed trees till we cut plankes, our Pulpit a bar of wood nailed to two neighbouring trees. In foule weather we shifted into an old rotten tent; for we had few better. . . . This was our Church, till we built a homely thing like a barne." Whether or not it was literally true, Smith's story was meant to be read as a parable of the establishment of civility in the New World. The tale is apparently about hardship, but is really about success in the use of a few European artifacts to bend the raw natural elements of Virginia to the purposes of the English god.[1]

No one doubted the necessity of religious observance to this effort, or that religious worship should be enforced by law in Virginia. A civil society—an ordered, disciplined society defined by political authority, a legal code, and a moral one — required a Church, and settlement strategies always provided for powerful religious authority. The colony's first code of laws, published in England in 1612, began by acknowledging "our highest and supreme duty . . . to him . . . from whom all power and authority is derived," and established severe corporal and capital penalties for challenges to sacred and temporal authority.[2]

Virginia's first rulers believed as strongly in the power of the physical environment to promote or thwart the sociopolitical intentions of the colonizers. Well-built towns would be the instruments for establishing civility in the New World, and a church was an essential element of a properly ordered town. In 1609, the Virginia Company Council ordered the establishment of three urban settlements at Henrico, Charles City, and James City, and instructed that "in every one of these there must be builte a Church." This utilitarian view of the environment soon took on a symbolic character. Not only did the proper kind of landscape conduce to the establishment of civil society, but a civil society manifested itself in part in the creation of a civil landscape. If the colonizers did their work right, the landscape would be transformed by and infused with the spirit of Christian civilization. Early accounts of Virginia, written to offer false assurance to backers of the colony at home, described the success of the enterprise in terms of its appearance. Sturdy churches were a standard part of the tale. The best-known account is Ralph Hamor's description of Henrico, with its rows of wood and brick houses, its walls and fortifications, and its brick church, fifty by one hundred feet, larger than any church subsequently built in Virginia before the American Revolution.[3]

Though Hamor ultimately confessed that his description had been a fraud, it reflected an assumption, never given up by colonial Virginia Anglicans, that a flourishing state Church was a necessity, and that a state Church required an appropriate physical setting. In 1624, the colony's fledgling General Assembly ordered "That there shall be in every plantation, where the people use to meete for the worship of God, a house or roome sequestered for that purpose and not to be for any temporal use whatsoever, and a place empaled in, sequestered only to the buryal of the dead." Eight years later, the legislature made its requirements more specific. It decreed religious uniformity throughout the colony, adherence "both in substance and circumstance" to the constitution and canons of the Church

of England "as neere as may bee"; established the office of church warden; required communion to be held at least three times yearly; and instituted a one-shilling fine for unexcused absences from church. Part XVII of the act ordered that "in all such places where any churches are wantinge, or decayed, the inhabitants shall be tyed to contribute towards the buildinge of a church, or repayringe any decayed church."[4]

The Church of England was the established Church in Virginia from the beginning of settlement, but it took a half century of legislation and practice for the particular character of the Virginia Establishment to be defined. However, by the 1660s, the date of the earliest surviving parish records in Virginia, the Virginia Church had taken the form that it would retain, with few changes, until the American Revolution.[5]

The Church in Virginia had a peculiar relation to the Church in England. Virginia was not part of any English diocese, but it was not a diocese itself. There was no bishop in Virginia (or indeed anywhere in the American colonies) until after the Revolution. The Virginia Church was loosely under the jurisdiction of the bishop of London, and it was to him that Virginians might turn for guidance when serious disputes arose. Yet many of the regulatory functions normally exercised by ecclesiastical officials in England were taken over by political entities in Virginia. As a result, the affairs of the Church were often more directly tied to day-to-day politics than they were in England. Early on, the governor of the colony assumed many of the duties of the bishop's ordinary, or executive, and it was to the governor rather than to the bishop that disputes in local parishes were normally carried. In addition, governors held the power to examine the letters of ordination of incoming clergy; to induct, or grant security of employment to, those clergy recommended by their parishes (although the aversion of parishes to induction was a continuing source of controversy); to issue marriage licenses in lieu of the publication of banns; and to probate wills. In the eighteenth century, governors also claimed the right to assign clergy to parishes where the vestry had failed to exercise their right of choice within a reasonable amount of time. The latter power expanded and contracted with the influence of individual governors. Thus, while the vestrymen could theoretically choose any qualified person they wished, some governors thought that when there was a choice among candidates, their own opinions should determine the matter. In 1756, the vestry of Elizabeth City Parish were considering two candidates and chose a Mr. Selden, who had approached them directly. Lieutenant Governor Robert Dinwiddie and Thomas Dawson, the Anglican commissary, sent them a curt letter, noting that "we are very sorry to find you pay so little Regard to the Power of the Crown and the Right of the Bishop [of London, through his representative Dawson], as not to receive Mr Warrington for your Minister especially as the Votes in the Vestry were equal. How different was the Conduct of Your Vestry in the Year 1731 who readily upon Governour Gooch's letter Rec'd the Revd. Mr Fyfe tho' a majority of them had declared for the Revd. Mr Smith. And the Vestry of York in the case of Mr Camm applied to Governour Gooch for his Letter of Collation, or leave to remove, before they received him from Warwick Parish." At its subsequent meeting, "this Present Vestry were Unanimous" in acceding to Dinwiddie's and Dawson's demands.[6]

The governor might act through his royal Council as well, or the Council might intervene on its own. As the highest court of the colony, for example, the Council acted in the absence of a governor and prosecuted the vestry of Charles Parish in 1709 for disturbing the worship service.[7]

The General Assembly, the colonial legislature, established parish boundaries; enacted laws paralleling the canon laws of the Church of England, including those governing the liturgy and physical accouterments of churches; passed occasional special acts at the request of individual parishes; and sometimes dissolved vestries when there seemed to be cause to do so. The legislators dissolved the vestry of Frederick Parish in 1752 for converting to its members' own use funds levied for the construction of a church, and it removed from office the vestry of Cople Parish in 1755 as a result, in Landon Carter's opinion, of the spiteful machinations of the enemies of Thomas Lee, a former vestryman.[8]

In the counties, the county courts prosecuted offenders against the moral law when they were "presented" by the church wardens, and the county clerk compiled the annual list of "tithables," or taxable parishioners, on which the parish levies were based. Often the county sheriff served as parish tax collector. The sheriff was chosen from among the commissioners, or justices, who comprised the county court;

the commissioners were often members of the parish vestry as well. In one late seventeenth-century dispute in Christ Church Parish, Middlesex County, Matthew Kemp acted in separate, occasionally conflicting, roles as vestryman, church warden, county commissioner, and county sheriff.

Although many agencies of colonial government had a role in church polity, it was the parish vestry who had the most responsibility for the operation of the Church in Virginia. The established Church in the colony lacked a bishop, a cathedral, or Church courts, and only after the late seventeenth century had a relatively weak central official in the person of the commissary, the bishop of London's personal agent in Virginia. For all practical purposes, then, this episcopal Church in Virginia was really congregational, or more properly parochial. Activities centered in the parish, the affairs of which were conducted by the vestry. The vestry in an English parish had originally been a meeting of the entire male populace. Over the centuries it had coalesced to an informal group of parish leaders. In the first half century of Virginia settlement, this customary practice was regularized and incorporated in the colony's laws. The *Lawes Divine, Morall and Martiall*, the 1612 legal code of Virginia, had provided that "Every Minister where he is resident . . . shall chuse unto him, foure of the most religious and better disposed [residents] as well to informe of the abuses and neglects of the people in their duties, and service to God, as also to the due reparation, and keeping of the Church handsome, and fitted with all reverent observances thereunto belonging." These advisors combined some of the traditional duties of vestries with the moral policing responsibilities church wardens customarily exercised. In the 1632 act of uniformity that ordered the building of churches, their construction and maintenance were to be attended to by the county "commissioners together with the mynisters, church wardens and cheife [inhabitants] of the parish." This passage effectively described the composition of English vestries, but it was not until the mid-1630s that the English name was used in Virginia, and not until 1643 that each parish was ordered to choose a vestry consisting of "the most sufficient and selected men," acting together with the minister and the church wardens. Two years later, the method of selection was specified as election by "the major part of the parishioners." By the end of the century, the vestry was firmly established as a group of twelve men plus the minister. The independence of action that characterized the vestries was secured in 1662, when the legislature granted them the right of cooptation, or choosing their own new members, after an initial election at the time the parish was established. Henceforth vestrymen served for life, or until they resigned or were legally removed from office. Despite sporadic attempts to institute regular elections, the vestrymen continued to enjoy the right of cooptation as long as the Establishment survived.[9]

Vestries conducted all the business of the parish. Not only did they plan and supervise the construction of churches, but they selected ministers, oversaw the relief of the parish poor, paid the minister's salary, built and maintained his glebe farm, and, through their church wardens, policed morals and church attendance. The vestry assigned seats in church. Every four years, in obedience to an order of the county court, they organized the "processioning" of the parish, a ritual viewing and renewal of the property lines in the parish. The results were normally recorded in their record book.[10]

Vestrymen met the parish expenses by an annual "levy," or parish tax. Every male Virginian over sixteen years of age and every female slave over sixteen was a tithable, and was assessed an equal share of the tax burden. Thus, while a large slaveowner had a larger tax burden than a small planter through the sheer weight of numbers, the tax was a head tax and did not reflect landholdings or other measures of relative wealth in its distribution of the parish tax burden. Almost all parishes levied their taxes in tobacco until the time of the Revolution, and so most vestries met once a year, usually in October when the tobacco harvest was in. (A few also had a spring meeting.) At their fall meeting, the vestry made decisions about major building and repair projects, selected clerks (lay readers) for each of the churches in the parish, heard applications for poor relief, and reimbursed the church wardens for any out-of-pocket expenditures that they had made during the previous year. The vestry then totaled the debts and anticipated expenses and divided the total by the number of tithables to determine the year's levy. In the mid-seventeenth century the annual levy had been fixed by law at ten pounds of tobacco per poll, but this was quickly amended to allow the vestries "to augment the aforesaid rate of tenne pounds of tobo per poll to such competency as they in their discretion shall think fitt." [11]

Day-to-day business of the parish was carried out by the church wardens. As an ancient office in the Church of England, the position of church warden had been established in Virginia even before the vestries, but after the latter were instituted the warden became their servant. By canon law, church wardens were to be elected every year, but some parishes found it expedient to retain their church wardens for several years at a time. In other parishes, the office rotated annually on a regular schedule. The definition of the church warden's duties changed little during the colonial era. On the eve of the Revolution they were summarized from the Virginia statutes by the methodical Robert Carter of Nomini Hall for his own use. Carter's manuscript "Rules for the Conduct of churchwardens" lists the warden's tasks as collecting the minister's salary; making formal legal complaint against all who swear, are drunk, "deny a God, Trinity or monotheism," or who are willfully absent from church; regulating processioning; certifying the levy payment and the accuracy of the list of tithables; ridding the parish of beggars and other nonresident poor people; and overseeing parish relief. Church wardens were to see that the church was provided with the necessary "ornaments" or fittings, to undertake minor repairs where necessary, and to oversee such major repairs as the vestry ordered. Because the church warden's job, though a demanding one, offered such an intimate view of parish life, new vestrymen were often made church wardens on the day that they were sworn in.[12]

In addition to the vestrymen and clergy, each parish had a parish clerk who recorded the vestry minutes and readers, also called clerks, in each church and chapel to assist the minister with the service, to read a service in the minister's absence, and even to catechize children, record vital statistics, and clean the church and communion plate. The lack of ministers in many parishes and the necessity of ministers' serving several churches in rotation made the reader's job an important one. One mid-seventeenth-century grand jury charged an entire county with breaking the Sabbath by failing to provide a reader. Some parishes employed sextons for routine maintenance and cleaning. The sexton's job was reserved for poor people, usually for someone on parish relief, and it was the one church position held by women.[13]

Not only was the Anglican Church a less centralized institution in Virginia than it was in England, but its territorial scope was different. Like the English Church, it was organized into parishes, but the connotation of the word was necessarily different. Except in the north of the country, English parishes were village-sized units, often only a few hundred acres in extent. The first Virginia parishes were constructed on this model, and were frequently confined to the territory of a single plantation or settlement, but such small parishes soon proved economically unable to function. The colony's government began to combine them into larger entities. The great age of parish creation was from 1640 to 1660. Never again would so many parishes be established in such a brief time (Tab. 1). In those two decades, thirty-three large parishes were set up. They formed the structure of the colony's parochial system through the remainder of the colonial era, as subsequent parishes were carved from their territory. After 1650, Virginia parishes were usually county- and half-county-sized, although some frontier parishes were much larger than that. A survey of colonial parishes initiated by the bishop of London asked, among other questions, "Of what

extent is your parish, and how many families are there in it?" The replies from Virginia indicated parish sizes ranging from 10 miles square in the compact, densely settled Bruton Parish, up to 20 by 100 miles and 10 by 120 miles for the adjacent parishes of Southwark and Lawnes Creek, south of the James River. Both parishes abutted the river but stretched south and west indefinitely into the back country. In the northern part of the colony James Scott of Overwharton Parish explained that his was a frontier parish and that he could not be certain how large it was. Most parishes in the settled Tidewater counties ranged from 20 to 40 miles long, and were 5 to 10 miles wide: they were usually coterminous with the county boundaries.[14]

Just as the size of the parishes varied, so did their populations. The 1724 survey counted parish population by families, and the number ranged from 78 families in James City Parish to 1,200 families in St. Paul's Parish, Hanover County. The minister of Henrico Parish equated 1,100 tithables with 400 families. Using this ratio we can postulate a population of tithables ranging from about 215 in James City Parish to 3,300 in St. Paul's Parish. The evidence of the surviving vestry record books reveals that most parishes in the long-established portions of Tidewater Virginia ranged from 500 to 700 tithables in the early part of the eighteenth century to 1,000 to 1,200 tithables in the quarter century before the Revolution. Wicomico Parish in Northumberland County, for example, grew gradually from 541 tithables in 1712 to a maximum of 1,211 in 1769. In St. Mary's White Chapel Parish in neighboring Lancaster County, there were about 700 tithables in the early 1730s, but the taxable population rose to around 1,900 in the 1760s, after the parish was merged with Christ Church Parish, Lancaster County. In Elizabeth City Parish, Elizabeth City County, the number of tithables in the third quarter of the eighteenth century varied from 1,035 to 1,326, while in farflung Albemarle Parish, Sussex County, at the southern edge of eastern Virginia settlement, the number of taxable inhabitants ranged from 1,581 in 1744 to 2,800 in 1773. The highest numbers of tithables and the greatest numerical variation could be found in the Shenandoah Valley frontier parishes of Frederick and Augusta, where the population was dispersed over vast areas. Frederick Parish had 4,824 tithables at its peak in 1770, while Augusta Parish grew from 1,670 tithables in 1747 to 4,415 in 1769.[15]

The unequal sizes of parishes and their consequent unequal financial abilities were a constant source of concern

TABLE 1: *Parish Creation, 1607–1780*

1607–19	9
1620–29	4
1630–39	8
1640–49	16
1650–59	17
1660–69	9
1670–79	4
1680–89	4
1690–99	0
1700–09	4
1710–19	2
1720–29	6
1730–39	10
1740–49	10
1750–59	7
1760–69	10
1770–80	14

Sources: Charles Francis Cocke, *Parish Lines, Diocese of Southwestern Virginia* (Richmond: VSL, 1960), pp. 43–46; Cocke, *Parish Lines, Diocese of Southern Virginia* (Richmond: VSL, 1964), pp. 195–98; Cocke, *Parish Lines, Diocese of Virginia* (Richmond: VSL 1967), pp. 263–68.

in colonial Virginia. Because the parish was the smallest effective unit of community public life, the colonial government devoted much effort to achieving a workable geographic and demographic balance in each parish. In 1662 the legislature provided for the combination of sparsely settled parishes to alleviate the financial burden of building churches and supporting clergy in those areas. This established a precedent for the constant enlargement, division, reduction, and recombination of parishes that went on through the remainder of the colonial period, but the problem was never satisfactorily resolved. The anonymous author of the 1724 "Proposition for supplying the country of Virginia with a sufficient number of much better Clergymen than have usually come into it" suggested a scheme based strictly on population. He recommended the combination of smaller parishes or their attachment to larger ones such as the 1662 act had ordered, but he then suggested that a mechanism be established that would maintain each parish at a population of four hundred to eight hundred tithables. He reckoned that four hundred tithables was the smallest number of taxpayers who could pay the legally established ministerial salary of sixteen thousand pounds of tobacco per year, and that eight hundred tithables represented the maximum number of parishioners that any minister could effectively serve. Thus, when a parish exceeded the upper limit, a division into two parishes would be made, but the separation would not be effected until the current minister died or left his place. At that time, two new ministers would be sought.[16]

The Church performed a variety of social functions. In addition to policing morals, supporting the indigent, and helping to maintain property rights (through processioning), the parish recorded vital statistics in its register, which the canons directed should be kept in the church under three locks and keys, and it supervised the education of orphans. But its central function was religious and its most conspicuous activity was Divine Service.[17]

The Anglican liturgy consisted of the reading of a series of set prayers and biblical passages, prefaced by sentences and invocations intended to prepare the mind for the holy words, interspersed with responsive readings and sung psalms, and often highlighted by a sermon or homily (a sermon read from a book of model sermons published for the use of uneducated ministers and lay readers). After 1549

the services were in English and the language of the liturgy resolutely based on biblical language. From the beginning, English church reformers were concerned to expose people to the unadulterated message of the Bible, and to eliminate what they understood as the extraneous and even superstitious interpolations of subsequent centuries. The Anglican reformers had reduced the hours, the multiplicity of daily Roman Catholic services, to two daily services, morning and evening prayer, and to the regular celebration of communion, although they also retained a number of occasional ceremonies. The Anglican liturgy was contained in the *Book of Common Prayer*, a document first created after the Reformation to replace the missals, collect books, graduals, and other liturgical documents in use in Catholic England. The prayer book had been revised several times during the religious struggles of the sixteenth and seventeenth centuries, but the version drafted in 1662, shortly after the restoration of Charles II, remained in use in America until it was revised by the newly independent Episcopal Church after the American Revolution.[18]

Having reduced the complexity of services and rendered them in the vernacular, the authorities demanded that they be performed in their entirety so that their theological import might be appreciated. Virginia law specified "That the canons sett downe in the liturgie of the church of England for celebrating divine service and administration of the sacraments be duly observed and that the whole liturgie according to the said injunctions be by the minister or reader at church and chappell every sunday thoroughly read." As early as the sixteenth century, however, the repetition of set prayers, which Anglican apologists defended on biblical and pedagogical grounds, rendered the service predictable and boring to some worshippers. Bishop William Meade described the standard Virginia service as one in which the clerk alone "sung or drawled . . . out" the responsive parts of the service that the congregation were intended to recite and in which the only psalm ever sung was the hundredth. In practice, many ministers combined and collapsed the liturgy into compact form, omitting whole sections. Meade reported that at the beginning of his career, in the early nineteenth century, it was common practice to abridge the service to avoid alienating the attention of parishioners. Some strict churchmen disapproved, but Meade thought it necessary, and obtained a letter from Bishop James Madison condoning the practice. He wrote of a clergyman who did not even take his prayer book into the pulpit, but memorized a few set prayers and recited them before his sermons. In fact, the predictability of the service made the sermon the most attractive part of Divine Worship. Virginians' comments on church services were usually directed to the sermon, and many attended only on the weeks when the minister would be present in church to preach.[19]

Abbreviated and perfunctory as it might be, it was for this ritual alone that the churches were built. In colonial Virginia, no other activities took place in the parish churches. The service made few demands on the building. There had to be a table for communion, which after the early seventeenth century had to be railed in to mark its significance. This railed table was the remnant of the medieval altar, and at it the clergyman was supposed to kneel when praying. By the seventeenth century, most of the service was led from the nave, so the minister and clerk both needed desks for their folio prayer books. For the all-important sermon, there was a higher pulpit, to give the clergyman the maximum visibility and audibility. These architectural requirements were minimal, yet Virginia vestries commonly filled them lavishly, for the church was much more than an auditorium. It expressed a variety of other meanings that nineteenth- and twentieth-century observers might call extraneous, but wrongly so. It was to these less tangible demands as much as to liturgical necessities that vestrymen responded when they set out to comply with their legal duties to build churches.

| 2 | Building |

The decision to build a church was a momentous one for any parish. It involved a commitment of supervisory time on the part of the vestrymen and of parish money far beyond that demanded under ordinary circumstances. Yet while the building process was a long and often arduous one, it was well defined. The institutional structure of the Virginia Establishment had crystallized by the third quarter of the seventeenth century, and a routine procedure for building churches had developed that varied little during the remainder of the colonial era. If the parish was a new one, the vestry initially arranged for a location for church meetings in a parishioner's house or barn, and then proceeded to erect one or more churches for the use of the parish, unless it had inherited an outlying church from an older parish to which it had belonged. The number and size of churches in any parish depended, of course, on the size and population density of the parish. The large frontier parish of Cumberland, in Lunenburg County, built four churches and one small "reading house" during the first three years of its existence. Even in established parishes, the constant enlargement, division, reduction, and recombination occasioned by the fluid, responsive character of the colonial Church necessitated the frequent construction and alteration of churches. New church buildings were wanted in the older parishes for a variety of reasons: an old church had become too small for the congregation, or it was "rotten and unfit for repairs," or the growth of settlement on the fringes of a large parish justified the construction of a subsidiary church — called a "chapel of ease" or simply a "chapel" — in that neighborhood.[1]

The decision to build was itself sometimes a hard one to make. Because of the expense and the time involved, parish vestries often delayed construction as long as possible. The Truro Parish vestry had Pohick church repaired in 1750 "to enable it to Continue a few years." In fact, it lasted almost twenty years longer. In Christ Church Parish, Middlesex County, a new upper chapel was not ordered until the old one was ruinous, and construction was still not begun for four years after the initial order to build (see below).

Similarly, the vestry of the Upper Parish of Nansemond County waited until its old brick church was "useless" and had to be abandoned before they considered replacing it.[2]

In the fragmentary statistical evidence available for the buildings, some patterns may be dimly discerned. Hard though the individual vestries' decisions to build might be, most made a major building commitment about once a generation. Judging by the thirty-six churches whose dates of construction and demolition are known, the average life span of a church throughout the colonial period was 35.9 years. If we factor in additions as alternatives to demolition of outmoded churches, for sixty-four such instances the interval between major changes — building and addition, addition and demolition — is reduced to 28.4 years. Colonial records are such that we can see the results of these cycles only during the last half century before the Revolution. The 1730s and the 1760s were the great church-building eras (Tab. 2; Fig. 4). Their visibility results from two phenomena. One we might call, using the term favored by English vernacular architecture scholars, the "vernacular threshold." This is the point in any society's economic history when large numbers of buildings begin to be constructed substantially enough to survive until the present. Most of the parish churches that survive are brick — there are only three framed survivors — and most date from the 1730s on. This is no accident. An examination of the building materials of parish churches shows that framed buildings were most common throughout the colonial era, and that few brick buildings were built before the eighteenth century (Tab. 3). Thus a preponderance of survivors from the end of the colonial era is not surprising. But even these are not evenly or randomly distributed. The majority of both surviving and documented churches date from the 1730s and the 1760s. Why? Economic cycles are not the answer, as a comparison of church building with all parish building projects shows. The number of parish building projects of all types, including additions, rose after the 1730s, and were at their highest in the 1740s and 1750s, when new church building dipped. On the other hand, the total number of building

TABLE 2: *Parish Building Projects, 1607–1790*

	Churches			Glebes	OB	VH	PH	Total	All
	New	Additions	Total						
1607–19	4	0	4	0	0	0	0	0	4
1620–29	0	0	0	0	0	0	0	0	0
1630–39	1	0	1	1	0	0	0	1	2
1640–49	1	0	1	0	0	0	0	0	1
1650–59	2	0	2	0	0	0	0	0	2
1660–69	8	0	8	0	0	0	0	0	8
1670–79	3	0	3	1	0	0	0	1	4
1680–89	5	1	6	0	0	0	0	0	6
1690–99	4	1	5	1	0	1	0	2	7
1700–09	7	1	8	3	1	0	0	4	12
1710–19	7	1	8	1	0	1	0	2	10
1720–29	16	1	17	2	4	1	0	7	24
1730–39	30	7	37	3	18	2	0	23	60
1740–49	24	9	33	7	17	6	0	30	63
1750–59	26	12	38	9	21	7	6	43	81
1760–69	38	7	45	7	14	4	4	29	74
1770–79	18	6	24	6	9	4	3	22	46
1780–90	0	2	2	0	0	1	0	1	3
TOTAL	194	48	242	41	84	27	13	165	407

Key: VH = vestry house; OB = glebe outbuildings; PH = poor house

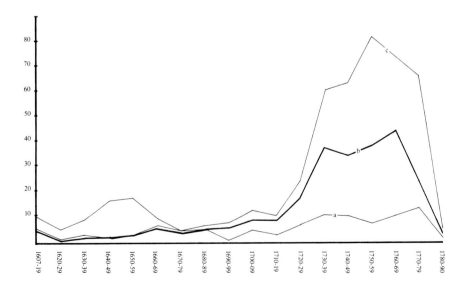

FIG. 4. Building cycles in Virginia, 1607–1790. Key: a = parishes established; b = churches built; c = all other parish building projects. (Drawing, Jocelyn Kwei.)

TABLE 3: *Parish Church Buildings and Additions, 1607–1790*

	Brick	Frame	Other	Unknown	Additions
1607–19	0	3	0	0	0
1620–29	0	0	0	0	0
1630–39	0	1	0	0	0
1640–49	0	1	0	0	0
1650–59	0	2	0	0	0
1660–69	1	7	0	0	0
1670–79	0	2	0	1	0
1680–89	3	2	0	0	1
1690–99	2	0	1	1	1
1700–09	4	2	0	0	1
1710–19	5	3	0	0	1
1720–29	4	12	0	0	1
1730–39	15	15	0	0	5
1740–49	6	18	0	0	9
1750–59	8	14	2	1	12
1760–69	11	24	3	0	7
1770–79	7	7	1	1	5
1780–89	0	0	0	0	2
Unknown	0	0	0	0	1
TOTAL	66	113	7	4	46

projects fell during the 1760s, when church building rose again. The peaks in the 1730s and 1760s should consequently be attributed to that generation-long building cycle (see Fig. 4). If the records and surviving buildings permitted it, we might push the cycle back to the 1640s and 1650s, the great era of parish establishment in Virginia. By the end of the seventeenth century, many parishes were building their second or even third churches; the surviving buildings, which date mostly from the 1730s on, are third- and even fourth-generation buildings.[3]

Once a vestry determined to build a new church, the next step was to choose a location. Many parishes used long-established sites over and over, but in the case of new or radically changing parishes, vestries attempted to plan new churches as close as possible to the geographical centers of the precincts they were intended to serve. Normally this choice was made by a committee of the vestry such as that appointed by Fredericksville Parish "to find the senter for fixing the Lower Church," but in some cases the parishioners themselves met as a group to make the

decision. An occasional, extremely scrupulous vestry worked even more precisely. The vestrymen of St. Andrew's Parish, noting in 1756 the necessity of building three new churches, ordered "That the Surveyor of the County of Brunswick do run a Centrical Line through this Parish and return a Platt of the said Line noteing the middle and the middle of each half." Of course, the geographical center was not necessarily the center of population, and sometimes the vestry was obliged to change the location, "the former place nominated being found to be inconvenient to the Majority."[4]

The two initial decisions—whether to build, and where—could be the most divisive of the entire building process. A protracted dispute in Shelburne Parish involved both issues. On September 29, 1772, the vestry voted that two churches would be enough for the parish, rather than the three suggested in an earlier unrecorded minute. The motion was seconded, but four vestrymen then demanded to be recorded as being absent from the meeting, to dissolve the quorum. The vote was taken, however, with the remaining vestrymen voting seven to one for the new proposal. The prevailing vestrymen entered the resolution "That it is the opinion of this Vestry that for any Vestryman to enter themselves Absent upon any Question upon a Supposition that a Majority will be against them merely by that means to prevent such Question from being put is in our opinion unfair, arbitrary, destructive of every Principle of Justice and must necessarily introduce Anarchy and Confusion." The majority's victory was only temporary for the balance shifted according to the attendance of individual vestrymen at subsequent meetings, and specifications for churches were repeatedly drawn up and rescinded and their locations changed.[5]

Vestrymen knew that to ignore parish opinion was to risk an appeal to the colonial government. In 1726 residents of Elizabeth City Parish petitioned the House of Burgesses to dissolve the vestry and cancel an order for a new church, "by reason of certain persons Assuming to themselves without lawfull authority and exercising in an unjust manner the power of Vestrymen of the said parish," and ordering the construction of a new church "remote from the greater Number of the sd. Inhabitants." The Burgesses decided that the church should be built at Hampton. The governor intervened in St. George's Parish, Spotsylvania County, after a petition from residents of the southern part of the county alleged that they were burdened with great hardship by the construction of two new churches remote from themselves and most of the parishioners. Although the vestry denied the charges, Governor William Gooch summoned representatives of both sides to meet with the council at the October 1733 General Court, and in the meantime he ordered the vestry to stop work on one of the churches. Gooch was wise to be cautious. A year earlier, parishioners in the adjacent parish, which had just been set off from St. George's, had destroyed the church at Germanna, the seat of former Governor Alexander Spotswood. Since 1724 those parishioners had complained that the location of the church and courthouse at Germanna was convenient to no one but Spotswood and his tenants. Finally, "some wicked and evil Disposed persons" burned down the church and "projected to have another instead thereof, in their neighborhood." [6]

Once a general location for the new church was chosen, it was then necessary for the vestry to select a specific site. The primary consideration was to find a location convenient to both roads and a spring, and to solicit the landowner to part with it. Occasionally the owner demanded too much money for a parcel or refused to sell it for other reasons. William Byrd II declined in 1740 to provide a site for a new Henrico Parish church—the present St. John's at Richmond—as requested because "there are so many roads already, thro' that land, that the damage to me would be too great to have another of a mile long cut thro' it. I should be very glad if you wou'd think Richmond a proper place, and considering the great number of people that live below it, and would pay their devotions there, but wou'd not care to go much higher. I can't but think it wou'd be agreeable to most of the people, and if they will agree to have it there, I will give them any pine timber they can find on that side Shockoe Creek, and wood for burning bricks into the bargain." Byrd's excuse was only that. He saw that siting the new parish church at Richmond would help stimulate settlement of that newly platted town, and the vestry complied with his wishes. For most property owners, however, there were smaller but more tangible incentives to relinquish the desired tract, since the conveyance of an acre or two to the parish often brought the right to sell the undertaker (building contractor) a variety of goods and services necessary to the construction of the new building. Thomas Jackson, who provided the land on which the extant St. Peter's Parish church stands, subsequently contracted to

make the bricks, to cart the shingles and other building supplies to the site, to find timbers for making plaster lath, to burn the lime for plaster and mortar, and to supply laborers to serve the plasterer. [7]

The next step was to hire an undertaker. The work to be done was advertised through notices posted on the doors of the parish churches until the 1730s. After the establishment of the *Virginia Gazette* at Williamsburg in 1736, it was customary to advertise in that newspaper and, in the northern Virginia parishes, in the *Maryland Gazette* as well. While many of the newspaper advertisements merely announced the construction of "a large Brick Church," others were quite detailed and indicated that the vestry had developed a clear idea of its requirements. The 1766 advertisement for St. Paul's church is one of the most detailed:

To be Let to the lowest Bidder, on Friday the 29th of August, The Building of a Brick Church in St. Paul's Parish, Stafford County, in the Form of a CROSS, of the following Dimensions; each Wing to be 16 Feet in the Clear [inside dimensions] for the Length, and 26 in Breadth, 2 Feet high to the Water Table, and 24 to the Cieling, with Galleries.

Any Persons inclining to undertake the same, are desired to meet at the Church of the said Parish at the Time above mentioned.

FIVE HUNDRED POUNDS will be paid in hand, the Undertaker giving Bond with sufficient Security for the faithful Performance of the said Building. [8]

The St. Paul's Parish advertisement illustrates several aspects of the standard building process. The bidding was open to anyone, although in practice it was only the larger and more expensive brick buildings that attracted interest from outside the parish. The contract was routinely let to the lowest bidder, who signed an agreement giving a bond, usually double the price of the church, for its completion in the manner and by the time specified. The undertaker was backed by a "security," a person who guaranteed his bond and the completion of the building in case the undertaker failed to do so. The security might be another craftsman or a relative, but more often it was an independent member of the gentry, sometimes a vestryman, who entered the agreement as an investment for a part of the profits. George Mason of Gunston Hall, for example, was security for Daniel French in the construction of Pohick church in

Truro Parish, and was responsible for having the work completed after French died.[9]

A church was an expensive project, and every penny had to be raised by taxation within the parish. The vestry could expect no supplementary contributions or governmental aid in constructing the new building. No parish church in pre-Revolutionary Virginia was built entirely at the expense of a private donor, and in only a few instances, mostly in the seventeenth century, did contributions other than levies and pew sales help to offset construction costs of parish churches. When Bruton Parish built a new brick church in 1677–83, "free donations" were solicited from parishioners to help pay for it, and thirteen gentlemen responded with contributions of £5 to £20 sterling. The construction of the parish's third church in 1711–15 was paid for in part by the General Assembly, since it was regularly attended by the governor and members of the legislature. Governor Alexander Spotswood personally financed the construction of twenty-two feet of the church's seventy-five-foot length. The government again helped to pay for additions to the church in 1752. Small legacies were sometimes left for anticipated church buildings. The most conspicuous exception to the rule of public finance was Christ church, Lancaster County. It was built with heavy contributions from Robert "King" Carter and his heirs, although the exact size of Carter's contribution is not certain. In his 1726 will, he bequeathed £200 sterling, or about £232.5 Virginia currency (his estimate), for the construction of the new church. This was about one-third to one-quarter of the cost of most large brick churches in eighteenth-century Virginia, and possibly less than that fraction of the exceptionally fine and exceptionally large Christ church. Petsworth Parish church in Gloucester County, for instance, was completed in 1724 at a cost of £1,190 current (£1,021 sterling at the prevailing exchange rate). An estimate of the probable cost of Christ church can be formed by comparing it with three other brick churches of the 1730s whose size and cost are both known. They were completed at costs ranging from £0.26 to £0.32 (current) per square foot in plan. At £0.29 per square foot, Christ church, containing thirty-three hundred square feet, would have cost £957 current or £795.1 sterling in the year of its completion. As another point of comparison, the vestry of Wicomico Parish projected its intended church of 1753, which was designed as an explicit copy of Christ

church, to cost £1,200 current (£926.4 sterling at prevailing rates) and actually contracted it for 145,300 pounds of tobacco, a fee amounting to £1,453 Virginia currency at the 1754 price of 20s. per hundredweight. Even without accounting for twenty years' inflation, the discrepancy between Carter's legacy and the probable cost of Christ church is apparent. What we don't know, however, is how much the family spent on the church after Carter's death. John Carter, the eldest son, wrote to his English factor, Micajah Perry, several times in the early 1730s ordering "some Things for our Church use," but these were ornaments and fittings. Another letter of August 8, 1734, requested plate and other things for the church "which I hope to finish soon after Christmass."[10]

Every other parish church of which there is a record was constructed entirely with tax monies. Because church buildings were so expensive, it was necessary to spread payments for them over several years. In two instances, Wicomico Parish began to make levies for building and to accumulate funds two or three years before the anticipated beginning of construction. Before contracting for a church in 1763, it had levied 25,000 pounds of tobacco toward building costs in each of the two preceding years, selling the tobacco and lending the proceeds at interest. Usually, however, the first levy was made in the year that the contract was let, and the cost of building was raised in three or four annual installments. Even by spreading the costs in this way, construction was burdensome to the parish. The 25,000-pound levy in Wicomico Parish doubled the parish budget, for only 24,660 pounds of tobacco were budgeted for all other expenses for the year. The burden on the individual parishioner increased in proportion. A survey of annual levies shows that in most parishes the annual levy was 20 to 30 pounds of tobacco per poll per year in non-building years, and that in years when churches were under construction, it was around 50 pounds of tobacco per poll. These figures remained stable throughout the colonial period. St. Mary's White Chapel Parish, for example, assessed 712 tithables 49 pounds of tobacco each in 1739, when a new parish church was under construction. In 1744–53, when the number of tithables was stable, the levy varied from 21½ to 29 pounds per year, with one year's assessment as high as 38 pounds. Lesser increases of this sort accompanied the construction of glebe houses and other small parish buildings, or major repairs to churches. In

Wicomico Parish, the annual levies between 1756 and 1760 ranged from 24 to 28 pounds per tithable, rose to 47, 50, 52, and 48 pounds, respectively, during the years 1761 through 1764 when the new church was being funded, then dropped back to the low thirties.[11]

Parishioners also paid rates to the county and, before the 1720s, to the colony. Consequently, vestrymen were careful not to overburden their constituents, who were not shy about complaining. Accomack residents objected to their vestry's plan to begin construction of a new parish church when little headway was being made on one already started, "as if it were an easy thing to build Churches." Taxation for building never exceeded the total budgeted for other parish purposes in any year, and where building projects threatened to surpass that limit, they were postponed or were financed in alternative ways. St. Andrew's Parish granted some of its inhabitants permission to have a chapel only on the grounds that they pay for it by subscription among themselves, while Albemarle Parish denied a similar request from the lower end of its parish "being of the Opinion that as there are already four Churches in this Parish they are Sufficient and that they cannot consistent with Justice and duty of their Office grant the Prayer of the said Petition." The parishioners of Dettingen Parish suggested that the vestry sell the pews in the gallery of a new parish church to lower the levy, a plan to which the vestry agreed, although there is no record of its ever having been done. When Fairfax Parish planned its new church at Alexandria in 1769, it chose to build a smaller church than it needed, "considering the Circumstances of its constituents," but then the vestry altered and enlarged the scheme when it was suggested that the undertaker add twenty percent to the size of the church and finance it privately by selling those pews at auction. After the new church was finished and paid for, the parish decided to reclaim the pews, reimburse the petitioners with interest for their pew payments, and sell the pews at auction for its own benefit. The proposal provoked a sharp protest from George Washington, one of the original subscribers to the gallery, in part because he objected to the resulting increase in the parish levy. Other vestries found it necessary to alter the financial arrangements of projected churches after they had commenced construction. Albemarle Parish did so in 1772, when it decided to pay for a new church over three years rather than two. The decision was made "Considering the large sum the new Church to be built at St. Mark Went at

and the bad prospect of a Crop of Tobacco Occasioned by the present Draught [drought]."[12]

The installment payment method had implications for the undertaker as well as for the parish. The usual practice was to make one payment at the time the contract was let, yearly payments thereafter, and a final accounting when the building was completed and "received," or legally accepted, by the vestry. This meant that the undertaker, who was responsible for hiring the laborers and subsidiary craftsmen, and, after the beginning of the eighteenth century, for obtaining all the building materials, had to carry the expense of building from year to year. While the security was officially responsible only for guaranteeing the undertaker's performance, it is likely that many helped to carry the annual building costs in return for a share of the proceeds. A newspaper article concerning the Portsmouth Parish church of 1764 traced the root of the problem to a vestryman's being "concerned" with the undertaker: "They went sharers." While some wealthy undertakers may not have needed this kind of backing, it must have been essential to smaller contractors. Equally advantageous to them was the receipt of the largest possible initial payment. Thus, in advertising the construction of a glebe house and gallery in the mother (main) church of Christ Church Parish, Middlesex County, the vestry ordered as an inducement to undertakers that "in the Notice given it is to be inserted that a considerable part of the money will be paid to the person who agrees for the same" at the time of the bargain.[13]

This mode of payment led to most colonial churches' taking longer than the specified contract time to complete. Some were never finished. A church did not take four years of steady work to build, no matter how elaborate, but because the payments were spread over several years, so was the work. When the Albemarle Parish vestry altered the payment schedule for rebuilding the front of its Nottoway church it also specified that "the Said front building [is] to be finised [sic] Within three years instead of two Years." The absence from church contracts of the stipulation that the undertaker work on no other projects at the same time, a common feature of house contracts, is significant. Financially, a contractor needed to work on several jobs at one time, and for economic reasons as well the vestry had no interest in having him finish in the shortest possible time. In 1739/40, the Bristol Parish vestry wished to talk to John Ravenscroft about a contract he had undertaken, but kept him waiting for so long that Ravenscroft left. His note explained that his other business required him to leave, "but to prevent any further misunderstanding about this Church . . . [and] to do the Parish Justice & preserve my own character I am willing to enter into bond with security for the performance of the work, & that any body may view it whilst tis carrying on[.] I hope this may prevent any further suspicion of fraud." Most churches that were unfinished or long in building, then, were neglected because the undertaker, having carried the expense of construction for several years and having received most of his money already, could often make more money by starting a new project and receiving the advance payment than he could by finishing an old job promptly for the relatively small final payment.[14]

This financing arrangement placed the undertaker at considerable risk. The building was his until it was received, and if anything happened to it before that time, he might default on his bond, and have to pay double the price of the building to the vestry as damages. While I have found no record of a church-building bond being legally forfeited, the penalty was suffered in effect if the undertaker rebuilt the structure. Mourning Richards, "undertaker and carpenter," was ruined by a disaster at Aquia church, Stafford County. He contracted to build the church in 1751, and during the three years it was under construction he also accepted work at the middle church of Christ Church Parish, Middlesex County, the construction of a glebe house in the same parish, and contracts for two churches for Dettingen Parish in Prince William County, along with the parish church of Wicomico Parish, Northumberland County. That is, he took on at least seven projects of which we know, distributed over more than one hundred miles in northern Virginia. Richards ultimately backed out of the Dettingen Parish contracts when he acquired the more remunerative Wicomico Parish job. But on February 17, 1754, when Richards was away at one of his other projects, and the Aquia church was within three days of completion, his carpenters left a heating fire too near some shavings, and the building was destroyed. The initial account in the *Virginia Gazette* reported that the fire had ruined Richards and his securities, and indeed he was reduced to a public plea for charity. He stated his case in the *Virginia Gazette* three months after the accident:

Mourning Richards humbly represents, That, in the Year 1751, he contracted with the Vestry of Overwharton Parish, in the County of Stafford, to build a large and beautiful church, near Aquia Creek, for 111,000 Pounds of Tobacco, which building he carried on with all possible Diligence, and made sundry Alterations and Additions, at the Request of the Vestry, who proposed paying him for so doing 20,000 Pounds of Tobacco more than the first Contract: That he had got the Church in such Forwardness that he should have been able to deliver the same to the Vestry in a short Time, and then was to receive the Ballance of his Tobacco, having received only 75,000 Pounds; but on the 17th Day of February last, while he was absent on his necessary Business, the whole building was accidentally consumed by Fire, which has reduced him and his Family to very great Distress, he being utterly unable to rebuild the said Church. And, therefore, he most humbly prays your Aid and Assistance.

The fire cost Richards the fifty-six thousand pounds of tobacco for the completed church that he had not yet been paid by the vestry, and he was forced to forfeit his bond or to rebuild the church at his own expense. Richards was able to complete the new church, and a marble plaque recounting the incident was set in the tympanum over the main entrance. In 1757, the legislature passed a special act allowing the vestry, which was "willing to pay a reasonable satisfaction" for the rebuilt church, to make a levy to reimburse Richards "in one or more years, and in such proportion as they think least burthensome to the said inhabitants." Yet Richards's contracting business seems to have been destroyed. He never began his work at Wicomico Parish, scheduled to get under way just as the Aquia fire occurred, and while he continued to accept carpentry apprentices there is no record of his having undertaken any major buildings after the second Aquia church.[15]

If no disaster struck and the undertaker finished his work, it then had to be formally "received" by the vestry, who certified that the contractor had fulfilled his bargain and ordered the church wardens or the parish collector to release the remaining funds. Or the vestry might find that there were several defects in the building, and withhold payment until they had been corrected. An unusually lengthy report from a committee of the Wicomico Parish vestry listed many defects that remained in John Wily's work in 1772, nine years after the initial decision to build a church and eight years after the contract had been let. These included his failure to pave fifty-six feet of the aisles, to finish the pulpit and desk, and to repair imperfections in the brickwork and glazing. Arbitration between the under-taker and his security on the one hand, and two of the vestrymen on the other, resulted in an agreement that other workmen would be hired to complete the church and the cost deducted from Wily's final payment. The security had already placed an advertisement in the *Virginia Gazette* in 1769 soliciting bids for the remainder of the work. He noted that Wily had failed to complete the church and that "bad consequences may arise if the church is not completed this year, which it is probable cannot be done by him." The decision to accept was not as clear cut in most instances, where the defects were smaller and it was a matter of judgment whether or not the building had been satisfactorily completed. In 1756 five vestrymen of Dettingen Parish objected to the reception of a new church, believing that the undertaker had not carried out his agreement. They objected as well to the minister's participation in the decision.[16]

As the Dettingen Parish vote suggests, the discretionary powers granted the vestry in receiving the church could be misused. This was the case in Portsmouth Parish in the 1760s, according to a series of items published in Purdie and Dixon's *Virginia Gazette* in 1766 and 1767, which concerned the new parish's church, received in 1764. The first item was a brief letter to the editor from "A Donator" that ostensibly reported the election of a new mayor of the town, "a Gentleman remarkable for the many good offices done that town." But this was merely a pretext for the writer, who went on to wish that he "could say as much for the Gentlemen of the Vestry of that parish: A church there, built within these three years, is now ready to tumble down! which has obliged the Church-Wardens to advertise it for repairs. I hope that none of the vestry were concerned with the undertaker that built the church. One of the Gentlemen is Sexton; a business more becoming a poor man, who is supported by the parish. Whether the Vestry of any parish can be guilty of sacrilege is submitted to the publick." Two months later, a "Timothy Trimsharp" added a purported transcript of a conversation overheard on the docks of Norfolk. On inquiring about the identity of a man being ferried over from Portsmouth to Norfolk, an English visitor learns that he is "G[eorge]. V[ea]l[e], . . . a man void of shame, honour, and honesty," the vestryman who was involved with the undertaker. Veale had persuaded his colleagues to accept the church "although split from top to bottom; it is now in such a condition, though only three years old, that no person can with safety go into it." The

vestryman was accompanied in the ferry by a gentleman in a great coat who was identified as the vestryman/sexton. The two would "rake hell for a shilling, and send soul and body to the Devil for money." A third correspondent conveyed another fraudulent document, a letter ostensibly found in a small house in Portsmouth. It was a communication from a third vestryman to a Dr. David Pursilly, the vestry's overseer of the church-building project. The vestryman's point, framed in semiliterate English, was that his vote to receive the church was a product of ignorance and gullibility, not venality. The letter averred that the vestryman "did not want to have any consern with it att all; had it not been that the most knoing man of the whole Vistri, and a freind of mine, caas'd me to accept, he promising to take mangment on him, which he always has done: So that if any done rong, it's no falt of mine. i declare that i never gad [got] on[e] farding by being a Vestryman; hop all the rest will clear themselves as well as i can. . . . Thank God my hands are clear; i have not been guilt of sacralige, nor robing the poor of our parish [one of Trim-sharp's charges]; neither am i Sexton or grave-digger." Trimsharp had accused Veale of having "a powerful party" of vestrymen in collusion with him, and the semiliterate vestryman concluded his abdication of responsibility with a confirmation of the bonds of interest, assuring Pursilly that "if you'l rite a diffence for me, i will onestly reward you; & for the futur, when any of my hands or famely are sik, will imploy you. . . . Should you clear our Vistri, the[y] will all imploy you when the[y] want a Doctor." The newspaper controversy was abruptly ended when the editors pleaded that Trimsharp, in fairness to them, reveal his identity and divert from them the anger of "many of the Gentlemen of Norfolk" County.[17]

If there was error in most vestries' actions, it was in being overly strict, rather than in corrupt laxness. Many defects in new church buildings were insignificant, yet the parishes were reluctant to receive the buildings until the letter of the contracts was fulfilled. Once the building had been accepted, any defects not previously noted were the vestry's responsibility. After the Dettingen Parish's Quantico church had been received over the objections of the five vestrymen, it was noted that the undertaker, William Waite, had not put leads and pulleys in the windows, but the vestrymen were "Convinced that the sd Church has been Legally received." They could only deduct the cost of correcting the building from what they owed him for additional work; they could no longer require him to remedy the defect or withhold part of his bond. Where the church had not yet been received, the vestry could hold up the entire final payment until it was satisfied. However, the undertaker had leverage as well. If the building was his financial liability until it was legally received, it was also his property. He could, if he wished, refuse to allow the parish to use it until he was paid. Thus there was incentive on both sides to compromise. James Anderson of Amelia County was granted concessions in finishing a chapel for Albemarle Parish in return for giving the parish permission to use it while it was being completed. Similarly, Truro Parish's vestry found that its new church had been completed "Except the Brick Pediments on the Outside of the two Doors which are not finished. And being of Opinion that the House can Receive no Damage from the Weather for want of the Pediments, And understanding that it is the general Desire of the People in this part of the Parish to have the Church received, on account of the great Inconvenience they at present Suffer for Want of it [they were meeting in a tobacco barn], We do accordingly receive the said Church for the Use of the Parish, except the Pediments which the said Edward Payne is still liable for & obliged to finish pursuant to the Articles of Agreement above mentioned." [18]

Despite their strict interpretation of the contracts, however, the vestries often allowed the completion negotiations to drag on, as in the case of John Wily, rather than exercise their right under the contract to sue the undertaker or to replace him promptly. They preferred to threaten for years, and then to hire a substitute as a last resort, paying the new builder out of whatever remained due to the old undertaker. In 1772 Fairfax Parish asked James Parsons what his intentions were with respect to finishing its church at Alexandria. Parsons was unwilling to say that he would not finish it, thereby raising the possibility of forfeiting his bond. Instead, he coyly "Answered that he did not think it proper to give a direct Answer, but he did not think that if the Vestry did proceed in the manner they proposed that it would be taken Notice of" by legal action. In other words, if the vestry did not sue Parsons for failing to fulfill his contract, Parsons would not sue the vestry for taking over a building to which they had no legal title. Only in the Revolutionary years, when craftsmen were presumably scarce and parish funds tight, did vestries routinely attempt to force the original undertakers to comply with their

bargains. Even then they preferred to compromise rather than to sue. John Woodward and Captain Lawrence House each agreed to build for Albemarle Parish in 1772. When the projects were still incomplete after seven years, the vestry initiated lawsuits. As late as 1786 the vestrymen had not pressed the suits, and offered to drop them if the work were completed. By 1788 even that condition was abandoned, and the parish decided to move an old church to a new site. [19]

With the receipt of the building, the construction process came to an end if no adjustments were required. Yet it was often difficult to predict at the time a building was first projected when it would be received. The infrequency of vestry meetings, coupled with the involved process of planning and building a church, meant that most parishes could expect at least a five-year delay between the perception of the need for a new building and the occupation of the completed structure. For many parishes, the wait was much longer. A sense of how the total process worked, of what it meant to construct a church, can be found in the experience of Christ Church Parish, Middlesex County, in the early eighteenth century. The parish had been created in 1666 by the merger of Lancaster and Piankatanke parishes, and its vestry book is the oldest one surviving in Virginia. Three churches, a "mother," or main church, also known as the middle church, and upper and lower chapels had been built at the time of Christ Church Parish's establishment. All were frame buildings, and at least one was post built. They required constant repair, and the upper chapel was enlarged twice in the 1680s. By the first decade of the eighteenth century, all three buildings had outlasted their usefulness. In 1707, the upper chapel, "now gone to ruin," was ordered replaced. The vestry, "after mature deliberation," determined to construct a wooden building fifty-six by forty-eight feet, an aisled structure unlike any public building ever erected in the colony (Tab. 4). Four years later, however, nothing had been done. In January 1711, the vestry ordered all three of the parish's churches replaced, occasioning a protest from the parishioners to the General Assembly. The assembly directed the vestry to build the three churches in sequence, and the vestrymen began with the upper one. A frame building was still planned, but it was now to be sixty by twenty feet, an aisleless structure closer to the traditional Virginia form. To

TABLE 4: *Three Churches for Christ Church Parish, Middlesex County*

	Lower	Middle (Mother)	Upper
July 2, 1707	——	——	New church ordered
July 24, 1707	——	——	Specifications and place set
January 4, 1711	New church ordered	New church ordered	New church ordered
January 23, 1711	——	——	Specifications set
February 5, 1711	——	——	Contract let
	——	——	Specifications altered
April 7, 1712	——	Specifications set	——
	——	Contract let to carpenter	——
June 9, 1712	——	Carpenter gives bond, masonry contract let, mason gives bond	——
	——	Specifications interpreted	——
July 21, 1713	——	Mason's orders changed	——
July 7, 1714	Specifications set	——	——
November 11, 1714	Specifications altered	——	——
December 6, 1714	Specifications altered	Specifications altered	——
January 3, 1715	Specifications altered	——	——
	Contract let	——	——
August 5, 1717	"Inconvenient pews" ordered changed	——	——
October 18, 1717	Yard to be fenced	Yard to be fenced	Yard to be fenced
	——	——	Altarpiece installed
	——	——	Begins to be used
March 31, 1718	——	New plate ordered	New plate ordered
	——	Bell given, cupola to be built	——
June 6, 1718	——	Church tarred, ladder to cupola to be built	——
	——	Ornaments ordered	——
	——	Plate order revised	Plate order canceled
October 7, 1719	——	Cupola not built, order reiterated	——
	——	Painted	——
	——	Altarpiece divided and moved	——
March 7, 1720	——	Undertaker complains of nonpayment	——
October 10, 1720	Glazed	Stand made	——
	——	Glazed	——
October 9, 1721	——	——	Horse block repaired
	——	——	Benches made
October 11, 1722	——	——	Ornaments set up

finance the church, the vestrymen ordered one hundred thousand pounds of tobacco added to the next levy. Three weeks later they met and drafted a detailed set of specifications. Now the new church would be sixty by twenty-five feet, and the dimensions of each of its framing members were specified, along with the number, size, and placement of windows, doors, and pews, the layout of the chancel, pulpit, and screen, and the trim and painting. They adjourned for two more weeks, and then met with workmen in February to make a contract. Once again, the specifications were altered. Some changes in the materials were made and more detailed instructions were given for the interior disposition of the church. The generous contract was let to John Clark for 110,000 pounds of tobacco, 90,000 of which was to be paid immediately. Clark was to finish his job in fifteen months, by April 30, 1712. Three vestrymen were appointed overseers, to make certain the work progressed according to contract and to explain any of the vestry's orders that might be unclear. No further vestry orders relating to the upper chapel were made for five years. In October 1717 the church yard was fenced in, the altarpiece was installed, and the church began to be used. New communion plate was ordered in March 1718 for the upper and middle churches, but that order was canceled when the vestry made a deal with one of its members to supply a single set of plate in trade for both sets of old plate. In 1719 Clark's estate was sued for 4,990 pounds of tobacco which the vestry claimed had been overpaid him. In October 1722 the "ornaments" (Bible, prayer books, cloth hangings for the pulpit and communion table) were installed, eleven years after the church was begun and a year after its first minor repair.[20]

In April 1712, the month the upper chapel was supposed to be completed, the vestry met to draw up specifications for the middle, or mother, church. It was to be a sixty-by-thirty-foot brick structure, on the site of the original. Again, the form of the building was specified in detail. Alexander Graves was hired to do the brickwork on the condition that he finish by the end of October 1713. He was to be paid sixty thousand pounds of tobacco for his work. Despite John Clark's delay in completing the upper chapel, he was hired to do the carpentry on the mother church, for fifty thousand pounds of tobacco. This time the vestry specified that if he failed to complete his work by December 1713, the overseers might hire someone else to do so. Two months later the vestrymen clarified their specifications, ordering

that the sixty-by-thirty-foot dimensions were to be "in the clear," or inside measurements. They noted that Clark had failed to provide security, and turned the job over to John Hipkins, Sr., who was to be paid sixty thousand pounds of tobacco for it. Hipkins was to have two years, rather than eighteen months, to complete his work, which was due on June 10, 1714. At the same meeting, the instructions to the bricklayer Alexander Graves were amplified, and he was granted an additional two thousand pounds of tobacco for the new work. Again in July 1713, Graves was ordered to build the walls of the church five courses of brick higher than originally specified, and he was given another four thousand pounds for that work. The church yard was empaled at the same time as that of the upper chapel. In March 1718 the parish received a bell as a gift from the bishop of London, and decided to build a small cupola on the roof of the mother church to receive it. The church wardens were instructed to hire someone to build a cupola, to tar the roof of the church, and to make a ladder up to the cupola. At the same time the vestry sent an order for ornaments to England. None of the new building was attended to, and the order was reiterated in October 1719. The woodwork was painted then, and one of the vestrymen, John Grymes, was allowed to divide the altarpiece and rehang it (it was blocking the single east window). The mother church could now be occupied, but John Hipkins was obliged to complain to the vestry in March 1720 that he had not yet received his final payment, which one of the church wardens was withholding on a technicality. In October 1720 the windows were glazed, eight years after the church was begun and ten years after its construction was first ordered.[21]

With two church building projects dragging along, the vestry initiated the third in July 1714, a month after the middle church was supposed to have been completed. The new lower chapel was to stand on the north side of the seventeenth-century building. It would be a brick structure fifty by twenty-five feet, and in many respects similar to the middle church. In November, the vestrymen decided that the structure was ten feet too short, and extended the length of the proposed church accordingly. A month later, at the time appointed to let the contract, the vestry determined that the sixty-by-twenty-five-foot plan, "not being Uniforme," should be changed to fifty-two by thirty feet. At the same time they altered the arrangement of the interior. The pulpit was originally to stand at the north end of the chancel aisle. Now they decided it should stand in the middle of the east-west aisle and ordered Hipkins to make the same change at the mother church. On the new day for making a contract, they altered the plan again, returning the pulpit to its position "on the North Side opposite to the South doore." More refinements were added to the specifications, and the contract was awarded to Captain Henry Armstead and Major Edmond Berkley. They were to be paid ninety thousand pounds of sweet-scented tobacco (the more valuable of the two Virginia varieties), and to finish by January 3, 1717, two years later. The vestry ordered that the undertakers be given "Two faire Abstracts of the dimensions of the [illegible] Chappell and likewise one Copy of all the rough Orders of Vestry relating to the building [of the] said Chappell." (The former contained the terms of their contract, and those are what survive in the vestry book. The latter would have given the undertakers a clearer idea of the vestry's intent as the specifications were negotiated, and these do not survive.) In August 1717, eight months after the scheduled completion of the church, it was still not ready. The vestry noted that Armstead and Berkley were "putting up Inconvenient Pews contrary to agreement," and asked the overseers to make them correct the discrepancy. The church yard was enclosed at the same time as the other two, but the building was not glazed until 1720.[22]

From the time of the decision to build until the last church was completed and fully fitted with its legally required ornaments, fifteen years had elapsed. The parish's ambitious building plan was fumbled badly. The design of the churches was constantly altered. Unrealistically short time limits were set for the construction of each building, but then, despite the parish's strict bond to keep the undertakers on schedule, construction was allowed to drag on for an unconscionable time. Much of the community's public money and attention had been focused on completing the three buildings whose total cost, the historians Darrett and Anita Rutman have observed, was only a little less than half the combined parish and county budgets for the entire preceding decade. Though the seventeenth-century records of this parish show that the construction process for these eighteenth-century buildings was already well established by the 1660s, the structure of the parish and of the building industry prevented it from being carried through smoothly. The vestry met only once a year and depended for inspection of the work on the efforts of uncompensated vestrymen who were not professional builders. The undertakers themselves were subject to the usual financial constraints, and it was not in their interest to work as quickly as the vestry demanded. Yet to enforce the bonds extracted from the undertakers at the time of the contract would have required lengthy and expensive trips to the General Court at Williamsburg, and acrimonious legal action against neighbors. The parishioners had experienced bitter controversies twice in the late seventeenth century, in a dispute over church seating and another over corruption in the collection of parish taxes, and twice more in the early eighteenth century, over the plan to build three new churches, and over the construction of a new county courthouse. The vestrymen were not willing to risk another divisive controversy. Better to let the churches wait.[23]

3 | Builder and Designer

The church-building process revolved around the undertaker. The parish vestry often took an active part in planning and supervising construction, drafting detailed specifications before an undertaker was hired, but more often they made a general plan and asked the church wardens to "receive proposals" for the ultimate form of the building from prospective undertakers. Once an agreement was made, the undertaker's financial resources, his skill in organizing the preparation of the site and the manufacture and purchase of building materials, the number and quality of the workmen he could command, and the workers' ability to translate a verbal description into a finished building, all governed the speed and success with which the project was accomplished.[1]

Who were the undertakers? Occasionally they were vestrymen like Severn Guttridge, or Guttrey (d. 1777) of St. George's Parish, Accomack County. Guttridge contracted to build that parish's new church in 1766. But as a vestryman he was an exception. A joiner and carpenter who built the county prison and did other public work during a recorded career of twenty-seven years, he was an obvious and appropriate choice for the job. Guttridge was also asked to design and draw a plan for a new parish poorhouse. Vestrymen who were not professional builders did not hesitate to award themselves contracts for parish services and for building smaller parish buildings ranging from glebe outbuildings to glebe dwelling houses, but churches were generally beyond their ability and beyond that of any but the most experienced building contractors like Guttridge to manage and to construct. For a novice to undertake a church was at worst to experience financial disaster and public abuse, and at best to risk the embarrassment of having to ask to be excused from his contract, as John Deskin, Gent., a vestryman of Dettingen Parish, did "Considering his Incampasity of Doing them."[2]

The undertakers are an elusive group. While several were men of high social standing, none left an extensive record. Their careers must be pieced together from odd bits of evidence. In parish and county records and in newspapers, 357 individuals are recorded as having worked on the buildings of over fifty parishes in some capacity between 1640 and 1780. Nearly half of these did repairs, minor building, and small jobs like tarring a roof or fixing a broken pew door. Of the 186 men who worked on major parish construction, building new churches or glebe houses or adding to older churches, most confined their activities to their home parishes, although some were the dominant builders in their localities. John Hipkins, Sr. (d. 1737), for example, was a partner with James Curtis in the contract for a Middlesex County courthouse of 1692, which was never built, but he did succeed in erecting a courthouse and a prison for the county in 1706–7. He went on to perform the carpentry on the middle church of Christ Church Parish in the same county six years later. James Jones built both the new parish church of St. Mary's White Chapel Parish in Lancaster County in 1739–41 and the county's new courthouse in the same years. Peter Legrand, a vestryman of St. Patrick's Parish, built glebe buildings and a chapel, made alterations to another church, built a gallery, and drew a church plan for his parish. Legrand styled himself a gentleman, and served as sheriff of Prince Edward County in 1770.[3]

Of the twenty-three builders who worked outside their home counties, about half were "considerable Undertakers," with regional businesses, who obtained a significant number of the public contracts of their day. Several had fathers or sons who were also contractors. Henry Cary, Jr. (d. 1733), who built parish churches on the Peninsula in Elizabeth City and St. Paul's parishes, as well as the chapel at the College of William and Mary, was the son of the overseer, or clerk of the works, at the Governor's Palace and the Capitol in Williamsburg. Henry Cary, Sr., also bid unsuccessfully on the contract for Bruton Parish church in 1711. The carpenter and joiner William Rand of Gloucester County worked in at least two of the three parishes in his home county in the second quarter of the eighteenth century, then moved to Smithfield and constructed parish and other public buildings in Nansemond and Isle of Wight counties. He sometimes undertook projects in partnership with the bricklayer John Moore, who obtained contracts in Middlesex, James City, and Louisa counties between 1728 and 1763. William Walker, "builder" of Stafford County, constructed a glebe house for St. Paul's Parish, Hanover County, and the tower of St. Peter's Parish church, as well as a bridge in Richmond County and a prison in Westmoreland County. At the time of his death in 1751, he had just obtained the contract to rebuild the colony's Capitol after a fire. As striking was the career of Captain Francis Smith of Hanover County, who between 1745 and 1767 worked on parish buildings from Hanover County to Augusta County in the Shenandoah Valley. He not only undertook the Augusta Parish church at Staunton in 1760, but he contracted to collect the taxes levied to build it![4]

These men stood above most parish building contractors in the degree of their social and material success, but even they were outstripped by a few whose careers are more visibly, if not abundantly, documented. The fortunes of three men will illustrate the upper ranges of success that eighteenth-century Virginia builders achieved.

During a long, active career, Larkin Chew (d. 1729) of King and Queen (later Spotsylvania) County built many important public buildings in the Middle Peninsula, including the King and Queen County courthouse of 1700, the Essex County courthouse of 1702, an addition to the Petsworth Parish church in 1701, and presumably the Mattapony church of St. George's Parish, Spotsylvania County, in 1725, since it stood on land purchased from him. Chew was a member of the House of Burgesses, a county justice, and sheriff of Spotsylvania County in his later years. In those capacities he came into conflict with former Governor Alexander Spotswood, a man with architectural pretensions of his own, who contributed to the design of the third Bruton Parish church. Spotswood and Chew battled over the removal of the county court from Spotswood's house, and Chew may have been an instigator of an unsigned petition of 1724, directed to the colonial legislature, accusing Spotswood of misappropriating £1,500 in colony funds intended to support the construction of a church and a courthouse in Spotsylvania County. In that year, Spotswood denounced Chew in a letter to the Lords Commissioners of Trade in England as "a base drunken infamous Fellow" whom the current governor, Hugh Drysdale, had chosen "to bring him the Character of Persons and the reports of Transactions in this Neighbourhood." Spotswood had heard Chew "Drinking damnation Healths

within my hearing; Roaring out a Chew (for thats his Name) or a Spotswood [for whom the county had been named] for the first man of the County; Boasting, upon this behavior of his, of the extraordinary Countenance he meets with at Court." The former governor's complaints to Drysdale had met with inaction, even though "this same fellow, who had served me as a Common Carpenter for Wages, had had the insolence in his drink to lay violent hands on me, and collar me at my own door before my Servants." Although Spotswood depicted Chew as a man vastly inferior to himself in social standing and in behavior, the carpenter's tenure as a Burgess and a county justice mark him as a member of the local elite, and it was perhaps his political position and his favor with Drysdale that made him a partner in 1728 in three grants of Shenandoah Valley land totaling sixteen thousand acres. When Chew's son Larkin died in 1770, his executors referred to him in a *Virginia Gazette* advertisement as a gentleman. As perhaps befit the son of a heavy drinker, the younger Chew kept an ordinary, or tavern, in Spotsylvania County. He may have practiced his father's trade as well, for the advertisement mentioned "sundry coopers, carpenters, and joiners Tools" among the goods for sale.[5]

Lewis Deloney (d. 1751) worked as a carpenter on the third Bruton Parish church when it was under construction in 1711–15. Deloney later undertook churches for Blisland Parish (in partnership with John Moore) and St. Andrew's Parish, along with other construction work for those parishes and for the parishes of Albemarle and Cumberland. By the end of his life, Deloney was styling himself "Mister." He lived on a two-thousand-acre tract in Cumberland Parish, Lunenburg County, and was granted the right to build himself a private pew in the parish church in 1746. In their rise from craftsmen to plantation owners, county gentry, and building contractors, Deloney and Chew followed a path that many aspired to, and a few achieved, in the woodworking and masonry trades in eighteenth-century Virginia.[6]

Major Harry Gaines of King William County, like some of the other eighteenth-century undertakers, was part of a father-son succession. His father, Mr. Henry Gaines, worked on churches in Stratton Major and Christ Church, Middlesex County, parishes. The elder Gaines died in 1734 while building an addition to the upper chapel in Christ Church Parish. The son may have been a minor when his father died, since another relative finished the upper chapel addition. Harry Gaines first appeared in the church records as the undertaker of a gallery in St. Paul's Parish, Hanover County, in 1744. He built a vestry house and a church for Stratton Major Parish, the largest church ever constructed in colonial Virginia. He also worked at Westover, the famous Charles City County plantation house of the Byrd family, in the early 1750s. Indeed, Gaines may have been the builder of Westover. At the end of his life, he was a member of the House of Burgesses, and through that connection he was implicated in the scandal that followed the death of Speaker and Treasurer John Robinson. Robinson's executors found that he had used his position as treasurer of the colony to loan large sums of government money to his friends. Gaines was one of the many recipients of Robinson's misplaced largesse, and he attempted to sell his seventeen-hundred-acre plantation to repay the loan. After Gaines's death in 1767, which followed Robinson's by less than a year, the speaker's executors sold all Gaines's real estate and his slaves to recover the debt. Robinson's estate was the beneficiary as well of the final payment on the Stratton Major Parish church, which was under construction at the time Gaines died and which William Muir was hired to complete.[7]

Larkin Chew and Lewis Deloney probably practiced carpentry and brickmasonry personally, at least in the early years of their careers, but it is unlikely that Harry Gaines did. Gaines owned 200 slaves at the time of his death, "among whom are several valuable tradesmen." For him, undertaking large construction projects was a business enterprise rather than a personal craft. It is difficult to judge from the vestry records the proportion of undertakers for whom this was true. Among the 186 men who contracted to build parish buildings between 1640 and 1780, only 19 were identified by their crafts. There were 12 carpenters, 4 bricklayers, as well as 2 joiners and 1 builder who contracted to practice their trades. Alterations and repairs and other small tasks were performed by 164 other men, of whom 3 were identified as carpenters, 3 as joiners, 2 as bricklayers, and 2 as painters. There was 1 glazier, 1 plasterer, and 1 man identified simply as a workman (Tab. 5). Undoubtedly many of those who were called undertakers were more than mere gentlemen entrepreneurs, but it is not possible to ascertain this from the documents.[8]

Whether or not the undertaker was himself a skilled worker, he was supported by a varied group of slaves, indentured servants, apprentices, and hired black and white

TABLE 5: *Trades of Parish Contractors*

Churches, Church Additions, Glebe Houses	
Unspecified	167
Carpenter	12
Joiner	2
Bricklayer	4
Builder	1
Minor Buildings, Repairs, Miscellaneous Tasks	
Unspecified	151
Carpenter	3
Joiner	3
Bricklayer	2
Painter	2
Glazier	1
Plasterer	1
Workman	1
Designs Only	8

workers who formed his crew. Much of the skill and artistic sense that made parish churches and glebe houses the stylish buildings many of them were was the rank-and-file craftsman's, yet sketching their careers is nearly impossible. We can name only a few, usually because they ran away from their masters and were named in advertisements in the *Virginia Gazette*. These were men like Sam Howel, "a good sawer," who ran away from Wade Netherland in 1766 to sue for his freedom in the General Court. Howel was a mulatto indentured until he was thirty-one years old, but who believed that he was entitled to earlier release. He lost the suit, and ran away again in 1770. James Morris and William Blethyn were Welsh house carpenters and joiners who absconded from Harry Gaines's Westover project in 1752. Thomas Field, a servant joiner born in Ireland, ran away from William Rand in Gloucester County in 1736. Field was last seen in Nansemond County where, like many runaway servants, he had assumed a new name, James Ingraham, and was believed to be headed for North Carolina. Other workmen appear incidentally in vestry dealings with undertakers, as when the St. Paul's Parish vestry expressed its dissatisfaction with the quality of brickwork done by William Frazer, who had been hired by undertaker William Walker to help with the construction of the parish glebe house. Mr. Samuel Peacock was a fancy painter, employed in Gloucester County by the Petsworth Parish vestry to paint and repair the woodwork of its Poplar Spring Church, and to gild the altarpiece. When Peacock failed to fulfill his bargain, the vestry hired the time of Richard Cooke, a servant of Charles Carter. William Copein was a bricklayer who worked with Mourning Richards on Aquia church, according to the plaque installed by Richards to commemorate the reconstruction, and inscribed by Copein. Copein was also employed at Pohick church nearly twenty years later, where he carved a stone baptismal font and appraised the woodcarving of William Bernard Sears (d. 1818).[9]

Sears was in his early career a member of William Buckland's crew. Although that most famous of Virginia builders did little church work beyond finishing a glebe house for Truro Parish and possibly building a glebe house for Lunenburg Parish, his fame has led to several efforts to identify his workmen. Buckland (1734–74) was trained in London as a joiner and brought to America in 1755 to work on George Mason's Gunston Hall in Fairfax County. He built up a shop that included, at various times: Sears; another "London Carver a Masterly Hand"; James Brent; a convict joiner, John Ewen (b. ca. 1746); and a convict house carpenter and joiner, Samuel Bailey (b. ca. 1741). Both Ewen and Bailey ran away from Buckland in 1770 and again in 1771, but Bailey at least returned. While he lived in Virginia, Buckland also took as apprentices John Ariss Callis and John Randall. When he died in 1774, Buckland, who had moved to Annapolis three years earlier, still owned Bailey's service along with that of two bricklayers, one painter, one carver (Lawrence Ohern, who may have been an apprentice), one adult male slave, and one black boy. Of this group, Sears was the only one who had an independent career that we know of. In 1772, after Buckland had moved to Maryland, Sears was employed to do carving work at Pohick church, undertaken by Daniel French and finished after French's death by Buckland's and Sears's old employer George Mason. In 1775, Sears worked at Mount Vernon in company with Gawan Langfier, who had been called in with Copein to appraise the value of Sears's carved work at Pohick church.[10]

Despite the paucity of information about individual builders, it is possible to derive from the evidence available a portrait of eighteenth-century Virginia building differing in several respects from that usually presented. Architecture in pre-Revolutionary Virginia was a large and highly organized business. It was, as we have seen, a well-staffed one. The hundreds of undertakers whose names appear in the parish records were supported by several times as many craftsmen whose names do not appear. In addition, it was possible to participate independently in building activities at several levels. There were some small jobs that could be undertaken as side ventures by ordinary planters using their own skills. These were the men who agreed to grub, clean, and fence the churchyard after the church was finished, to tar the building, or to repair broken doors and horseblocks. Most appear in the records once and never again. Larger tasks could sometimes be undertaken by a wealthy planter who owned a crew of skilled slave craftsmen for his own plantation use. Landon Carter undertook the Richmond County courthouse in 1749. So far as we know, Carter's other building projects were confined to his own land. Most houses and public buildings were erected by men for whom construction was a major portion of their economic activity, men with active local businesses like Peter Legrand of Prince Edward County, John Hipkins, Sr., of Middlesex County, or Wade and John Netherland of Cumberland and Powhatan counties. They enjoyed high social standing in their communities, as attested by the regular use of the honorific title "Mister." Some practiced the trade personally, others simply owned the business. All used slaves and indentured servants in their work, men who were able to carry on the project while the master was not on the site. In 1743, Major Edward Daingerfield undertook to make brick and a brick churchyard wall for Blisland Parish. Ten years later he was dead, but work on the parish glebe was performed by "Mrs Daingerfield's Workmen." Finally, above the level of these local builders was the stratum of major colonial building contractors, the Larkin Chews and the Harry Gaineses. These were gentlemen of considerable wealth and standing in the colony, who ranked among the most successful Virginians of their era. Building craftsmen were thus widely distributed and readily available throughout Virginia after the late seventeenth century. Labor was expensive, but it was not particularly scarce.[11]

In short, while builders might have agricultural and other business interests in the eighteenth century (as indeed they might have in the nineteenth, after the emergence of the architectural and building trades in recognizably modern form), it is a mistake to pigeonhole them as "farmer-carpenters," "gentlemen architects," "master builders," or in other categories suggesting quasi-professional status or a limited understanding of the full range of building and design. Building was a major economic activity for those who built the churches, and the undertakers, whatever their personal skills, were actively involved at every level of the building process in negotiating the contract and organizing the project. The construction industry in colonial Virginia was a highly organized, businesslike one. It was practiced by numerous skilled individuals, and supervised by equally knowledgeable men, who were in no sense the captives of minimal standards of workmanship or mindless traditionalism, as has often been argued.[12]

Much of our understanding of eighteenth-century Virginia architecture has been obscured by a notion of design responsibility developed in the early twentieth century. It arose in part from a misunderstanding of the nature of the building process, as we have observed it, and of the relationship of that process to the social structure of the colony. Recognizing that there was a difference between eighteenth-century and twentieth-century building, Fiske Kimball, a pioneering scholar of early American architecture, placed great emphasis on the concept of the eighteenth-century designer as someone who, if he had no fully developed architectural skills himself, was at least familiar with the current architectural trends of Europe and was motivated to imitate them. This familiarity came through the designer's education and, in some instances, travel, but more often it was acquired from architectural treatises and handbooks. While architects as a sociologically defined profession did not exist, and "characteristics personal to designers" are difficult to identify in standing buildings, "Armed with books, a cultivated owner or an ambitious mechanic was often able to erect buildings which would have honored an architect by profession, and to deserve honor as an architect."[13]

This analysis carries a hidden assumption, common to studies of pre-Revolutionary American architecture. It is that colonial Virginians not only knew of European developments, but wished to emulate them as closely as possible. Whether "naturally," from a desire to curry favor with cosmopolitan royal officials, from the imposition of

taste by those officials, or from what John Clive and Bernard Bailyn call "the sense of inferiority that expressed itself in imitation of English ways, and a sense of guilt regarding local mannerisms," "taste" ultimately triumphed over "tradition." The architect for whom Kimball and his successors looked was not so much a person who possessed an "artistic" sensibility as a person who felt compelled to force local building into a received European mode. The historiography of colonial American public buildings and large houses has thus been directed largely toward the identification of published or built prototypes of individual structures, and the chronicling of the emergence of an identifiable *auteur*, from the tasteful "gentlemen architect" and highly skilled "master builder" of the eighteenth century to the trained professional of the early nineteenth century whom we recognize as similar to the architect of our own day.[14]

This enterprise is faulty both logically and empirically. In its one-sided emphasis on the authority of European forms, it ignores the paradox of colonial life, described by Clive and Bailyn, that double impulse of attraction to and revulsion from the imperial center. Colonials saw the metropolis not only as a source of cultural, political, and economic good, but also as a locus of corruption compared with the colonies' unspoiled virtue. Too often students of architecture deny the tension by resolving it, treating the apparent colonial fondness for the imported style and for the local vernacular as mutually exclusive. The cosmopolitan impulse embodied in the gentleman architect, they say, must vanquish the barbarities of the master builder. The gentleman works from taste (is there only one?) while the builder is straitjacketed by tradition. Indeed, academic buildings are designed, while "most colonial buildings were not designed at all, but were simply built."[15]

The search for the *auteur*, in particular for the gentleman architect "almost always" responsible for "the most ambitious and formal structures" of colonial America, proceeds not from the careful examination of buildings and their histories but from a conceptual structure that has little to do with the history of architecture and much to do with the celebration of a hierarchical ideal. Architectural historians tend to believe that the architectural ideas of the upper classes are inherently superior to others current in any society. "Aesthetic appreciation of an object," Eric Mercer has pointed out, "is not always clearly separable from, and is often heightened by, awestruck admiration of the vast, and usually exaggerated, sums that it is said to cost." Moreover, architectural historians tend to identify with the elite who commissioned the buildings they study, and to project this identification onto the past. Thus, they assume that lower social groups inevitably look to their betters for architectural ideas and that elite taste inevitably vanquishes popular taste, however crude the translation.[16]

Our one-to-one equation of styles with social classes, and our assumptions about the mutual exclusivity of high style and local vernacular, cause us to miss the complexity of the process through which colonial buildings, and particularly churches, were designed and built. These striking buildings embodied the contradictions of the colonial society, the dual loyalty both to the metropolitan style and to the local one, not accidentally, not helplessly, not ignorantly, but knowingly and expressively. They were carefully considered buildings, and their mixture of fashionable decoration and local forms reflects the complicity of client and craftsman and their mutual participation in a richly varied architectural tradition. The churches sprang from the Anglo-Virginian parish community as social products that actualized the profoundest sort of symbolic discourse in a dramatic public statement. If we judge the churches according to an abstracted external standard of "taste," we will fail to comprehend them: indeed we would dismiss them as insignificant. To understand their architecture, we need to take into account all levels of significance, from the most cosmopolitan to the parochial; to understand the process of their design, we need to recognize the striving of their collective designers to satisfy all those levels of reference.

Colonial churches were highly nuanced buildings. When they used the European high style, it was for Virginian purposes. When they drew on tradition, it was by choice. Their design was a process in which many people — the vestry, the undertaker, the craftsmen, and, occasionally, even the parishioners — played a role. The responsibilities that we customarily assign to the professional architect — the planning and detailing of the building, the production of drawings, the determination of the structural system, the drafting of a bill of materials, the provision of materials, the siting of the building, the hiring and supervising of workmen, the assessment of the finished structure — were handled by a bewildering variety of people. Moreover, we cannot easily separate the tastes and contributions of the builders from those of their social superiors. In distinguish-

ing master builder from gentleman architect, we forget that most of the master builders — the people who took on the building contracts — were themselves gentlemen by colonial Virginia standards. Some of them were personally skilled in the building arts, and some were not. Furthermore, the physical production of stylistic elements lay in the hands of the manual workers, black and white. The nature of the process and the evidence of it are such that it is empirically impossible to oppose gentry sensibilities to worker backwardness in the design of Virginia's colonial churches. At the same time, there ran through the society — through vestrymen, undertakers, and craftsmen — a core of knowledge of the vernacular building traditions of Virginia that informed the vestrymen's initial attempts to decide what sort of church to build, infused the detailed negotiations between vestry and undertaker, and allowed for the production of specifications that left much to custom and skill. Finally, there were liturgical intentions everyone understood, which further helped to define the shape of the finished building. Liturgy, tradition, and current style were elements of an architectural lexicon that was familiar, in varying degrees of specificity, to all the participants in the building process. If we cannot conceive of traditional craftsman reeducated by cultivated gentleman, we cannot locate design entirely in the builder to the exclusion of his client either. Who designed the churches? They all did. The fracture of high style and vernacular, of design and execution, along clear class or craft lines is impossible. Responsibility was diffuse, but clients and builders shared an architectural language whose meanings and intentions required less explicit exposition than might otherwise be the case in a larger community, and its assumptions, coupled with negotiations as the work progressed, produced the buildings that we see scattered throughout eastern Virginia today.[17]

In designing a new parish church, the vestry and their contractors negotiated the ultimate form of the building after agreeing to certain basic conditions. But these were often the last in a series of decisions begun as soon as it was determined that a new church would be constructed. Usually the general size of the projected building was established when the original decision to build was made, based on the number of parishioners who were expected to attend the new church. It is clear that the vestry knew how many people they wanted to accommodate, and how many their new church could be expected to hold. No formulas for the calculation of these data have come down to us in the vestry records, but the calculation was probably based on square footage, the measurement used in newspaper advertisements, from which prospective undertakers were expected to devise plans. Otherwise the vestry minutes simply note, as one from St. Peter's Parish did, the decision "that as Soon as Conveniently may be a new Church of Brick Sixty foot Long and twenty fower foot wide in the Cleer and fowerteen foot pitch with a Gallery Sixteen foot Long be built and Erected upon the maine Roade by the School House neer Thomas Jackson's." Occasionally, virtually complete specifications, extending to the number and size of the windows, the kinds and quality of interior finish, and the colors that the trim was to be painted, were drafted before any workmen were involved. In other instances, the original design was itself the product of discussions between the vestry and the undertaker. The Bristol Parish vestry ordered its church wardens "to consult with Skilfull workmen, about the most Convenient way" to add to its parish church. Most often, the basic dimensions of the church were determined, and then an advertisement issued an invitation to any interested workmen "to come in [to the vestry meeting] & bring there Planes & Prepossials" on a specific date, usually in the spring. The phrasing and punctuation of the ensuing contracts as recorded in the vestry books often seem to reflect the progress of these negotiations. After agreeing to the size of the building, the undertaker and the vestry entered into an item-by-item consideration of the structure, layout, and finish of the new church. Following a discussion, the foundation structure was agreed on. The negotiations moved on, and the clerk wrote in summary: "a strong substantial Girt Floor laid with sound well season'd quarter'd Pine Plank in bredth not above 10 Inches," adding after more consultation, "all the Pews to be 6 feet wide & 10 feet long, except two Vizt. one on each side of the Communion Table." There was more discussion: "which are to be 9 by 7 the Ally to be 6 feet wide." The haggling continued to the number and size of the doors, the details of the finish of the pews, the arrangements of the chancel and pulpit, the position of the font, the exterior details. The finish of the interior walls was remembered, and added. Then the roof and the paint were negotiated. The question of a gallery was raised and decided. Finally a price was agreed on, a completion date set, and the contract signed.[18]

At whatever stage the undertaker was brought into the design process, the ultimate product was a lengthy document drawn up in the form of a contract or "Articles of Agreement." Many of these documents were transcribed in the vestry books (for an example, see Appendix). They make clear several aspects of the design of colonial churches that are important to understand. As Alan Gowans pointed out in his discussion of Christ church, Lancaster County, a building contract was a very mundane thing. The "art" of the church is absent from the contract. The specifications for Wicomico Parish church, drawn up in 1753 and revived in 1763, are a case in point. The builder was directed to base the church on Christ church (Fig. 5), often considered the most beautiful of the Virginia churches, yet there was no mention of the proportions, most of the details, the brickwork, or other elements of the church normally considered to be its fine points. Instead, it was the overall image of Christ church—the distinctive combination of elements such as the cross plan, the ox-eye windows, and the hipped roof—that constituted for the Wicomico vestry the essential connection between the model and the copy. Moreover, as in all building contracts, much was left to the judgment and experience of the builder, subject to consultation with the vestry or its representative overseers as the work progressed. When the specifications were changed, as they usually were, it was up to the prospective undertaker to alter the dimensions of the doors and windows "in Proportion to the heigh [sic] of the Wall." Undertakers of other churches were instructed that their buildings were to be "completely finished According to art," that "the Rafters over the single pews for the body of the Church [are] to be according to Architect[ure]," that the new features were to be "correspondent to the Church." There was thus play for the builder's imagination and aesthetic sense, but within a narrowly specified context, since much of the form of the building was determined before his arrival. The details—the exact shape and proportions of moldings and panels, of pulpits and altarpieces and doorways—were left to him. Yet he was also subject to constant "viewing" of his work by vestry overseers, and to aesthetic criticism and correction by his clients and even by the public. An anonymous correspondent wrote to Purdie and Dixon's *Virginia Gazette* in 1770 comparing the steeple then being constructed by Benjamin Powell to "the Emperour of Morocco's pigeon house, or the thing upon the Turkish mosques which they

FIG. 5. Christ church (ca. 1732–35), Lancaster County. The wall is a 20th-century reconstruction on 18th-century foundations. (Photograph, Dell Upton.)

call a minaret, where a fellow knocks upon a piece of wood with a mallet to call the Mussulmen to prayers." [19]

Eighteenth-century Virginia churches and other large buildings are often thought to have been designed according to elaborately comprehensive proportional systems. These may have been employed in the planning of a few churches — an argument has been made by Marcus Whiffen for a proportional design in the original version of the third Bruton Parish church — but it is difficult to take such systems seriously in comprehending the finished products. The vestry and their contractor thought in terms of standard compositional elements — compass ceilings and windows, wainscot pews, water tables, moldings — which were reconciled in the design less by a proportional system than by their common employment of traditional dimensioning modules. For example, the thickness and height of brick walls were determined by the standard size of bricks and by traditional rules about the relationship of wall thickness to wall height. Bricks were about 8 inches long by 4 inches deep by 2½ inches thick. Four courses of bricks plus the intervening mortar joints made a foot of height. A one-story brick building, or the brick foundation of a frame building, usually had walls 1½ bricks thick — about 13 inches with mortar and plaster. Timbers, too, were cut to conventional sizes and were framed in conventional ways, with little variation from one building to another. Molding elements were equally uniform. Most panels, for example, were framed with quarter-inch and half-inch ovolos. Even window glass was employed in a limited number of standard pane and sash sizes, and while some vestries might order "Shash [*sic*] windows proportioned to the Building," most specified "eighteen-light sash" or simply 8-by-10 inch panes. Within the limits of these standard modules, everything from a molding to the size of the building lay under the control of several different people; any and all of the parts were routinely altered in the course of construction. Thus abstract schemes could be of little use in most churches.[20]

In addition to these structural uniformities, the appearance of church buildings was governed by long-established conventions of planning dictated by Anglican religious practice, and by similar conventions of fittings and decoration specified both in custom and in law. Every church had to have certain features, including a pulpit, a communion table, a reader's desk, a Bible, prayer books, an altarpiece, and the Royal Arms, because civil and ecclesiastical laws

required them and because the church rituals could not be performed without them. Thus, designing a church could be for the vestry and the undertaker a matter of employing those customary and legally mandated elements in a particular form that suited the parish's needs and ability to pay. The high degree of standardization possible allowed the vestry of Upper Parish, Nansemond County, simply to order the construction of a building "to be Compleated as Soon as Can be after the Usuall Manner of building Chappells." The vestrymen were seldom this formulaic, but there was a recognizable usual manner as early as 1665, when the vestry of Christ Church Parish, Middlesex County, directed that its church be built "in Such decent mañer & Form as is usuall, and that [the undertakers] provide all Things fitting." A century later, the Frederick Parish vestry ordered Charles Smith to supply its Winchester church with "every other useful and necessary piece of work which is customary in such a building and not herein particularly specified." [21]

The vestries' participation in church design was facilitated by the traditional practice of modeling a new building on a standing one. A variety of sources might provide a design. Some vestries chose a distant model to emulate. The new mother church of Christ Church Parish, Middlesex County, built in 1665, was "In every respect to be done and Finished according to the Middle plantacon [later Williamsburg] Church." The attraction is not certain: Middle Plantation was not yet the colonial capital, and we know nothing about its church, built about 1660, that would help us to understand. For the Wicomico Parish church of 1763, the model, as we have seen, was a prominent structure that stood nearby. It is easy to understand why the parish would turn to Christ church, Lancaster County, one of the largest and most elaborate in the colony, and situated in an adjacent parish, to which many of the Wicomico Parish elite had kinship ties. Most often, another church in the same parish was chosen, as when Lynnhaven Parish ordered that its new Eastern Shore chapel of 1753 was "to be finished in a Workman-like manner after the Moddel of the [main] Church." Although a copy might bring with it a visually pleasing idea, the vestries never chose a foreign or a published model. Their intentions were too context-specific for that. When the vestry ordered the construction of a building "pewed & raild in the manner of the Mother Church," it provided a concrete basis for judging both the intended and the final result. The undertaker could refer to the standing church in drawing up an estimate preparatory to bidding on the contract, as a kind of full-size model of what was wanted, and as an indicator of the desired quality. Vague phrases like "a proper facing & moulding" to the pews acquired substance when it was understood that they were to be "finished in a plain Manner after the Moddle of Curls Church." The model served as a means of quality control, and also as a guide for making subsequent price adjustments. Churches were undertaken for a fixed price, but alterations were routinely made in the course of the work, and supplementary payments made. Sometimes outside workmen were called on to figure such items as "the Value of two Windows [and] the difference between a plain Cornice and Mundillion" one. It was much easier when there was a fixed standard. The 1665 Middlesex County church exceeded the required standard, and the vestry assigned two of its members to "View the Middle Plantacõn Church and make report to this Vestry how much it is Short of this [newly built] Church In workmanship, And . . . allowance [will] be made [to] the Undertaker accordingly." [22]

In virtually every completed church, the undertaker received additional compensation for work not specified in the original contract, as did William Waite, who built Quantico church in Dettingen Parish in the 1750s. He was paid fourteen thousand pounds of tobacco extra for "Doors with glass over them & Plain Neet Cutt Windows," and three thousand more for a plaster cornice. The most common reason for making these amendments was that the original design was thought to be inadequate to the parish's spatial needs. Fredericksville Parish came to this conclusion about its "Church above the Mountains," and lengthened it eight feet before construction was begun. Other specifications were altered because the engineering was judged faulty by prospective undertakers. It was "represented to this Vestry" in Lynnhaven Parish that the wall thickness of its Pungo chapel was "to[o] slender and weak for a Building of Such Dimensions." The vestry and the undertaker agreed on a thicker wall and a corresponding alteration in the fee was made. Sometimes the design was changed because the vestry thought it would improve the appearance or function of the building. Most often these changes involved single features rather than a comprehensive adjustment of the entire scheme. David Kinked was ordered to change the plans for a new church for St. Mark's Parish by moving the north door to the south side and setting the

building east-west as required by canon law. Alexander Graves was directed to raise the walls of the middle church of Christ Church Parish, Middlesex County, five courses of bricks higher then originally ordered. The much-altered specifications for Wicomico church were changed again during construction when John Wily was instructed to put pediments over each door and to insert two gallery windows in each end of the church. The vestry of the Upper Parish of Nansemond County had the wall thickness of its Suffolk church altered, and at the same time agreed to an extra payment to change the window openings from square to compass heads. When they ordered the alteration to the wall thickness at Pungo chapel, Lynnhaven Parish's vestry agreed to pay the undertaker Hardress Waller £5 to put a four-foot circular window in each gable, believing that "the same will be as well useful as Ornamental in the said Chapel." Even after a church was finished, it continued to be subject to these piecemeal remodelings. Dettingen Parish decided to have two extra windows cut in Broadrun chapel several years after it was built. Suffolk Parish had the windows of its parish church reworked to match those of an addition. These were routine occurrences, and they were facilitated by the use of the modular system of design based on conventional dimensions. [23]

Although the designs of pre-Revolutionary Virginia parish churches were made as a result of negotiations among a number of people working within a traditional system of building practices, ecclesiastical ritual, and aesthetic assumptions, and were subject to constant change, the process could not be an improvisatory one. Churches were large and complex buildings, and the projects had to be carefully considered, if only for the parties' financial security. There is abundant evidence that throughout the eighteenth century, and probably in the seventeenth as well, architectural drawings supplemented written specifications in the planning, bidding, and construction of virtually every one of these vernacular buildings. What they were like is a matter of conjecture. Most of the vestry book entries say "plan" rather than "plans," and we must surmise that most drawings were confined to a floor plan, with perhaps an elevation of a principal facade used in some cases, as in the only extant drawing, a nineteenth-century copy of the plan and elevation drawing for Pohick church (Fig. 6). In at least two instances — those of the Wicomico church and of

Pohick church—a roof framing plan was used. Both had hipped roofs, the framing of which was a complex geometrical problem. The carpenter had to determine the length and cutting angle of timbers that sloped in more than one plane. Most eighteenth- and early nineteenth-century builders' handbooks included instructions for calculating the length of hip rafters as a standard feature, and illustrated framing plans (Fig. 7) that were probably similar to those used at the Virginia churches.[24]

The earliest evidence of the use of drawings comes from St. Peter's Parish, where they were employed in the bidding and construction of the parish church that still stands there. The building was first projected in 1700, and was constructed over the next four years. Immediately after a decision to build the church was made and its basic dimensions established by the vestry, a copy of the order was given to one of the vestrymen who was "Requested to Show the Same to will Hughes and Desire him to draw a

FIG. 6. Pohick church (1769–73; Daniel French, undertaker), Fairfax County. Redrawn by Benson J. Lossing from an 18th-century original, "before me while I write." Present location unknown. Lossing attributed the design of the church to George Washington, but the similarity of Pohick church to Falls church, whose design was provided by James Wren, suggests that the vestry simply appropriated Wren's design. (From Benson J. Lossing, *The Home of Washington* [Hartford: A. S. Hale and Co., 1871], p. 88.)

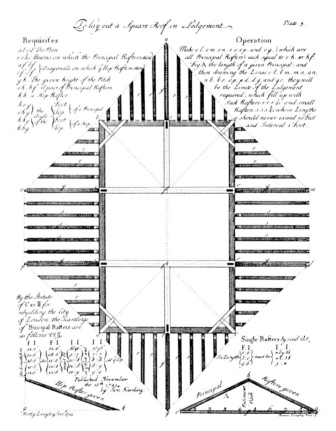

FIG. 7. Framing of a hipped roof. A drawing similar to this was probably used to construct the roof of Pohick church. (From Batty Langley, *The Builder's Treasury of Designs*, pl. 5, courtesy College of Environmental Design Library, University of California, Berkeley.)

Draft of the Said Church and to bee at the next vestry."
After the parish was unable to attract workmen to undertake
the church at the price it was willing to pay, it chose to
contract the work piecemeal, and persuaded Hughes, a carpenter, to take on the carpenter's, joiner's, and turner's
work of the building, "according to the Sevrall Drafts this
day Subscribed by the Said Hughes," who must have
presented elevations of the new building, with its stylish
curvilinear gables, as well as a plan, and perhaps a drawing
of an altarpiece or gallery. There is nothing in the account
to suggest that the use of drawings was a novel idea on this
vestry's part. Rather, their procurement is treated as a
routine part of the vestry's task.[25]

Like specifications, the drawings could be made by
many different people. Sometimes the vestrymen themselves
provided them. The 1772 Albemarle Parish church was to
be built "according to a plan to be designed, prepared and
laid down by the Church Wardens," while two vestrymen,
the builder Severn Guttridge and Clement Parker, Gent.,
drew one for a new poorhouse in St. George's Parish,
Accomack County, in 1768. Some vestries knew what they
wanted but had to find someone capable of making the
drawing, as in Hughes's case, or in a similar instance in Suffolk Parish where the vestry drew up lengthy specifications
for its new Chuckatuck church, then asked the church
wardens to find "Some skillful person in Building" to make
a drawing.[26]

The responsibility for drawing depended less on skills
than on the vestry's certainty about its requirements.
William Walker, "Builder" of Stafford County, constructed
the tower of St. Peter's Parish church "According to a Plan
Delivered into the Vestry drawn by the Sd: Walker," but
he built the glebe house of adjacent St. Paul's Parish from
plans produced by the prospective occupant, the Reverend
Patrick Henry. Where their intentions were less clear, the
vestrymen might purchase a plan from someone. John
Jones was paid by Albemarle Parish "for drawing 2 plans at
building," Samuel Murfee by St. Patrick's Parish "For a
Plan of the Church," and Appollis Cooper by Shelburne
Parish for plans for a glebe house and a church. Most of the
men from whom the vestry purchased plans were builders.
The best known of these men, as a result of Thomas T.
Waterman's work, is John Ayres, or Ariss, an English-born
builder who provided the designs for churches in Truro and
Frederick parishes in the decade before the Revolution.
Plans were purchased in advance when the vestrymen
wanted drawings in hand on which to base negotiations
with undertakers, but were not yet ready to make a contract
with the designer or with anyone else. In all the vestry
books from 1660 to 1775, there are only ten recorded
instances, involving eight individuals, of the purchase of
plans from someone who did not then undertake the
building (see Tab. 5). The gentleman architect is a figure
who is conspicuously missing from the annals of the design
of Virginia's largest public buildings. Only Governor
Alexander Spotswood, who in 1711 supplied "a platt or
draught of a Church" for the vestry of Bruton Parish, is a
possible candidate. The vestry book says simply that the
parish clerk had "received" a plan from him, which
accompanied the governor's offer to pay for part of the
construction costs. The plans were later altered and redrawn.[27]

By far the most common tactic was for the vestries to
publish general dimensions, and to require each bidding
undertaker to bring a plan that met the specifications along
with a bid for building his design. They thus had their
choice of several alternative schemes. Truro Parish determined to build a church that would contain "1600 [square]
Feet on the Floor," and advertised that it "will then be
expected of each Workman to produce a Plan and estimate
of the Expence." At a similar meeting to contract for two
parish churches, the Fairfax Parish vestry chose to use
James Wren's plan for both, hiring him to build Falls church
from his own plan, and paying him forty shillings for the
use of his plan in the construction of the church at Alexandria.[28]

The design and construction of parish churches was an
exercise of political power in eighteenth-century Virginia.
The vestries, though sensitive to their constituents' senti-
ments, initiated building projects, sited, designed, and built
churches with the assistance of undertakers who were their
social peers, and taxed the parishioners to support the
projects. These churches thus used state power to house the
liturgical apparatus of the state Church in forms that spoke
eloquently of the values of Virginia's ruling order.

4 | Structure

Though few of the physical elements of Virginia's Anglican churches were unique to the colony, the interaction of economics, technology, society, and religion produced a distinctive church architecture in pre-Revolutionary Virginia, and a distinctive way of using it. As religious buildings, the churches were shaped by the requirements of what Anglicans called "Prayer Book worship." As public buildings, they were required to meet certain needs of the state. As Virginia buildings, they shared with dwelling houses the use of a simplified, though variable, Virginia building technology. This structural system, a seventeenth-century product of the intersection of English practice with the peculiar economic and demographic uncertainties of the colony's early history, formed the physical armature within which the other considerations were accommodated.

Almost all seventeenth-century Virginia churches, as well as eighteenth-century churches of outlying parishes and the chapels of poorer parishes in the older settled areas, were wooden buildings (see Tab. 3). Seventeenth-century parish churches were for the most part as fragile as the houses of their parishioners, since, like the houses, they were built of a particularly flimsy kind of frame construction. The timbers of these buildings came into direct contact with the ground or were, at best, supported on wooden blocks that served as a foundation. Earthfast post construction, in which the principal wooden uprights were set into the ground, was used at several parish churches in seventeenth-century Virginia, including the lower churches of St. Peter's and Petsworth parishes, which were reposted in 1688 and 1695 respectively. Petsworth Parish's Poplar Spring church of 1677 may have been a post building as well, for the parish paid church warden Phillip Lightfoot for thirty-three cedar posts used in its construction. Poplar Spring church was the most elaborately decorated seventeenth-century Virginia church that we know of. It was fitted with wainscot (paneled) pews and pulpit and a chancel screen with turned balusters, and embellished with painted cherubim, yet the structure was a cheap one. When the builder Samuel Duning erected the building, he cut too many corners, and had to be instructed to "put crosse beames to every small

rafter & fitt the small peeces for the plaister worke, as allsoe amend and rectifie all & every the defects & faults in the covering and weatherboards of the Church." Duning's economy was not blameworthy, only overzealous, for the vestry was glad to pay him extra money for these improvements. This building had its posts replaced by Robert Pryer in 1695, less than twenty years after it was constructed. It was enlarged in 1701, and survived until 1723, when its replacement was completed.[1]

It is likely that most post churches used a variation of earthfast construction known as interrupted-sill building (Fig. 8), which made possible the installation of a substantial wooden floor of the sort ordered by the Petsworth Parish vestry. Interrupted-sill buildings had sills, as normal framed buildings did, but rather than have the posts sitting on top of the sills, the sills were framed into the sides of the posts, which then penetrated the ground as in other forms of earthfast construction. The "Great Church" of Christ Church Parish, Middlesex County, built 1666–67, utilized interrupted-sill construction. In 1684 the vestry asked Christopher Robinson, its church warden, to have the building repaired, specifying "That the Earth be firmly Ram'd, under the Sells [sills], and a Convenient pent house [a small cantilevered roof mid-height on the wall] made to keepe the Raine off them." The reference to ramming the earth under the sills suggests that they were held off the ground by the building's posts, and that they did not have a protective continuous masonry underpinning. This ancient variation on post building characterized the most soundly built of post houses as well.[2]

The Petsworth Parish reposting of 1695 marks the last use of holeset post building recorded for churches, although St. Peter's Parish built a post glebe house in 1704, and post building continued to be used for minor parish construction. Block construction, a late seventeenth-century variant of all-wood building, lasted longer in churches. In block construction, a conventionally framed structure standing on sills was set on wooden piers or pilings rather than on a masonry foundation (see Fig. 8). This technique was utilized for chapels and minor parish buildings like vestry

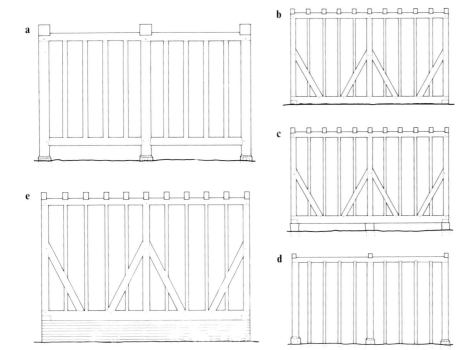

FIG. 8. Post building variations. Schematic elevations of (a) framing with interrupted sills; (b) standard Chesapeake framing with groundlaid sills; (c) standard Chesapeake framing on blocks; (d) earthfast framing; (e) standard Chesapeake framing with brick underpinning. (Drawing, Dell Upton.)

houses and glebe outbuildings until the Revolution. St. Peter's Parish, whose lower church was post built, erected an upper church set on blocks in 1688 and replaced the blocks in 1697. Newport Parish had its upper chapel lengthened and fitted with "good Lightwood Blocks" in 1742, and a year later built a new chapel "on good sound Cyprus blocks." The Bristol Parish vestry of 1725 was indifferent whether its two new chapels were "underpinned with good Blocks or rock-stones," a choice the Southam Parish vestry also gave the undertaker of its two new chapels in 1745. The present Pohick church in Truro Parish replaces a wooden building of 1733 that was ordered to be straightened and reblocked "to enable it to Continue a few years," and in 1758 the Upper Parish of Nansemond County reblocked one of its chapels. By the second quarter of the eighteenth century, though, most wooden churches were set on brick or, less frequently, stone foundations.[3]

At the edges of settlement, log construction was occasionally employed, especially for chapels in parishes where the main church was frame. In 1752, Abraham Keller

of Frederick County agreed to build for Frederick Parish a thirty-by-twenty-two-foot chapel of squared and dovetailed logs that in other respects differed little in its specifications from the frame and brick buildings in the eastern part of Virginia. The vestry of Camden Parish in 1769 ordered the construction of two identical round-log chapels with clapboard roofs.[4]

Of the wooden churches, the best preserved is Slash church (Figs. 9, 10), built in 1729 as the upper church of St. Paul's Parish, Hanover County, by Thomas Pinchback and Edward Chambers, Jr. A rectangular building with a gable roof, it has suffered relatively few exterior changes although the gallery is all that remains of the original church on the interior. Similar to it is the former Tillotson Parish church (Figs. 11, 12), now Buckingham Baptist church, built sometime after the parish's establishment in 1757. This hip-roofed structure was nearly doubled in size by the addition of a north leanto in the 1830s, and only the gallery and some benches are left on the interior, but it is intact structurally. The parish church of Henrico Parish (Figs. 13, 14), begun in 1739 and enlarged in 1773, and known since

Fig. 9. Slash church (1730–32; Thomas Pinchback and Edward Chambers, Jr., undertakers), Hanover County. The gallery windows at the west have been moved several times, and the wing to the left (north) is a modern addition. (Photograph, Dell Upton.)

Fig. 11. Tillotson Parish (Buckingham Baptist) church (ca. 1760), Buckingham County. The original church has been covered with aluminum siding. It was extended by a leanto along the north side in 1833 and by a further extension in the 20th century. (Photograph, Dell Upton.)

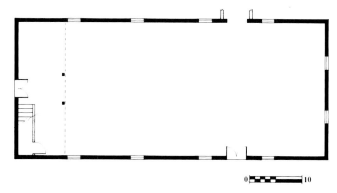

Fig. 10. Slash church. Plan. The north door was probably cut when the 1954 Sunday school wing was built. (Drawing, Dell Upton.)

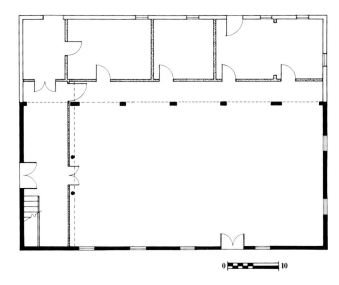

Fig. 12. Tillotson Parish church. Plan. The vestibule at the west and the Sunday school rooms at the north are modern. (Drawing, Dell Upton.)

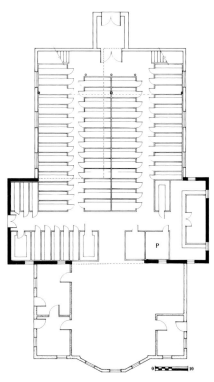

FIG. 13. Henrico Parish church (1739–41; Richard Randolph, Gent., undertaker; enlarged beginning 1773), Richmond. The west facade of the original church is the right transept. The 1773 north wing was enlarged in 1830–34 to form the nave visible in this illustration, and the tower was added at the same time. The church was further enlarged to the south in 1905. (From William Meade, *Old Churches, Ministers, and Families of Virginia* [1857; reprint ed., Philadelphia: J. B. Lippincott, 1910], n.p.)

FIG. 14. Henrico Parish church. Plan. The pews in the nave date from the 19th-century enlargement; those in the original section are modern reproductions of 18th-century forms. Key: P = present location of pulpit. (Drawing, Dell Upton.)

the nineteenth century as St. John's church, Richmond, was originally very close in size and appearance to Slash church, but postcolonial alterations have eliminated or disguised most of its colonial features, and little remains of the eighteenth-century fabric except its gable ends and some pieces of the wall. These three survivors are all that remain of the timber buildings that once dominated the Anglican landscape of Virginia.[5]

The earliest brick churches appeared in the third quarter of the seventeenth century. Three extant churches lay claim to dates between the 1630s and the 1650s, but these dates are unacceptable, for reasons discussed in chapter 5. The first firmly dated brick church about which we know more than the name was the second Bruton

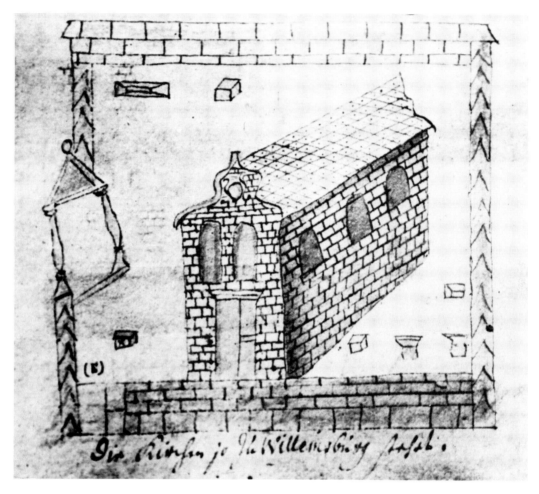

Fɪɢ. 15. Second Bruton Parish church (1681–83; Capt. Francis Page, undertaker), Middle Plantation (now Williamsburg). Drawing of 1702 by Franz Ludwig Michel. (Photograph, Colonial Williamsburg and Burgerbibliothek, Bern.)

Parish church (Fig. 15), planned in 1678 and built at Middle Plantation (now Williamsburg) in 1681–84. A rectangular structure with curvilinear gables and, according to archaeological evidence, buttresses, the church stood until the second decade of the eighteenth century, when it was described as ruinous and replaced by the extant (third) Bruton Parish church. Beginning with the 1681 structure, but especially after 1700, it was increasingly common for at least the principal church in each well-established parish to be built of brick.[6]

Whether post built, blocked, framed on a masonry foundation, or built entirely of brick or stone, the parish churches presented engineering problems not encountered in other buildings in pre-Revolutionary Virginia. In no other building was the craftsman faced with enclosing such a large undivided space. Courthouses included a large open room, but they were usually one-story buildings and relatively small when compared with the churches. Some mansions were nearly as large as good-sized churches, but mansions were divided by vertical partitions and horizontal floors that provided bracing and additional support for walls and roofs. In a church, the tall walls had to brace themselves, and the roof ideally had to span the enclosure without intermediate support. The church builders found that, with a few modifications, notably in the way they customarily framed roofs, the traditional building system was adequate to the task.

By the early eighteenth century, Virginia's builders had developed a framing system (Fig. 16) utilizing traditional Anglo-American forms in a manner that was informed by the labor-saving intelligence of post building. Where most buildings in the Anglo-American tradition employed heavy three-dimensional frames, Virginia's builders worked around a regular ten-foot bay and a frame consisting of pairs of long walls linked at the top by lap-jointed joists. Joinery was simplified, and the vocabulary of joints was restricted for the most part to lap joints and simple mortise-and-tenon joints throughout the frame. Part sizes were standardized. Most frame buildings used posts, braces, and joists about four by eight inches, studs and common rafters three by four inches, and sills about ten inches square. This simplification and standardization allowed building to proceed smoothly, with a minimum of labor-costly complexity in framing and joinery, and it permitted the parts to be manufactured rapidly to a small number of standard dimensions by the gangs of sawyers builders used.[7]

Virginia's church builders tended not to deviate from the traditional wall-framing system except to increase the size of the members on some occasions. Contracts for large frame churches often specified the sizes of the timbers to be used, and sometimes the kind of wood and the method of manufacturing the parts as well. Part sizes might be increased dramatically over the customary dimensions. The vestry of St. George's Parish, Spotsylvania County, specified that its two new sixty-by-twenty-four-foot churches were to have fourteen-foot-high walls. The post, plate, and ceiling joist size was increased from the customary four by eight inches to nine by twelve inches, the studs to four by nine, the braces to nine inches square, and the sills and floor girders to a foot square. Christ Church Parish, Middlesex County, ordered a sixty-by-twenty-five-foot upper church to have six-by-twelve-inch posts, six-by-nine-inch plates, and four large nine-by-eleven-inch tie beams. The vestry specified as well that the floor timbers were to "be of the best White Oake to be of quartered Stuff," though the latter condition was amended to "the best Ring Oake Squared with the Saw," when quartered oak proved to be unobtainable. The vestry further assumed the use of the usual ten-foot bays in directing that seven floor girders be used for the sixty-foot structure. The builders of Providence Presbyterian church, the only frame colonial church to survive other than the three Anglican ones, used a different strategy. They employed six-inch-square studs on two-foot centers, but the posts were the same size: the building was effectively unbayed. In contrast to these sturdy structures, for a forty-by-twenty-four-foot church with fourteen-foot walls — a building taller but no larger than a house — the Fredericksville Parish vestry was satisfied in 1745 with parts of the size customary in domestic construction, except that the floor was to be reinforced and the plate was to be increased to eight by nine inches to accommodate the heavier roof frame that would cover the church.[8]

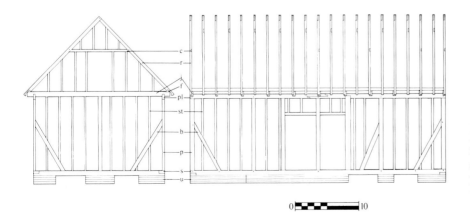

Fig. 16. Granary (early 19th century), Rich Neck, Surry County. A traditional Virginia frame. Key: u = brick underpinning; s = sills; p = post; b = braces; st = studs; pl = plate; f = (tilted) false plate; j = joists; r = rafters; c = collars. (Drawing, Dell Upton.)

0 ▬▬▬▬ 10

Considerations of strength also affected the use of brick. According to eighteenth-century prescriptive sources, one and one-half bricks (fourteen inches) was standard brick wall thickness, and field examination of domestic architecture shows this to have been the norm for one-story brick houses in Virginia as well. Virginia church builders specified wall thicknesses ranging from two bricks (eighteen inches) to four bricks (three feet) thick. Although there was evidently no hard-and-fast rule, two-brick-thick walls seem to have been restricted to structures with a wall height of twenty feet or under. An exception was the third Bruton Parish church, where the legislature ordered that the twenty-three-foot-high walls of the wings were to be two bricks thick. The rule of thumb seems to have been invoked in Lynnhaven Parish in 1773, where the walls of Pungo chapel, which were to be twenty feet high, were increased from two to two and one-half bricks thick before construction started, when the vestry decided that two-brick-thick walls would be "to[o] slender and weak for a building of Such Dimensions." No church recorded in the surviving records had a wall height exceeding twenty-eight feet, but in the twenty- to twenty-eight-foot range, wall thickness varied widely. Two-and-one-half-brick-thick walls were most popular, while in larger and more expensive churches they could be as thick as four bricks. In every church, the walls were a half-brick thicker below the water table, and at least another half brick was added to the thickness below grade. Although these relationships were constant, it is clear that for very large buildings the vestrymen knew no rule for the relationship of wall thickness to height, and that an intuitive sense of strength and considerations of cost, which was calculated by wall volume for brick buildings, governed each vestry's choice. Mistakes could easily be made, and it is probable that the cracks that developed in the brick walls of the 1762–64 Portsmouth Parish church and the 1743 Cypress church of Southwark Parish before the buildings were finished resulted from the use of inadequate foundations for their swampy sites.[9]

The most demanding task the Virginia builder faced was to span the open room safely, preferably without columns. The characteristic Virginia framing system described above typically utilized an all-common-rafter roof system, in which small rafters of about three by four inches were set at two-foot intervals, and usually connected by collar beams — the cross bar of the A formed by each pair of rafters — the same size as the rafters (see Fig. 16). A roof of

this sort could easily span an eighteen- to twenty-foot-deep house, but few builders trusted it to cover a larger structure. Thus it was seldom employed in church construction. One survives, however, on Providence Presbyterian church (Fig. 17). The rafters are on two-foot centers, but the timbers, like those in the walls, are six inches square. Common-rafter roofs were also employed at the Fredericksburg and Mattapony churches of St. George's Parish, Spotsylvania County, built in 1731, for the bill of scantling only called for relatively small four-by-five-inch rafters. A version of the common-rafter roof called a clasped purlin roof (Fig. 18), with long horizontal members (the purlins) wedged into the angle between the rafter and the collar, may have been used in a church built for Fredericksville Parish in 1745. Again, the specifications only call for four-by-five-inch rafters, but they also list wind braces and purlins of the same size.[10]

It is more likely that the Fredericksville specifications were an uninformed attempt to order a girt, principal rafter, "or as the Workmen Call it a princeapal Roof," one of the two types of roof structures most often found on Virginia's surviving pre-Revolutionary churches. A principal-rafter roof was constructed on a bay system, with large rafters at six- to ten-foot intervals supporting heavy purlins. The purlins and principals were normally fashioned into a rigid frame by some sort of wind bracing set diagonally between them, and this frame in turn supported the small common rafters that were set at two-foot intervals between the principals. The common rafters might simply lie across the

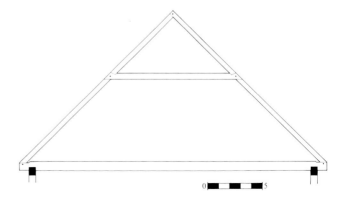

FIG. 17. Providence Presbyterian church (ca. 1750), Louisa County. The all-common-rafter roof is unusual for having no false plate. (Drawing, Dell Upton.)

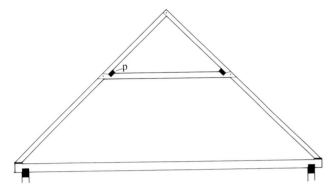

Fig. 18. Clasped-purlin roof. Key: p = purlin. (Drawing, Dell Upton.)

backs of the purlins, or they might be mortised into them. Further reinforcement in roofs of this kind was supplied by collar beams connecting each pair of principal rafters and often the common rafters as well. Principal-rafter roofs were used on many of the earliest surviving American buildings, including the brick Bacon's Castle (1665), Surry County, Virginia, and the post-built Cedar Park (1702), Anne Arundel County, Maryland. Principal-rafter roofs are the earliest church roof form of which we have a clear record. St. Luke's church had one that collapsed in 1887, although the restorers of 1955–57 installed a common-rafter structure. The 1677 Petsworth Parish vestry order to Samuel Duning to "put cross beames to every small rafter" implies that there were also large rafters, and therefore a principal-rafter roof, on the Poplar Spring church that Duning was building. The use of principal rafters was clearly specified in the contract for the Lynnhaven Parish church of 1691, and for each of the three new churches built by Christ Church Parish, Middlesex County, in the second decade of the eighteenth century. Two of these buildings are gone, two lost their roofs in the nineteenth century, and the roof of the fifth is inaccessible, so the earliest example of a principal-rafter roof available for inspection is that on the 1711–15 Bruton Parish church (Fig. 19). The Bruton roof is characteristic of its type. The large principal rafters taper from their feet to their apex, and are braced by collars set about two-thirds of the way up from the tie beams. Two sets of purlins, one in the plane of the roof and one set back from it, support the common rafters, which are tenoned into the upper purlin and pass over the lower one. There are small

queen-post struts reinforcing the angles of the principals and the tie beams, and the whole is disposed in bays of six common rafters, with four trusses (three bays) covering each of the east-west arms and two trusses (one bay) spanning each of the transepts. Principal-rafter roofs continued to be specified throughout the colonial period. Southam Parish ordered a "girt roof with principal rafters" for its two new chapels of 1745, and Fairfax Parish did the same in the specifications for its two new churches of 1767.[11]

A principal-rafter roof was much stronger than a common-rafter roof, but it relied chiefly on the stiffness of the timbers in the plane of the roof to support it. For very wide churches this was not adequate, and while the Christ Church Parish vestry, in the absence of a better solution, was willing to specify a principal-rafter roof for its thirty-foot-wide mother church of 1712, no subsequent vestries used them for churches over twenty-four or twenty-five feet wide. One possible solution to the spanning of wider buildings was to use intermediate posts. The Stratton Major Parish vestry ordered five pairs of columns to be used in its fifty-foot-wide parish church of 1760, but ultimately decided that they were unnecessary.[12]

It was probably in the 1720s that Virginia's builders began to roof large churches with king-post trusses. King-post frames resembled principal-rafter roofs in every respect except that a large post stood on the tie beam in the center of the span and the ends of the principal rafters were

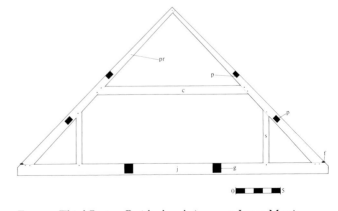

Fig. 19. Third Bruton Parish church (1711–15; James Morris, undertaker), Williamsburg. Principal-rafter roof truss. Key: pr = principal rafter; p = purlin; c = collar; s = strut; j = joist/tie beam; g = girder; f = false plate. (Drawing, Dell Upton.)

tenoned into it at the apex of the roof rather than being joined to each other (Figs. 20–22). Thus the cross frame was a true truss, and supported the roof plane at right angles to it. Normally the king post was cut with shoulders near the bottom to accommodate diagonal struts that further reinforced the angle between the king post and the principals (technically called top chords). King-post trusses were a northern English vernacular form that passed into general English practice in the seventeenth century, at which time they acquired the upward-raking struts that the American examples have. The strutted form was popularized in seventeenth-century books like Joseph Moxon's *Mechanick Exercises* (Fig. 23), published in installments between 1678 and 1680. Moxon's purpose was to explain the standard practices, or "mysteries," of several common trades, including the building trades, to the lay public, so it can be assumed that here as elsewhere he was illustrating a common practice. By the early eighteenth century, the strutted king-post truss was routine builder's handbook fare, and *The Builder's Dictionary* of 1734 illustrates several versions. King-post structures were introduced into New England in the second decade of the eighteenth century and were customary on American churches from the 1720s on. It is likely that they came to Virginia in that decade, although it may be that the Petsworth Parish vestry was thinking of that relatively novel form when it referred in 1694 to "an english fraim'd roof." King posts were not explicitly mentioned in the documents until the 1760s when the specifications for the 1760 Staunton church of Augusta Parish and for Pohick church, built by Truro Parish beginning in 1769, both called for them. Yet of the standing churches, every one built after 1720 that retains its original roof has some version of the king-post truss. The earliest surviving example may be that at Merchant's Hope church in Prince George County (Fig. 24). The date of the church is in dispute; it is certainly not 1657 as is often claimed. The brickwork, compass windows, raised-panel doors, two east windows, and the few details that survive inside suggest a date in the second quarter of the eighteenth century. Merchant's Hope resembles nearby Westover and Blandford churches, both built in the early 1730s, and Westover church has a version of the same roof used at Merchant's Hope. It may be that the Prince George County church was begun shortly after the redefinition of the boundaries of Martin's Brandon Parish in 1720. Its roof employs a king-post truss modified to accommodate the arched "com-

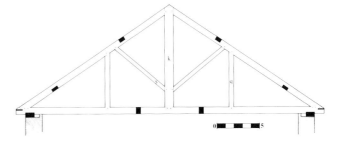

Fig. 20. Fork church (begun ca. 1737), Hanover County. King-post roof truss. Key: k = king post; s = strut; q = queen post. (Drawing, Dell Upton.)

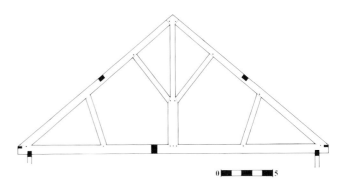

Fig. 21. Tillotson Parish church (ca. 1760), Buckingham County. King-post roof truss. (Drawing, Dell Upton.)

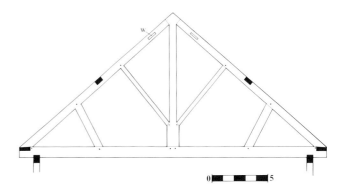

Fig. 22. Henrico Parish church (1739–41; Richard Randolph, Gent., undertaker), Richmond. West king-post truss. Only the trusses at the east and west gable ends survive. Key: w = mortise for wind brace. (Drawing, Dell Upton.)

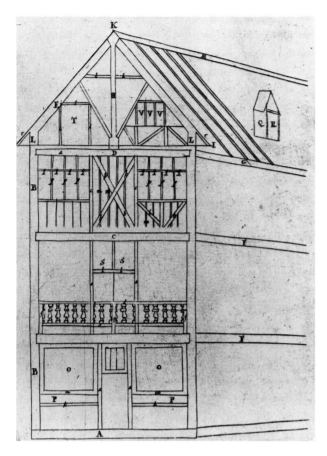

FIG. 23. King-post truss. (From Joseph Moxon, *Mechanick Exercises* [London, 1703], p. 145, courtesy Henry Francis du Pont Winterthur Museum Library: Collection of Printed Books.)

earliest firmly dated example of the king-post truss on a Virginia church. Each of the arms of this cruciform church has a single king-post truss except the western arm, which is slightly longer and has two trusses. The trusses are fully developed versions of the traditional form. They differ in no noticeable respect from the king-post roofs one finds all over the East Coast in eighteenth-century buildings. At the crossing, the carpenters solved the problem of the valleys by using a complete truss set diagonally across the space, and supporting the other two valleys with half-trusses butted up against the complete one.

Many pre-Revolutionary Virginia churches had compass, or arched, ceilings, and the carpenter had to consider how to accommodate them within the structure of the building. With common-rafter and principal-rafter roofs, which were not trussed, the problem was less acute since the plastered or plank-lined vault could be carried up the undersides of the rafters and across the collars. This was done at the Newport Parish church, and at Lynnhaven Parish in 1691, where Jacob Johnson agreed to make "the Inside of the Roofe from the wind beams [collars] to the plates well Sealed with good Oaken boards Arch wise and whited with good white lime." A similar solution was used at the former upper church of Suffolk Parish, built in 1753 and now called St. John's church, Chuckatuck. The current roof structure is an early nineteenth-century replacement, but close examination suggests that it was part of a careful

pass" ceiling that projects into its roof space. The principal rafters at Merchant's Hope are bent at the feet, a vernacular practice of considerable age in England, and one that appears on a few early eighteenth-century Chesapeake-region buildings such as Cloverfields (ca. 1730), Queen Anne's County, Maryland, and Sweet Hall (ca. 1720), King William County, Virginia. "Knees" of this sort appear in the earliest published illustrations of king-post roofs in the English handbooks.[13]

While the date of Merchant's Hope church is in dispute, that of Christ church, Lancaster County, is more clearly established. It was finished in 1735, and stands as the

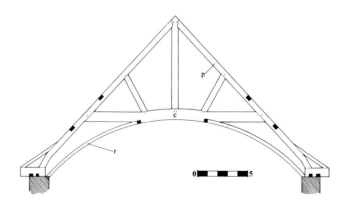

FIG. 24. Merchant's Hope church (ca. 1725), Prince George County. King-post truss. Key: p = bent principal rafters; c = collar curved to accommodate plaster vault; r = ribs for vault tenoned into truss. (Drawing, Dell Upton.)

FIG. 25. Yeocomico church (1706; enlarged second quarter 18th century), Westmoreland County. Interior of original portion. Two large tie beams keep the roof from spreading. The lining of the compass ceiling is noteworthy. The roof of the original section is lined with riven clapboards applied with their butt ends up, while the wing, visible at the right, is lined with beaded boards. (Photograph, Francis Marion Wigmore, 1927, courtesy Virginia State Library.)

attempt to "restore" the church by reproducing its eighteenth-century form. Such roofs, which lacked tie beams connecting the rafter feet, were in danger of spreading and toppling the walls, however. A compass ceiling was installed in the king-post roof in Merchant's Hope church in essentially the same manner as in the later churches just mentioned (see Fig. 24). The king posts sit on collars. The collars are elaborately shaped and, together with the ribs, carefully joined to their undersides and fitted with their own purlins, form the arch of the ceiling. Merchant's Hope originally had tie beams, but these were cut out and the walls did begin to topple. Some vestries discovered the problem early in their churches' lives, and were forced to install tie beams that penetrated the vault and, in their eyes, marred its appearance. The Albemarle Parish vestry instructed the undertaker Colonel John Wall to build its St. Mark's church in 1744 with "the Roof to be Arch'd without beams across (at least such as will appear)." Two years later they found it necessary to make an additional payment to Wall of £118.17.6 current money for "placing & putting in

two strong and Substantial Crosbeams in the sd. Chapel for the better supporting & strengthening the Roof" and some other incidental alterations. Similar beams are still visible in Yeocomico church, Westmoreland County (Fig. 25). At Christ church, Lancaster County, the carpenter simply accommodated the compass ceiling entirely within the vertical walls. The ribs at the apex of the vault are attached to the underside of the tie beams of the trusses.[14]

The traditional structural system was one of the fundamental elements of style in Virginia building. It anchored the Anglican parish churches firmly into the architectural landscape of colonial Virginia: they could only be seen as Virginia buildings, not as versions of some outside model. At the same time, it had more direct implications, affecting what could be done technically to meet the demands made on the churches. The roof-framing system in particular had implications for the planning of Virginia churches, for it restrained their width and led to a characteristic and distinctive way of expanding churches that helped to set them apart from those of the other American colonies.[15]

5 | Churches |

"Solemn duties of public service to be done unto God must have their places set and prepared in such sort, as beseemeth actions of that regard," wrote the great sixteenth-century Anglican theologian Richard Hooker. In the sixteenth and seventeenth centuries, the Church of England developed a tripartite formula for church planning that was based on three ritual centers: the pulpit, the communion table, and the baptismal font. Specific arrangements might take many forms, but all were based on a fundamental Anglican belief, enunciated in Hooker's treatise *Of the Laws of Ecclesiastical Polity*, in the complementary importance of priest and people. While Anglicans rejected the abolition of all differences between clergy and laity that more radical Protestants advocated, they regarded the cleric as the first among spiritual equals, as a leader of fellow believers, not as a privileged individual with a special relationship to God. In practice, the congregation was thus a vital part of the service, not deriving its benefit merely from being in the presence of a magical rite. The service continued to focus on the priest, but on his teaching rather than on the liturgy. The eighteenth-century commentator Charles Wheatly captured the mixture of priestly learning and popular participation Anglicans desired when he described the Prayer Book ritual as one in which "a scholar can discern close logick, pleasing rhetorick, pure divinity, and the very marrow of the antient doctrine and discipline; and yet all made so familiar, that the unlearned may safely say Amen." In the first century of the English Reformation, the church was redefined in accordance with this concept. The Anglican parish church in Virginia played many and complex roles in the Virginia parish, but first and most explicitly it was intended to accommodate worship according to these principles. The planning of Virginia's churches was a special case of the general seventeenth- and eighteenth-century attempt to arrange churches to engage the worshippers in the ritual and to place them in a manner conducive to learning from liturgy and sermon.[1]

The Henrician Reformation was less methodical than the Calvinist and Lutheran ones. The decision to break away from Roman control was in many respects political and economic. Although Anglican theologians came to see the Bible as their ultimate authority, it seemed expedient to Henry VIII and his advisors to continue to claim an unbroken succession of institutional authority in a Catholic Church, if not the *Roman* Catholic one. The piecemeal character of English reform left the way open for clerical and lay reformers of all stripes to argue their positions on doctrinal, ceremonial, and architectural matters. A rich polemical literature marked the course of reformation under Henry and his successor, Edward VI, as further departures from Roman practice were instituted by royal and institutional decree. Even before spending time on the Continent during the Marian interlude, influential English churchmen were familiar with the ideas of European Protestants, and this served to encourage further diversity of opinion on English ecclesiastical reform. Yet the more cautious stance adopted by Elizabeth at her accession left many of the most radical reformers in opposition, while the dominant Anglican position was presented as a middle way between Catholic doctrine and Reformed and Lutheran ideas. It was Richard Hooker who presented the case most forcefully for orderly, minimal change, and for the desirability of continuity with ancient practice. Over the course of the seventeenth century his views gained hold on Anglicans.[2]

As it affected the parish church, the Anglican Reformation after the late sixteenth century was characterized by the attempt to retain as many traditional practices and trappings as possible, while adapting them to the Anglican concern for popular participation in church services. The service and the building were designed so that both clergy and laity might understand and participate fully according to their stations. One fruit of the new attitude was the casting of the liturgy into English, beginning with the 1549 *Book of Common Prayer*. Another was the reconception of the church building.[3]

G.W.O. Addleshaw and Frederick Etchells pointed out in their detailed and comprehensive study *The Architectural Setting of Anglican Worship* that the medieval church had consisted of a group of discrete areas: font, nave, chantry chapels, chancel. Not only did each of these areas serve a separate function, but access was limited to different groups in the parish community. The font was the location for baptisms, with priest and family participating. The nave was the parish's space. Chantry chapels were tiny enclosures used for saying masses on behalf of their donors. They stood in the nave but were used by the priests charged with saying those masses. The chancel, containing the altar, was also for clerical use. While all were enclosed within a single set of walls, they were less a coherent space than a series of places linked by a general religious purpose. The looseness of their integration is graphically depicted in the confusing plans of most medieval parish churches (Fig. 26), which were expanded and subdivided over the years for a variety of purposes, and at the instigation of many different members of the parish. Pre-Reformation churches were less unified communal efforts than products of uncoordinated activities by various groups within the parish. The Anglican Church retained many of the customary spaces, but it redefined their use. In theory, the division was no longer one of role in the Church but of function in the religious enterprise. The various parts of the church served as spaces appropriate to the performance of specific offices and services by the entire community. Richard Hooker made the point by contrasting the old dispensation of the Jews

with Anglican practice: "Our churches are places provided that the people might there assemble themselves in due and decent manner, according to their several degrees and orders. Which thing being common unto us with Jews, we have in this respect our churches divided by certain partitions, although not so many in number as theirs. They had their several for men, their several for women, their several for priests, and for the high priest alone their several. There being in ours a local distinction between the clergy and the rest (which yet we do not with any great strictness or curiosity observe neither) but one partition [between nave and chancel]." Hooker recognized the origin of the division, but said that it was different from the elaborate socioreligious distinctions of the Jews. In the nave of an Anglican church, both clergy and laity heard prayers. In the chancel, both participated in the communion service. At the font, all celebrated baptism. Anglicans officially asserted the necessity of the public celebration of communion and baptism as recognitions of the community of the Church.[4]

With the transformation of many chantry chapels to private pews, the new Anglican churches became buildings with three ceremonial centers: the nave, or body, of the church, a font at the west, and the chancel at the east end. The roods (crucifixes) and rood lofts that surmounted the chancel screens of medieval churches were taken down. The screens themselves were not only tolerated but protected, and throughout the seventeenth and eighteenth centuries new churches were built with them, and old churches supplied with them where they had been lost (Fig. 27). These screens were intended to fulfill two related functions: to allow the communicants to come close to the place where the communion was administered — to see and hear clearly what was being done — and to shield them from distractions to contemplation and solemnity. In Hooker's words, "the cause whereof at the first (as it seemeth) was, that as many as were capable of the holy mysteries might there assemble themselves and no other creep in amongst them." Hooker defended the physical separation of nave and chancel, dismissing the Puritan charge that it was a throwback to Judaism, which had been abolished by the coming of Christ, "as though we retained a most holy place, whereinto there might not any but the high priest alone enter." Hooker's was an indirect admission that the reverence and dignity that were supposed to infuse communicants might not pervade everyone present in church. This was more explicitly acknowledged in bishops'

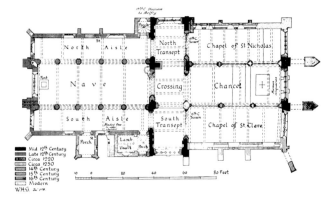

FIG. 26. Rye church (12th–16th centuries), Sussex, England. Plan, showing progressive enlargements. (From John L. Denman, *A Short Survey of the Structural Development of Sussex Churches* [Brighton, England: Sussex Historic Churches Trust, 1967], p. 47.)

FIG. 27. St. Mary the Virgin church, Croscombe, Somerset, England. A medieval church with a chancel screen, pulpit, and pews of 1616. (From *Artotypes of Devon Churches*, [n.d.].)

visitation articles in the seventeenth century, some of which inquired, as the bishop of Norfolk's did in 1638: "Is your chancel divided from the nave or body of your church, with a partition [screen] of stone, boards, wainscot, grates, or otherwise? wherein is there a decent strong door to open and shut, (as occasion serveth) with lock and key, to keep out boys, girls, or irreverent men and women? and are dogs kept from coming to besoil or profane the Lord's table?"[5]

Other physical changes resulted from the English Reformation, two of them direct consequences of the partitioning principle. The stone altar of the medieval church was replaced by a wooden table (Fig. 28), commonly called the Lord's Table. The alteration was made for several reasons. First, the site of the communion was moved out farther into the chancel to make it more visible to all. The old stone altar stood against the east wall at the far end of a sometimes lengthy chancel and was, of course, not portable. Second, the communion was recast as a meal, a spiritual feast, rather than as a reenacted (or renewed) sacrifice. A movable table permitted the communicants to gather around and not be distant spectators. Finally, a table suggested a meal, while a stone mensa connoted a sacrifice. The decision to change was not easily made, and conservative Anglicans were disturbed by the possibility, which was sometimes realized, that enthusiastic parishioners would

FIG. 28. Communion table (ca. 1635), St. Mary's church, Puddletown, Dorset, England. (Photograph, Dell Upton.)

dispose of the old altar, thereby showing more contempt for old authority than the new rulers found comfortable. In the seventeenth century, in order to reestablish what he thought of as a sense of stability and due reverence for the table and to facilitate new ways of administering the communion—as well as for more abstruse theological reasons—Archbishop William Laud ordered the table moved back to the east end of the chancel and enclosed with a rail to give it a greater air of permanence and dignity.[6]

With the chancel reserved for communion, the nave became the site of ordinary services. Pulpits for delivering sermons had been found in some parish churches since the late Middle Ages. Now, however, they became universal, and reading desks, in accordance with Canon LXXXII of 1603 ordering "that a convenient seat be made for the minister to read service in," and often clerks' seats, were added to them (Figs. 29, 30).[7]

The font had traditionally been placed close to the west door. While some reformers argued that it was more convenient and desirable to have it adjacent to the table or the pulpit, Church authorities decreed that entry into the holy community through baptism was appropriately signified by the old arrangement. The font should continue to stand "in the ancient usual places," and it should be made of stone, to discourage moving it.[8]

Finally, the form of decoration in the church was drastically altered. Where the medieval church had been filled with visual images—in its stained glass, in its doom (a painting depicting the Last Judgment) over the chancel arch, in the altar and wall paintings throughout the interior, in internal and external statuary, in the rood itself—the Anglican church was stripped of most of these. Conservative reformers recognized that "Images were first brought into the Church and set up [not to be worshipped but] to be the unlearned men's book. Then ought unlearned men to use them in such sort as learned men use books of holy scripture, and none otherwise." While these men were willing to tolerate images on that basis, so long as they were neither venerated on bended knee nor esteemed "any . . . better than other, [either] for the antiquity, [or] for the goodly carving, painting or gilding of them," more radical reformers won out, and images were abolished except for those in the stained glass, which was largely left intact. In place of representational images, texts were inscribed on the walls of the church (Figs. 31, 32), beginning in the mid-sixteenth century, in the reign of Edward VI.

FIG. 29. St. Mary's church, Badley, Suffolk, England. A medieval church with 17th- and 18th-century appointments. Note the cut-down medieval chancel screen with its neoclassical finials, the late medieval benches and bench ends in the foreground, the 17th-century close pew at the left and reading pew at the right, and the altarpieces on the east wall. (Photograph, Dell Upton.)

Fig. 30. St. Andrew's church, Winterborne Tomson, Dorset. A Norman church with fittings installed 1716–36. Note the chancel screen, the altar rail, the pulpit and type, and the great pews. (Photograph, Dell Upton.)

Fɪɢ. 31. St. Mary the Virgin church, Cerne Abbas, Dorset, England. Wall text (Hosea 6:1), signed "1679 TR." (Photograph, Dell Upton.)

Fɪɢ. 32. St. Mary the Virgin church. Wall texts from various biblical sources (early 18th century). (Photograph, Dell Upton.)

FIG. 33. St. Mary's church, Puddletown, Dorset, England. Lord's Prayer wall text (late 17th or early 18th century). (Photograph, Dell Upton.)

FIG. 34. Lord's Prayer altarpiece (1635), Terrington St. Clement church, Norfolk, England. Painted on board, signed "GB RM [probably church wardens] 1635" at bottom. (Photograph, Dell Upton.)

FIG. 35. Arms of James I on crest of 1616 screen, St. Mary the Virgin church, Croscombe, Somerset, England. (Photograph, Dell Upton.)

Fɪɢ. 36. Arms of Queen Anne (reigned 1702–14), Terrington St. Clement church. Painted on board. (Photograph, Dell Upton.)

Similarly, in place of altar paintings the reformers installed plaques or tablets bearing the Ten Commandments, and often the Apostles' Creed, the Lord's Prayer (Figs. 33, 34), or the Beatitudes. These practices, too, were initiated during Edward VI's reign, and they were officially encouraged in Elizabeth I's. In 1560 she ordered Archbishop Matthew Parker to see that "the tables of the Commandments be comely set or hung up in the east end of the chancel, for edification, ornament, and to promote a religious demeanor among the parishioners." To this more explicitly didactic decoration was added another element — the Royal Arms (Figs. 35, 36). Royal Arms began to be hung in churches during the reign of Henry VIII. A royal order of 1561 acknowledged them to be a proper "crest" for

screens (see Fig. 27). To conservatives, the message was plain. Where the pre-Reformation Church had been in some senses a parallel institution to the state, acting, at least in theory, as an independent representative of a higher power, the reformed Anglican Church was just that — the Church of *England*, an arm of the state, part of an interpenetrated temporal and spiritual power, over both of which the monarch was supreme earthly head. An opponent asked the Elizabethan Anglican controversialist John Jewel, "Is it the word of God setteth up a dog and a dragon in the place of the Blessed Virgin Mary, Mother of God, and St John the Evangelist, which were wont to stand on either side of Christ crucified?" Another opponent claimed that "It was like a declaration on their part, that they were worshippers

F IG. 37. All Saints' church (1703–13), North Runcton, Norfolk, England. (Photograph, Dell Upton.)

F IG. 38. King Charles the Martyr church (1767?), Shelland Green, Suffolk, England. Because the village core is to the north, the main entrance faces that way; a vestry room has been built where the south porch would normally be located. (Photograph, Dell Upton.)

not of our Lord, whose image they had contemptuously thrown aside, but of an earthly king whose armorial bearings they had substituted for it." The Royal Arms became a compulsory feature of church fittings in 1660.[9]

This was the Anglican parish church bequeathed by the sixteenth century to the new colony of Virginia—a building conceived in three parts, with the font at the west end, a chancel fitted with a movable wooden communion table, and a nave with a pulpit and reading desk, the latter two sections separated by a transparent screen. It had biblical passages of appropriate content painted on its whitewashed walls, the Ten Commandments and other key texts displayed, usually over the communion table but sometimes over the screen, and the Royal Arms attached (most commonly) to the screen.

How was the three-part structure realized physically? At the time the first Englishmen came to Virginia, just after the death of Elizabeth I, the principal plan type consisted of a building containing the nave and the font, with the chancel housed in an attached but structurally separate wing. This was, of course, the medieval plan. In England many such churches were modestly adapted medieval buildings, but Anglicans in Europe and America continued to build that way into the eighteenth century. The renowned medieval vertical-timber church at Greensted-juxta-Ongar, Essex, for instance, has a brick Elizabethan chancel, while the eighteenth-century All Saints' church (Fig. 37), North Runcton, Norfolk, and King Charles the Martyr church (Fig. 38), Shelland Green, Suffolk, were also built with chancels. A second kind of church, known as the room, or auditory, church (Figs. 39, 40), appeared at the beginning of the seventeenth century. Here, there was no structural differentiation between the chancel and the nave, though most of the seventeenth-century examples continued to employ screens to mark the division. The auditory form is most strikingly employed in Christopher Wren's city churches, built in the late seventeenth century. Wren's buildings tended to be deeper in relation to their length than were the earlier rural buildings, and often had galleries on several sides. The depth of his churches made it impracticable to stretch a screen entirely across one end, and Wren was said to be opposed to them on principle in any case. Thus, most of his churches relied on a communion rail to establish the nave-chancel division. James Gibbs and other

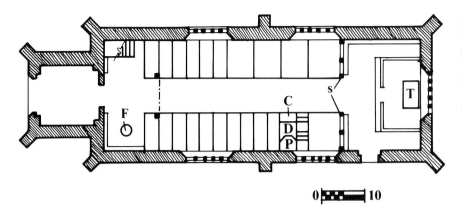

FIG. 39. Foremark church (1662), Derbyshire. Plan. A room church with a screen. Key: F = font; P = pulpit; D = reading desk; C = clerk's desk; s = screen; T = table. (Redrawn by Dell Upton from Addleshaw and Etchells, *Architectural Setting*, plan 6.)

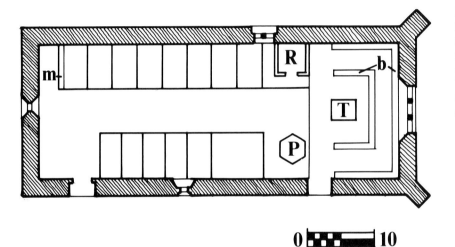

FIG. 40. Langley chapel (ca. 1601), Shropshire. Plan. A room church without a screen, the earliest known example of the room-church plan. Key: m = musicians' desk; R = reading pew; P = pulpit; T = table; b = communicants' benches. (Redrawn by Dell Upton from Addleshaw and Etchells, *Architectural Setting*, plan 29.)

eighteenth-century heirs of Wren's ideas sometimes pressed the chancel into a recess that resembled the old chancel building from the interior but was unexpressed, or minimally expressed, on the exterior (Figs. 41, 42). The room church dominated Virginia church building throughout the colonial period, but it took the form of the smaller, longer rectangular room of rural England rather than the spacious rectangle of Wren's churches. When Wren-like proportions and some details were adopted in the mid-eighteenth century, they were still fitted with Virginian plans.[10]

There is no evidence that Virginians ever built churches with separate chancels. William Strachey's 1625 description

of the 1610 church at Jamestown already depicts a room church, although the earliest dated English example was built only in 1601 (see Fig. 40). Strachey's church sounds too magnificent for Jamestown at that date, and it resembles Ralph Hamor's description of the contemporary church at Henrico, later disowned by its author as a fiction. Nevertheless, Strachey's account is interesting for its similarity to the colony's later seventeenth- and eighteenth-century churches. The Jamestown church was, he said, sixty feet long and twenty-four feet wide, a common eighteenth-century church size. St. Andrew's Parish, Brunswick County, ordered one of those dimensions almost one hundred fifty

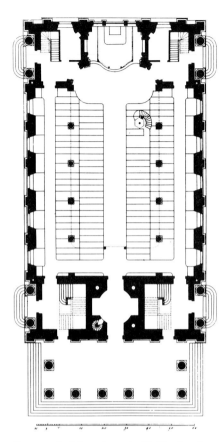

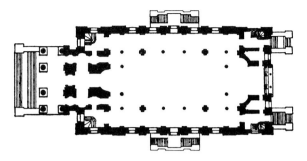

FIG. 42. Christ church (1715–24; Nicholas Hawksmoor, designer), Spitalfields, London. Plan. (From Kerry Downes, *Hawksmoor* [2d ed.; Cambridge: the MIT Press, 1980], p. 179.)

FIG. 41. St. Martin's in the Fields church (1721–27; James Gibbs, designer), London. Plan. (From James Gibbs, A *Book of Architecture* [London, 1728], pl. 2, courtesy Henry Francis du Pont Winterthur Museum Library: Collection of Printed Books.)

FIG. 43. Newport Parish (St. Luke's) church (ca. 1685), Isle of Wight County. A view before its 19th-century restoration. (From *American Architect and Building News* 15, no. 434 [April 19, 1884], unnumbered plate.)

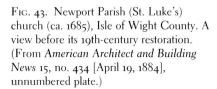

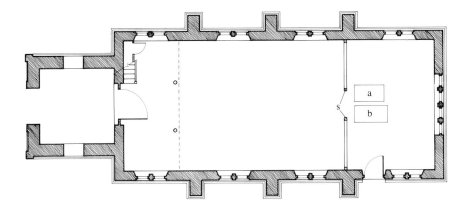

FIG. 44. St. Luke's church. Plan. Key:
s = screen, reconstructed on old sill;
a = graveslab of Joseph Bridger (d. 1686);
b = graveslab of Anne Randall (d. 1696).
(Drawing, Dell Upton.)

years after the Jamestown church was built. Strachey depicted a church fitted with cedar pews, "fair broad windows to shut and open, as the weather shall occasion," a cedar pulpit, and "a font hewn hollow, like a canoe." It had two bells at the west end, a black walnut communion table, and "a chancel in it of cedar." That the chancel was to be *in* the church suggests that Strachey was thinking of an auditory building.[11]

After Strachey's description, almost no evidence for the form of Virginia's parish churches survives from before the 1660s, and little useful information is available before the fourth quarter of the seventeenth century. By then the Virginia vernacular church had taken the form it was to have until the Establishment was dissolved. The essential elements are all present in Newport Parish (St. Luke's) church (Figs. 43, 44), Isle of Wight County, Virginia's oldest surviving church. Like its many successors, St. Luke's is a rectangular building, nearly twice as long as it is wide, and "oriented," or set with its chancel toward the east, in the traditional manner. Buttresses divide the long walls into four bays, each of which is fitted with a tall double-lancet window with molded-brick Y-tracery. In the mid-nineteenth century, the horizontal iron bars that supported the original glazing were still in place, although the openings had been bricked up. At the east end is another brick-mullioned window, this one four lights wide and divided into three tiers (Fig. 45). Above the great east window is a small circular one. There is a small door on the eastern side of

FIG. 45. St. Luke's church. East end. (Photograph, Dell Upton.)

the easternmost buttress in the south wall (Fig. 46). The main entrance is at the west end, sheltered by an open porch in the base of the three-story tower. These elements — the single-story sidewall elevation, the east window, and the south and west doors — define the rectangular Virginia church of the colonial period.[12]

If we may take St. Luke's church as our starting point, the question arises, how old is it? It is traditionally claimed to have been built in 1632, but the origins of the building have been the subject of great debate. The 1632 date, which was originally put forth conjecturally in the mid-nineteenth century, has since been bolstered by a variety of unsatisfactory evidence. This has included a brick, altered in the late nineteenth century and no longer attached to the building, that bears an ambiguous inscription, and a now long-lost vestry book in which someone is reported to have seen the date just before the book crumbled. The restorers of the 1950s assumed the early date without question, and let it guide their interpretation of the architectural evidence. They stated, "That such fully Gothic designs [the Y-tracery and buttresses] should have been so employed at the end of the century does not invite acceptance on the basis of our

knowledge of existing comparable structures." Their argument can be dismissed easily. Buttresses are found on English parish churches built in the seventeenth and eighteenth centuries. A pair with classical profiles, for example, support the north corners of All Saints' church, North Runcton, built 1715. Buttresses were also common into the nineteenth century in Bermuda (Fig. 47), an island with architectural and personal ties to Virginia. Y-tracery windows very similar to those at St. Luke's church can be found in England in King Charles the Martyr church, dated 1767 by Nikolaus Pevsner (see Fig. 38). While the Virginia church belongs to a tradition of church planning and design established in the early seventeenth century, it does not *have* to date from those early years. Other circumstantial evidence places it later. Our current knowledge of architectural and economic conditions in Virginia in the 1630s makes it seem unlikely that *any* brick building, much less such a large and elaborate one, was built then. A report of Governor John Harvey to the Privy Council in 1639 suggests that the resources of the colony were strained in attempting to build one in Jamestown, and in fact the church was not completed until 1647. The later one dates

Fig. 46. St. Luke's church. Southeast corner, showing buttresses and restored chancel door. (Photograph, Dell Upton.)

Fig. 47. The Crossways (early 19th century), Sandys Parish, Bermuda. Corner buttress. (Photograph, Dell Upton.)

St. Luke's church from this point of view, the more likely one is to be right.[13]

If St. Luke's church does not date from the early seventeenth century, what is a more likely date for it? Although the only certainty is that "the brick church" was standing in 1734 when the earliest surviving vestry records of Newport Parish open, the external ornament provided by the tracery, the applied pediment on the tower, the oval windows, buttresses, quoins, pilasters, and stepped gables, as well as the complexity of massing created by the shapes of the buttresses and the double, high water tables, mark this as an early church, built before the shift to plain exteriors that characterized Virginia churches beginning in the second decade of the eighteenth century. The tower is the only one known to have been built as an original feature of a Virginia church, a circumstantial indicator that it was built in the formative years of Virginia vernacular church building. Indeed, St. Luke's is one of the few Virginia churches to have a tower at all. The chancel door is an incidental feature of the composition, as it was in most English churches. In contrast, in eighteenth-century Virginia churches, the south door was enlarged and incorporated into the overall pattern of openings (Fig. 48). Its ornamental surround was the only significant exterior decoration.

These features suggest a date late in the seventeenth century for St. Luke's. Other elements link it more closely with a group of churches of known date built in the period 1675–1710. The buttresses are St. Luke's most prominent feature. Buttresses were found during the 1939 excavation of the Bruton Parish church (Fig. 49), constructed in 1681–83.

FIG. 48. St. John's Parish church (ca. 1731–34), King William County. West door. (Photograph, Dell Upton.)

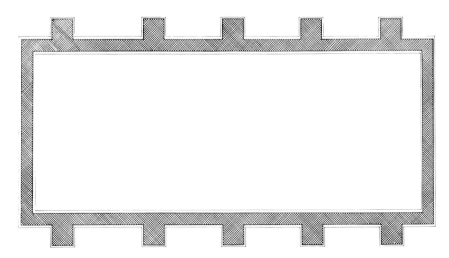

FIG. 49. Second Bruton Parish church (1681–83; Capt. Francis Page, undertaker), Middle Plantation (now Williamsburg). Plan, as excavated 1939. (Drawing, Colonial Williamsburg Foundation.)

Buttresses were also excavated at the Jamestown church, of which only the tower, probably added at the very end of the seventeenth century, stands (Fig. 50). It has long been asserted that the Jamestown church was erected from 1639 to 1647, and repaired after damage by Nathaniel Bacon's supporters in 1676. In fact, no evidence has ever been offered in support of the 1639–47 construction date, other than a low appropriation made for repairs in 1680. The fragmentary state of Virginia's seventeenth-century records makes it impossible to know whether this was the only appropriation, however. It is worth noting as well that none of the archaeological explorers has ever found evidence of a fire in the remains. One must conclude that a new church was erected after 1676, and that Jamestown, Bruton, and St. Luke's churches were contemporaries. At all three, the buttresses are set back from the ends, although at Jamestown they are recessed only a few feet from the east end. St. Luke's and Bruton are nearly identical in size, although the number of buttresses differs. Bruton and St. Luke's both have shaped gables, and the disposition of the tower at

Jamestown makes it likely that it did as well. The stepped, parapeted gables of St. Luke's church are part of an ornamental tradition imported to England from the Low Countries in the late sixteenth century and popular on vernacular buildings throughout the seventeenth century. The crude drawing of the Bruton church made in 1702 by the Swiss visitor Franz Ludwig Michel (see Fig. 15) shows a building resembling St. Luke's in other respects. In the apex of its west gable, Bruton church has a circular window similar to that in the east gable of the Isle of Wight County church. A square-headed door, resembling the one in the chancel at St. Luke's, forms the west entrance of Bruton. Over it there are a pair of windows marking the location of the west gallery. Three bays of windows pierce the side of the Bruton church. The crudeness of the drawing is such that these could be windows like the round-headed traceried windows at St. Luke's, or they could be compass windows, the semicircular arched windows standard on Virginia brick churches in the eighteenth century. If the latter, they antedate the next known examples by thirty years. The

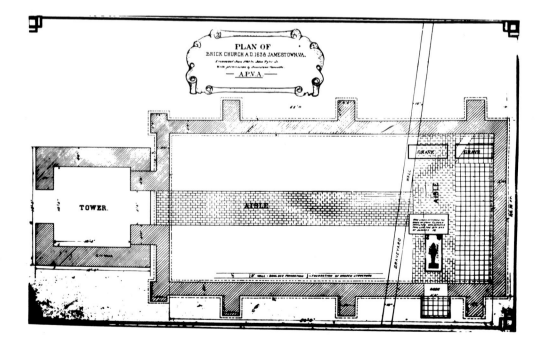

FIG. 50. James City Parish church (ca. 1680; tower ca. 1699), Jamestown. Plan, as excavated 1901. (From John L. Cotter, *Archaeological Excavations at Jamestown, Virginia* [Washington, D.C.: National Park Service, 1958], p. 20.)

FIG. 51. St. Peter's Parish church (1701–3; Will Hughes, carpenter; Cornelius Hall, bricklayer; tower 1739–40, William Walker, undertaker), New Kent County. The sash and doors are modern. (Photograph, Dell Upton.)

buttresses are not represented in the Michel drawing, but since that drawing also shows a three-bay church, while the excavations revealed one of four full bays and two half bays, and since the chancel door ordered by the vestry is omitted from the drawing, the discrepancy probably results from the artist's inaccuracy. The gables here are not crowstepped, but are curved in the "Flemish" manner popular in large seventeenth-century vernacular buildings and used in several American houses, most notably Bacon's Castle (1665), Surry County, Virginia.[14]

Another shaped-gable church very similar to St. Luke's is St. Peter's Parish church (Figs. 51, 52), built 1701–3. Like

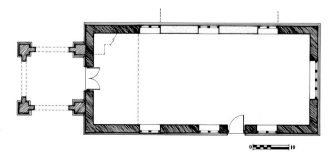

FIG. 52. St. Peter's Parish church. Plan. (Drawing, Dell Upton.)

FIG. 53. St. Peter's Parish church. Curvilinear gables reconstructed from ghosts on the tower. The originals were gone by the time of the Civil War. (Photograph, Dell Upton.)

FIG. 54. St. Peter's Parish church. Nineteenth-century woodcut, showing transom windows in place and sliding sash in tower. Note stairs to vestry room, now supplanted by interior access. (From *St. Peter's Parish* [n.p.: St. Peter's Parish, 1979], courtesy of St. Peter's Parish.)

St. Luke's church, St. Peter's is a rectangular building, in this case slightly more than twice as long as it is wide. There is a west door and a south door. The shaped "Flemish" parapeted gables (Fig. 53) were removed by the time of the Civil War but they have since been restored from ghosts found on the tower. The south side is four bays long, with the chancel door enlarged and surmounted by a round window to form a more prominent visual element, while the north wall is three bays long. Both are conjectural restorations in some respects. The north wall is a reconstruction occasioned by the removal in the nineteenth century of a wing added in the eighteenth century. The nineteenth-century wall was in turn replaced by the recent restorers with one of eighteenth-century form. The south door had also been closed and was reopened in the twentieth-century restoration, and the three bays of windows were repositioned slightly at that time. A nineteenth-century woodcut (Fig. 54) illustrates that the basic pattern is correct, and the double-light transom window frames are partly original (Fig. 55). The woodcut shows a small circular window over the south door, rather than the large oval one reproduced there. As with St. Luke's church and all other pre-1720 churches for which evidence survives, a large, multilight window (Fig. 56) fills the east end. The opening was partly closed and fitted with two smaller rectangular windows later in the church's history, and the present frame is thus a reproduction, but the opening itself is unaltered. The resemblance to the Isle of Wight County church is made the more striking by the high water table and by the tower. The latter, however, was added in 1740 by William Walker.[15]

St. Luke's similarities to this group of second-generation churches suggests a date in the fourth quarter of the

FIG. 55. St. Peter's Parish church. Detail of southwest window. A line clearly demarcates the original frame at the top from the restored frame at the bottom. Note the carpenter's mark, made by two chisels, in the upper corner. The sash are modern. (Photograph, Dell Upton.)

FIG. 56. St. Peter's Parish church. East end. The difference between the original brickwork and the reconstructed gable is clearly visible. (Photograph, Dell Upton.)

seventeenth century for the Isle of Wight County building. As a group, these churches point to the years around 1680 as the period when a rectangular building based on the room churches, developed in rural England early in the same century, became the characteristic form of the Virginia vernacular church.[16]

Church builders in eighteenth-century Virginia refined the form established in the late seventeenth-century

buildings. Beginning early in the eighteenth century, the massive appearance and decorative features of the exterior of the early churches were stripped down. Yeocomico church (Figs. 57, 58), the lower church of Cople Parish in Westmoreland County, is dated 1706 by a molded brick plaque set into the south wall of the building; it was probably begun in 1703, when a new upper church was also undertaken. Here, in a church begun while St. Peter's was

FIG. 57. Yeocomico church (1706; enlarged ca. 1740), Westmoreland County. The molded-brick plaque in the gable carries 8 sets of initials, probably those of the vestry. The plaque under the eaves on the south side near the west end reads "G/I*I/1706." (Photograph, Dell Upton.)

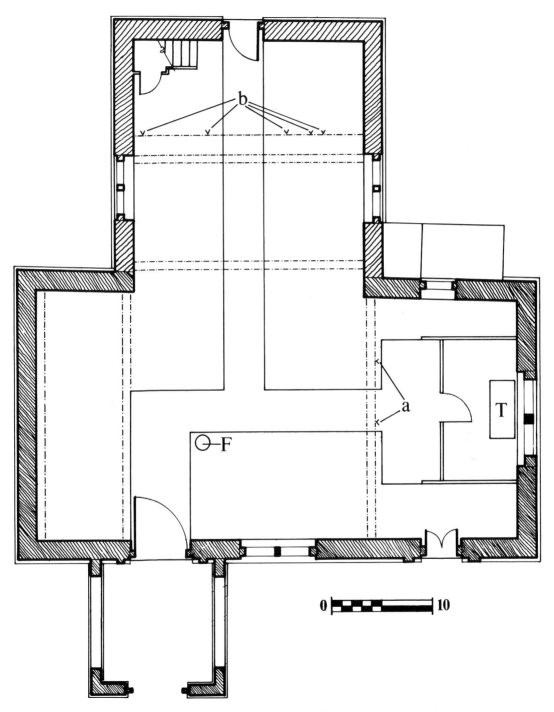

FIG. 58. Yeocomico church. Plan. Key: T = table; F = font; a = notches in tie beam that may indicate former presence of a screen; b = position of pew partition notches on inside of gallery rail. (Drawing, Dell Upton.)

FIG. 59. Yeocomico church. South porch.
The brick plaque is inscribed "S♀M."
(Photograph, Dell Upton.)

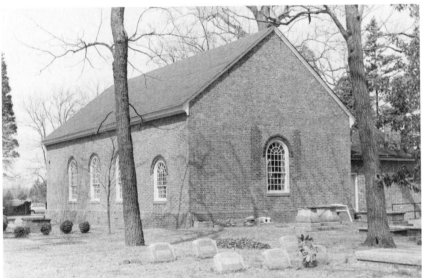

FIG. 60. Middle (Christ) church (begun 1712; Alexander Graves, bricklayer; John Hipkins, Sr., carpenter), Christ Church Parish, Middlesex County. Substantially reconstructed above the springing of the windows in the 19th and 20th centuries. The small window is the original chancel door. Patches are evident where the large chancel window was reduced in size. The west porch is modern, and the church originally had clipped gables. (Photograph, Dell Upton.)

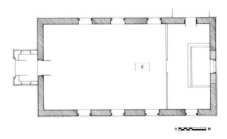

FIG. 61. Christ church. Plan. The northeast door was originally a window, and the southeast window was the south door. The chancel rail and the communion enclosure are modern, but reproduce the location and approximate size of the original screen and communion enclosure, respectively. Key: g = graveslab of Mr. Edward Thompson (d. 1674), a London merchant. (Drawing, Dell Upton.)

being built, the process of change is already visible. The exterior ornamentation is restricted to some diaperwork and plastered arches on the porch (Fig. 59), the date plaque, and the plain molded-brick pilasters flanking the two entrance doors. Like the other early churches, it has a large east window with a circular opening over it. The pattern is convincing, but it is necessary to be cautious about the form of the double sash windows that now fill all the openings, since the records of the church preservation association reveal that the exterior walls have undergone constant and sometimes drastic reworking since the beginning of this century. A nineteenth-century correspondent, writing from memory twenty years after his last visit, reported "a large Gothic window much broken" in the east end. The massiveness of the earlier churches has been replaced by a baroque feeling for masses and complex shapes, most notably in the pronounced "kick" at the eaves, and in the way the porch, a miniature of the church building, is joined to it. The kicks constitute the first datable use of a feature that remained popular in the Northern Neck of Virginia, where Yeocomico church stands, until the Revolution, and that appears occasionally in other parts of the colony as well.[17]

The new forms are most clearly evident in the trio of churches built for Christ Church Parish, Middlesex County, in the second decade of the eighteenth century. Although conservative in plan, they were radical in appearance. In the two that still stand — the middle, or mother, church (Figs. 60, 61), begun 1712, and the lower chapel (Fig. 62), begun 1714 — there were more similarities than are now apparent. The mother church deteriorated in the nineteenth century, at last subsiding into a roofless and floorless ruin. It was repaired in 1848 and again in 1900, as a plaque on the modern west porch records. The church now lacks several courses of its original wall height, and has a gable roof, although it was built with a clipped-gable roof like the lower chapel. Both churches have west doors and south chancel doors, and were ordered to have large east windows like the churches discussed above. The east window at the lower church has been replaced by a projecting chancel the width of the original opening. The single small window at the middle church replaces two windows closed in the nineteenth century, which in turn replaced the original. The lower chapel is in considerably better condition, and retains its original roof shape. As at Yeocomico

FIG. 62. Lower chapel (begun 1714; Capt Henry Armstead and Maj. Edmond Berkley, undertakers), Christ Church Parish, Middlesex County. The steps, rails, and low wall are modern. (Photograph, Dell Upton.)

church, the baroque complexity of shape is augmented by the use of eaves kicks. More notable is the total absence on the exterior of either church of any decoration, even of the restrained variety found at Yeocomico church. The visual interest derives entirely from the juxtaposition of the compass windows against the brick wall.[18]

Later changes in Virginia church building continued to be more visual than formal. Beginning in the 1720s, most brick churches and some frame churches employed classical doorways of molded brick or wood (Fig. 63) as their single exterior decorative elements, and the size of the doorway was enlarged to accommodate the decoration and to make it more striking. The doorways were comparable in size and visual emphasis to the windows, rather than inconspicuous, as at St. Luke's church, or visible but subordinate, as at Yeocomico church or Christ church, Middlesex County. The first documented use of pediments appears in the 1723 instructions given by the Petsworth Parish vestry to under-

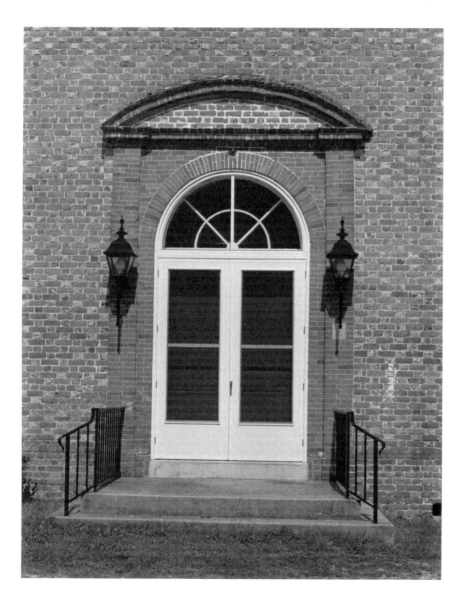

FIG. 63. Lower (Mattaponi Baptist) church (ca. 1730–34), St. Stephen's Parish, King and Queen County. West doorway. To the right of the doorway, just below cornice level, can be seen a brick inscribed "David Minetree." (Photograph, Dell Upton.)

taker James Skelton, who was ordered to "Civer the pedements over the dors with Lead," an afterthought for which he was paid extra. From the 1720s on, "Pediment Heads" were a regular, though not an inevitable, feature of parish churches, and the Fairfax Parish vestry went so far as to specify that at its Falls and Alexandria (Christ) churches of 1767 they were to be in the Tuscan order.[19]

After the 1720s, the majority of church builders also preferred to use smaller east end windows, but to use two or even three of them. Sometimes the chancel window was indistinguishable from the other windows in size and decoration. Paired or triple windows were favored. Ware church, Gloucester County, traditionally dated 1690 but probably (on the basis of the information offered so far) built in the second quarter of the eighteenth century, has two compass-head double windows, while Merchant's Hope church (Fig. 64), probably built in the third decade of the eighteenth century, has a pair of compass windows identical to those on the side walls. The same pattern was used at the lower church of Southwark Parish, built in the 1750s (Fig. 65).

Within the basic model, there were differences in specific plans, and a major change occurred around 1700, at about the time the appearance of Virginia's churches also changed. The principal access to the nave of the church

was through a large door that, in English parish churches, had traditionally been placed in the south wall near the west end. In that location, it had been sheltered by a large porch in which the parishioners gathered, marriages were contracted, notices posted, and ecclesiastical and sometimes civil trials were held. In the largest and latest examples, a room over the porch held the parish records and served as a vestry room. Vestiges of this tradition survived in Virginia. The clearest example is at Yeocomico church (see Figs. 57, 58), which has a southwest door. An open porch shelters it and leads to a wicket door—a wide door with a smaller door set into it—which is the only entry into the original church other than the chancel door. Porches were relatively common in Virginia in the seventeenth and early eighteenth centuries. The vestry of Petsworth Parish ordered its church wardens in 1680 to "Erect & Build a good & Substantiall Porch to the [1677] Church at Poplar Spring, of Such dimensions as they shall think convenient; & correspondent to the Church." The 1680 Wicomico Parish church had a porch whose repairs were frequently noted in the vestry records for the next seventy years, and William Byrd noted of a 1710 funeral in Westover Parish that "as soon as the service was begun it rained very hard so that we were forced to leave the parson and go into the church porch but

FIG. 64. Merchant's Hope church (ca. 1725), Prince George County. View from the northeast, showing double chancel windows of the same size as those on the long wall. (Photograph, Dell Upton.)

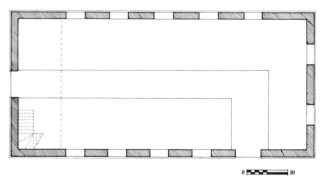

FIG. 65. Lower church (begun ca. 1751), Southwark Parish, Surry County. Plan. The outlines of the alleys survive in the ruined church as mounds, and the locations of the stairs and gallery can be discovered from evidence on the walls. (Drawing, Dell Upton.)

Mr. Anderson [the parson] stayed till the service was finished." Porches might also be included in the first stages of bell towers, as they were at St. Luke's church, and in the Jamestown church tower (Fig. 66) of ca. 1699. By the second quarter of the eighteenth century, these were the only kinds of porches built. The 1740 tower at St. Peter's Parish church with its open porch and the glazed porch in the 1770 tower of Bruton Parish church are examples. In both cases the second stories were used as vestry rooms, as was traditional in English practice. Most parishes did

FIG. 66. James City Parish church (ca. 1680; tower ca. 1699), Jamestown. Tower before construction of 1902 church. (From *Colonial Churches in the Original Colony of Virginia* [2d ed., Richmond: Southern Churchman, 1908], n.p.)

without towers and porches and built small freestanding houses for the vestry to use.[20]

The southwest door left its mark on Virginia's parish churches. Except at Yeocomico church, no eighteenth-century Virginia builders directly applied this traditional practice. Yet even in west-end-entry churches, some vestrymen continued to refer to the south side as the front and the north side as the back of the church. At Christ church, Middlesex County, the continued importance of the south side in a west-end-entry church is evident in the brickwork. The Flemish bond on the west and south sides has glazed headers, while that on the north and east does not. The church was meant to be seen from the south and west.[21]

Although most of Virginia's colonial churches were simple rectangles, their interior spaces were specialized and differentiated according to Anglican religious practice. On the exterior this differentiation was displayed not by massing, as in the English nave-and-chancel churches, but by the placement of the openings. The presence of the chancel was indicated by the east window(s) and by the chancel door. Many churches had west galleries whose location was marked by small windows in the west gable; sometimes these were decorative oval or circular bull's-eye, or ox-eye, windows as in the third Bruton Parish church of 1711–15 or in the Wicomico Parish church of 1763–72. The pulpit in a rectangular church was normally set against the north wall, and the fenestration pattern was often altered by omitting a window to create a blank wall against which to place the pulpit or by inserting a smaller pulpit window to light it. A smaller pulpit window exists at Mangohick church (Figs. 67, 68) built as a chapel of St. Margaret's Parish around 1731. Colonel John Wall was paid ten shillings extra in 1744 "for Erecting a small Window in the back side" of the chapel he built for Albemarle Parish.[22]

The distinction between chancel and nave, manifested in the medieval church in the structural separation of the two, embodied not only a division between holy and profane space, between priests' domain and lay turf, but a literal division of financial responsibility. Traditionally the clergy constructed and maintained the chancel, and the parish took charge of the nave. Chantry chapels within the nave were financed by the donors on whose behalf they were erected. Early Anglicans continued to conceive the church as a building composed of two rooms, although they

FIG. 67. Mangohick church (ca. 1731), King William County. Brick at west end inscribed "T A Brown"; brick over south door has illegible initials and date. Note the smaller pulpit window on the north side. The east addition is modern. (Photograph, Dell Upton.)

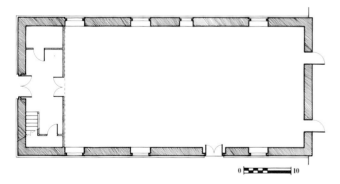

FIG. 68. Mangohick church. Plan. The vestibule and west rooms are modern. (Drawing, Dell Upton.)

redefined the spaces. They retained chancel screens and sometimes even the division of financial responsibility as well. Both these elements of seventeenth-century Anglicanism were brought to Virginia. At the second Bruton Parish church, a building that, as we have seen, had no structural division between the parts, the burial fees and the responsibility for repairing the damage occasioned by a burial were divided between the minister and the vestry: "For the privilege of Burials either in the Chancell, or in the new Church, it is ordered by this Vestry, that for breaking up the ground in the Chancell, the Fees payable to the Minister shall be one thousand pounds of Tobacco, or five pounds sterling; and in the Church the Fee payable to the Parish shall be five hundred pounds of Tobacco, or fifty shillings in money; and that the Minister shall be at the charge to relay the Chancell [pavement], and the Parish for the same [relaying the pavement in the body of the church]." It is worth noting that the linguistic distinction between chancel and church is maintained here, although Virginians never used the word nave.[23]

Most seventeenth-century Virginia parish churches of which we have a record were fitted with screens. The remains of the great sill beam of a screen were found during the restoration of St. Luke's church (see Fig. 44), and there are several references to screens in the documentary record of Virginia Anglicanism. One was installed in the Petsworth Parish church of 1677, setting off the easternmost fifteen feet of the rectangular building as a chancel. When the upper chapel of Christ Church Parish, Middlesex County, was enlarged in 1687, the vestry ordered for the twenty-year-old building that "20 Foot in length [is] to be added to the West End Thereof the Pulpit and Screan to be Removed [i.e., moved], and the Coñunion Table to be Rayled in." The French traveler Médéric-Louis-Élie Moreau de Saint-Mèry even claimed to have seen one in the 1764 Portsmouth Parish church, but he probably meant a chancel rail.[24]

There is little evidence for the appearance of these screens. Post-Reformation screens in England tended to resemble their medieval predecessors, which were normally composed of a solid lower section, often paneled, with painted figures or other designs in each panel; a pierced middle section that allowed some sight through the partition; and a cornice on top that concealed the large beam supporting the rood. In larger versions, the screen might be fitted with a loft for seating. Anglican screens tended to keep the three-part morphology, omitting the rood and loft, and reducing the proportions of the cornice. The open section was more transparent than in the medieval screens, and the Royal Arms were sometimes mounted on top. The elaborate screen at St. Mary the Virgin church (see Fig. 27), Croscombe, Somerset, is the classic example of the post-Reformation screen. Installed in 1616 along with the pulpit, reading desk, and pews, the screen has a solid lower range, surmounted by a two-tiered openwork section. The lower of the two tiers consists of three large arches, the upper of three pairs of double arches with central pendants. The whole is richly carved with strapwork, gadrooning, and other mannerist ornament, encrusting a basically classical formal structure. The screen is topped with pierced strapwork, obelisks, and the crest of James I. At the other end of the spectrum is the screen installed a century later in St. Andrew's church, Winterborne Tomson, Dorset (see Fig. 30). It too is divided into three parts, with the lower sections on either side forming the walls of the minister's pew and a pew across the aisle from it. There is an open

doorway the width of the aisle in the center. The left (north) open section is completely transparent except for a central muntin. The right opening is obscured at the south by the pulpit, while the northern half forms a "window" that supports the reading desk, framing the minister as he stands in his pew on the chancel side of the screen. The upper section and cornice are reduced to a single beam with a small molding. The Virginia screens were certainly more like Winterborne Tomson than Croscombe, but all followed a common formula. The 1677 Poplar Spring church of Petsworth Parish had "a Scrime to be runn a Crosse the Church with ballisters; . . . 2 wainscoate double pews one of each side of the Chancell, Joyninge to the Scrime with ballisters suitable for the said Scrime. 1: double pew above the pulpitt & deske Joyninge to the Scrime." In other words, it was to be a screen with a closed lower portion, and a baluster screen above. As at Winterborne Tomson, the lower portion would form one of the walls of two double pews within the chancel, and one outside it. These pews were to have a small balustrade around their tops, matching the balusters of the screen and of the communion rail as well. Each of the three early eighteenth-century churches of Christ Church Parish, Middlesex County, built between 1710 and 1720, was to have "a comendable Screene to divide the Church from the Chancell." No description was offered beyond the notation that the third screen, at the lower chapel, should be "open pursuant to the directions of the Overseers of the worke."[25]

Just as the appearance and the structures of Virginia's parish churches changed in the early eighteenth century, so did their internal arrangements. We can observe the change in the three second-decade churches of Christ Church Parish, Middlesex County, whose significance in the history of exterior form has been noted. For seven years, the Christ Church vestry struggled with planning problems in ways that were as conservative as the results were up-to-date in appearance. In their deliberations can be read the transition from a screened church to the more open one of eighteenth-century Virginia. The first building projected, the new upper church proposed in 1707 to replace the ruinous building of the 1660s, was to have an aisled plan. It was ordered "that the said Church be fifty Six foot long and forty eight foot wide, and that the posts be twelve foot pitch and the pillars twenty four foot long, the Rafters over the single pews and for the body of the Church to be according to Architect[ure] and from the post of Each Side to the pillar Eight foot the body of the Church to be thirty two foot wide the Pulpit Chancell & pews to be Laid of[f] at the discretion of the Vestry." The reference to the inner posts as "pillars" implies that a continuous roof slope was intended; if so, it would have had a fifty-five degree pitch. The rafters over the single pews and the reference to the center section as the "body of the church" also hold out the possibility that this was to be a clerestoried structure. Strikingly old fashioned as the form was, the instruction to lay off the chancel indicates that it was to be contained within the body of the church.[26]

Nothing was done about constructing this building, and in 1710 a new plan was drawn up that projected a frame church (Fig. 69) nearly fifty percent smaller than the original scheme (1,500 square feet as opposed to 2,688 square feet enclosed by the 1707 plan). Its 60-by-25-foot proportions were more in accord with the customary Virginia rectangular church plan, however. The plans called for three 8-by-4-foot windows on each side, with sliding sashes (a novel feature in Virginia), and an east window 10 feet wide running from the arched ceiling to "within Six foot of the Sill." There were to be western and southern doors. In keeping with the screened-church tradition, the south door opened directly into the chancel, as in all English churches with separate chancel structures, and as, apparently, in all but the last screened Virginia church. The screen set off the easternmost 12 feet of the church for the chancel. Within that space a 14-by-7-foot railed enclosure was made for the communion table, in accordance with the practice initiated by Archbishop Laud in 1616 and customary in Virginia from the late seventeenth century. Five "high framed pews" were set near the chancel, and the pulpit and desks were placed on the north side, west of two of the high pews and nearly halfway down the length of the church from the east end. The new upper church was a straightforward example of the old screened version of the rectangular church, such as had been built in most late-seventeenth-century Virginia parishes. The south door led into the screened-off chancel, and the pulpit stood approximately in the center of the church, separated from the chancel. The chancel had an enclosed communion table and the main door was in the west end.[27]

Two years later, in 1712, the middle church was planned. The vestry clearly worked from the upper church specifications for the middle church (and from the middle church specifications in planning the third church in 1714), for in each case the same phrases were repeated in the same order. This middle church (Fig. 70), the mother church, was the largest of the three, at sixty by thirty feet. Its windows were of the same size and disposition as those of the upper church, and there is no mention of the compass windows with which this brick church was fitted, although undoubtedly the frame church did not have them. Again, a screen set off the easternmost twelve feet of the building as

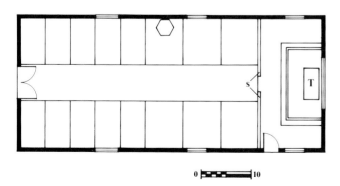

FIG. 69. Upper chapel (1710) of Christ Church Parish, Middlesex County. Reconstructed plan. Key: s = screen; T = table. (Drawing, Dell Upton.)

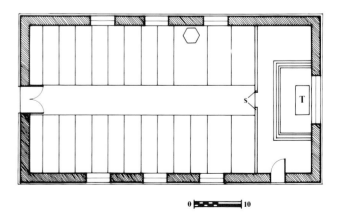

FIG. 70. Middle church (begun 1712), Christ Church Parish, Middlesex County. Reconstructed plan. Key: T = table, s = screen. (Drawing, Dell Upton.)

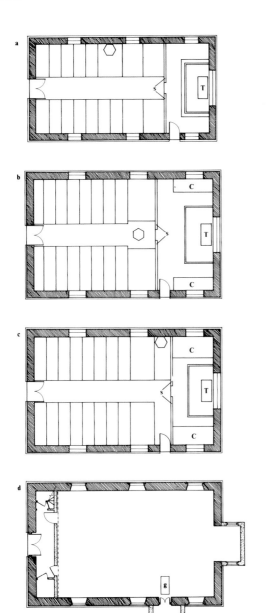

FIG. 71. Lower chapel (begun 1714), Christ Church Parish, Middlesex County. Reconstructed plans: (a) first design; (b) second design; (c) final design; (d) current plan. Key: s = screen; T = table; C = chancel pews, possibly for communicants; g = graveslab of Mary Beverley (d. 1678). (Drawing, Dell Upton.)

a chancel and there was a fourteen-by-seven-foot communion rail around the table. The chancel, however, was raised a step from the rest of the church, and the table another two steps. The arrangement of pulpit and pews was the same as in the upper church. The new church was thus a somewhat larger brick version of the familiar formula employed at the upper church.[28]

When it came time to begin work on the lower church, the same plan was proposed, although the dimensions were changed (Fig. 71a). The fenestration and door openings followed the example of the middle church, and the chancel, communion table, pews, and pulpit were treated identically with the 1712 design. When the dimensions were enlarged from fifty by twenty-five feet to fifty-two by thirty feet after the vacillations detailed in chapter 2, the chancel depth was increased to sixteen feet, and the "communion place" to sixteen by ten feet (Fig. 71b), with pews inside the chancel enclosure. The pulpit was moved east and placed in the middle of the "alley" or aisle. This was an arrangement used often in early eighteenth-century English churches and less frequently in American ones, but nowhere else in Virginia. At the same time, John Hipkins, the undertaker of the middle church, was ordered to alter his building to follow this new arrangement, which necessitated paying him for removing the pulpit he had already built against the north wall. In the final scheme (Fig. 71c), the chancel and communion rail at the lower church were reduced to their original dimensions, but two further, more important changes were made. The south door was moved west, and opened into the body of the church rather than the chancel. The pulpit was pushed back out of the aisle against the north wall, but remained east of center, opposite the new location of the south door, not close to the center of the building as in most seventeenth-century Virginia churches. No orders were given to Hipkins to change the mother church again; perhaps he had gone too far in the new work, or had not begun it at all. For reasons not revealed, the vestrymen of Christ Church Parish had experimented with two new plans for their lower church, abandoning the old seventeenth-century arrangement in favor of a form that characterized all subsequent Virginia rectangular churches. The chancel was no longer a rigidly defined part of the building. Although the lower church still had a screen, it is the last to appear in Virginia church records. Henceforth the "chancel" was reduced to the "communion place," the small railed-in enclosure around the table. It was defined by its rail and by the two steps that invariably raised it from the surrounding floor. With no architecturally significant chancel in the church, the chancel door now opened into a cross aisle that intersected the main east-west aisle and usually led directly to the pulpit opposite. The disparate features of the seventeenth-century Anglo-Virginian parish churches, embodied in the upper and middle churches of the parish, had been rearranged subtly in a way that coordinated all the parts of the parish church into a clearly articulated plan.[29]

It is difficult to say whether the Christ Church Parish vestry invented the new plan or whether, as is more likely, they had learned of a recently developed form and were experimenting with a more modern church. In any case, their lower church is the first we know of with the new plan, which meshes nicely with the change of appearance, and it is the more valuable for being documented and extant. With the 1711–15 Bruton Parish church, the lower church stands at the beginning of the Georgian era in Virginia building. Their successors were many.

The spiritual, intellectual, and civil aspects of the Anglican church were presented in the chancel and its furnishings, in the pulpit and desks, and in the "ornaments," or furnishings, of the church. The Virginia church plan was designed to display these elements effectively, although most of the space inside was devoted to seats for the congregation. From the time of the Reformation, Anglican officials had devoted considerable attention to rearranging the church and its ceremonies in a way "that the people may hear." The English notion of the auditory church directly addressed this question. The same issue confronted Virginia church builders: how could the building be arranged so that everyone in the congregation might hear? In the rectangular church, this was achieved by limitations on size. Only a few exceptional churches reached eighty feet in length. They included the Stratton Major Parish church of 1760; Ware Parish church; St. George's Parish church, Accomack County; and Hungar's Parish church. Few others surpassed seventy feet.[30]

At some time in its history, every parish confronted the problem of enlarging a church or building one with a capacity greater than a seventy-foot rectangular building could provide. The simplest method of enlargement was to lengthen the building, but this was satisfactory only for a

few relatively small structures. The Ham chapel of Southam Parish was enlarged from forty to sixty-four feet in length, for instance, while the Sapponey and Nansemond chapels of Bristol Parish were enlarged from forty to sixty feet. With one exception, no church was lengthened beyond the unwritten seventy-foot limit.[31]

The four very large churches mentioned above were the products of new construction, and were created by expanding traditional dimensions proportionately. The Stratton Major church (see Fig. 216), for example, was eighty by fifty feet, or double the common dimension of forty by twenty-five feet. The building, which substituted for earlier upper and lower churches, was conceived as tandem churches. There were south and west doors, but also a north door. There were also two east-west aisles. The parishioners from the upper church were seated on either side of the north aisle: those from the lower church on the south aisle. The pews were numbered in parallel, rather than continuously through the church. The churches in Hungar's, St. George's (see Fig. 215), and Ware (Fig. 72) parishes all had doubled dimensions and double aisles as well, although there is no evidence that they interpreted the doubling quite so literally as in Stratton Major Parish.[32]

Expanded proportionately, rather than lengthened, these large churches point toward the preferred method of

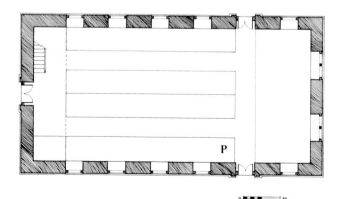

Fig. 72. Ware church (mid-18th century), Gloucester County. Plan, showing alleys, pew blocks, and pulpit position as reported in a 19th-century description. According to that account, ten burials were found east of the chancel aisle when the church was repaired. (Drawing, Dell Upton.)

FIG. 73. Vauter's church (ca. 1719; enlarged 1731), Essex County. View from the southeast. (Photograph, Dell Upton.)

enlarging existing churches, and of building exceptionally capacious ones in eighteenth-century Virginia: the centralizing plan. Wren's London churches followed the centralizing principle, employing plans that were deep in relation to their lengths. Until close to the end of the colonial era, however, no Virginia builders chose this strategy. Most frequently they erected additions at right angles to the main building, forming a T plan (Figs. 73–75). The first T addition of which we have a record was built on the Poplar Spring church of Petsworth Parish in 1701, when Larkin Chew was hired to construct "the back worke on the north Side to be built in Length five and twenty foot and the inside twenty foot clear work from wall to wall." It has been suggested that T additions derived from cruciform-plan Virginia churches, but the Poplar Spring addition was constructed fourteen years before the first cruciform church in Virginia. Possibly Virginia's T plans owed something to Scots kirks. Kirks incorporated "aisles," or perpendicular north additions, from the Middle Ages on, and in the

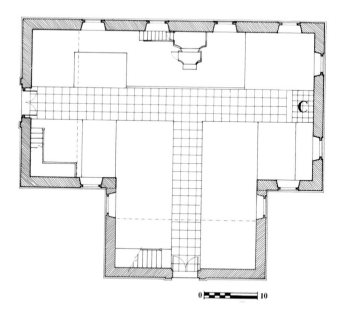

FIG. 74. Vauter's church. Plan, showing original location of chancel (C). The pew enclosures (indicated by single lines) and the pulpit date from about 1830. (Drawing, Dell Upton.)

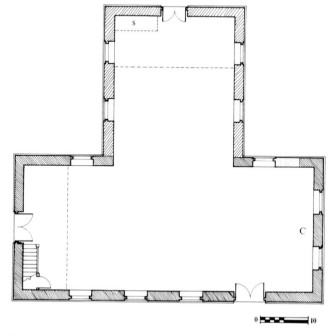

FIG. 75. Blandford church (1734–37; Col. Thomas Ravenscroft, undertaker; enlarged 1752–70; Col. Richard Bland, undertaker). Plan. Key: C = location of chancel; s = former gallery stair. (Drawing, Dell Upton.)

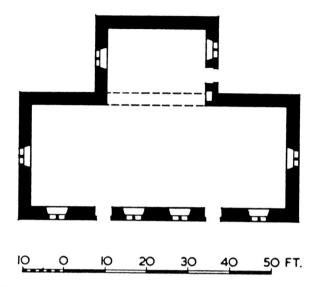

FIG. 76. Drainie kirk (1654–75), Moray, Scotland. Plan. (From George Hay, *The Architecture of Scottish Post-Reformation Churches, 1560–1843* [Oxford: Clarendon Press, 1957], p. 56.)

seventeenth century aisled plans were widely built by Scots Presbyterians (Fig. 76). These north wings were often burial aisles or the private seating and retiring rooms of local lairds, but they sometimes had pews on their ground floors as well. If kirks were a source of Virginia T plans, no particular individual can be credited with introducing the form. A healthy proportion of Virginia's population was of Scots origin, including the commissary and about one quarter of the early eighteenth-century clergy, and any or several of them might have suggested the idea. It is equally possible that the concept came by other routes, or was a local invention. A T plan, with the addition as a separate room, was used in the original construction of the Third Haven Friends' meeting house (Fig. 77) on the Eastern Shore of Maryland in 1682, and additions at right angles were regularly made to Virginia houses in the late seventeenth century. It is most likely that the Virginia T addition combined all these sources in the syncretic manner that produced much of the New World's vernacular architecture.[33]

It is more important to ask why the form appealed to Virginia's builders. A deep centralized church could have been constructed using a "double roof," or parallel gable roofs, such as many late seventeenth-century English

provincial meeting houses employed. Double roofs were known to Virginians, but they required columns that obstructed the congregation's view. An unobstructed view could have been achieved without centralizing by lengthening the church, but this would have made it difficult for the congregation to hear, and was probably the reason for limiting the length of churches to no more than eighty feet. Virginians preferred a central focus *and* an unobstructed view. T additions allowed the builder to bring as many people as possible close to the pulpit while maintaining a relatively narrow span in each wing. The engineering problems of roofing a deep church were minimized, and the building could be covered without resort to interior columns or other supports.[34]

Every T-plan church resulted from an addition to an existing rectangular church. The single exception was the 1718–19 lower church built for St. Paul's Parish by Henry Cary, which was to have a sixty-by-twenty-foot building with "A Twenty foot Square room, on the Backside." But this may have been a vestry room rather than an extension of the auditorium, for the vestry later referred to "the Church and Back Building."[35]

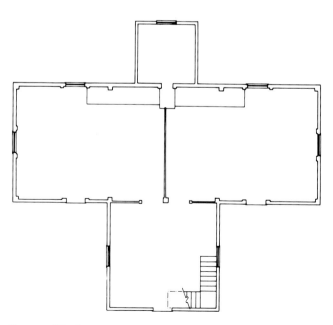

FIG. 77. Third Haven Friends' meeting house (ca. 1682), Easton, Maryland. Plan. (Drawing, Orlando Ridout V.)

Although a T addition was constructed at Poplar Spring church at the very beginning of the eighteenth century, T additions were relatively rare until the great spate of church building and enlarging in the second quarter of the century. The earliest surviving T addition is the one at Vauter's church (see Figs. 73, 74), Essex County. The original building was probably finished around 1719, and the ell, unusual in being a south rather than a north wing, is dated 1731 above its doorway. Visually the T is indistinguishable from the original structure. It has a triangular pedimented doorway, a pair of small segmental-headed windows to light an original gallery, and compass-head main windows. An addition, possibly a T, was projected for the wooden upper chapel of Christ Church Parish, Middlesex County, in 1731, and undertaken by Henry Gaines. Permission was granted in 1733 for twenty-foot-square private additions to the north sides of each of the other two churches in the parish as well. These would have been T additions, their private character close to the Scots tradition, but they were never constructed. T plans spread throughout the eastern part of Virginia in the 1740s. Related to them was the addition built to the lower church of Suffolk Parish, now known as the Glebe church, in 1759 (Figs. 78, 79). Where the T additions were normally set slightly off center to the east, this was pushed all the way to the east, forming an L-shaped plan. The addition was demolished in the 1850s but the church still stands.[36]

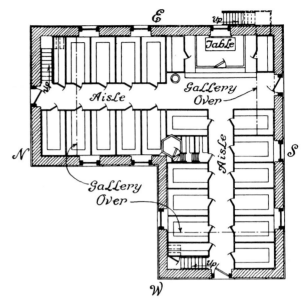

The Glebe Church
Erected in 1737-38 as
Bennett's Creek Church
of Suffolk Parish in
Nansemond County, Virginia.
—— // ——
As Enlarged in 1759 by the
Addition of a North Wing.
—— // ——

FIG. 79. Lower church, Suffolk Parish. Plan as reconstructed by George Carrington Mason. (From Mason, *Colonial Churches of Tidewater Virginia*, pl. 40.)

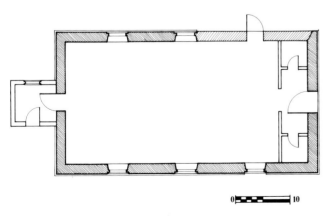

FIG. 78. Lower (Glebe) church (ca. 1737; enlarged b. 1759), Suffolk Parish, Suffolk. Plan, showing church without demolished addition. (Drawing, Dell Upton.)

The cruciform plan used for constructing large parish churches was derived from the T addition. Rectangular west-end-entry churches ranged in floor area from 480 square feet up; only a handful exceeded 3,000 square feet. T-plan churches stood at the upper end of that range, but never topped it. The smallest recorded had an area of 1,775 square feet after enlargement, the largest 2,500 square feet. The smallest cruciform church, on the other hand, was St. Paul's in King George County, at 2,340 square feet, and

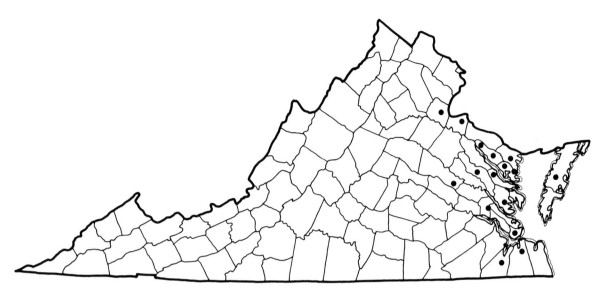

FIG. 80. Cruciform churches in Virginia. (Drawing, Dell Upton.)

churches of this plan ranged (in their original form) up to 3,600 square feet at Abingdon church. All the cruciform churches were built in long-established, wealthy parishes along one of the three principal rivers (Fig. 80). The only exceptions were the church planned in 1748 and built in the 1750s by the Upper Parish of Nansemond County, which lay inland from the James River but was connected to it by the Nansemond River, and the 1738 Pungoteague church of Accomack Parish on the Eastern Shore. It is worth noting, as well, that all cruciform churches were built in that form. No church was ever enlarged to the four-armed plan in the colonial period.[37]

The first church built with a cross-shaped plan was the third Bruton Parish church at Williamsburg, projected in 1710, planned in 1711, and built between 1711 and 1715 (Figs. 81, 82). The original design was for a church seventy-five by twenty-eight feet, with two wings twenty-two feet wide and nineteen feet long. Governor Alexander Spotswood "proposed to the Vestry to build only 53 of the 75 foot, and that he would take care for the remaining part." A. Lawrence Kocher was led to conclude from this that the vestry planned a Greek-cross church fifty-three feet each way, but the wording of the vestry minute shows that a Latin-cross plan was always intended, and that Spotswood merely helped with its cost, rather than enlarging the

original plan. Spotswood also supplied "a platt or draught" of the proposed building, but it can only have been a rough scheme. Most vestry book records indicate that complete plans of the sort required from undertakers consisted of a plan and often elevation drawings, along with a bill of materials, or "scantling," and a cost estimate. Spotswood's plan was not complete, however, for the clerk of the vestry was "impowered to agree with some skillful workman, to lay down the said scantlings: also to calculate the number of bricks sufficient for a wall of 56 foot long, 28 foot wide, and 23 foot high above the ground, and report the same to the next Vestry, in order to a full consideration thereof," and another vestryman was sent "to acquaint the Honble. Alexr. Spottswood with the proceedings of the Vestry concerning his draught." Two years later, when the length of the wings was reduced from nineteen feet to fourteen feet six inches, the vestry had the plans redrawn. Nevertheless, Spotswood continued to take an aggressively active role in the building process, acting as liaison to the legislature, which was financing the wings, and offering, with vestryman Colonel Edmund Jennings, to supply bricks "in order to beat down" the estimates given by the builders John Tillett and Henry Cary, which the domineering Governor judged "extravagant." In December 1715 it was noted that the church was nearly complete, and in November of the next year the

FIG. 81. Bruton Parish church (1711–15; James Morris, undertaker; enlarged 1752–54; tower 1769; Benjamin Powell, undertaker), Williamsburg. View from the northwest, showing churchyard with 18th-century monuments. (From *Colonial Churches in the Original Colony of Virginia*, n.p.)

church wardens were ordered to sell the materials of the 1683 building. It was not until 1717, however, that the church received a shingle covering over its beaded-weatherboard roof.[38]

No crucifix symbolism was intended by the Bruton plan: the concern was with audibility in a very large urban church. It would be ten years before other cruciform churches were built, and they, too, appeared in urban settings. The first was Elizabeth City Parish church (Figs. 83–85), Hampton, completed around 1728 by Henry Cary, Jr., builder of the T-plan lower church of St. Paul's Parish. About ten years later the Elizabeth River Parish church, now known as St. Paul's, Norfolk (Figs. 86, 87), was erected. The Elizabeth River church followed the Bruton precedent closely in its three-bay body, one-bay chancel, and large bull's-eye windows over the transept doors. The Elizabeth City church, now known as St. John's, reduced

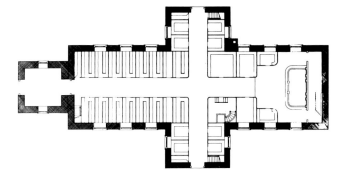

FIG. 82. Bruton Parish church. Plan as restored by Colonial Williamsburg. In the 18th century, the chancel was against the east wall. (Drawing, Colonial Williamsburg Foundation.)

Fig. 83. Elizabeth City Parish (St. John's) church (begun ca. 1728; Henry Cary, Jr., undertaker; tower 1761; Charles Cooper, bricklayer, Thomas Craghead, carpenter), Hampton. Mid-19th century view showing tower before destruction in Civil War. (From Meade, *Old Churches*, n.p.)

Fig. 84. Elizabeth City Parish church. The tower, the porches, and the small window in the angle are 19th-century alterations. (Photograph, Dell Upton.)

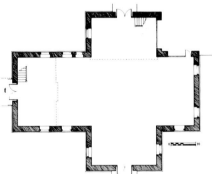

Fig. 85. Elizabeth City Parish church. Plan. Key: t = location of 1761 tower. (Drawing, Dell Upton.)

Fig. 86. Elizabeth River Parish (St. Paul's) church (1739), Norfolk. Mid-19th-century view. "SB 1739" formed in glazed bricks in gable of south wing. (From Meade, *Old Churches*, n.p.)

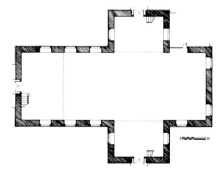

Fig. 87. Elizabeth River Parish church. Plan. (Drawing, Dell Upton.)

FIG. 88. Lower (Mattaponi Baptist) church (ca. 1730–34), St. Stephen's Parish, King and Queen County. (Photograph, Dell Upton.)

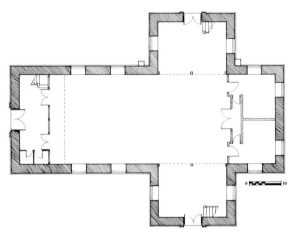

FIG. 89. Mattaponi church. Plan. The church burned out in the early 20th century and the present interior is all modern, but the west gallery is in the location of the 18th-century original. (Drawing, Dell Upton.)

the length of the western portion to two bays. It had a tower added in 1761, eight years before construction of the present tower at Bruton Parish church. A third church on the Bruton model was the lower church of St. Stephen's Parish, now known as Mattaponi Baptist church (Figs. 88, 89), built ca. 1730–34 with a two-bay nave like that at Elizabeth City Parish church. Both the latter churches, and possibly the Elizabeth River church, were embellished with the pedimented doorways that had not yet come into use when Bruton Parish church was built.[39]

No other cruciform churches in Virginia bear a direct resemblance to Bruton church, and to the extent that it was an example, it must be accounted so for showing how the perpendicular wing might be treated in a relatively formal way, not for its Latin cross plan or for any of its details. Far more influential was Christ church, Lancaster County, built about 1732–35 (Fig. 90; see Fig. 5). The seventy-foot east-west portion of Christ church is five feet shorter than the original Bruton Parish church. But while Bruton church was projected to be nine feet longer from east to west than it was from north to south, and was eighteen feet longer as built, the north-south dimensions of Christ church are the same as the length of the building. Furthermore, while the transepts at Christ church are set only slightly to the east of center, at Bruton Parish church and its imitators they are

noticeably set so. Christ church appears as a Greek cross, even if it is technically a Latin one. The high walls and steep, double-pitched roof add to the illusion of vertical centrality, in contrast to Bruton church's long, low axiality in its original form, which was augmented by its mid-eighteenth-century addition.[40]

An inspection of the plan reveals why the wings of Christ church are set slightly to the east. This adds length to the body of the church, and reduces the eastern arm to a relatively small chancel housing the communion place and the two large pews, at least one of which belonged to the Carter family. Furthermore, the centralizing intent of the plan was fulfilled by the pulpit's being set, as in the T-plan churches, in the southwest corner at the intersection of the arms. It could be seen from every seat in the church, something that could not be said of the altarpiece and the communion rail.[41]

Churches inspired by Christ church were built even before it was completed. The parish churches of North Farnham and Lunenburg parishes in Richmond County, the next county west of Lancaster on the Northern Neck, were both finished around 1737, just two years after Christ church, and so must have been begun during the construction of King Carter's church. The Lunenburg church was demolished in the early nineteenth century, but Farnham

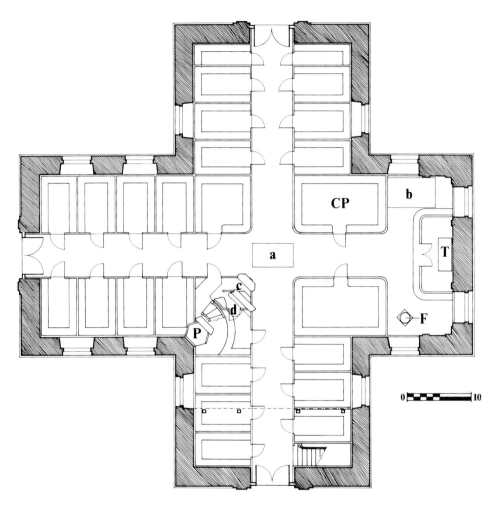

Fig. 90. Christ church (ca. 1732–35), Lancaster County. Plan. Key: P = pulpit; d = reading desk; c = clerk's desk; F = font; T = table; CP = Carter pew; a = tomb slab of David Miles (d. 1674); b = tomb slab of John Carter, Esq. (d. 1669), and his wives, Jane Glyn, Ann Carter, and Sarah Ludlowe, and his children, George, Elinor, and Sarah Carter, all of whom died before he did. (Drawing, Dell Upton.)

church (Figs. 91, 92) survived as a ruin and was extensively rebuilt in the mid-nineteenth and again in the early twentieth centuries. Like Christ church, Farnham church is a Latin cross, closer in proportion to Bruton than to Christ, but appearing, because of its height, to be a Greek cross. The arms are about five feet shorter in total span than the east-west body of the church, and are located farther east than those at Christ church. The original hipped roof must have contributed to the centralized appearance, but it was already gone by the time Bishop Meade saw the church in the mid-nineteenth century. The elevations are close to those of Christ church, although it is clear that the builders of Farnham church were inspired by the older building rather than directly imitating it.[42]

The same is true of the parish church of St. Mary's White Chapel Parish, Lancaster County. The church was under construction when the surviving vestry book opens in 1739, four years after Christ church was completed. Only the north and south transepts survive. The east and west arms were demolished in the nineteenth century and the space between the transepts filled in. The extant portions of the building bear only the vaguest resemblance to Christ church; even more than at Farnham church, it was the idea, not the specific forms, that appealed to the builders. The parishes of St. Mary's White Chapel and Christ Church had closely intertwined histories, and in 1752 they

FIG. 92. Farnham church. Plan. (Drawing, Dell Upton.)

FIG. 91. Farnham church (begun ca. 1734), Richmond County. The church was abandoned and reconstructed several times in the 19th century, most recently after an 1888 fire. The original hipped roof had been replaced by gables by the time Bishop Meade visited it. The doorways and other architectural decoration are modern. (Photograph, Dell Upton.)

were formally merged by the legislature upon the discovery that they had never been legally separated. Family ties and geography made the connection closer still: many of the same families were prominent in the two parishes, and the churches were relatively near by Virginia standards.[43]

Equally near to the Lancaster county parish churches was the Wicomico Parish church in adjacent Northumberland County. Where St. Mary's White Chapel church was only formally similar to Christ church, the Wicomico Parish church was an explicit copy of the Lancaster County building, as we have seen in chapter 3. The vestry first decided to replace its seventeenth-century church in 1753, when they drew up specifications for a church "built near the old One," seventy-five by thirty feet, "with a Cross of the same length and weadth, from out to out," twenty-five feet high. The length was five feet longer than Christ church, but the width of each wing was the same as the original. The doors and windows were to be of "the same Dimentions as those in Christ Church in Lancaster County"; there were to be ox-eye windows over each door as in Christ church; and "the Pews [were] to be of the same Height, and the benches of the same Weadth as the Pews in Christ Church." But where Christ church had only one gallery, and that a later eighteenth-century addition, Wicomico church was to have three galleries, in this respect

resembling St. Mary's White Chapel church. No church was constructed in 1753, but ten years later the old scheme was resurrected and updated, and the intended resemblance to the model stated more explicitly. The Wicomico church was to have brown interior woodwork, white exterior woodwork, and a vaulted ceiling like its model. The pulpit, however, was to be placed at the northwest interior corner, not the southwest corner as in Christ church.[44]

Cruciform churches resembling Christ church continued to be built in the Northern Neck and Middle Peninsula parishes into the third quarter of the eighteenth century. Christ Church Parish, Middlesex County, advertised for the construction of a new brick upper church "in the Form of a Cross, sixty by thirty each Way in the Clear, with one Gallery" in 1772. Two years later, St. Paul's Parish in Hanover County decided to build "a large Commodious Brick Church eighty foot long and thirty five foot Wide with a Cross projecting twenty foot on each side and thirty five foot Wide," or a Greek/Latin cross eighty by seventy-five, at Hanover Town. However, the undertaker, Paul Thilman, died, and the Revolution began before the parish could make a new contract. One of these late brick buildings survives—Abingdon church in Gloucester County (Figs. 93–95). The contract was advertised in 1751, and a brick on the south corner of the west front reads "WB 1755." Like

FIG. 93. Abingdon church (ca. 1751–55), Gloucester County. Early 20th-century view showing the colonial wall with its ramped piers and a gate that may be colonial. (From *Colonial Churches in the Original Colony of Virginia*, n.p.)

FIG. 94. Abingdon church. Brick at right edge of west facade inscribed "WB 1755." (Photograph, Dell Upton.)

FIG. 95. Abingdon church. Plan. Key: P = original location of pulpit. (Drawing, Dell Upton.)

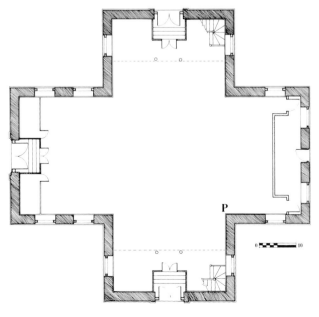

Christ church, Abingdon is a Latin cross that looks like a Greek cross, and its nave is five feet longer than the chancel. It resembles the Hanover Town church in measuring eighty by seventy-five by thirty-five feet, and it may have been the immediate model of the St. Paul's Parish building. The slight increase in the width of the arms over Christ church (from thirty to thirty-five feet) and the slight decrease in wall thickness result in a crossing so large that the feeling of a cruciform plan is nearly lost on the interior. Instead, from the original galleries in the north and south arms, the space is experienced as a large central area with shallow recesses on the sides. Like many post-1750 parish churches, Abingdon church was built with a flat ceiling.

The pulpit here was originally located at the southeast corner of the crossing.[45]

At least two northern Virginia churches of the late colonial period were built with cruciform plans. Aquia church (Figs. 96, 97) was begun by Mourning Richards in 1751, at the same time as Abingdon church. Aquia is a true Greek-cross church, with two intersecting sixty-four-by-thirty-two-foot sections. Again, the crossing is large, and one gains a feeling of a central open space, if not as much as at Abingdon church (Fig. 98). At Aquia there is an original west gallery and the pulpit, as at Abingdon, is in the southeast corner of the crossing. In 1762 and again in 1766 the vestry of St. Paul's Parish, also in Stafford (now King

FIG. 96. Aquia church (1754–57; Mourning Richards, undertaker). West entrance. (Photograph, Dell Upton.)

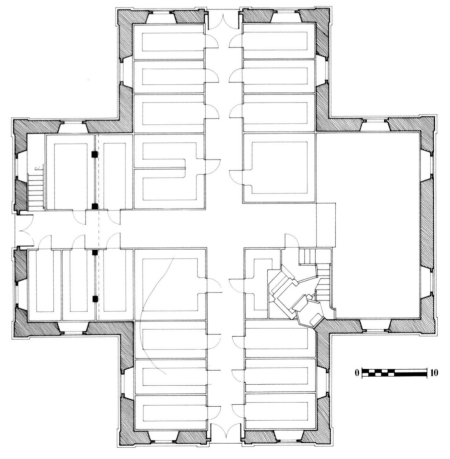

FIG. 97. Aquia church. Plan. The pews were reduced in height in the 19th century and the chancel reorganized in the 20th century; otherwise the interior arrangement is original. (Drawing, Dell Upton.)

FIG. 98. Aquia church. Interior. (Courtesy, Virginia State Library.)

FIG. 99. St. Paul's Parish church (begun ca. 1766), King George (formerly Stafford) County. Exterior. (Photograph, Dell Upton.)

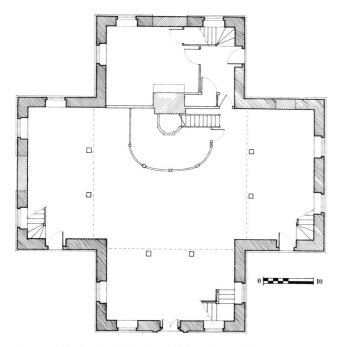

FIG. 100. St. Paul's Parish church. Plan. The building was converted to a school in 1813. The rooms in the north wing date from that conversion, while the pulpit and chancel were installed ca. 1830. (Drawing, Dell Upton.)

George) County, advertised the construction of a cruciform brick church (Figs. 99, 100). This building is sixty-two by thirty feet each way, or just two feet smaller in every dimension than Aquia church.[46]

Both Aquia and St. Paul's churches have two-story facade elevations that break with Virginia tradition, and windows on the entrance facades as well as on the side walls and east ends, where one would expect to find them. Aquia church's two-story fenestration is the first example of a northern Virginia regional pattern that was growing in popularity when the Revolution intervened. Pohick church, Falls church, and Alexandria (Christ) church all have square-headed lower windows and compass-head upper ones as Aquia does. Most surviving contracts, like that for Pohick church, are silent on the fenestration, although two rows of windows are illustrated in the elevation drawing for Pohick church (see Fig. 6). The specifications for the churches at Alexandria and the Falls built for Fairfax Parish beginning in 1767 gave dimensions for upper and lower windows, however, and the vestrymen in Shelburne Parish, Loudoun County, in 1774 ordered the construction of a church "of sufficient Pitch for two Rows of Windows."[47]

FIG. 101. Pohick church (1769–74; Daniel French, undertaker), Fairfax County. (Photograph, Dell Upton.)

FIG. 102. Pohick church. View ca. 1900. Note the remnants of the painted window surrounds ordered by the vestry during construction. The chimneys for heating stoves are not original. (Photograph, Virginia State Library.)

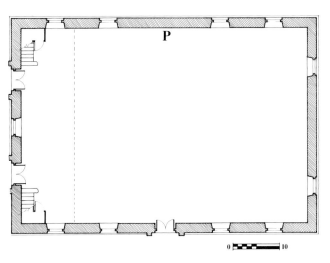

FIG. 103. Pohick church. Plan. Key: P = original location of pulpit. (Drawing, Dell Upton.)

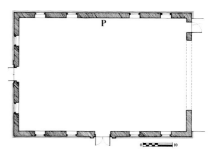

FIG. 105. Falls church. Plan. The east wall was cut out to accommodate a larger chancel in 1959. Key: P = original location of pulpit. (Drawing, Dell Upton.)

FIG. 104. Falls church (1767–70; James Wren, designer and undertaker), Fairfax County. The wooden doorway probably dates from the mid-19th century. (Photograph, Dell Upton.)

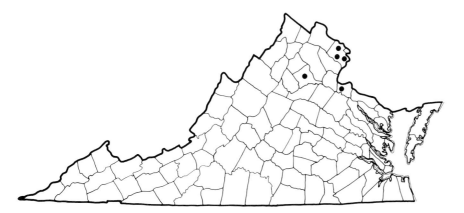

FIG. 106. South-entry churches in Virginia. (Drawing, Dell Upton.)

Pohick (Figs. 101–103) and Falls (Figs. 104, 105) churches are the survivors of a group of churches that were novel in plan as well as in appearance. These were deeper than traditional Virginia rectangular churches, with forty- to fifty-foot widths two-thirds to four-fifths of their lengths. The known examples contained twenty-four hundred to three thousand square feet in plan, placing them at the upper limits of the rectangular church range. Despite their Wren-like proportions, these buildings did not adopt London city-church plans, but adapted the Virginia rectangular plan in a significant way, moving the south door to the center of the south side, and setting the pulpit opposite it. Thus, a kind of symmetry infuses the architectural history of Virginia's churches, as these latest and most stylish of Virginia Anglican churches revived a pulpit placement that had characterized the colony's churches before the classic eighteenth-century reformation embodied in the lower chapel of Christ Church Parish, Middlesex County.

The connection of the northern Virginia churches to the more traditional rectangular plan is evident in three hybrid churches, two built at the southern edge of the deep-church group (Fig. 106): Lamb's Creek church (Figs.

FIG. 107. Lamb's Creek church (ca. 1770), King George County. The painted date over the west door is modern. (Photograph, Dell Upton.)

107, 108) of Brunswick Parish; which is believed to have been built about 1770, and Little Fork church (Figs. 109, 110) of St. Mark's Parish, which was built by William Phillips between 1774 and 1776 to replace the burned Little Fork chapel of 1750. Both retain the traditional rectangular shape, but they are swollen to eighty-foot lengths. Each is seven bays long and has a central south entry, a west door, and a blank central bay at the north against which the pulpit stood. Otherwise the plan is indistinguishable from most earlier Virginia churches. Little Fork church has a pair of small windows, like gallery windows, at the west end, but neither church apparently had an original gallery. The third church, Payne's church (Fig. 111), designed by John Ayres and built by Edward Payne as the upper church of Truro Parish in 1766–68, was closer to the traditional dimensions of a rectangular Virginia church, at fifty-three by thirty feet. It, too, had the new central placement of the south door.[48]

While Little Fork and Lamb's Creek churches demonstrate the identity of the northern Virginia central-entry

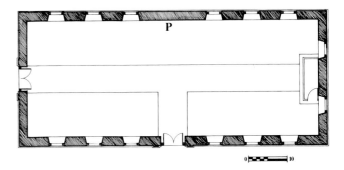

FIG. 108. Lamb's Creek church. Plan. Key: P = original location of pulpit. (Drawing, Dell Upton.)

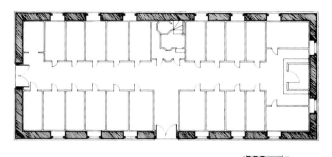

Fig. 110. Little Fork church. Plan, showing reconstructed pews and pulpit. (Drawing, Dell Upton.)

Fig. 109. Little Fork church (1773–76; William Phillips, undertaker), Culpeper County. (Photograph, Dell Upton.)

Fig. 111. Payne's church (1766–68; John Ayres, designer; Edward Payne, under-taker), Fairfax County. The only known photograph of the demolished church shows that it had a pedimented doorway in the center of the south side. (From *Colonial Churches in the Original Colony of Virginia*, n.p.)

churches as transformations of the traditional Virginia rectangular church, more complex relationships to Middle Colonies traditions exist as well. The deep northern churches, which were built from Prince William County as far north as Frederick County, resemble churches built in the Middle Colonies along lines that reflect the influence of dissenting meeting-house plans. The central-entry meeting-house form, familiar from New England, was used by Protestant dissenters in England as well as in the Middle Colonies. Old Drawyer's Presbyterian church (1773) near

Odessa, Delaware, is an example (Fig. 112). From the mid-eighteenth century on, a number of similar churches were built in Pennsylvania, Delaware, and Maryland Anglican parishes. Unlike the Presbyterian churches, the Anglican churches continued to have communion places at their east ends. St. Anne's church (1765–71), Middletown, Delaware, has a Palladian window at the east similar to those used on the chancels of the eighteenth-century Philadelphia Anglican churches, Christ and St. Peter's (Fig. 113). Like those urban churches and the northern Virginia churches, it has two tiers of windows, although its upper windows are square headed. It has a central south door and a prominent west entry, and on the north side, as at Pohick church and Falls church in Virginia, there is a blank central bay against which the pulpit stood. A similar plan is found at St. James's church, built in 1768 in Anne Arundel County, Maryland. This one-story building has a hipped roof like the Virginia buildings, as opposed to the Delaware and Maryland buildings, which have gable roofs. Where St. Anne's church acknowledges its new orientation by placing a gallery along the south wall, the Virginia churches like Pohick retained the traditional west gallery.[49]

Alexandria (Christ) church and Falls church were both intended to be built from the same set of plans, supplied by James Wren, for a deep rectangular church. The plan of Pohick church (see Fig. 6) and the elevations of the existing building show that it was also intended to resemble Falls church on the exterior. However, the Fairfax Parish vestry decided during construction to enlarge Christ church by widening it, and in the process they constructed a building with two west doors and parallel east-west alleys. The Truro Parish vestry had already decided to use two aisles at Pohick church, and during construction they altered the original plan by replacing the original central west entry with a separate door for each alley. These churches thus combined elements of the deep church with the large double-alley churches like Ware and Stratton Major discussed earlier in the chapter (Fig. 114). At the same time, there are ties to the northeast. St. Paul's church (Figs. 115, 116), Quantico, Maryland, and Christ church, Sussex County, Delaware, originally built as chapels of Stepney Parish, Maryland, at about the same time that Pohick church was being constructed, also have double west doors and their pulpits are placed in the center of the north wall, though neither has a corresponding south entry. Once again, as happened with the T additions, ideas from a variety of sources were

FIG. 112. Old Drawyer's Presbyterian church (1773), near Odessa, Delaware. (Photograph, Dell Upton.)

FIG. 113. St. Anne's church (1765), Middletown, Delaware. (Photograph, Dell Upton.)

synthesized into a new Virginia church plan. What is significant is that the outside element in the synthesis is not European, but northeastern. Northern Virginia's ties with Maryland and Delaware, and through them to Pennsylvania and the north, evident in the economic and settlement history of the two regions and in the domestic architecture

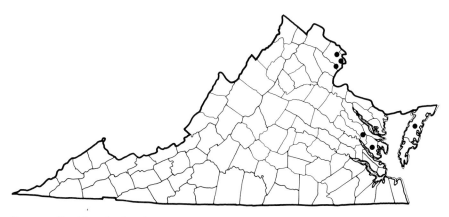

FIG. 114. Double aisle churches in Virginia. (Drawing, Dell Upton.)

FIG. 115. St. Paul's church (1773), Quantico, Maryland. A double-aisle-plan church. (Photograph, Dell Upton.)

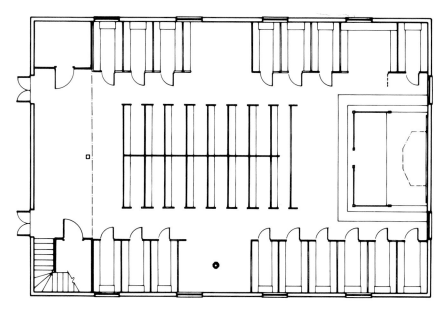

FIG. 116. St. Paul's church. The pulpit originally stood in the middle of the north wall. (Drawing, Johanna Mennucci.)

of such towns as Alexandria, Georgetown, Annapolis, Centreville, New Castle, and Philadelphia, were manifested in church building as well. Northern Virginia served as a conduit for the introduction of new ideas into late colonial Virginia. Its churches were Virginia buildings, but they looked to the Middle Colonies for new planning ideas and, as we shall see, for architectural fashions as well.[50]

The Anglicans of sixteenth-century England bequeathed to the new colony of Virginia a three-part church plan, with the font at the west end, a chancel fitted with a movable wooden communion table at the east end, and a nave containing a pulpit and a reading desk. Using these elements and ideas drawn from several sources, Virginians created three characteristic church plans and several hybrid versions of them (Fig. 117). The first was a rectangular building with a south chancel door and a west main entry very similar to the rural auditory churches that began to be built in England early in the seventeenth century. Seventeenth- and early eighteenth-century versions tended to incorporate a chancel screen; after the second decade of the eighteenth century an open rectangular room was more common. In the early eighteenth century, when larger churches were desired, Virginians developed a perpendicular addition probably derived from similar architectural ideas in domestic planning and in Scots Presbyterian church design, and intended to combine the advantages of a traditional structure, clear visibility of the pulpit, and easy hearing in a centrally focused structure. The third Bruton Parish church, built at the same time that the rectangular plan was being perfected and the T-plan variant developed, disciplined the perpendicular addition to a formal visual image, introducing the second Virginia type, the cruciform church, as the standard large-church plan in Virginia. It reigned until late in the colonial period both in the Bruton-like Latin-cross version and in the more popular pseudo-Greek cross form introduced at Christ church, Lancaster County, after 1730. Another large-church plan was introduced at the end of the pre-Revolutionary era. It altered the proportions of the rectangular plan, retaining the major elements of it, but increasing the depth of the church. This plan moved the south entry to the center of the long side, and the pulpit to the center of the north. Once again the south side was visibly the front of the church, as it had literally been in English parish churches and as Virginians had thought of it throughout the eighteenth century. A double-aisled variation was introduced both to the traditional rectangular church and to the deep church in the last decades before the Revolution, and during the same years the central south door was adapted to the rectangular church.

The continuities and differences in the plans raise two important points. Like its English counterparts, the Virginia parish church embodied two dichotomies. One juxtaposed the traditional Catholic mystery of the communion sacrament — the sacrifice of the mass — with the Protestant emphasis on the spoken word as an instrument of religious transformation. The stone altar of sacrifice and mystical transubstantiation had been replaced by the wooden table of the shared ritual meal in the sixteenth century, but in the seventeenth century Anglicans continued to discuss the proper attitude toward the sacrament, and by extension

toward the chancel. Many argued that the table deserved some form of reverence as a holy place. Anglican historians have argued that no emphasis of pulpit over chancel was intended in seventeenth- and eighteenth-century Anglicanism, which may be true, but there can be no doubt that that was the effect. More and more, clergy tended to conduct all their offices from the pulpit, except in the case of baptism and communion. Landon Carter noted this in the conduct of Isaac William Giberne, rector of Carter's home parish of Lunenburg. He attributed Giberne's unwillingness to perform baptisms during the regular church service to his "aversion to trouble for it is easier after divine service is over to go to the font than to be walking backwards and forwards during divine service which I fancy my friend is not fond of for he goes as seldom to the Alta[r] in the church service [to pray] as any Min[is]ter as I have ever been acquain[ted] with."[51]

The second dichotomy was that between the Church as a transcendent institution conferring authority on worldly institutions, and the Church as an arm of a worldly body, the state. The Church-state juxtaposition should lead to a unified existence with spiritual and temporal institutions reinforcing one another. This was a Puritan as well as an Anglican concept. But in Virginia practice the Church was subordinate not only to the state but to local powers as well. To a great extent, this was true of the Church of England everywhere. Seventeenth- and eighteenth-century Anglicanism was both a spiritual and an intellectual religion, but it was above all a civil one. English people and Americans were convinced of the necessity of an established Church as a support for civil rule, and Virginia's Anglicans, no less than England's, or than New England's Calvinists, thought it beneficial to enact laws requiring attendance at church, like that passed by the Virginia legislature in September 1632. The reason was simple. Public worship, as Richard Hooker pointed out, was necessary because without it "dangerous practices" resulted.[52]

To see the relationship between Church and state simply as one of moral instruction of the citizenry, or more cynically as their indoctrination, with the civil aspects of Anglicanism excluding the spiritual and intellectual, is to miss the point, however. In the Anglican church, the parishioners learned about the higher purposes of civil society. At the same time, in their daily lives they saw manifested, in concrete form, the reality of which religion was the abstract description. The two were linked through the

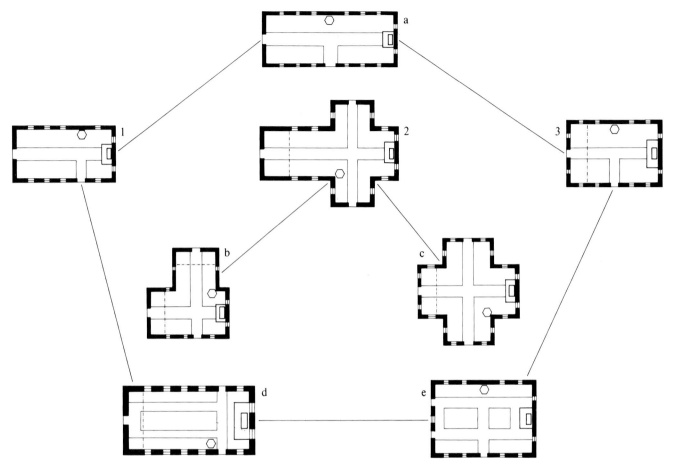

FIG. 117. Virginia church plans. The three basic types are (1) rectangular; (2) cruciform; and (3) deep; their variants are (a) rectangular with central south entry; (b) T-plan; (c) Greek cross; (d) rectangular with double-aisle plan; (e) deep with double-aisle plan. The lines connecting the plans are intended not to suggest a chronological evolution, but to propose conceptual similarities between the basic plans and the variants. (Drawing, Dell Upton.)

presence of the Royal Arms in church. The arms were juxtaposed with the Ten Commandments. The meaning of the Commandments was channeled and concretized by the presence of the arms. The arms were displayed, wrote one seventeenth-century English commentator, "to professe the subjection of every soule to the higher power. . . . [They] do put us in minde of that *Defender of the Faith* and of our duty to him who is *next and immediately under God* supream governor over al persons and cases as well Eccle-

siasticall and Temporall in all his Majesties Realmes & Dominions." An eighteenth-century writer added that the juxtaposition of arms and Commandments was intended "to satisfy all those who tread the courts of the Lord's House and are diligent in the performance of their duty agreeably to the contents of these grand rules of the Christian religion (viz., the Ten Commandments, the Lord's Prayer, and the Creed) that they shall meet with encouragement and protection from the state." All the complex interrelations of divine and earthly lordship and law were thus neatly bound up in the superposition of Royal Arms and altarpiece. But it was a relationship that was intended to serve the ends of the state. The form of the Anglican parish church bequeathed to Virginians was intended to make understanding consumers of Christian doctrine of the parishioners, and in that way to make good citizens of them. The parish church was officially a lesson in power.[53]

The Anglican parish church was "about" the power of Church and state, about the justification of temporal power by spiritual claims, about the reinforcement of ecclesiastical power by the arm of the state. But in some respects all religions are about power. What was special about the Anglican parish church in colonial Virginia? This question underlies an inquiry into the visual character as well as the forms of Anglican parish churches in the colony. Why do churches have compass ceilings and windows? Why is exterior decoration restricted to the doorways of eighteenth-century churches? Why do pulpits and altarpieces look the way they do? One's conditioned response is to answer, "fashion." But fashion is a question rather than an answer. Power cannot explain fashion, nor can the workings of power be explained simply by recounting the arrangement of its elements. To understand both, one must turn to the specific embodiment of power in Virginia in architectural and artifactual style.

| II | Hospitality |

| 6 | Holy Things and Profane |

When Rebecca Snead, one of the imaginary Virginians we encountered in chapter 1, cast a glance around her parish church, there were many things she might have seen. Some were familiar from her daily experience. The plastered walls, the shape of the balusters and hand rails, the beaded edges of the ceiling boards and pew panels, and the moldings around the doors and windows were probably too commonplace to make a conscious impression. But the curved ceiling, the pediments over the doors and the altarpiece, the pilasters on the altarpiece, the carving on the pulpit, the silver flagons and cups used at communion, the velvet hangings with their gold embroidery, and the elaborate decoration on the leather bindings of the church's Bible and prayer books might have caught her eye, for they were not encountered often. She saw them in church, and associated several of them with specific settings outside church as well. Perhaps some were familiar from a rare trip to the county court with her husband, Zachariah; others from a vividly remembered occasion in the house of burgess James James. Though Rebecca might have been more aware of the pediments and silver than the plaster and beading, all parts of the church contributed to her experience of the building. Virginia's parish churches were not the unified products of single individuals—not works of art in the customary sense—but the visual qualities of the churches were essential to their builders' social and ritual aims, and the structures were decorated and furnished in a carefully calculated manner.

Traditionally, scholars analyze the visual qualities of architecture and decorative arts in terms of style. They examine the sources of an artifact's appearance and they criticize the coherence with which forms from a variety of sources are combined in the work at hand. In the case of Virginia's parish churches, the forms were drawn from both European classical and Anglo-American vernacular traditions. However, the architecture and furnishings of Virginian Anglicanism are best understood by reversing the customary emphasis of historical inquiry. Where traditional methods presume that an object is significant to the extent that it can be related to cosmopolitan norms, the proper approach to these artifacts focuses on their local context. It is not the builders' relationship to Christopher Wren but to Rebecca Snead and her neighbors that is most significant. Whatever the sources of particular formal elements in the church, what functions do they serve in the parish? Some classical and vernacular elements are common to all buildings in Virginia, and they create the unifying background that Rebecca Snead overlooked. These elements I call style. Against this background are set other elements that help to create distinctions within and among buildings, and they attracted Rebecca's attention. These elements I call mode.

My concept of style combines ideas derived from art history and archaeology. The art historian Meyer Schapiro defines style as "the constant form—and sometimes the constant elements, qualities and expression—in the art of an individual or group." The archaeologist James M. Sackett writes that style is "a highly specific and characteristic manner of doing something." Style encompasses the visually characteristic attributes that, he writes further, "act as a signpost or banner advertising the arena" for which the object is intended. For art historians and archaeologists, style characterizes an entire population, an age, or a place. In Schapiro's words, style "is a manifestation of the culture as a whole, the visible sign of its unity."[1]

These statements imply style's unifying mental temperament, but give slight consideration to the uses of style. Sackett, for instance, sees style as "passive," and contrasts it with the "active" attributes of an object—attributes that adapt it to its purpose—which he calls function. Yet much of the visual unity of style arises not from undefined cultural harmony, but from generally accepted conventions that did have real functions. Conventional sizes of bricks and timbers, standard ratios of wall thickness to height, preferred window shapes, particular classical details, molding planes of fixed profiles, such as those encountered in chapter 4, allowed the carpenter, the mason, and the joiner to work with a finite amount of training and tools to create a varied but coherent group of buildings. Convention also communicates meaning. In the Virginia church, for example, contrasts between materials and finishes— between common and expensive woods, planed and rough boards, painted and whitewashed surfaces, between silver and velvet or redware and fustian—were conventions that conveyed messages, as were the contextual contrasts between high and low, light and dark, decorated and plain. For the builder, convention eliminates the need to rethink every architectural problem. For the user, it helps to project the meaning of specific buildings. For the historian, it shapes the characteristic look, or style, of a group of artifacts.[2]

Style is pervasive. It provides a context, or system of common understanding, within which the active participants of a society can operate in a coordinated manner, however imperfect that coordination might be. To make an analogy with linguistic scholarship, style is a kind of code, a concise, bonding body of implicitly understood assumptions that need not be rehearsed; allusions suffice. Style is in some sense consensual.[3]

The word "style" is often used in a narrower sense, one that is incompatible with the pervasive, consensual definition. It is applied to small groups' preferences for artifacts with a limited number of very specific attributes. At Rebecca Snead's parish church, for example, the simple moldings and beaded edges were known to all Virginians in their churches, but the communion chalice embellished with billowing convex gadroons in a "baroque style" was familiar only to the local gentry, whose homes were filled with English goods decorated in a similar manner. Referring to these narrow, very specific preferences as "styles" is confusing, since for their users they served to distinguish, not to unify. Owning such goods set one off from one's neighbors, and intentionally so. Consequently, it is helpful to describe the use of visual elements in this manner by a different name—mode. Mode refers to the divisions within

society; it emphasizes and perpetuates old differences, recalling them to attention by clothing them in striking new garb, and it works to create new differences, casting an identifying cloak over individuals not apparently related, or set apart, before.

Though the modes of elite and avant-garde groups are most likely to attract historians, modes can be created by groups of any social status wishing to set themselves apart. The preference for Chippendale furniture, oriental rugs, and Chinese porcelain is a mode among certain wealthy twentieth-century Americans of conservative taste; the adoption of country music, Western dress, and pick-up trucks among the urban and suburban working class is also a mode. The distinctive costume of doctrinally plain religious groups like the Amish Mennonites is another. All serve to identify individuals within a subgroup of people with one another, and to demonstrate to the individuals and to outsiders their differences from the larger society.[4]

Our analysis of the visual qualities of Virginia's parish churches will take into account both style and mode. The church contracts show that Virginia's vestries and undertakers thought out each part of the structures separately, naming in the agreement the parts that affected the price of the buildings. Architectural inspection of surviving buildings offers insights into other choices that were negotiated on the site or left to the craftsmen. From all these choices emerged buildings that combined style and mode in eloquent ways. A complex environment was created that used a framework of style to assert a building's universality, but then employed mode to articulate separations and distinctions among the people who used the building. Horton Davies has stressed the importance of the *Book of Common Prayer* in Anglican life. The Anglican Church erased distinctions between clergy and laity by placing the same document, written in English, in the hands of individuals in both groups. The use of mode in the Virginia parish church replaced the old division with two new distinctions. One was the artifactual distinction between Virginia churches and other Virginia buildings. Second, and more important, was the distinction within the parish among groups of lay people, between those who controlled the church and those who merely attended it.[5]

Many of the components of style in the parish churches of Virginia have appeared in the chapter on church building.

Structural systems, standard dimensions of parts, and rules of thumb for such things as roof pitch were developed in Virginia from the beginning of settlement and contributed to the underlying visual coherence of the buildings. Similar conventions existed for the materials and finish of a building: a repertoire of choices was available. The building could be built of brick or frame or—at the northern and western fringes of settlement—of stone or log. Frame buildings were clad in riven (hand-split) clapboards or sawn weatherboards. Weatherboards (Fig. 118) were finished at their lower edges with beads or, less often, with quarter-round moldings. Roofs were covered with clapboards or with

shingles sixteen inches to three feet long, rounded at their butts (lower ends). The shingles were attached with nails or pegs to narrow laths about one by four inches, fixed horizontally across the backs of the rafters. Less often, shingles were laid over lapped weatherboards or clapboards, or over cyphered (flush bevel-edged) planks. Vestries frequently specified which they preferred in the building contracts. Exposed wall surfaces were whitewashed or tarred, and roofs were tarred or painted. Exterior trim was most commonly painted white, but occasionally unspecified "oyle & colours" or "proper Colours" were called for.[6]

Bricks were laid in one of two bonds (Fig. 119). English-

Fig. 118. Beaded (a) and molded (b) weatherboards. On a real building, the two would not be mixed as they are in this drawing. (Drawing, Dell Upton.)

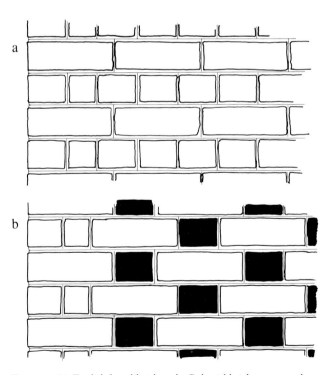

Fig. 119. (a) English-bond brickwork. Colonial bricks were made in wooden molds lined with sand, producing uneven edges. Brickmasons commonly ruled the mortar joints with a straightedge and a sharp tool to give the appearance of even courses. (b) Flemish-bond brickwork. The headers are glazed. (Drawing, Dell Upton.)

bond walls, with alternating courses containing all headers, or short bricks, and all stretchers, or long bricks, were used in the walls of most of the early churches. Flemish bond, with headers and stretchers alternating in each row, was used at St. Luke's church, but otherwise it was standard in churches built from the second decade of the eighteenth century on. Some eighteenth-century builders used combinations of Flemish-bond walls and English-bond underpinnings, but no other bonds were used in Virginia's colonial churches, in contrast to colonies where cross-bond and American-, or common-, bond brickwork could also be found.[7]

Flemish-bond brickwork incorporated an intrinsic checkerboard pattern that eighteenth-century builders often emphasized by using fire-glazed blue-black bricks for the headers (Figs. 120, 121). Glazed headers could also be used in raking courses paralleling the eaves of the church, and occasionally formed other decorative patterns. For example, in the west wall of Lynnhaven Parish (Old Donation) church double glazed headers were used to create diamond or sideways chevron patterns. (Alterations in the facade and the addition of a west porch have made the original pattern difficult to discern.) In addition to glazed bricks, the surface of a brick building might be enlivened with bricks rubbed to give a smoother surface and a lighter color. Rubbed bricks were normally used as highlights around window and door openings and at building corners. Specially molded bricks formed door frames, window mullions, and water tables, the course near the base of the building that marked the diminution of the wall thickness from the foundation to the main wall. Water-table bricks were commonly of three shapes (Fig. 122). A bevel was most often used, but a cavetto (concave quarter-round) or an ovolo (convex quarter-round) shape was used on more pretentious churches, sometimes in combination to produce a more complex shape. Some second- and third-quarter eigh-teenth-century churches had a course of beveled bricks called throating under the window sills (see Fig. 121), and a few late colonial churches in northern Virginia used Aquia sandstone for door frames, corner quoins, and keystones over windows (see Fig. 96).[8]

While there were other kinds of exterior finish used in individual cases, this catalog covers the standard practices in Virginia's parish churches. What is striking is that the list is so short. There was variety in the exterior appearance of individual churches; they could not be called monotonous.

FIG. 120. Upper church (before 1729), Stratton Major Parish, King and Queen County. Representative bay showing compass window with rubbed and gauged arch and rubbed jambs. The walls are laid in Flemish bond with glazed headers above the beveled, rubbed-brick water table, and in English bond, with original air holes, below the water table. The course of bricks under the window sill was installed when the windows were replaced in the 19th century. (Photograph, Dell Upton.)

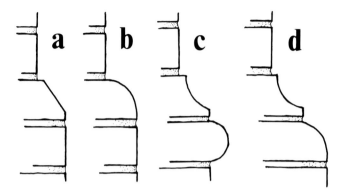

FIG. 122. Water tables. Key: a = beveled; b = ovolo; c = cavetto and torus (after Farnham church); d = cavetto and ovolo (after Falls and Pohick churches). (Drawing, Dell Upton.)

FIG. 121. Merchant's Hope church (ca. 1725), Prince George County. Representative bay showing compass window with rubbed and gauged arch, rubbed jambs, and bevel-brick throating under the sill. The walls are laid in Flemish bond above the beveled water table, English bond below it. Note the blocked air hole in the underpinning below the left corner of the window. The window frame and sash are original. (Photograph, Dell Upton.)

Yet the repertoire of the Virginia builder was a narrow one. This self-limitation of the builder's choices describes much of the Virginia style and goes a long way toward accounting for the coherent appearance of the churches as a group, as well as for their similarity to the domestic and secular buildings of colonial Virginia.

The catalog of interior finishes was also restricted. Pew, chancel, and gallery floors were made of pine plank. Alleys or aisles were commonly paved with slabs about eighteen inches square, called flags or flagstones in the vestry books, and made of sandstone or freestone, although several parishes preferred "white Bristol stone" paving. An alternative to stone was to use brick tile, square blocks about eight inches on a side and four inches thick (i.e., the size of two bricks), made of kiln-fired clay cast in molds the same way as ordinary bricks. While a few churches, like the log chapel built in Frederick Parish in 1752, had no wall finish, the standard for modest parish churches was to have walls and ceilings covered with plaster. Many vestries specified something more elaborate. Walls and ceilings were to be "ceiled"—the word referred not only to "the Top of a Room," as it does now, but also to any interior finish above the floor—with flush beaded or cyphered planks carried at least as high as the tops of the pews, boards and batten, clapboards (see Fig. 25), or even beaded weatherboards such as the "Feather Edge Plank plain'd & beaded" that the Albemarle Parish vestry specified for the interior of one of

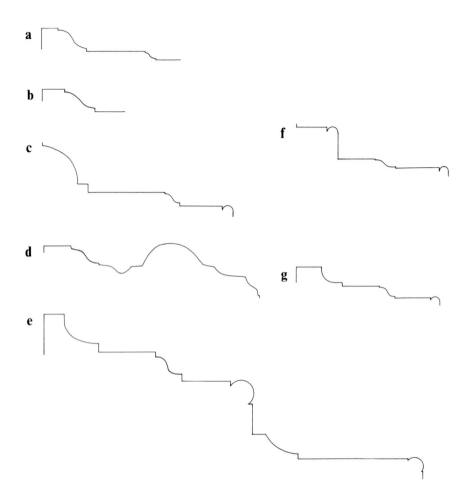

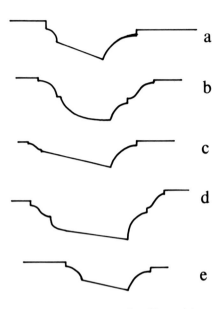

FIG. 123. Door and window frames. (a) Merchant's Hope church (ca. 1725), Prince George County, south door; (b) Merchant's Hope church, window; (c) Christ church (ca. 1732–35), Lancaster County, south door; (d) Fork church (begun ca. 1737), Hanover County, west door; (e) Aquia church (1754–57), Stafford County, west door; (f) Aquia church window; (g) Little Fork church (1773–76), Culpeper County, window. (Drawing, Dell Upton.)

FIG. 124. Wainscot panel moldings: (a) Christ church, Lancaster County, pews; (b) Christ church pulpit; (c) Ware Parish church (mid-18th century), Gloucester County, stair spandrel; (d) Abingdon church (ca. 1751–55), Gloucester County, pulpit; (e) Aquia church (1754–57), Stafford County, pulpit. In every case, the panel is at the left, and the stile at the right. (Drawing, Dell Upton.)

its churches. The most elaborate interior cladding was joined wainscot, which was used not only for pew walls, but for wall dados, pulpits, doors, and sometimes as a substitute for balustrades on stairs and gallery fronts.[9]

Not only materials, but most moldings fell within the bounds of style. Window and door frames were commonly finished with a quarter-round or cyma backband at the outer edge, and a bead at the inner edge (Fig. 123). In all but the most elaborate buildings, ovolo and bead moldings finished the majority of wooden edges (Fig. 124), while stair, gallery, and communion railings used a standard arch-topped composite form with the balusters set into a channel in the soffit (underside) or simply nailed to it (Figs. 125b–d). A few later stairs used a simple cylindrical or elliptical rail. A version of the standard handrail form also served as capping for pew partitions (Fig. 125a).

Formal variation appeared most often in turned balusters, where chisels of a fixed profile approximated the standardization of the joiner's plane, but where the entire piece was of such size that no fixed template could be used. Turners could transfer the general dimensions of the design from paper to wood by using calipers and compasses or a strike pole, a stick with nails protruding at appropriate intervals that scored the turning block of wood. Yet even in churches where all the balusters were of a single design, the balustrades of stair, gallery, and communion rail might be different heights, which required that the turner reproportion the baluster for each location. Once the basic marks were made, the success of the piece depended on the turner's skill in manipulating his tools. Because turning involved more of what David Pye has called the "workmanship of risk" (as opposed to the workmanship of certainty, where all dimensions and relationships are fixed and results guaranteed by mechanical means), lack of care was more likely to affect the quality of the work. The haste with which Aquia church was reconstructed after its 1754 fire is

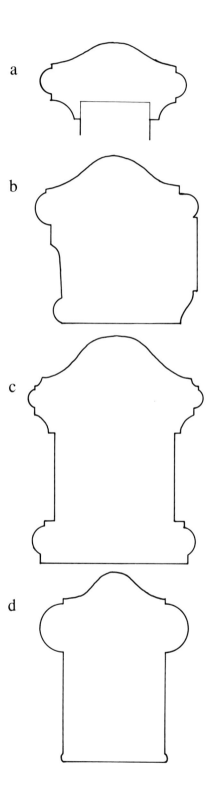

FIG. 125. Handrails and pew caps: (a) Abingdon church north gallery pew cap; (b) Merchant's Hope church (ca. 1725), Prince George County, gallery rail (plainer side faces in); (c) Slash church (1730–32), Hanover County, gallery rail; (d) Tillotson Parish church (ca. 1760), Buckingham County, gallery rail. (Drawing, Dell Upton.)

Fig. 126. Aquia church (1754–57; Mourning Richards, undertaker), Stafford County. The lower turnings on the elaborate balusters do not match as closely as they should, suggesting the haste with which the building was reconstructed. (Photograph, Dell Upton.)

evident in the balusters used in the building (Fig. 126). The moldings on adjacent balusters are not aligned correctly, suggesting that the turner or turners did little checking of the work. But as the eighteenth-century *Builder's Dictionary* pointed out, turning was an opportunity for the exercise of "the Fancy of the Workman," since there was no fixed pattern and no economic reason to restrain the imagination. The article on turning in the *Dictionary* records that turners were paid a penny an inch regardless of complexity, and that painters were similarly paid according to the overall length of the balustrade, not the actual surface area. Each baluster consisted of a taller upper portion and a shorter lower one (Figs. 127, 128). The upper section was shaped

like a tall vase or, later, a Tuscan column, and was relatively plain. The lower part might have at its center an urn, a ball, or a concave reel, with other moldings bracketing or elaborating the core shape.[10]

Interior finish was usually painted or whitewashed. Whitewashing was the only coloring applied to plaster, except for rare instances of pictorial representation. Woodwork might be whitewashed or left plain on occasion, but it was most often colored with oil-based paints. White was standard for ceilings and walls; white, "a neat brown," and "wainscot color" (equated by William Salmon with oak color) were most common for pews and other woodwork. A few parishes chose "Sky Colour," or light blue, interior trim. The choice of colors was partly symbolic and partly economic. Palladio called white "particularly grateful to God" as a mark of purity, and the Anglican apologist Charles Wheatly defended its use for vestments for the same reason: it "aptly represents the innocence and righteousness wherewith God's Ministers ought to be cloath'd." White was conveniently the cheapest of paint colors. Salmon priced it at fourpence per pound in mid-eighteenth-century London. Wainscot color was about the same price, four- to fivepence per pound. The late seventeenth-century writer Randle Holme identified blue as the color of piety and sincerity, but it cost eight- to twelvepence per pound in the eighteenth century, and was less likely to be used.[11]

Again, the alternatives from which the interior of the parish church was selected were relatively restricted. No two buildings were exactly alike; sheathing, wainscoting, handrails, and balusters differed slightly, but a widely shared group of compositional conventions accounts for most of the fabric in nearly all the standing and well-documented buildings. There are several important points that these conventions raise.

It is evident that the frames, balusters, and other decorative moldings were based, however remotely, on Roman classical forms, yet to search for their sources is useless. Similar embellishments were illustrated in every architectural publication, but none can be identified as the specific source of a particular Virginia example. The illustrations were derived from an international formal vocabulary shared by seventeenth- and eighteenth-century joiners and turners. They are seen in most Western European countries, and in the vernacular buildings of all the European ethnic groups of seventeenth- and eigh-

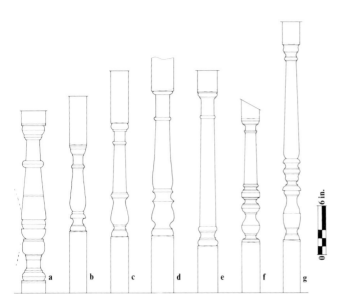

FIG. 127. Representative balusters: (a) Newport Parish church (ca. 1685), Isle of Wight County, gallery; (b) Slash church (1730–32), Hanover County, gallery; (c) Mangohick church (ca. 1731), King William County, gallery; (d) Yeocomico church (1706; enlarged ca. 1740), Westmoreland County, north wing gallery; (e) Fork church (begun ca. 1737), Hanover County, gallery; (f) Abingdon church (ca. 1751–55), Gloucester County, pulpit stair; (g) Tillotson Parish church (ca. 1760), Buckingham County, gallery. (Drawing, Dell Upton.)

FIG. 128. Christ church (ca. 1732–35), Lancaster County. The balusters of the communion rail are among the most elaborate balusters found in Virginia's churches. (Virginia State Library.)

teenth-century America. They are conventional, and appear in the churches as elements of style rather than mode. To their users their potential meanings lay within the local community as badges of dignity, rather than as attempts to identify with an external elite. It is important not to mistake their function as modish simply because of their classical origins. Other elements that derived from classical sources have that intent, but not these. They belong to the category of the "decent" and "proper"—the appropriate or decorous, within the larger order of things—as those words were used in the building contracts. Altars were to be "decently railed," and pews to have "proper" moldings. Among the deficiencies to be corrected in a new parish church, the Wicomico Parish vestry noted, "The Moldings on the Top of the Pews to be taken off and Proper ones to be Put on in a Workman like manner."[12]

Change, through the influx of new ideas, individual invention, and accident ("flow," "mutation," and "drift," respectively, in the language archaeologists borrow from Darwinism), is inevitable in stylistic elements. Thus, it is not hard to distinguish between the bulbous proportions of the late seventeenth-century balusters of St. Luke's church and the more carefully and more "correctly" proportioned ones of the mid-eighteenth-century churches (see Fig. 127). Early eighteenth-century handrails like those on the galleries at Bruton Parish and Merchant's Hope churches were sometimes asymmetrical; those of the mid-eighteenth century were invariably symmetrical (see Fig. 125). These changes are of use to the architectural historian in dating a building—which is also the chief utility of style for archaeologists—but within the larger realm of style in the Virginia churches such temporal variations are of minor import.[13]

If chronological variation signifies little in this connection, contrasts within the repertoire had great meaning for eighteenth-century Virginians. The selection of a specific structural system or surface treatment naturally varied with the skills of the artisans, the knowledge and whims of the vestry or their overseers, and the amount of money the parish was willing to expend. But even in such relatively commonplace decisions as these, Virginians maintained a clear hierarchy of preferences. Some choices were better than others for reasons other than cost: they served as distinguishing markers. Certain of these preferences are not surprising. We are not startled to learn that, on the whole, brick was thought more dignified than frame building. George Hardy bequeathed one thousand pounds of tobacco to Newport Parish in 1655 as a contribution to the construction of a new parish church only if it were built of brick. More than a century later, Edmund Pendleton informed a neighbor of the proposed construction of two churches in the new parish of St. Asaph, writing jovially that "we intend . . . to be humble and build them of wood."[14]

Customary distinctions were equally important in surface finish. From the late seventeenth century on, surfaces of uniform or regular appearance were thought to be more desirable than those of irregular appearance. Riven clapboards, for instance, tended to be wavy edged and rough surfaced, while sawn boards were more regular. In 1686, Argall Blackstone bequeathed timber from his lands for reroofing a new York Parish church "if they would cover the church with plank sawed featheredged instead of clapboards." In upgrading a projected chapel to a church, the St. Mark's Parish vestry agreed in 1752 to make an extra payment to the undertaker to ceil the inside of the building with flush plank rather than lapped clapboards. Three years later the overseers of a new church in adjacent St. George's Parish, Spotsylvania County, were annoyed to "find that instead of neat Cealing with pine plank the greatest part of the same at 5.6ths is done with Popler Plank in the nature of Battons or instead of the plank being Laid Edge to Edge to make smooth neat Wall the same is laid one upon another." The equation of neat with smooth and uniform extended to masonry as well. The Truro Parish vestry ordered the Aquia stone quoins of the new Pohick church painted white because they were "coarse grain'd and rather too soft," and the rubbed bricks of the window jambs "painted so near as possible the same colour with the Arches" (see Fig. 102).[15]

None of our information about the relative desirability of interior and exterior surface treatment dates from before the late seventeenth century. Though we have no direct evidence for earlier seventeenth-century churches, we know from domestic architecture that smoothness and regularity

of surface were less valued then than they were in the eighteenth century, and that fewer distinctions were made among suitable treatments for different surfaces. A seventeenth-century builder saw nothing wrong with making interior and exterior walls, the roof, the ceiling (see Fig. 25), and even some interior floors of clapboard, for example. Instances of similar treatment are found in eighteenth-century Virginia buildings, and they were probably widespread among the now-vanished houses of ordinary Virginians, but the gentry builders who planned the churches increasingly required different finishes for different surfaces. The particular standards changed, but the point is the same: Virginians distinguished the dignity of architectural forms on customary as much as economic grounds.[16]

Although Virginians recognized a hierarchy of finishes, this does not imply that they always chose the "best" or most expensive ones their budgets allowed. Examples of choices of lesser finishes abound, even in brick (and therefore costly) churches. Bristol Parish specified for a chapel the use of weatherboards "Rough from the [saw] pitt," and St. Patrick's Parish changed a planned compass, or vaulted, ceiling to a "square" or flat one. Many vestries ordered work in "the Best plain manner," as Bristol Parish did for the 1752 addition to its brick Blandford church. Neither did vestries feel compelled to emulate English modes as closely as possible. Style and mode were used carefully in the parish church to create a desired impression on those who used the building.[17]

We have seen that most of the parish church was made of common ingredients, which I call style. Wall surfaces, doors, windows, pew walls, gallery and communion rails were all formed from conventional elements. The effect of this combination of conventional elements, however, was intended to be unconventional, to set the church off as a distinctive place. Though vestries felt no necessity to use the most elaborate or expensive forms in every church, they did create a totality that in size and quality of finish was substantially different from the houses of most colonial Virginians. It is easy to miss this point if we consider only standing houses. All surviving colonial houses, even the smallest and plainest, were built by prosperous white Virginians; all but a handful were constructed by people at the level of the county gentry — of the vestrymen and their social peers — or higher. In these standing houses, plastered

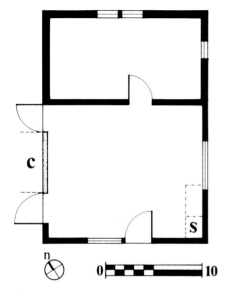

FIG. 129. Ball-Sellers house (late 18th century), Arlington County. Plan. Both rooms were built at the same time, but the main house is made of split logs and the rear leanto is framed. Key: c = original location of chimney; s = original location of ladder stair. (Drawing, Dell Upton.)

FIG. 130. Ball-Sellers house. Interior of roof showing riven rafters and riven clapboard gable and roof covering. The whitewashing indicates that this was used as a living space. (Photograph, Dell Upton.)

walls and well-finished parts seem modest and commonplace. Yet this was not true for most Virginians. J.F.D. Smyth, traveling in Virginia just after the Revolution, depicted the houses of most white planters as wooden structures, clad with thin boards, covered with shingles, "and not always lathed and plaistered within; only those of the better sort are finished in that manner, and painted on the outside. The chimneys are sometimes of brick, but more commonly of wood, coated on the inside with clay. The windows of the best sort have glass in them; the rest have none, and only wooden shutters." George Washington described the houses south of Petersburg in even bleaker terms, as log buildings with wooden chimneys. Passing through Hampton Roads in 1793, Harry Toulmin recorded small slaveholders living in wooden houses with no upstairs rooms and no glass, with their slaves' houses, built of logs without finish of any sort, erected adjacent to them.[18]

Descriptions of this tenor are numerous, but the houses

that inspired them, once dominant in the landscape, are now gone. Some sense of their nature can be found in a few extant buildings, though it is necessary to recall that even they are superior to what most black and white Virginians knew. The Ball-Sellers house (Figs. 129, 130) in Arlington County was probably built in the third quarter of the eighteenth century by John Ball on a 166-acre tract of land. The sixteen-by-eighteen-foot main room was constructed of halved, saddle-notched logs, with their flat sides turned out as a surface to which riven clapboards could be nailed. The interior is finished with an irregular, paper-thin plaster rendering applied over a brown coat of plain mud; the ceiling joists are crooked and only roughly squared. The clapboard roof was attached to rafters made by splitting a single pole in pie-shaped sections, and the eaves are packed with mud to seal off the whitewashed roof space as living quarters. A wooden chimney probably served the house, and a ladder stair led to the loft. Ball's 166-acre tract places him

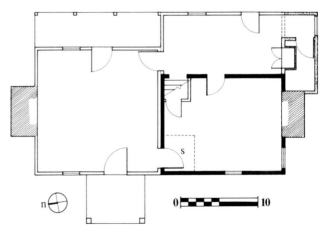

FIG. 131. Perkinsons (late 18th century; enlarged ca. 1800), Chesterfield County. The small portion in the foreground is the original house; the larger wing to the left and the leanto attached to the original were added around 1800. The porch and chimneys date from about 1850, and the kitchen ell from the turn of the century. (Photograph, Dell Upton.)

slightly above the average for mid-eighteenth-century landholders in the Potomac River Basin.[19]

A series of small houses in Chesterfield County, south of Richmond, offers similar insights. The third-quarter eighteenth-century house known as Perkinsons is, at twelve by sixteen feet, barely larger than a great pew (Figs. 131, 132). It is the smallest surviving colonial Virginia house, but it is well finished with beaded-board sheathing on the interior walls, clapboard exterior cladding, and exposed, well-made but undecorated joists (one would expect beaded edges). The ceiling of the original house is seven feet two inches high, and that of the late eighteenth-century leanto addition six feet high. A surviving colonial door, which connects the two, is five feet five inches high. During the period when the house was probably built, the Perkinson family owned 201 acres of land that it had been granted in 1704. The nearby Wilson Farm (Fig. 133) is nearly as small as Perkinsons at fourteen by sixteen feet. Its framing members are well made and beaded, but whitewash on the interior surfaces of the weatherboard cladding indicates that the one-room house never had any plastering on it. The house was probably built by the Wilson family, owners of a 275-acre tract, in the late eighteenth century.[20]

FIG. 132. Perkinsons. Plan. Key: s = original location of stair. (Drawing, Dell Upton.)

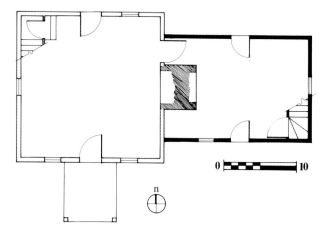

FIG. 133. Wilson Farm (late 18th century; early 19th century), Chesterfield County. Plan. (Drawing, Dell Upton.)

At about the time the Perkinson and Wilson families were building their houses, John Edwards was constructing one fifty miles to the east in Isle of Wight County (Fig. 134). It was a one-story structure sixteen by twenty feet, a common size for a one-room building. It had a wooden floor in the western half, but in the east, in front of the fireplace, was a large, brick-lined storage pit, and loose boards laid across it served as a floor. The joists of the Edwards' house were chamfered and decorated with lambs-tongue stops (see Fig. 223), but the walls were unplastered and there was no ceiling: one could look right to the under side of the roof. During the period when he probably built the house, Edwards owned 100 acres of land, but increased his holding to 237 acres by the end of the century. That increased prosperity allowed Edwards's son Isham Edwards to construct a new house. Isham's house was the same size as the earlier dwelling, but it was set on a high brick

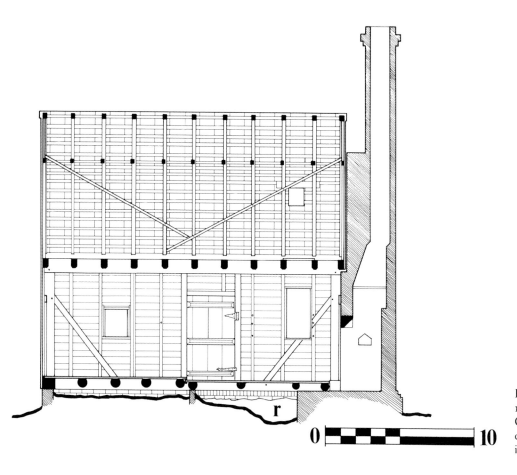

FIG. 134. Edwards house (late 18th century), Isle of Wight County. Section. Key: r = root cellar, partly filled in. (Drawing, Dell Upton.)

basement and the interior was treated with plaster walls and ceilings. The old house was given a new chimney and converted to a kitchen.[21]

These are the homes of middling, not poor, Virginians. Calculations of landholding in Chesterfield County suggest that the Perkinsons and Wilsons were wealthier than forty-five to sixty percent of their neighbors. John Edwards was better off than a fifth of his neighbors in the 1780s; by the turn of the century his good fortune and his neighbors' impoverishment raised him to the sixtieth percentile.[22]

In this light, such unremarkable aspects of a parish church as its size, its plaster finish, and its glazed windows take on a new significance, for they would have made the church a strange and striking building to most Virginians. Some sense of this wonder is gained from Samuel Kercheval's account of a childhood visit to a Shenandoah Valley tavern in the late eighteenth century. It was young Kercheval's first contact with a stone building and with plastered ceilings and walls: "I was struck with astonishment at the appearance of the house. I had no idea that there was any house in the world which was not built of logs; but here I looked round the house and could see no logs, and above I could see no joists; whether such a thing had been made by the hands of man, or had grown so of itself, I could not conjecture. I had not the courage to inquire anything about it."[23]

It is unlikely that adults were as mystified by a plastered interior as young Samuel Kercheval was, but most Virginians found the inside of a church an alien place. It might not seem supernaturally created to them, but it would seem a thing apart. In addition to the high-quality finish, other elements served to reinforce the building's apparent singularity, some of which were unique to churches in colonial Virginia. Most prevalent was the use of compass elements—windows, ceilings, pediments—and an occasional curved communion rail. Arched ceilings, round-headed windows, and curvilinear balustrades were unknown in domestic building in colonial Virginia and, except for a few unglazed arcades, arched openings were unknown in any secular buildings in the colony. Their use alone set the church apart.[24]

The choice of these shapes was not accidental. Curved shapes were derived from a language of honor that was as much a part of the conventions of the Church as beaded weatherboards were of Virginia carpenters. The compass ceiling of many churches belonged to a long tradition of treating the interior of a roof like the sky. Domes and vaults had been likened to the celestial vault for centuries, and the practice was a continuing, if an increasingly abstract, one in English parish church building. While carpenters of a medieval parish church like St. Wendreda (Fig. 135) at March, Cambridgeshire, filled the roof structure with angels, builders of seventeenth- and eighteenth-century churches like King Charles the Martyr, Shelland Green, Suffolk, or All Saints', North Runcton, Norfolk, used arched or domed ceilings, blue paint, and a few understated cherubs.[25]

The earliest recorded compass ceiling in Virginia was installed in the 1677 Poplar Spring church of Petsworth Parish, where the undertaker was ordered to put cross beams on the rafters and "small peeces for the plaister worke." A wood-lined vault originally covered St. Luke's church. Similar ceilings were employed in the 1679 Hungar's Parish church, in which Simon Thomas agreed to lay planks on ceiling arches, and in the 1691 Lynnhaven Parish church, where Jacob Johnson installed a lining of "good Sealing Oake boards Arch wise." Explicit references to the sky similar to those in English churches could be found in Virginia as well. The second Poplar Spring church of 1721–23 had a cornice "painted with the resemblance of a bright blue sky, and clouds rolling off on either hand." The use of sky color "where tis requisite" in Lynnhaven Parish's 1753 Eastern Shore chapel may be a clue to another instance.[26]

The depiction of the heavens in the Poplar Spring painting was unnecessary. The compass ceiling itself was a sufficient marker of distinction and dignity, a sign of a special place. In ancient times, the dome was intended as a microcosm of the natural world. It asserted by analogy that those who controlled the space under it also held dominion over the world under the sky. By the eighteenth century, the analogy had lost its power. The dome or vault itself conveyed importance. It was part of a customary system of ordering the physical world, which no longer required an explicit, or even a conscious, reference to the heavens to work. Yet the old analogy was close enough to the surface to be resurrected as an enrichment when needed.[27]

The vault, dome, and compass ceiling were part of a larger family of devices placing the honored under its own roof, whether dome, canopy, gable, or pediment. The common term compass for ceilings, windows, and segmental pediments connects those three standard elements of

FIG. 135. Church of St. Wendreda, March, Cambridgeshire. Double-hammerbeam roof of ca. 1500, embellished with angels. (Photograph, Dell Upton.)

FIG. 136. Newport Parish (St. Luke's) church (ca. 1685), Isle of Wight County. Plastered pediment over compass-headed entry to tower. The wicket door visible inside the tower is a modern reproduction based on the eighteenth-century door at Yeocomico church. (Photograph, Dell Upton.)

FIG. 137. Abingdon church (ca. 1751–55), Gloucester County. West door. The stones of the walk may originally have paved the alleys inside. (Photograph, Dell Upton.)

FIG. 138. Abingdon church. South door. (Photograph, Dell Upton.)

church building to the old symbolism. The pedimented doorways used on many churches are part of a continuous tradition running from Rome through early Christian and medieval building to post-Reformation England; they recall the gateway symbolism of Mediterranean and medieval European architecture, and in turn refer, largely unconsciously, to the triumphal arches of imperial Rome. They signal the transition from the secular world to the exalted world of the Church. In this spirit the detached triangular pediment at St. Luke's church floats above the compass-head entry to the tower like the crown it is popularly believed to be (Fig. 136). As with so many elements of that church, it seems to exist out of historical context in Virginia. The next evidence for the use of pediments dates from about 1720. The original section of Vauter's church, Essex County, has a pedimented frontispiece doorway. The second Poplar Spring church of 1721–23 had pediments, as well. Pediments were most common on brick churches, but were not confined to them. The Albemarle Parish vestry ordered for its frame St. Andrew's church of 1747 "a Fronton or Pediment over each Door."[28]

Pedimented doorways thus partook of the vault/dome/canopy tradition in dignifying the approach to the honored place, and in their shape. The pediment—"this noble Part," in the words of *The Builder's Dictionary*—conveyed honor in itself. At the same time, although no vestry record mentions, much less explains, it, every surviving pedimented church before the 1750s uses a segmental pediment for the main (west) door and a triangular pediment over any secondary doorways (Figs. 137–139). In doing so, the gateway/canopy of the pediment was linked to the compass ceiling and the more general principle that curved or compass forms were more dignified than straight or "square" ones. On brick churches lacking pediments, like Lower Southwark and Merchant's Hope (Fig. 140) churches, the west door had a compass head and the south door had a flat head. The compass window, found in Virginia only on churches, conveyed the same importance. Like the pediment, it was found most often on brick churches, but an occasional frame church, like the Henrico Parish (St. John's) church, Richmond, incorporated segmental window heads even when the full semicircle did not appear.[29]

Pediments, compass ceilings, and compass-head openings can be read as inflections in the builder's vocabulary. All derived from longstanding traditions in church

Fig. 139. St. John's Parish church (ca. 1731–34; enlarged mid-18th century), King William County. Note the segmental pediment over the west door and the triangular pediment over the door into the north addition. (Photograph, Dell Upton.)

Fig. 140. Merchant's Hope church (ca. 1725), Prince George County. (Photograph, Dell Upton.)

building, but none was so deeply rooted as to be obligatory. Their use depended in part on money, of course, but where pedimented and compass windows were added as afterthoughts to costly brick churches, they were employed as contextual or marking devices for setting churches off from their surroundings. Even plastered walls and glazed windows could do so in modest churches, particularly those on the fringes of settlement, but in parishes like those in the rich counties between the Potomac and James rivers, more emphatic accents were required (Fig. 141).[30]

The architectural elements considered so far set the church apart as a special and important place but did not identify it as a sacred space. That function was served by characteristic fittings and furnishings, since explicitly religious imagery was minimal in the Church of England. Crosses and crucifixes, for example, were not used between the Refor-

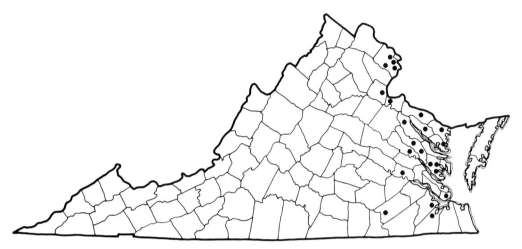

FIG. 141. Pedimented doorways in Virginia. (Drawing, Dell Upton.)

mation and the nineteenth century, except by a tiny group of High Churchmen in mid-seventeenth-century England. Indeed, religious iconography of any sort was strongly discouraged in post-Reformation Anglicanism. By the seventeenth century some representational imagery began to be returned to parish churches, but in Virginia churches it was rare. The Petsworth Parish vestry, always leaders in sumptuous church building, paid Thomas Powell "for draweing the Cherubin" in the post-built Poplar Spring church of 1677. Small winged cherub heads, similar to those common on eighteenth-century tombstones, flank the compass-head tablets on the Abingdon church altarpiece. The 1723 Poplar Spring church, painted in 1739 by Charles Carter's indentured servant Richard Cooke, was more lavishly decorated. A woman who had been taken to the ruined church by her mother in the early years of the nineteenth century wrote to Bishop Meade of "the remains of the fine painting, over what had been the chancel. . . . I think I then first received a correct idea of the solemn use and importance of a church, as I must have been very young." Below its cloud-painted cornice "were fragments of the plaster, extending farther down at the corners, and representing an immense crimson curtain drawn back. I remember seeing part of what seemed a very large cord and tassel. Mamma said there used to be an angel just where the curtain was drawn on one side, with a trumpet in his hand, and rolling on toward him were vast bodies of clouds with angels in them, and that she used to fancy one of the faces

was like her dear little brother John, who was drowned when only ten years old. . . . I feel sure that then I first understood about the last Judgement."[31]

There are two points of interest about Cooke's painting at Poplar Spring. The first is its rarity. One school of Anglican thought approved of heavenly images to promote the idea of the church as, in Horton Davies's term, a "numinous" building, manifesting divine presence, and not merely a functional one, facilitating the practice of certain rites. While this viewpoint represented a powerful strain in Anglican ecclesiology, it seems not to have affected many Virginians' conception of their churches. The Poplar Spring painting and a similar representation of "Angels floating in the clouds" at Lamb's Creek church were not duplicated anywhere else in Virginia so far as we know.[32]

If the formal theological concept of numinosity failed to influence many Virginians, older popular images did. Bishop Meade's correspondent, for example, saw in the Poplar Spring decoration images of the Last Judgment. The painting served for her the same function that dooms—those grimmer, more graphic portraits of the Last Judgment that were traditionally placed over chancel arches in medieval English churches—had for churchgoers in medieval times. Dooms were officially renounced after the Reformation, but they may have survived in popular use. Gabriel Williamson Galt, a member of an old Williamsburg family, wrote of two pictures that were once in Bruton Parish church. One hung over the students' gallery and made "a vivid impression on me[.] there were talons & beaks &c in the midst of horrible flames." The second depicted a similar scene. They were "sufficient in them days to give me a most dreadful idea of the Old Wretch and his place of abode." The two images of life after death stood in the same complementary relationship as the death's heads and succeeding, more hopeful, cherubs did on New England gravestones and Virginia tombs of the same period (Fig. 142).[33]

The second point about Richard Cooke's painting — as well as the one at Lamb's Creek church — is that it depicted angels pulling back curtains to reveal the altarpiece inscribed with the Ten Commandments, rather than a pictorial image. The Commandments stood in the strongest iconographic tradition in the Virginia parish church, of displaying religious texts for affective purposes. English parishes in the sixteenth and seventeenth centuries were encouraged to paint edifying passages on the walls of the church, matching each text to its location (see Figs. 31–33). Next to the pulpit, for example, one might set a Bible verse about preaching. While this strikes us as less impressive than displaying talons and beaks, or even angels, it is necessary to bear in mind what Rhys Isaac has called the great "dramaturgical possibilities available through the display of formal documents in a society where the written word was not yet commonplace," but where the prestige ascribed to learning in a Protestant society was nevertheless present. Some Virginia churches may have contained wall texts. Twenty years after painting the cherubs in the first Poplar Spring church, Thomas Powell was paid in 1699 "for

writing the vers. on the Guarder [girder?]. Request of mr. Hoults [the minister]." It was on the altarpiece, lettered with the Ten Commandments and sometimes with the Apostles' Creed and the Lord's Prayer, however, that the display of texts was most common. That the document was valued not merely for its contents, but as an image, was made clear by the manner of its presentation. English wall texts were usually drawn as if on parchments. The Commandments and other altar texts were inscribed on tablets (the word eighteenth-century Virginians used). All surviving Virginia examples but one take this form; Christ church, Alexandria, is the exception. The distinction between displaying the contents of the text and the text as an artifact was blurred in this manner. The very act of placing the Decalogue on tablets, whether or not they were affixed to an elaborate architectural altarpiece, was an iconographic act, calling to mind the tablets on which Moses originally received the Commandments. The reference was made explicit in some churches by the bracketing of the tablets with paintings of Moses and Aaron. In 1774 Elizabeth Stith of Surry County bequeathed £50 Virginia money to Southwark Parish to purchase an altarpiece for the parish's twenty-year-old lower church. It was to have "Moses and Aaron drawn at full length holding up between them the Ten commandments." A similar painting survived in nearby St. Luke's church until the early nineteenth century. The visual power of words themselves was also recognized. Vestries were willing to pay generous sums for inscribing the tablets to artisans specially skilled in lettering.[34]

The parish church was distinguished most clearly by its two major architectural fittings — the altarpiece and the pulpit. The altarpiece might be very modest. Altarpieces up to the early eighteenth century invariably seem to have been boards hung upon the wall, like the earlier English examples (see Fig. 34). This is suggested by the language of documents, such as the 1689 will of Colonel John Stringer who left money to have the Lord's Prayer and the Ten Commandments "Sett Up" in a new parish church. Christ Church Parish, Middlesex County, paid William Brookes for "fastning Comdts" in its upper church and allowed John Grimes to "Divide the Altar Piece and Sett up the Same Each Side of the East Window" at its middle church in 1719. The earliest surviving Virginia altarpiece is one of this sort: a pair of framed walnut tablets with astragal heads in St. Mary's White Chapel church (Fig. 143). The Ten Commandments are lettered on them. The tablets are seven

FIG. 142. Tomb of Robert Carter (ca. 1735), Christ church, Lancaster County. Cherub. (Photograph, Dell Upton.)

FIG. 143. St. Mary's White Chapel church (1739–41), Lancaster County. Altarpieces. The Ten Commandments were bequeathed by David Fox in 1702, and the Lord's Prayer and Apostle's Creed by his son William Fox in 1718. All are painted wood. The tablets were restored and probably repainted in 1882; the red and gold painting of the frames certainly dates from then. (Photograph, Dell Upton.)

feet high and three and one-half feet wide and consist of two boards held together by nailing a frame and then a molding (Fig. 144a) to their faces. The moldings are painted gold on red, but this dates from an 1882 refurbishing. The lettering is gold on a black background, and at the bottom of the right tablet the name of the donor, David Fox, and the date, 1702, are recorded in black on gold. Flanking these are two compass-head tablets six and one-half feet high and two feet nine inches wide. They are made of three boards held in a joined, bolection-molded frame by cleats (Fig. 144b). These tablets were the legacy of

William Fox, and may have been imported: in 1718 Fox left a sum of money for his wife to "send for the Lords Prayer & Creed well drawn in Gold letters & my name under each of them, set in decent black frames." The frames are now painted gold and red like those of the Commandments.[35]

Architectural and documentary evidence alike suggest that the altarpieces in most Virginia churches throughout the colonial period were wall tablets of this kind. Four large tablets, five feet eight inches high by two feet four inches wide, survive in Mattaponi church. Like the William Fox tablets, they have compass heads and are framed with

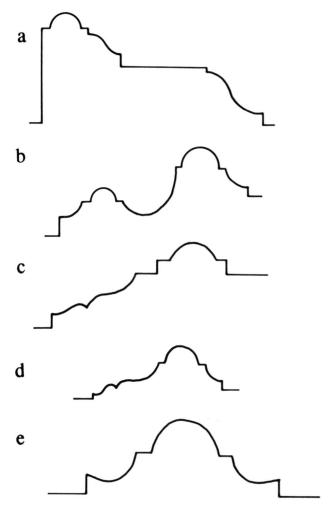

FIG. 144. Altarpiece moldings: (a) architrave molding, Ten Commandments (ca. 1702), St. Mary's White Chapel church; (b) bolection molding, Apostles' Creed (ca. 1718), St. Mary's White Chapel church; (c) bolection molding, altarpiece, Lower (Mattaponi) church, St. Stephen's Parish (ca. 1730–34), King and Queen County; (d) bolection molding, altarpiece (third quarter 18th century), St. John's Parish church, King William County (now in St. Paul's church, Norfolk); (e) bolection molding, altarpiece, Abingdon Parish church (ca. 1751–55), Gloucester County. (Drawing, Dell Upton.)

bolection moldings (Fig. 144c). They are lettered in gold on a black ground, with a gold border on the inner edge of the frame, the remainder of which is green with black highlighting. The three original end windows at Lynnhaven Parish (Old Donation) church left room for nothing larger than hanging tablets. Mid-nineteenth-century accounts of Yeocomico church described canvas-covered framed tablets hanging on its walls. Most church-building contracts, though they often directed the builder to provide a communion table, failed to say anything about the altarpiece, suggesting that hanging tablets were to be used. In many cases these may have been salvaged from an older church, as the St. Mary's White Chapel tablets were when the present church was built in 1739–42.[36]

After about 1730 some churches began to mount their tablets in large pedimented architectural altarpieces on the east wall. Six of these survive, and there is photographic evidence of two others. All were originally constructed in brick churches. They fall into two formal groups. The four altarpieces in the first group, ranging in date from Christ church, Lancaster County, finished in 1735, through Little Fork church, built 1773–76, have two to four tablets under a single pediment. The Christ church altarpiece has a compass pediment (Fig. 145). It forms part of a larger composition of wainscoting that wraps around all three walls of the eastern arms, terminating in triangular pediments that are asymmetrical when seen head on, in order to look symmetrical when seen in perspective from the west (Fig. 146). The other three altarpieces have triangular pediments; those at Abingdon (Fig. 147; see Fig. 144e) and Little Fork (Fig. 148) churches are broken while that at Aquia church (Fig. 149) is complete. In every case, pilasters — of Doric, Ionic, or composite order — support the pediments and form tabernacles in which tablets similar to those hung on the walls of other churches are set. The tablets vary in shape and in number. The two at Christ church have astragal heads, although the panels themselves are replacements of the originals. Compass heads were used for the four panels at Aquia church and were drawn onto the four square-headed panels at Abingdon church. Plain square heads were used at Little Fork church. Except in Abingdon church, the altarpieces consist of a single bay. The joiner of the Abingdon altarpiece used extra pilasters to create a large central bay containing the Commandments, with narrower side bays for the other texts. In this respect the altarpiece resembles those in the second group.

FIG. 145. Christ church (ca. 1732–35), Lancaster County. Altarpiece. The tablets are modern. (Photograph, Dell Upton.)

FIG. 146. Christ church. Chancel paneling. The pediment is asymmetrical to offset the effects of perspective when the chancel is viewed from the west. (Photograph, Dell Upton.)

Fig. 147. Abingdon church (ca. 1751–55), Gloucester County. Altarpiece. The legend in the frieze was added in 1861. The upper corners of the two central tablets are embellished with cherubs. (Photograph, Dell Upton.)

FIG. 148. Little Fork church (1773–76; William Phillips, undertaker), Culpeper County. Altarpiece. The cross and the lettering are modern, as are the communion rail and pews. (Photograph, Dell Upton.)

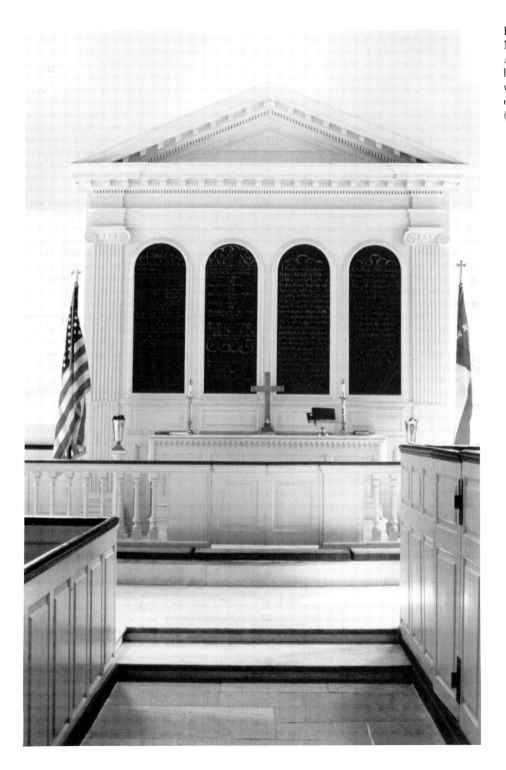

FIG. 149. Aquia church (1754–57; Mourning Richards, undertaker). Altarpiece. The lettering was done by William Copein, who signed his work. The communion rail and other altar furniture are modern. (Photograph, Dell Upton.)

Fig. 150. Falls church (1767–70; James Wren, designer and undertaker), Fairfax County. Civil War-era photograph of ruined interior showing altarpiece in place. (Photograph, Brady Collection, National Archives.)

The altarpieces in the second group have a pedimented central bay flanked by flat-corniced side bays. Two survive, those formerly at St. John's church, King William County, and at Christ church, Alexandria, and two, at Falls church and Bruton Parish church, are known from photographs. They vary in detail, but there is much more consistency among them than among those in the first group. Two of the four, at Falls church and St. John's church (Figs. 150, 151; see Fig. 144d—the latter has been installed in St. Paul's church, Norfolk, since 1984), had triangular pedi-

ments. The Bruton Parish church altarpiece (Fig. 152) had a compass pediment, and the altarpiece at Christ church, Alexandria (Fig. 153), incorporated a Palladian window, substituting the compass arch of the central window for a pediment. All but the St. John's church altarpiece employed the Ionic order, in accord with *The Builder's Dictionary*'s note that the Ionic "is at present us'd properly in Churches and religious Houses . . . and other places of Tranquillity and Devotion." All used square-headed tablets, although those at the two Fairfax Parish churches, Falls church and

FIG. 151. St. John's Parish church (ca. 1731–34; enlarged mid-18th century), King William County. Altarpiece (third quarter 18th century) before removal to St. Paul's church, Norfolk. (Photograph by Grace Heffelfinger for Virginia Historic Landmarks Commission, 1972.)

FIG. 152. Bruton Parish church (1711–15; James Morris, undertaker; enlarged 1752–54), Williamsburg. Early 20th-century photograph of altarpiece before destruction. (Photograph, Colonial Williamsburg Foundation.)

FIG. 153. Christ church (1767–73; James Wren, designer; James Parsons, under-taker), Alexandria. Chancel showing pulpit and stair, type, rail, and Palladian window built into altarpiece. The communion table, font, and finials on the rails date from the early 19th century; the other furnishings date from the 20th century or were installed then. (Photograph, Dell Upton.)

Christ church, were crossetted. The altarpieces at the latter churches are known to have been made around 1770. Bruton Parish church and St. John's church were built in 1715 and the early 1730s, respectively, but both were enlarged in the 1750s, and it is likely that their altarpieces were installed at that time. They are ascribed to the third quarter because the central-pediment form is the first we have seen that can be attributed to specific English sources. Central-pediment altarpieces were illustrated in several variants in Batty Langley's *City and Country Builder's and Workman's Treasury of Designs*, published in 1740 (Figs. 154, 155). While other pattern-book writers occasionally included church details, Langley's book was heavily illustrated with altarpieces, pulpits, fonts, canopies, and wall monuments. Anglican church builders in Virginia and in other colonies found it a useful source. The ways in which Langley was used in the northern Virginia churches, in particular, are noteworthy. The vestry of Fairfax Parish di-

FIG. 154. *Tuscan Altar Piece.* (From Batty Langley, *The City and Country Builder's and Workman's Treasury of Designs* [3d ed., London: 1750], pl. CIX, courtesy Henry Francis du Pont Winterthur Museum Library: Collection of Printed Books.)

FIG. 155. *An Ionick Altar Piece.* (From Langley, *Designs*, pl. CX, courtesy Henry Francis du Pont Winterthur Museum Library: Collection of Printed Books.)

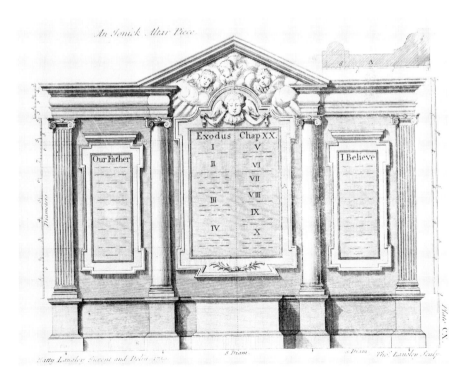

FIG. 156. Falls church (1767–70; James Wren, designer and undertaker), Falls Church Parish. West doorway. (Photograph, Dell Upton.)

FIG. 157. Christ church (1767–73; James Wren, designer; James Parsons, undertaker), Alexandria. Northwest doorway. (Photograph, Dell Upton.)

rected the undertakers of Falls church and Christ church, Alexandria, to install Ionic altarpieces. James Wren at Falls church simply lifted his design from the Ionic altarpiece illustrated in plate CX of the *Designs* (as eighteenth-century Virginians called the book), reducing the central columns to pilasters, but retaining the complex shape of the central tablet and the crossetted tabernacle frames of the side tablets. At Christ church, the alteration of the original church design brought changes in the decoration, which was upgraded considerably. The brick pedimented doorways

in the Tuscan order specified by the vestry and used at Falls church (Fig. 156) became rusticated sandstone Tuscan doorways at Christ church (Fig. 157), and the altarpiece was incorporated into an elaborate Palladian pulpit window with an exterior stone frame and interior pilasters (Fig. 158). The Ionic order was retained on the interior, however, and Langley-type crossetted tabernacle frames like those at Falls church were employed for the tablets. These Fairfax Parish churches may not have been the only ones to model their altarpieces after Langley details. Payne's church and Pohick

FIG. 158. Christ church, Alexandria. Aquia sandstone pulpit (east) window. (Photograph, Dell Upton.)

church, begun in Truro Parish shortly after Fairfax Parish was set off from it, were also to have Ionic altarpieces, and in the newly completed church at Pohick, William Bernard Sears was paid for gilding the ornaments on the tabernacle frames. The physical similarity of Pohick to Falls church and the use of Langley's book in another context (discussed below) in Pohick church argue for the existence here of another altarpiece derived from the *Designs*.[37]

The elaborate classical decoration of architectural altarpieces was often matched by their finish. At their most elaborate, Virginia altarpieces could be magnificent. When Richard Cooke was hired by the Petsworth vestry to paint Poplar Spring church, he raised the vestry's expectations considerably over those of his predecessor Samuel Peacock. Cooke, who was probably the decorative painter at the Page family's mansion Rosewell near Poplar Spring church (see below), may have been more skilled than Peacock, inspiring the vestry to attempt a more ambitious undertaking than they had assigned Peacock. Cooke's cherubs drew back their curtains to reveal an altarpiece that was to be "Neatly Painted: the Ground work of the Pannels to be Jappand; the Creed Lords Prayor & Ten Comandments to be Done In A Leagable hand In fair Gold letters and All the Carvingwork to be Guilded."[38]

The Word was enshrined not only in altarpieces but in pulpits. Fewer pulpits than altarpieces survive. There are four complete ones, and parts of two others. Evidence for the placement of now-destroyed pulpits is preserved in plaster scars at some churches, and there are documentary accounts as well. Virginia pulpits varied in their appearance, but there were constants of design that linked them to one another and tied them to their architectural contexts. The "triple-decker" pulpit embedded in the popular imagination, with the pulpit proper soaring above a reading desk from which the minister conducted all of the service except for the sermon, and a floor-level clerk's desk, from which the lay reader led responsive readings and hymns, was the most elaborate type. Three-level pulpits were being built in Virginia by the late seventeenth century. The first Poplar Spring church of Petsworth Parish had a pulpit "of wainscoate 4 foote diameter, & made with 6 sides, 6 foot allowed for the reading desks & passag into the pulpitt: the ministers pew to be under the pulpitt, & raised 18 Inches and the readers deske under it," according to a 1677 vestry minute. Triple-decker pulpits survive in the two most lavish of standing Virginia churches, Christ church, Lancaster County (Fig. 159), and Aquia church (Fig. 160). It was not necessary to combine all three parts into a single towering pile. Desks could be installed in adjacent pews, and pulpits could be free standing, especially where they were elaborately decorated. The pulpit at St. John's church, Richmond, which probably dates from the original construction of 1739–41, is a freestanding hexagonal stack (Fig. 161). Its wainscoting is not patterned to allow for the installation of a mid-level reading desk, so it was probably not a three-tiered pulpit. The pulpit at Christ church, Alexandria, stands on a

FIG. 159. Christ church (ca. 1732–35), Lancaster County. Pulpit. (Photograph, Dell Upton.)

FIG. 160. Aquia church (1754–57; Mourning Richards, undertaker), Stafford County. Pulpit. The dome of the type is covered with plaster. (Photograph, Dell Upton.)

pedestal in front of the east window, above the communion table (see Fig. 153). There are no original associated desks. The arrangement is one used in large town churches in late eighteenth-century Anglo-America, but this is the only Virginia example. The squat Tuscan column that supports it is an indicator of the pulpit's intended freestanding position. Some triple deckers had pulpits (Virginians reserved the term for the upper level, calling the other two levels the desks) supported on plain central piers, but most

followed the English vernacular practice of carrying the pulpit's side walls down to the floor, as at St. John's church, Richmond, or of cantilevering the pulpit out from the wall, as at Christ church, Lancaster County.[39]

All surviving pulpits are hexagonal, in accord with the preference for "round"—not square—elements in important locations. Above the pulpit, and sometimes connected with it by a backboard, hung what is now called a sounding board, but in colonial times was called a canopy, type, or

FIG. 161. Henrico Parish (St. John's) church (1739–41; Richard Randolph, Gent., undertaker), Richmond. Pulpit. The book ledge, brackets, and stairs are modern. (Photograph, Dell Upton.)

FIG. 162. Speaker's chair (ca. 1730), Virginia Capitol, Williamsburg. (Photograph, Colonial Williamsburg Foundation.)

top. The older terms tie the use of the type (defined by the *Oxford English Dictionary* as "a small cupola or dome") to furniture of state—chairs, beds, cupboards, and pews covered with canopies of cloth or some more durable material —which signaled its owner's great status. Originally reserved for royalty, furniture of state was common among high-status civil and ecclesiastical personages in the late Middle Ages and early modern period, and it survived into the eighteenth century in occasional use. For most Virgin-

ians, the only contact with furniture of state was in church, although members of the gentry might encounter it in the pedimented Speaker's chair in the House of Burgesses (Fig. 162), and parishioners of Bruton Parish church would have been confronted with the juxtaposition of the canopied pulpit with the governor's pew opposite it. In the governor's pew was a traditional chair of estate, with a silk curtain hanging on three sides, suspended from a canopy supported on "two fluted, Gilt Pillars." The canopy over the pulpit

Fig. 163. St. Mary the Virgin church, Croscombe, Somerset, England. Pulpit (1616). Installed as part of the redecoration of the medieval church. Note the coffered soffit of the type and the arms of Bishop Lake, the donor, and of the Diocese of Bath and Wells. (Photograph, Dell Upton.)

FIG. 164. Christ church (ca. 1732–35), Lancaster County. Type. The frieze has remnants of original decorative painting; the dome may originally have been plastered. (Photograph, Dell Upton.)

FIG. 165. Christ church (1767–73; James Wren, designer; James Parsons, undertaker), Alexandria. Type. Wooden armature, cornice and finial with plastered dome. (Photograph, Dell Upton.)

belonged to this tradition of state furniture, as seventeenth-century types, which had no flat surfaces to reflect sound, demonstrated (Fig. 163). The type honored the minister's office and the words he spoke, rather than the individual. A traditional ornament, a sun inlaid in the soffit, mixed the dome of heaven imagery with a visual pun on Christ the son in the types at Christ, St. John's, and Aquia churches (see Fig. 161). Virginia canopies were either flat topped, as in the survivors at St. Luke's and St. John's churches, or actually domed, with finials. Of the latter, that at Christ church, Lancaster County, was made entirely of wood and probably plastered (Fig. 164), while the plaster survives on the wooden armatures at Aquia church and Christ church, Alexandria (Fig. 165). Often the corners of the pulpit and the backboard were fitted with pilasters, and the whole

treated in a way that formed an ensemble with the altarpiece. Fairfax and Truro parishes specified for their new Falls, Christ, and Pohick churches of the late 1760s that pulpit, altarpiece, and canopy were to be "compleated in the Ionic Order." Uniformity might also be achieved by using similar, costly materials for the ensemble, like black walnut for the pulpit and altar rail at Truro Parish's Payne's church or for the pulpit and communion table that Captain Joseph Terry made for Antrim Parish.[40]

While pulpits were less likely than altarpieces to reflect published design sources, the 1774 pulpit at Pohick church (Fig. 166), as sketched by Benson J. Lossing in the 1850s, resembled designs published by Batty Langley (Fig. 167) in its shape and its decoration of dove, all-seeing eye, and gilt palm branches and draperies.[41]

FIG. 166. Pohick church (1769–74; Daniel French, undertaker). Pulpit. The drawing was made by 19th-century historian Benson J. Lossing, who visited the church before its interior was destroyed in the Civil War. (From Lossing, *The Home of Washington*, p. 93.)

FIG. 167. A *Hexangular Pulpit*. (From Langley, *Designs*, pl. CXIV, courtesy Henry Francis du Pont Winterthur Museum Library: Collection of Printed Books.)

Like the pulpit and the altarpiece, most of the furnishings of the church were required by canon law, as embodied in Virginia statutes. Acts of March 1661 and March 1662 ordered church wardens to provide the "ornaments" of the church "according to the act of parliament before [in front of] the common prayer booke." The ornaments included a Bible and two prayer books in folio, communion vessels, cloths to cover the pulpit and altar table, a cushion for the pulpit, and a bell. Also required by canon law, although not specified in these acts, were a chest, a font, a communion table, a surplice for the minister to wear, and a pulpit and reading desk. This list comprises the minimum legal appurtenances of an Anglican parish church in Virginia. The vestry records show evidence of routine efforts to comply with the law, but as late as 1719 Virginia clerics complained of the lack of "the decent habits, and proper

Ornaments and Vessels, which our Established Liturgy requires." Throughout the colonial period, many churches lacked some elements of the mandatory equipment. Elizabeth Stith's legacy of money to buy an altarpiece for the lower church of Southwark Parish, for example, suggests that the church had been allowed to stand for two decades without that elementary fitting.[42]

Chests had been required furnishings in English churches since the Middle Ages. There is evidence in the vestry books for their existence in ten Virginia parishes between the 1630s and the 1770s, but only one survives. This remarkable chest (Figs. 168, 169) was provided in 1677 for the lower chapel of Christ Church Parish, Middlesex County, by church warden Richard Perrott, Jr. (1651–1735). It outlasted the original lower chapel, and survived in the chapel's successor of 1714, even during the period the

FIG. 168. Church chest (1677; Richard Perrott, Jr.), Lower chapel, Christ Church Parish, Middlesex County. (Photograph courtesy of the Museum of Early Southern Decorative Arts.)

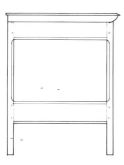
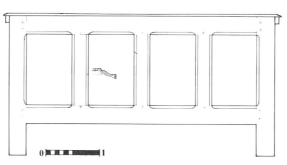

FIG. 169. Lower chapel chest. (Drawing, Dell Upton.)

building was unused. Perrott probably made the chest himself. An entry in the parish register records that he had made a private pew and built a stable at the upper chapel of the parish eight years earlier. The entry is dated 1669, but it is entered between the list of marriages for 1686 and the christenings for 1687, and the date is probably an error. Furthermore, at the time the vestry ordered that "Mr Richard Perrott Junr be pd for the Chest" at the lower chapel, it paid the church warden of the upper chapel for a chest "that he hath provided" for that church. The difference in wording reinforces the idea of Perrott's authorship of the lower chapel chest.[43]

Perrott's chest is made of oak. It is five feet long, two feet deep, and two and one-half feet high, with four panels across the front and rear, and one panel at each end. There is a till at the right end that is missing its lid (Fig. 170); otherwise the chest is intact. It was evidently made to stand against the wall, for the front panels are recessed and flat on the outside, but slightly raised on the inside, while the back panels have their finished sides inside, facing the front, and their rough sides toward the rear. Six rabbetted boards, nailed up under the rear rail and nailed to a rabbet in the front rail, form the bottom, in accord with a common seventeenth-century practice. The chest is elaborately carved with a rope design on both the stiles and the muntins, an interlace on the bottom front rail, and an incised gadroon on the top front rail. The heart at the center of the gadroon is partly obscured by a lock, installed in 1762. Abstract gouged diamond patterns are worked into the panels.[44]

The Middlesex County chest is similar in its decoration to large domestic chests surviving from England and from New England. It is a little bigger, however, than most large domestic chests and it was probably significantly larger and more elaborate than the majority of southern church chests. Another rare survivor, in St. Paul's church, Quantico, Maryland (Fig. 171), is only a foot and a half deep, three feet long, and a little over a foot high. It is made of nailed boards, and is undecorated. While Perrott was paid 300 pounds of tobacco for his chest, the upper church warden was paid only 160 pounds for his. Parishes in the eighteenth century paid prices ranging from 30 to 176 pounds of tobacco for their chests.[45]

Perrott's chest is domestic in more than its appearance. Chests served houses until the eighteenth century in lieu of closets, particularly for storing valuable textiles, tableware,

and other small movables. They were often kept in the bedchamber or other secluded rooms of the house for protection. Church chests had the same protective function. Anglican Canon LXX required that parishes have a chest or coffer with three locks and three keys, one for the minister and one each for the two church wardens, in which to keep the parish register. Every week, the three men had to remove the book, enter the week's business in it, and return it to the locked chest.[46]

By the eighteenth century, this regulation was no longer strictly observed in any of its particulars. As cupboards and closets became more common in domestic settings, they made their appearance in churches as well. A large compass-head closet in All Saints' church, North Runcton, Norfolk, probably substituted for the chest in that eighteenth-century English church (Fig. 172), and the cupboards

Fig. 170. Lower chapel chest, interior. Note the original hinges, the till, now missing its lid, and the molded finish of the rear panels. (Photograph, Dell Upton.)

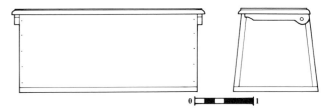

Fig. 171. Church chest (ca. 1770), St. Paul's church, Quantico, Maryland. (Drawing, Dell Upton.)

FIG. 172. All Saints' church (1703–13), North Runcton, Norfolk, England. Closet. (Photograph, Dell Upton.)

underneath the pulpit in Virginia churches like St. John's, Richmond, may have served the same purpose.[47]

Linen and books were stored in chests in churches throughout the colonial period. Book chests were mentioned by Shelburne and Frederick parishes, and linen chests by Christ Church Parish, Middlesex County (these included the Perrott chest). In contrast to their imported contents, most church chests were made locally. Only Petsworth Parish is known to have imported one, when it sent for church ornaments in 1751 "to come in a Very Strong Oak Chest, for the use of the Parish."[48]

The books stored in the chests were of several kinds, in addition to the register, an important legal document, and included a Bible and two prayer books in folio (one for the use of the minister and one for the clerk). Parishes were also encouraged to maintain libraries, but the bishop of London's 1724 inquiries, addressed to all colonial parishes, revealed none in Virginia. By the time of disestablishment, a few parishes owned collections of sermons, from which the

clerk read on the Sundays the minister was officiating at another church. In 1785 Lynnhaven Parish reported owning a seven-volume set of Socker's sermons for each church, and one volume of the late seventeenth-century Anglican theologian John Tillotson's sermons. St. James-Northam Parish owned nine volumes of Tillotson's sermons.[49]

Church books were acquired from England, in accordance with the Virginia vestries' custom. No resident printers or bookbinders existed in Virginia before 1730, but after that date they were readily available, and some did church work. William Hunter of Williamsburg bound church Bibles for David Mossom, the minister of St. Peter's Parish, in 1765. Yet even when books were printed and bound in the colony and others were imported for sale by Virginia printers, the vestries preferred to order them from England. Often the resulting books were elaborately ornamental, as was a pair of "Folio Prayer Books covered with blue Turkey Leather with the Name of the Parish thereon in Gold Letters" ordered by George Washington on behalf of Truro Parish in 1774. Similarly decorated books were acquired by Hungar's Parish in 1763, including a Bible (Fig. 173) and four prayer books, all of which survive. Printed in Cam-

FIG. 173. Bible (1758), Hungar's Parish, Northampton County. Bible, ordered from England by the parish in 1763. (Photograph, Edward Chappell.)

FIG. 174. Westover Parish baptismal bowl (1694–95, London), now owned by St. John's church, Richmond. The SABE monogram is original, but the other inscriptions were added in the 19th century. (Courtesy of St. John's church, Richmond, and the Virginia Museum of Fine Arts, Richmond.)

bridge in 1758, they are bound in black leather with gilt spines and cover ornamentation and cover panels inscribed "Hungar's Parish 1763."[50]

Like the churches, pulpits, altarpieces, and chests were built of the vernacular stuff of Anglo-Virginian building, particularly joined wainscoting. But the use of classical detail on pulpits and altarpieces went beyond standardized moldings to the incorporation of classical orders, of decoration such as gilding and japanning, which was associated with upper-class material life, and, after 1750, forms based on current architectural publications. The same may be said of the elaborate gilding and decoration of the imported books. Our focus begins to shift from style to mode, and many of the modish elements were imported from England.

This preference for imported ornaments extended to communion plate and even baptismal fonts, all of which were usually "sent for." Fonts were the focus of the last of the three ritual centers in Anglican churches. Puritanically inclined reformers were given to removing English fonts and replacing them with metal baptismal bowls kept near the communion table, a practice that Church officials tried unsuccessfully to stop in the seventeenth century. Although Church officials ordered the use of stone fonts in "the ancient usual place" by the west door, metal basins continued to be employed, and there is evidence of their use in Virginia. The vestry of Antrim Parish in 1757 ordered its church wardens to purchase a basin for the use of its new church. An extant example is the "large silver Bason instead of a font," the gift of Sarah Braine in 1697, that the rector of Westover Parish reported to the bishop of London in 1724 (Fig. 174). Several other surviving pieces of colonial Virginia church silver were baptismal basins, but they are outnumbered by surviving stone fonts.[51]

Ten fonts and one bowless pedestal remain from eighteenth-century Virginia. Three of the earliest fonts have integral stone bases. One is the former Jamestown church font, now at Bruton Parish church, which is an octagonal stone piece with its bowl set on a bulbous vase-shaped pedestal (Fig. 175). The use of stone and the octagonal shape have characterized English fonts since the

FIG. 175. Font (early 18th century?), reputedly from James City Parish church, now at Bruton Parish church, Williamsburg. Photograph ca. 1888–1903. (Photograph, Colonial Williamsburg Foundation.)

FIG. 176. Font (ca. 1718), St. Mary's White Chapel Parish church, Lancaster County. (Drawing, Dell Upton.)

Middle Ages, but the balusterlike pedestal is a post-Reformation characteristic. The Jamestown font is traditionally believed to have been made in the seventeenth century, although it closely resembles the font in St. Mary's White Chapel church (Fig. 176), which was part of William Fox's legacy to the parish at the time of his death in 1718. The St. Mary's White Chapel font is circular and may have been made in three parts; it is in three parts now. At nearby Christ church, Lancaster County, the light gray marble font (Fig. 177) also has a circular bowl, but it is decorated with

FIG. 178. Font (ca. 1740), Yeocomico church, Westmoreland County. The bowl is polished gray marble, and the base, of uncertain date, is made of sandstone painted white. (Photograph, Dell Upton.)

FIG. 177. Font (ca. 1735), Christ church, Lancaster County. (Photograph, Dell Upton.)

four cherubs' heads in high relief around the rim, and acanthus leaves circle the base of the bowl. It stands on a tall, attenuated column.[52]

These fonts differ from all other colonial Virginia fonts in having original pedestals integral with their bowls. The sandstone base of the Yeocomico church font (Fig. 178) resembles published font and sundial designs in Langley's book (Figs. 179, 180), as well as existing English fonts like those at All Saints' church, North Runcton, Norfolk (Fig. 181), and St. Michael's, Chesterton, Huntingdonshire, both made at about the time that the Yeocomico font was presumably carved. However, the history of the base is puzzling. It was in the church as early as 1906, but nine-teenth-century accounts refer only to a marble font, and to

tales of its having been carried away for use as a punch bowl.[53]

None of the other surviving fonts have colonial bases, and they may never have had stone pedestals in the eighteenth century. The Albemarle Parish vestry's order to undertaker James Anderson to include in a new church "A neat turn'd Post erected in the [baptismal] Area with handsom Mouldings round the Top, whreon to place the font or Bason, & a Desk adjoining to it to lay the Book on" may reflect common practice in Virginia parish churches. In other instances, sandstone bases like the one at Yeocomico church or the one preserved at St. John's church, King William County (though not originally belonging to that church), may have been made in the colony to accommodate imported marble bowls (Fig. 182).[54]

FIG. 179. *Fonts for Churches*. (From Langley, *Designs*, pl. CL, courtesy Henry Francis du Pont Winterthur Museum Library: Collection of Printed Books.)

FIG. 180. *Pedestals for Sun Dials*. (From Langley, *Designs*, pl. CLI, courtesy Henry Francis du Pont Winterthur Museum Library: Collection of Printed Books.)

FIG. 181. Font (18th century), All Saints' church, North Runcton, Norfolk, England. Formerly in St. Margaret's church, King's Lynn, Norfolk. (Photograph, Dell Upton.)

FIG. 182. Yellow sandstone font pedestal (late 17th century?), at St. John's Parish church, King William County, since 1978, and believed to have belonged to Acquinton church, King William County. (Photograph, Dell Upton.)

Of the fonts that survive, one, at Abingdon church (Fig. 183), resembles the bowl of the Jamestown font, and another, one of two at Pohick church, is circular with four circular lobes projecting horizontally from the lip (Fig. 184). All of the others are remarkably similar in appearance and probably in date. They are marble, have circular or octagonal bowls of hemispherical or more often of ogee profile, and are decorated with bands of moldings or baroque decoration in the form of gadrooning. They were probably made in the 1730s and 1740s, judging from contextual evidence. Those at Old Donation (Fig. 185), St. John's, Richmond, and Fork (Fig. 186; originally at Mattaponi) churches are associated with buildings constructed between the mid-1730s and early 1740s. The font at St. John's church in Richmond, now altered, may have been a duplicate of the Yeocomico font, which was probably installed during a remodeling around 1740. The second of the two Pohick fonts is similar in shape to the Mattaponi font (Fig. 187). It was made in 1773 by William Copein for £6. The vestry instructed Copein to make it "according to a Draught in the 150th plate in Langleys Designs being the upermost on the left hand," but Copein seems to have adapted both the top two designs freely (see Fig. 179). At any rate, as the other surviving fonts demonstrate, the form was a common one; no instruction from Langley was really necessary.[55]

Fonts were occasionally made by undertakers as part of their contracts. John Moore and Lewis Deloney, for example, agreed to install in the new Blisland Parish church of 1734–36 "a table & Font as Useall." But most of the survivors and many of those recorded in the vestry books were imported.[56]

None of the surviving eighteenth-century fonts draws on the common Virginia formal language. Instead, all but the early Pohick font look to European baroque design, as the largest and most elaborate pulpits and altarpieces had. That is, the most critical appurtenances of the Anglican ritual were dignified by the visual modes of the elite. Mode was equally important, therefore, in the design of communion furnishings.

Immediately after the Reformation, as we have seen, Anglicans began to replace the stone altars of medieval churches with wooden tables, although the practice was technically illegal until it was sanctioned by Bishop Nicholas Ridley in 1550. The abandonment of stone altars was made official policy throughout the Church of England at the

FIG. 183. Marble font (date unknown), Abingdon church, Gloucester County. (Photograph, Dell Upton.)

FIG. 184. Font (date unknown), Pohick church, Fairfax County. The date is that of the present church's completion (1774), and was inscribed on the font at an unknown time. This font is believed to have been used in the predecessor of the present church. (Photograph, Dell Upton.)

FIG. 185. Red marble font (second quarter 18th century), Lynnhaven Parish (Old Donation) church, Virginia Beach. The red-painted sandstone base is a 19th-century addition. (Photograph, Dell Upton.)

FIG. 186. Gray marble font (second quarter 18th century), formerly at Mattaponi church, now at Fork church. (Photograph, Dell Upton.)

FIG. 187. Font (1773; William Copein, carver), Pohick church. (Photograph, Dell Upton.)

accession of Elizabeth I. The Royal Injunctions of 1559 demanded a "decently made" holy table, as early Anglicans liked to call it, that could be moved to allow the communicants to gather round, and that would allude to the communion as a meal.[57]

Seventeenth-century Anglican officials thought the popular attitude toward the table was too casual, even disrespectful. They found instances where the communion table was used as a desk when schools were kept in church during the week. Parishioners placed their hats on it during services. It was pushed around carelessly, and treated as an object of no value. Dogs stole the communion bread, and urinated on the legs of the table. As a result, the officials demanded that the table be kept against the east wall in the traditional position of the altar when it was not being used, and that it be railed in with a low balustrade to give it a sense of permanence and dignity.[58]

Seventeenth- and eighteenth-century Virginians were accustomed to chancels containing a wooden table with a balustrade about eighteen inches to two feet high enclosing it. The rail was set far enough from the table to allow the minister to move around it; three feet was specified in one case. This enclosed area was referred to as the communion place, the chancel, or the altar. It was usually raised two steps above the floor level of the rest of the church, one step to the rail and one beyond it. This permitted kneeling by the communicants, even though some parishioners with Presbyterian sympathies refused to kneel at the rail, demanding instead that they be served in their seats.[59]

Tables, also called by Virginians communion tables or altars, were customarily built by undertakers of the church as part of their contract or as a supplementary service. When tables needed to be replaced, the vestries purchased them from local craftsmen. There is no evidence of a communion table ever having been imported by a Virginia parish. Distinction was conveyed to the communion table—which was nearly invisible under its hangings—by material rather than decoration. From the time of the founding of Jamestown, black walnut was the most popular wood, although Christ Church Parish, Middlesex County, gave the undertakers of its three early eighteenth-century churches the choice of black walnut or white oak to match the white oak communion rails. As a consequence of their origins, the tables tended to employ the formal language that was used for the buildings themselves. Two of the three surviving tables, at Yeocomico church (Fig. 188) and at Fork church (Fig. 189), are joined tables, with rectilinear tops, molded straight skirts, turned legs resembling the balusters of galleries and altar rails, and rectilinear stretchers fixed just above their turned feet. Joined tables and stools were common items of household furnishing that had originated in the mid-sixteenth century, and joined tables continued to be made as respectable furnishings throughout the colonial period in America, even though decorative arts scholars

FIG. 188. Communion table (18th century), Yeocomico church. Photograph taken by Susan Higginson Nash in the 1930s before the table was restored. (Photograph, Colonial Williamsburg Foundation.)

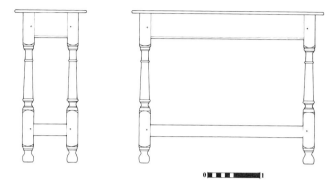

FIG. 189. Communion table (ca. 1740), Fork church, Hanover County. (Drawing, Dell Upton.)

have sometimes treated them as early pieces, or have ignored them in favor of more elaborate eighteenth-century forms of tables. The black walnut table at Yeocomico church has traditionally been thought original to the church, although its baluster legs might have been made at any time in the first half of the eighteenth century. The table at Fork church has column turnings like those seen on much other mid-eighteenth-century furniture. It may be as old as the church, but it more likely dates from a few decades later. The third surviving table, at Christ church, Lancaster County (Fig. 190), is a walnut table with cabriole legs and a pulvinated skirt. While it has suffered extensive repairs, it resembles in its form the dining table possibly built at about the same time for the church's benefactor, Robert Carter, and now kept in a former Carter house.[60]

The three tables not only look like dining tables, but are about the size of dining tables, except for the very narrow Fork table, which resembles a drop-leaf table without the leaves. The similarity to dining tables was intentional. The first Anglicans referred to the table as the Lord's board, or dining table.[61]

The metaphor of the meal extended from the table to its decoration. The required ornaments of the church included an altar carpet and linens, and a corresponding pulpit cloth and cushion. Both kinds of decoration stemmed from longstanding honorific customs. Textiles could be marks of honor because they were a legacy of a time when elite households were mobile and used portable fabrics as furnishings and because fine textiles remained in the eighteenth century a durable and relatively safe way of

FIG. 190. Communion table (ca. 1735), Christ church, Lancaster County. The walnut table has been heavily repaired; several of the feet are replacements. (Photograph, Dell Upton.)

FIG. 191. A 17th-century French domestic scene showing a table covered with a fringed carpet over which a linen cloth has been placed in preparation for dining. (Abraham Bosse, "L'Hyver," from *L'Oeuvre Gravé d'Abraham Bosse*, ed. André Blum [Paris: Editions Albert Morancé, 1924].)

storing accumulated wealth. Linens in particular were used for this purpose. To possess expensive textiles was to have means; to display them was to demand respect. To drape cloth over a canopy or an article of furniture in the post-medieval period, moreover, was to highlight the significance of what was under, or on, it. Cupboards for the display of silver and gold vessels were draped with cloths. Among the most expensive and prestigious of fabric furnishings in the seventeenth and eighteenth centuries were curtains, cushions, and table covers. Cushions connoted luxury and ease, and in the seventeenth and eighteenth centuries still intimated high status and dignity. When Sir Thomas Gates, one of Virginia's first governors, attended church at Jamestown, he was provided with a table with a cloth and a velvet cushion at which to kneel to pray. Cushions were often embellished with long tassels at the corners to heighten their visual prominence and evident expense. Thus for the Church to require that each pulpit be furnished with a cloth and a cushion was to reinforce the sense of dignity created by the pulpit's canopy. Similarly, the table was sometimes furnished with cushions on which the Bible

and prayer books might lie when not in use. The table was to be covered routinely with "silk, buckram or the like," and during communion services to have in addition "a fair white linen cloth upon it." This arrangement reproduced seventeenth- and eighteenth-century upper-class dining table furnishings (Fig. 191). Those who could afford it covered their tables, however elaborate the piece itself might be, with deep hanging cloths or carpets that were often sumptuously embroidered. During meal times a linen cloth was thrown over the permanent cover. The Anglican communion table thus carried through the meal imagery of the table while drawing on the prestigious connotations of fine fabric hangings.[62]

The disparity between the relatively low cost of furniture and the high cost of textiles that characterized aristocratic domestic life in the Middle Ages was not eradicated in the post-Reformation period. Expenditures on textiles could easily outstrip even elaborate architectural work in the parish churches. Petsworth Parish, in keeping with the luxurious standards it maintained in all things, paid vestryman Augustine Smith over £103 Virginia money plus a fifty percent commission for importing crimson velvet ornaments with gold fringe and lace in 1751. This was an outlandishly high price, and the parish levy was raised nearly by half to pay it. But the intent was a familiar one, even if the expense was disproportionate. Like the Petsworth vestry, most Virginia parishes preferred imported crimson or red velvet hangings. Less wealthy parishes chose ingrain broadcloth in crimson or purple. In either case, the hangings usually had a fringe of silk or gold, and the cushions were tasseled in the best manner. The pulpit cloth and altar carpet (now called a frontal but then usually referred to as a communion cloth) often had the parish monogram displayed on them. St. George's Parish, Spotsylvania County, ordered two sets of ornaments "to be of Crimson velvit with Gold tassels a Cypher upon Each pulpit Cloath St. G. P.," for example, and Wicomico Parish ordered a similar set of crimson velvet ornaments for pulpit, table, and altarpiece, the last to be mounted on paste board. "Note that the front of the Pulpit Cloth is to be mark'd Wiccocomoco Parish 1771 in Gold Letters," the vestry added. One green velvet altar cloth, at St. Mary's White Chapel Parish church, was reported in the nineteenth century to have had the Ball family coat of arms embroidered on it. Not only were great sums of money expended on these ornaments, but the textiles were frequently replaced, in part because wool velvet is highly susceptible to moth infestations, and quickly deteriorates. The vestry of Christ Church Parish, Middlesex County, ordered whole or partial sets of ornaments six times between 1669 and 1751.[63]

The napkins and fair linen cloth that lay on the table at communion time were usually less elaborate. Most were made of damask, the finest grade of linen, but some were of the second-best variety, diaper linen. Occasionally domestic furnishings may have been contributed for this purpose. Captain Henry Creeke gave Christ Church Parish, Middlesex County, a damask table cloth and two damask napkins with his initials on them. Creeke may simply have been commemorating the gift of new textiles by monogramming them, but his simultaneous gift of a piece of silver marked with Henry Corbin's coat of arms suggests that all the items came from his personal cupboard.[64]

The value and desirability of church textiles made them the targets of frequent thefts, particularly since their domestic character facilitated their appropriation to private use. Four parishes reported in the *Virginia Gazette* the loss of diaper and damask table cloths and napkins as well as

crimson and red velvet and purple broadcloth communion and pulpit cloths in the eighteenth century. Three incidents of the loss of the minister's ceremonial surplice and one of a silver cup with the parish monogram on it reflect the market for reusable fine materials that existed even when the stolen goods could not be reused intact. A green velvet pulpit cloth with gold fringe and the parish's monogram stolen from Lower Mattox church in 1715 was discovered to have been turned into a pair of breeches.[65]

The same combination of honorific and domestic associations was embodied in the final category of church ornaments, the communion plate. The word itself is significant. Plate was the generic term for vessels of silver and gold. Like textiles, plate was a favorite—perhaps the favorite—method of storing surplus wealth. To own plate was to show a significant surplus, and to be worthy of honor. The connotation was strengthened by the traditional conception of silver and gold as "noble" metals because they do not corrode, that is, they do not undergo reaction with the air, and are therefore easily refined. The seventeenth-century Virginia planter William Fitzhugh summed up silver's attraction in a well-known letter. He wrote to an English correspondent that, having built his own plantation, his house, and his slave labor force up to the proper level, and bought three more plantations besides, he now thought it "as well politic as reputable, to furnish my self with an handsom Cupboard of plate which gives my self the present use & Credit, is a sure friend at a dead lift, without much loss, or is a certain portion for a Child after my decease." To set out the church plate on the communion table was thus to invoke the habits of wealthy hosts who displayed their entire household plate on cloth-covered cupboards while entertaining. Allusions to grandeur were embedded in the idea of the communion service and *plate* became a generic term for any communion vessels, whether or not they were made of precious metals.[66]

The church plate lying on the altar reinforced the metaphor of the meal (Fig. 192). As they had done with the altar and the table, Anglicans in the sixteenth century at first tolerated, then forbade the use of the specialized vessels of the medieval mass. The Catholic chalice was replaced by the larger and usually plainer communion cup. The first surviving, specifically Protestant English plate was made in 1548, about the time the Anglicans began to make systematic adjustments on theological grounds to Catholic practices and to create an English liturgy. It was not until the

Fig. 192. Anglican communion service, showing carpeted table. (From Charles Wheatly, *A Rational Illustration of the Book of Common Prayer* [2d ed. London, 1714].)

beginning of Elizabeth's reign, however, that the use of pre-Reformation plate was forbidden. While every church was required to own suitable plate, there was no canonical group of pieces comparable to the Bible and the two prayer books. By the seventeenth century, the accepted standard seems to have been a communion cup; one or more plates or patens; and one or two tall flagons, for storing the quantity of wine needed now that the laity received wine as well as bread during communion (Fig. 193). Sometimes there was an alms basin as well. What Virginia parishes actually owned varied widely. While the two sets of communion plate ordered by Christ Church Parish, Middlesex County, in 1718 consisted of four flagons, two cups, and five plates, for many rural parishes it was an accomplishment to piece together a single set for several churches. It was necessary in some to pay someone "for Carrying the Communion pewter & Linen from one Church to another."[67]

The forms of the four basic vessels closely followed the development of their domestic counterparts throughout the seventeenth century. The common shape of the domestic wine cup on which the chalice was modeled changed from a plain, pronounced V-shaped bowl and circular foot to a more rectilinear body and a stem with an exaggerated knop or knob in the center. The mid-seventeenth-century cup of York Parish illustrates the first form (Fig. 194), while the gadrooned chalice given to Westover Parish in 1695 by Sarah Braine embodies the second (Fig. 195). Flagons were also indistinguishable from those displayed on domestic

Fig. 193. Christ Church Parish communion silver, Christ church, Lancaster County. The plate (1720–21; Thomas Folkingham, London) and flagon (1695–96; Sam Hood, London) were purchased by Robert Carter as agent for the parish in 1720. The chalice and paten (London, ca. 1680) were presumably purchased by the parish at an earlier date. (Photograph by Cornwall Photography, courtesy of Historic Christ Church, Inc.)

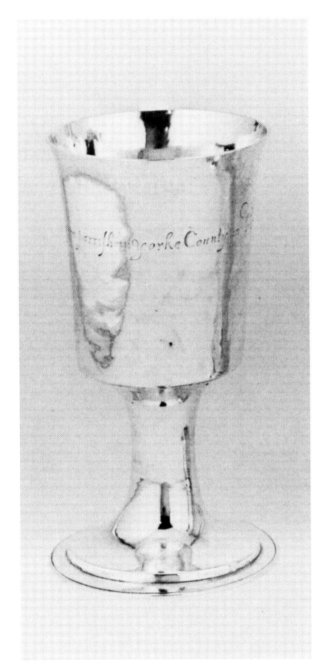

FIG. 194. York Parish communion chalice (1649–50; T.G., London), Grace Episcopal church, Yorktown. (Courtesy of Grace Episcopal church and Virginia Museum of Fine Arts, Richmond.)

FIG. 195. Westover Parish communion chalice and paten (1694–95; R, London), Westover church, Charles City County, Virginia. (Courtesy of Westover church and the Virginia Museum of Fine Arts, Richmond.)

cupboards and used to hold wine, cider, and beer at mealtimes, and basins resembled the washing basins used in elite halls. The fitted paten-covers introduced into the Elizabethan Church were more specifically ecclesiastical, and their traditional form never entirely lost favor with Virginians. In common with their English coreligionists, however, Virginia Anglicans tended increasingly toward the use of larger footed patens akin to domestic salvers (described in 1661 as "a new fashioned peece of wrought plate, broad and flat, with a foot underneath, and is used in giving Beer, or other liquid thing, to save the Carpit and Cloathes from drops"), and finally to patens sized and shaped like dinner plates.[68]

In the late seventeenth century, upper-class domestic practices began to shift away from the use of silver objects at the table, as glasses replaced wine cups, fine ceramics replaced trenchers, and forks obviated the use of washing basins. Some vessels like flagons and platters continued to be made for domestic use in other materials, but for the most part formal change in church silver was separated from domestic developments and the rate of change declined. In Virginia, up-to-date decoration of the kind used in the late seventeenth century on the Westover Parish plate tended to vanish. Churches acquired plate of elegant shapes, but embellished it with inscriptions rather than with applied or integrated decoration.[69]

Despite the separation of standard church plate from the domestic practice of the elite, it is clear that Virginians continued to make the connection. This point is lost when one thinks in terms of the customary category *church silver*. By the eighteenth century, church silver represented a traditional sign rather than a literal imitation of contemporary elite domestic life. But silver was only one part of most parishes' plate. Few parishes owned matched, complete services of silver vessels. Silver pieces were mixed with vessels of humbler and more up-to-date materials that did conform to current domestic practice. Pewter "plate" was common, though none seems to have survived, and ceramic objects like the "White mug" of St. Patrick's Parish, the earthen bowls of Southam Parish, or the glass tumblers of Lynnhaven Parish could be found as well.[70]

Virginians tended to use ecclesiastical and domestic terminology interchangeably in describing church plate. The official term *communion cup* was more likely to be replaced by the traditional *chalice* or, simply, *cup*. *Basin* and *bowl* were interchangeable terms, as were *plate*, *platter*, *salver*,

FIG. 196. East Lynnhaven Parish church flagon (1716–17; Robert Timbrell, London), Old Donation church, Virginia Beach, Virginia. (Courtesy of Old Donation church and the Virginia Museum of Fine Arts, Richmond.)

and *server* (*paten* was used only once in the vestry records). The silver "tankard" of 1785 listed in the Lynnhaven Parish records was probably identical with the flagon that survives (Fig. 196). A tankard was not a flagon. The former was a current eighteenth-century form, while the latter was used only in ecclesiastical contexts by that time. Yet to the writer the two lidded vessels seemed to belong in the same general category. The fluidity of ecclesiastical and domestic terminology was matched by the indifference to particular forms that parishes displayed. As a chalice a parish might use a cup, a two-handled cup (Fig. 197), a mug, or a tumbler. A "trencher plate" could serve as a paten. The result was a miscellaneous collection of wares of various ages, materials, conditions, and qualities that often looked much more like the contents of a domestic cupboard than a specially created set of ritual implements. Lynnhaven Parish's inventory of its possessions, made in 1785 at the order of the legislature, recorded for its mother church the large silver tankard (see Fig. 196), a silver salver, a silver cup washed with gold, and three pewter plates. At its Eastern Shore chapel were a silver tankard, silver cup, and small silver salver, three pewter plates, and a pewter basin, and at its Pungo chapel a pewter tankard, two glass tumblers, and two pewter plates.[71]

While recognizing the variety of communion vessels that individual churches possessed, it is important not to lose sight of the significance of silver plate. Silver vessels and fabric ornaments were always imported by Virginia vestries. Churches in northern colonies regularly purchased communion vessels from local smiths, and there were skilled artisans working in Virginia from the 1690s on who made some of their wares and imported others. At least sixteen worked in Williamsburg alone up to the time of the Revolution. Parishes from North Carolina commissioned communion vessels from them, but Virginia vestries and donors both invariably sent directly to England for their silver, buying through their commercial agents from established English silversmiths like Thomas Farren, whose products were owned by at least six Virginia parishes and who also made silver objects for the royal family.[72]

In silver, more than in almost any other artifact before the middle of the eighteenth century, modish appearance was desirable as a sign of continuing economic power. Secular owners routinely brought their plate to silversmiths to have it refashioned. A concern with the current mode was evident in Virginia church silver as well. Donated silver like Sarah Braine's chalice compares visually with contemporary domestic work in old and New England (see Fig. 195). Vestries, also, were concerned with being current when they bought silver. Christ Church Parish, Middlesex County, decided in 1718 to replace its upper and middle church silver, and made a deal with vestryman John Robinson to obtain a new set of communion plate for the upper church in trade for both sets of old plate. Another vestryman, John Grymes, donated plate to the lower

FIG. 197. Two-handled cup and cover (1686–87; Pierre Harache, London), Bruton Parish church, Williamsburg, Virginia. Given to the chapel of the College of William and Mary in 1775 by Lady Gooch, the widow of a former governor. (Courtesy of Bruton Parish church and the Virginia Museum of Fine Arts, Richmond.)

church. As was common in the eighteenth century, other parishes used their old plate as raw material for new.[73]

Whether by their size, material, context, or cost, the church and its contents were strikingly different from the buildings most Virginians knew. Many of the church's components were beyond the financial means of ordinary people; others incorporated centuries-old signs of honor and high status. One way to set the furnishings of a church off was to use items that were exotic because they were obtained outside Virginia or because they employed European decorative modes. At the same time, many church furnishings duplicated or resembled the current or recently set-aside domestic furnishings of the upper class. If the church was visibly different from most planters' houses, it was visibly similar to those of the ruling gentry. Style and mode led the viewer to make these comparisons.

Style located the church within Virginia life. At the same time, modish elements were used sparingly but not randomly within the church. Rather, they were played off

knowingly against common elements to make critical distinctions within church and parish. They served to identify the most important parts of the church liturgically, and they asserted the position of certain members of parish society.

A reexamination of changes in the exterior appearance of the churches illustrates this point. Before the second decade of the eighteenth century, churches were often highly ornamented on the outside. The Bruton Parish church of 1681–83 (see Fig. 15) and St. Peter's Parish church of 1701–3 (see Figs. 51, 56) had curvilinear parapeted gables and other brick decorations applied to the exterior. The late seventeenth-century Newport Parish church has stepped parapeted gables, quoins, pilaster strips, and a pediment on the tower (Fig. 198). At Yeocomico church, dated 1706, a small amount of diapering (lozenge-shaped patterns of glazed brick) and a plastered trefoil in keeping with the compass-head principle embellish the porch (see Fig. 59). Molded bricks recording initials and dates are distributed throughout the wall and pilasterlike piers without pediments or entablatures frame both doors. Brick "ornaments" of some kind embellished the gables of the present

FIG. 198. Newport Parish (St. Luke's) church (ca. 1685), Isle of Wight County. Late 19th-century repairs to the brickwork, particularly around the windows, are clearly visible in this photograph. (Photograph, Virginia State Library.)

Bruton Parish church, built 1711–15, until they were taken down in 1742. Wicomico church, built ca. 1685, had barge boards, possibly decoratively carved, and "spears" or pinnacles, all of which were replaced in 1721. The date is significant. Beginning with the three churches of Christ Church Parish, Middlesex County, church builders were deemphasizing the exteriors of their buildings. When compared to an urban eighteenth-century church like Christ church, Philadelphia (Fig. 199), for example, the Virginia churches have no facades. Other than the pedimented doorways used after 1720, their cornices and rubbed-brick jambs comprise the most assertive exterior decoration on urban or rural parish churches in eighteenth-century Virginia.[74]

The addition of frontispiece doorways to these geometrical buildings beginning in the 1720s called attention to the division between exterior and interior, setting off the inside from the outside and giving it greater importance. The fashionable detail that began to be introduced at Aquia church in the mid-1750s and that formed so conspicuous a part of the Truro and Fairfax parish churches of the 1760s was applied to the doorways and interiors according to the same principles. On the inside of the eighteenth-century church, as on the outside, most of the visible surface was high-quality vernacular work. But at critical points—the altarpiece, the pulpit and type, the font—modish classical elements, expensive materials, and up-to-date decoration were used. Similarly, the relatively plain communion vessels of the eighteenth century served as backgrounds for the engraved monograms, coats of arms, and inscriptions that most bore. The church as a whole should therefore be thought of as a neutral, if dignified, ground against which certain points could be made through the use of the high style or other distinctive means.

The selectivity was conscious and informed. The decoration was as carefully planned as the building itself. The vestry of Augusta Parish ordered Captain Francis Smith to make a pulpit "in a Fashionable and methodical manner with a Canopy over the Pulpit and Pialasters neatly Voluted the whole Jobb & every Part of it to [be] Finished & Compleated in a serviceable Beautifull and Workmanlike Manner." That is, the vestry wanted up-to-date decoration, and it was important that it be done correctly, according to the rules of high-style architecture. A growing awareness of mode was evident elsewhere in the colony in the middle of the eighteenth century. It was not enough simply to order

Fig. 199. Christ church (1727–44), Philadelphia. East end. (Photograph, Dell Upton.)

altarpieces in the Ionic order. During the construction of Pohick church, the Truro vestry discovered that "the Dimentions of the Alterpiece mentioned in the articles with the undertaker . . . are not according to the proportions of Architecture [and] the said undertaker is authorised & desired to make the same according to the true proportions of the Ionic order." To get it right was as important as to do it all.[75]

There were two reasons for the careful use of decoration. The first was to dignify the important elements of the church. The parts of the church that served as formal transfer points of Anglican theology were decorated to at-

FIG. 200. Westover (ca. 1750), Charles City County, Virginia. North (land) door. (Photograph, Dell Upton.)

tract attention and to engender respect. But there was a second purpose as well.

Other than in churches, pilasters and pediments and similar modish decorations were found only in the homes of Virginia's wealthiest planters (Figs. 200–202). In addition, furnishings and decorations in the parish churches also resembled those found in the homes of Virginia's ruling gentry. It has been estimated, for example, that only about five percent of colonial Americans owned significant quantities of silver objects. Fine table coverings and other textiles, too, distinguished the households of the gentry from those of their neighbors. If, as asserted at the beginning of this chapter, visual elements serve to identify the arena in which social actions are played out, then the decoration of altarpiece, pulpit, silver, and textiles with gilding, japanning, and modish forms equated the universal values of the Church with the specific values of the gentry. The ideal order and the existing social order were one.[76]

"Mixe not holy thinges with profane." The legend was engraved on a silver chalice and paten given to James City

FIG. 201. Westover. Southeast parlor. The paneling of walls other than those containing fireplaces and the use of pilasters were confined to the largest Virginia houses. The pilasters and the triangular panels over the doors combine to create the effect of pedimented doorways. The plaster elements in the ceiling are original, but were reinstalled and slightly rearranged in the 20th century. (Photograph, Barry Zarakov for the Virginia Historic Landmarks Commission.)

FIG. 202. Kittiewan (ca. 1760), Charles City County. Hall. The mantel is a late 18th-century alteration. (Photograph, Dell Upton.)

FIG. 204. Jamestown paten. Inscription. (Courtesy of Bruton Parish church and the Virginia Museum of Fine Arts, Richmond.)

FIG. 203. Jamestown communion chalice and paten (ca. 1660; London), Bruton Parish church, Williamsburg. Formerly the property of James City Parish. Francis Morrison's name and the date of the gift are marked on the base of each piece. (Courtesy of Bruton Parish church and the Virginia Museum of Fine Arts, Richmond.)

Parish in the mid-seventeenth century (Figs. 203, 204). But the two pieces, for containing the body and blood of Christ, offered in the feast that Thomas Bennet likened to an earthly lord's banquet, were also marked "Ex dono Francisci Morrison Armigeri. Anno: Domi: 1661." The Anglican parish church effected what modern observers might consider to be a mixture of the holy and the profane. Anglican reformers had gone far toward eliminating the distinction between clergy and laity in the Church of England, but new divisions had been created in the churches, divisions whose existence was attested by the appearance of the artifacts through which the rituals of the state Church were enacted. To say this is not to imply that the secular world could or should have been kept out of the Church: the notion of neutrality is an anachronism in this setting. It is, however, to attempt to appreciate the particular way in which a certain social order and a certain religious order were melded in the parish churches of Virginia. As we shall see, not all Virginians shared this vision. But in the Anglican churches, style and mode worked in an elegant way to meld the ideal order of theology with the dominant order of the Virginia parish, expressing complementary visions of sacred and secular life. The holy and the profane met for Virginians in the concept of hospitality.

7 | The House of God

It is tempting to interpret the use of gentry modes in the Virginia parish churches as a kind of hollow strutting on the part of the elite. Horton Davies identified social prestige—"by which the exterior and interior of religious buildings will be a mark of the standing in society of their donors and to some extent of those who worship in them"—as one of five interrelated factors that helped to determine the appearance of English churches. While social prestige was undeniably a motive for many individuals in the Virginia parish church, it is important not to lose sight of the larger social process that the churches embodied. The mixture of holy things and profane in the church was part of a continuing process of symbol-making by which Virginia Anglicans interpreted their society.[1]

Students of symbolism distinguish carefully between concepts of sign and symbol, a distinction not always made in colloquial usage. A sign, a conventional marker that stands for some more cumbersome concept, is a more limited and a more easily defined entity than a symbol. For example, the state might indicate its interest in the Church by having officers of the government present in every church every Sunday. In Virginia parish churches, the state's concern was signified more conveniently by installing the Royal Arms in each church. Similarly, the type over the pulpit was a sign that directed attention to the message proclaimed from beneath it. A biblical text asserting the importance of preaching, painted next to the pulpit, could be an equally effective sign. Presuming that the text was known to be about preaching, it could create an atmosphere of importance and expectation even without knowledge of the actual contents.

In contrast, recent studies of symbolism suggest that it is more useful to explore the symbolic *process* than to attempt to identify and interpret individual symbols. At bottom, symbolism is rooted in the human necessity for order. Our actions are based on the belief that our environment is not random, but structured and predictable. At the same time the structure of the world is a human invention. We learn it from other people, who teach us to see certain relationships in our social and physical surroundings. Consequently, the symbolic process is a reciprocal one: we look for the relationships we expect, and we find them because we put them there. In this sense symbolization is the act of creating and recreating the world: we continually invest our environment with an order that we find over and over again. Correspondences and resonances appear in unlikely places, and the imagined structure begins to take on a life of its own. When this happens, the symbolic order is effective.[2]

Meaning is essential to the symbolic process. The conventions that we called style in chapter 6 give order to the craft of building, but they are not symbolic (although they might be useful in symbolization, as we shall see). Symbolic orders must explain and justify the world, and make it possible to explain and judge individual actions within it. This is particularly necessary for religious philosophies, the most comprehensive and systematic of symbolic constructs.

Religious discourse makes universal claims, but to be effective these claims must be perceived to have some corresponding existence in the real world. Often this can be achieved, the anthropologist Victor Turner has suggested, by a metaphor likening a complex symbolic order to some smaller, more easily apprehended set of relationships. In the context of the symbolic process, Turner argues, people forge self-concepts that cast their routine actions in terms of the metaphor. In doing so, they give their actions meaning.[3]

Religious discourse is by definition ideological. In offering a description of the world in the light of ultimate truths, religion makes a statement of how it ought to be interpreted *from one point of view*. No interpretation is neutral, yet an ideological claim succeeds when its assumptions or propositions come to seem self-evident, when it is transformed into common sense. Then it appears to be a neutral depiction of the natural, rather than the expression of a value-laden viewpoint. It achieves legitimacy, sometimes called hegemony, in its domain, and it informs the conduct of those who accept it.[4]

Symbolic orders can only be understood through the

actions they inspire. For participants and for observers, the physical environment is a powerful aid to imagining the metaphorical connection between the larger order and the smaller one. Medieval Christians, for example, traditionally thought of their churches as microcosms, miniature models of the city of God or of the divine universe. They described the process as "anagogical," by which the concrete physical properties of the church led the mind upward, enabling it to understand more difficult, abstract theological precepts. The Christian was called on to act like a citizen of the divine city. Some Anglican writers were attracted by this idea. They argued for a numinous interpretation of the church as a building that *somehow* conveyed the presence of divinity. But they lacked a precise theory of the relationship between the building and the structure of the universe that would function like the civic, mathematical, and harmonic theories that underlay the Gothic arguments.[5]

The material world supports the ideological claims of religious propositions as well. An artifact is infinitely more powerful than words. To build a model of one reality is to vitiate all verbal descriptions of alternative realities. The profane elements of the Virginia parish church—the gentry artifactual style, the display of personal monograms and other marks on ritual objects, and, as we shall see in the next chapter, the social arrangement of seating—served this purpose. They *reified*, or made concrete and apparently objective, a particular relationship between religious values and the conduct of daily life. By being cast in physical form, the social and moral propositions asserted in ritual, sermon, and the behavior of the parishioners acquired an apparently independent existence. Their evident naturalness and their commonsense quality made them credible. The physical environment seemed to be an independent confirmation of theology.[6]

We can think of the interaction of word and artifact as the "argument" of the church, but in doing so must not mistake it for logical exposition. Here is where the metaphorical aspect of the symbolic process enters. The argument of the church is that a similar order underlies abstract theological propositions and a particular social structure. The assertion is made through actions conducted within the confines of a pair of complementary premises. According to the Church, the secular world ought to imitate the sacred world. Virginia's Anglican leaders conceived this demand in terms of a complementary premise: that the sacred world is like a household. The conduct of the eighteenth-century

gentry in church made this argument. The quasi-domestic appearance of the colonial Virginia parish church and the use of elite modes made the assertion architecturally. The religious duty was understood by Virginians through the metaphor of hospitality.

The traditional Christian locution that the church is the house of God was the obvious root of this metaphor. Richard Hooker used the domestic analogy to contrast church and daily life, to teach "what difference should be made between house and house." Virginians were as conscious of these ideas as Christians elsewhere. Landon Carter was unwilling to go with a dissatisfied mind to "the house of my God." But Virginians chose to see the congruities rather than the differences between the two houses. The satirist James Reid made clear that the comparison of God's house and the Virginian's was a conscious one. He referred disparagingly, if inaccurately, to the Virginia parish's "little brick-house, neither so large nor so good as an Esquire's." The church was ostensibly the house of God, but everything about it provoked the question, "Whose house is this?"[7]

It is not enough to say that the church was the house of God. It is the beginning of an understanding, but it needs to be filled out and made more specific. The house of God was not a slave's house or a common planter's house: it was a gentleman's house. The eighteenth-century English commentator Thomas Bennet remarked that at communion, as at the last supper, "Christ is still the Master of the Feast, and the principal Person present at it. We are his Guests; 'tis his Table at which we are entertained, his Provisions which we eat and drink; and we have the great Honor vouchsafed us of eating and drinking in his own Presence." Bennet was playing on his readers' familiarity with a complex, if fading, traditional social ritual of eating that informed the Anglican sense of communion. At great houses, social precedence was recognized in table seating. It was an honor to be allowed to sit at the lord's table, for the lord might choose to dine at a separate table, or even in a separate room from his guests. The Anglican Christ was an English lord. Virginians naturalized the image. For them, the house of God was the residence of the greatest gentleman in the neighborhood. The analogy took on meaning for Virginians when it was enlivened by the understanding of a particular way of life that went on in the planter's house and by that means acquired behavioral corollaries.[8]

Hospitality was deeply rooted in the Virginian's mind. It was an old concept in Anglo-American society. The "Ancient English Hospitality" was an admirable medieval quality to postmedieval Englishmen. The eighteenth-century traveler Edward Kimber likened Maryland's "universal Hospitality" to "the old roast-Beef Ages of our Fore-Fathers." But Virginians identified particularly intensely with the hospitable virtues, and, in their own and others' judgments, seemed to have perfected them to a higher degree than elsewhere. When they described themselves they emphasized their hospitable temperament, and when they traveled they looked for this quality and compared it with their own. "Here is the most Good-nature, and Hospitality practis'd in the World," Robert Beverley wrote in his 1705 history of Virginia. Traveling in Barbados in 1751, George Washington observed that "Hospitality & a Genteel behavior is shewn to every genteel stranger by the Gentlemen Inhab[itants]," but he attributed this to the small size of the island, which "preven[ted it] being much infested" with visitors. When outsiders traveled in Virginia they invariably wrote, as Thomas Anburey did, of "the liberality and hospitality so peculiar to this province." Indeed, hospitality was an obligatory theme that every Revolutionary-era and early national traveler in Virginia addressed. Sympathetic travelers like Benjamin Henry Latrobe and Luigi Castiglioni found Virginia's hospitable ways intact, while more critical ones like Johann David Schoepf and Alexander Macaulay thought that "the people are a little alter'd." [9]

At its core, hospitality incorporated several fundamental virtues. Foremost among them was that selfless quality Virginians called "good neighborhood." Good neighborhood recognized the commonality that binds all people together regardless of personal standing. It avoided sacrificing the general good to the personal good. Thomas Wilkinson complained to the court in 1693 that George York, lessee of a water mill up the creek from his own, "takes all advantages and at all unseasonable times to open his flood gates & Sluces, & so at once & wth great violence to let his water go, thereby to break & carry away the damm and waterworks of yor Peticonr to his great prejudice, detrmt & loss." Wilkinson accused York of acting "contrary to all the Laws of good neighborhood." Those were social laws, not judicial ones, and the petition was endorsed "nothing to be done." Self-centeredness and concern for one's own gain was the very opposite of the spirit of commonality built into the hospitable relationship; thus Edward Kimber attributed the lack of hospitality he found in Yorktown to "Schemes of Gain, or Parties of Gaming and Pleasure" that "muddy too much their Souls." Not only economic gain and personal pleasure but political differences contradicted good neighborhood, for they denied the unitary notion of the public good on which political theory was based. For Robert Beverley, good neighborhood in Virginia "has of late been much depraved by the present Governor, who practices the detestable Politicks of governing by Parties; by which, Feuds and Heart-burnings have been kindled in the Minds of the People; and Friendship, Hospitality, and Good-Neighbourhood, have been extreamly discouraged." Similarly, Anburey reported a case in which captured British officers had been entertained at Tuckahoe, Goochland County, to the consternation of "the illiberal part of their countrymen," who failed to perceive the principle of commonality. One of those officers, however, forfeited the privilege of Tuckahoe's hospitality by raising political matters in conversation, and thus breaking the common bond.[10]

As the case of the British prisoners of war illustrates, the notion of commonality meant that one distributed hospitality to friends and strangers, even enemies, impartially. "Strangers and travellers are here treated in the most free, plentiful, and hospitable manner; so that a few inns or ordinaries on the road are sufficient," wrote Hugh Jones, sounding a common theme. William Hugh Grove observed that "in places where there are no Ordinarys you ride in where 2 brick Chimbles [chimneys] shew there is a spare bed and lodging and Welcome." [11]

To refuse hospitality was a grave social sin. The "Churl, that either out of Covetousness, or Ill-nature," failed to comply was "abhorr'd by all," wrote Robert Beverley. But hospitality required that one go beyond the spare bed. Those whose hospitality was merely adequate were as much the objects of derision as those who showed none. Virginians complained to the English authorities that Governor Francis Nicholson's hospitality was "most scandalously penurious, no way suiting the dignity of her Ma'ties Governour, having but one Dish of meat at his table." True hospitality implied liberality to the point of self-sacrifice. According to Beverley, the poorest planter would sleep on a form or couch or even sit up all night to give his only bed to a traveler. For those with more means, excess was in order. Beverley regretted that hospitality was attended on occasion with "a little too much Intemperance." The French traveler Jean Pierre Brissot de Warville recorded Washington's complaint that pre-Revolutionary Virginia hosts made it a point of honor to send their guests home drunk. The Randolphs of Tuckahoe were the outstanding hosts of eighteenth-century Virginia, according to Thomas Anburey. Their entire house seemed to be "built solely to answer the purposes of hospitality, . . . being constructed in a diffent manner than in most other countries . . . : It is in the form of an H, and has the appearance of two houses, joined by a large saloon; each wing has two stories . . . in one the family reside, and the other is reserved solely for visitors." [12]

Hospitality carried general obligations of shelter and help, but it also had a ritual component by which it was defined — the meal. Dining was ideally suited to the expression of hospitality. It involved the provision of goods directly necessary to the survival of the guest; it was capable of being easily judged in quality and quantity; it was served on table coverings and with ware that demonstrated the host's economic standing; and it brought host and guest together in a face-to-face relationship in the performance of a mutually understood ritual of long standing. For these reasons, dining was widely recognized by Virginians as a ceremony of social cohesion. A remarkable agreement entered in the Lancaster County records authorized Isaac Allerton and Thomas Gerrard, on behalf of themselves and two other planters, to erect at the expense of the four, "a House . . . for the continuance of good Neighborhood." This "Banquetting House" was intended to stand as a boundary marker. In it "each man or his heirs, yearly, according to his due course, [was] to make an Honorable treatment fit to entertain the undertakers thereof, their wives, mistresses & friends yearly & every year, & to begin upon the 29th of May" 1671. [13]

Thus, whatever else it might entail, hospitality was judged by the quality of one's table, as the complaint against Governor Nicholson suggests. "Full Tables and Open Doors" was Edward Kimber's succinct characterization of Maryland hospitality. Visitors to Mount Vernon always reflected on Washington's "genteel table for strangers that almost daily visit him," although some judged it "a good table but not a sumptuous one." [14]

The connection between the planter's hospitality and the Anglican Church is easy to make on a formal level. Christian doctrine universally demanded open-handed and self-sacrificing charity of believers. Article XXXVIII of the Thirty-Nine Articles, the official summary of Anglican belief, declared that "every Man ought, of such things as he possesseth, liberally to give Alms to the Poor, according to his Ability." Hospitality might be conceived in this spirit as an exercise of Christian charity. Moreover, the parallels between the doctrine of salvation and the custom of hospitality are striking. Article XI of the Thirty-Nine Articles asserted the traditional Christian doctrine that "we are accounted righteous before God, only for the Merit of our Lord and Saviour Jesus Christ by Faith, and not for our own Works, or Deservings." Salvation is dispensed freely without regard for personal merit, which is absent, or for service to God, which is always inadequate. Similarly, hospitality is dispensed to friends and strangers alike, without regard for personal benefit or past service, which could not exist on the part of strangers. The commonality recognized by the hospitable might be interpreted as an expression of "the Love that Christians ought to have among themselves to one another." This love was manifested in the Church in the ritual of the Lord's Supper, which was also the "Sacrament of our Redemption," the heart of spiritual salvation, in the same way dining was the heart of hospitality. Just as the dispensation of salvation characterized the Church, so the dispensation of hospitality defined a house. Thus, Ben Carter informed Philip Fithian, "It is a custom here whenever any *person* or *Family* move into a *House*, or repair a house they have been living in before, they make a *Ball* & give a *Supper*." [15]

Hospitality depicted in its ideal form closely accorded with the universal Christian ideal of charity, and Virginians claimed hospitality as their characteristic attribute. Yet it clearly was not so universally practiced or impartially applied as suggested. A man like Captain John Lee could, by virtue of his social position, take advantage of the institution of hospitality to reside all but eight or ten weeks a year at other people's houses, but poorer Virginians like the drunken man who showed up at Nomini Hall one stormy night when Philip Fithian lived there would be lucky to sleep in an outbuilding with the house slaves. Other strangers found that "their much-praised hospitality is by no means unrestricted, but is confined to acquaintances and those who are recommended." J. D. Schoepf traveled twenty miles through Isle of Wight County before he could find a planter who would take him in. No one could expect to be received graciously by humble Virginians. Joseph

Hadfield, when marooned on the James River in 1785, encountered a man who threatened him with a gun. The best accommodations he could find were at a plantation so poor that it could offer only "a piece of hoe-cake, made of Indian Corn, such as they feed the niggers with." Hospitality was thus a social grace found primarily among rich Virginians of the sort who "have in abundance everything necessary for the conveniences of life . . . [and] are considered the leading gentry of the district." As practiced by Virginians, it owed less to Christian notions of charity than to secular ideas about gentry prerogatives.[16]

While the Christian concept of hospitality stressed selflessness and commonality, the secular idea of the gentleman injected large elements of personal assertion, self-display, and class consciousness. After the American Revolution, both J.F.D. Smyth and Thomas Anburey agreed that despite the growth of egalitarianism in Virginia, "There is a greater distinction supported between the different classes of life here, than perhaps in any of the rest of the colonies; nor does that spirit of equality, and levelling principle, which pervades the greatest part of America, prevail to such an extent here." Anburey affirmed that "before the war, the spirit of equality or levelling principle was not so prevalent in Virginia, as in the other provinces." While his experience at Tuckahoe convinced him that common planters had caught the spirit, as evidenced in their informal and unintimidated behavior toward their host, it was clear that the owner, Colonel Randolph, had not.[17]

The spirit of inequality underlay the concept of the gentleman, who thought of himself as a powerful and solitary figure. Like William Byrd II, he might depict himself romantically as an Old Testament patriarch, with his "family" of relatives and slaves gathered around him, subject to his distantly loving, disciplined direction. A less appealing image appears in Philip Fithian's journal. An old black man came to Nomini Hall to complain about his food rations. "He sat himself down on the Floor clasp'd his Hands together, with his face directly to Mr *Carter*, then began his Narration." The man's posture of submission deferred to the absolute and unfettered power Virginia gentlemen were taught to exercise over their dependents. It was another of the recurring themes sounded by eighteenth-century observers. "Their authority over their slaves renders them vain and imperious, and intire strangers to that elegance of sentiment, which is so peculiarly characteristic of refined and polished nations," Andrew Burnaby wrote. James Reid

described the process by which this feeling was instilled. "Before he is capable to be his own master, he is told that he is Master of others, and he begins to command without ever having learned to obey. . . . His dog & horse are his most favourite companions, and a negro about his own age, stature & mental qualifications, whom he abuses & kicks for every trifle, is his satelite."[18]

The old slave's posture at Nomini Hall was an exaggerated version of the kneeling position in which Anglicans were required to pray, but James Reid informs us that the planters who demanded such submission from their slaves refused it to their god, offering to kneel only to women, and then mockingly. Puritans rejected kneeling on doctrinal grounds, but for the Virginian "To bow the knee, except to a young Lady, is reckoned below the dignity of a polite Gentleman." The planter's elevation was derived from his economic power.

If a King Williamite has Money, Negroes and Land enough he is a compleat Gentleman. . . . His money gilds over all his stupidities, and although an Ass covered over with gold is still an Ass, yet in King William County a fool covered over with the same metal, changes his nature, and commences a GENTLEMAN. Learning and good sense; religion and refined Morals; charity and benevolence have nothing to do in the composition. These are qualifications only proper for a dull, plodding thoughtfull fellow, who can live in a closet by himself, and who cannot appear in polite company for want of Negroes.[19]

Reid's bitter cavil encapsulated the difference between a Christian and a Virginia gentleman. Virginia gentlemen could imagine no commonality. They were "haughty and jealous of their liberties, impatient of restraint, and can scarcely bear the thought of being controuled by any superior power," according to Andrew Burnaby. They demanded recognition, and they manifested a powerful complacency and love of self-display. The Virginia gentleman "hugs himself upon the glorious appelation 'Esquire,' and dreads to fall back into the ranks of the common planter." The gentleman's horse served the same purpose in white society as the self-abasing posture of the slave did in white-black relationships. It allowed the gentleman to rise above most of his neighbors, and to be on a par with only a few. It facilitated a graceful and impressive entry onto any scene, one that emphasized lack of physical effort.[20]

Competition was critical to the gentleman's self-image. Virginians strove to present an image of easy personal prowess and unlimited economic ability. Both men and women fancied elaborate dress, but while the planter acted the genteel host, his wife organized the necessary work of the household and his slaves performed it. Dancing and hunting, horse racing and cock fighting, card playing and gambling were universally described as the favorite pastimes of the Virginia gentleman. They allowed the demonstration of prowess in a competitive setting. Their indulgence was often in direct contradiction to the moral tenets espoused by the Church. Clergymen like William Stith, the rector of Henrico Parish, tried in vain to stem the excesses of gentry indulgence. Yet Stith's sermon "The Sinfulness and Pernicious Nature of Gaming," preached before the General Assembly and then published at Williamsburg in 1752, had no noticeable effect on the vice. "Gentlemen of good and respectable families" provoked one another to physical combat in gambling contests, and others ultimately squandered their health and their families' fortunes. Though slaves and movable property could be seized for gambling debts, Virginians tended to treat debts lightly. The duke de La Rochefoucault Liancourt reported that the very legislators who were responsible for a stringent 1792 law against gambling were among the new state's most avid gamblers.[21]

Seen in this light, the custom of hospitality appears very different from Christian charity. Hospitality indulged the convivial spirit prevalent among Virginians, a spirit promoted both by their rural isolation and by the chance for competitive self-display. In this arena, the poor and the unknown had little place. James Reid concluded accurately that "Self love must be the principle motive & cause of all their actions, seeing that they are only kind and complaisant to such as are able to repay the benefit. A rich man therefore is not entertained on account of his own account, or because of any intrinsic merit . . . but for the sake of his wealth. . . . When a wealthy man therefore receives a good dinner . . . instead of thanking the people who bestowed the favour, he should go home and thus address his cash—O Money! what thanks and praise do I owe to thee for heaping upon me so many kindnesses?" Hospitality was more likely to be extended to one's inferiors in ritual settings where power was celebrated or sought. It took the form of the "treat," the extravagant dispensation of food and drink on public occasions. When William Byrd II was installed as colonel and commander-in-chief of the militia in 1710, the officers dined with the governor, while the men were treated with a hogshead of liquor at the churchyard.

Treating was also the established means of soliciting votes in elections.[22]

The concept of hospitality was thus inspirited by two ostensibly related but in fact opposed concepts—those of the Christian and of the Virginia gentleman. It would be equally mistaken to imagine that the Christian was entirely overwhelmed by the Virginian as it would be to ignore the existence of the Virginian. The concept of hospitality embraced a collection of contradictory attitudes built around the notions of easy grace and stern patriarchy, free generosity and open self-promotion. It guided the gentleman's actions in the Church. As much as the Christian concept of charity infused the secular idea of hospitality, so much more did the Virginian notion of hospitality infuse the life of the parish. In the relations of vestry to parish, of vestry to clergy, of clergy to parishioners, of gentry to parish, the precepts of hospitality guided the participants' actions and their responses to what they saw.

As we have seen, the vestry was in many respects the parish gentlemen's club, and it shared many of the same personnel with the county court. Vestrymen convened in private at the house of one of the group or, more often in the eighteenth century, in a neutral vestry house, a small one-room building that was erected in the yard of the major church of the parish or included (at St. Peter's Parish and Bruton Parish churches) in an added tower. To conduct the business of the vestry in the convivial manner of a social occasion came naturally. James Reid observed that vestry meetings inevitably included meals. "When a Church is to be built, or any other public edifice, the Directors assemble, and instead of consulting upon it, they eat upon it, by which means the business goes forward with success. When the poor are to be relieved, the Officers appointed assemble and eat upon it; Nor has it ever been known that they filled the bellies of the poor till they had previously satisfied their own."[23]

The vestry itself was an institution of hospitality. Vestrymen did for their neighbors whatever needed to be done to keep the parish running. The parishioners expected the vestrymen to fulfill their duties honestly, thoughtfully, and diligently. The sense of duty in vestrymen was conceived as arising from their being part of a local community, whose interests they shared and who could call them to account for their failures. The vestrymen expected, and were expected, to discern the needs of the parish and to satisfy them in a timely fashion. When a church needed to be repaired, a church warden had the work done at his own expense, and was reimbursed. When some item needed to be sent for, a merchant vestryman placed the order. As representatives of the house of God, the vestrymen attended to the needs of its guests, their fellow parishioners. But if hospitality implied unlimited service, it also implied a silent gratitude on the part of the guest: the guest who presumed to tell a host how to conduct his affairs was soon unwelcome. The vestry expected obedience to their orders as masters of the parish, along with acquiescence to their decisions about church building, taxation, ministerial hiring, and the prerogatives of mastery in general. It required a massive uprising like that over seating in Lynnhaven Parish

Church in 1736 or an appeal to higher authorities in Jamestown or Williamsburg to change a vestry decision. When there was such an occurrence, the vestrymen were unlikely to accept it graciously. Landon Carter ascribed the lack of acquiescence to vestry conduct to "Malice and venom" and "Revenge" in connection with a Cople Parish case brought before the House of Burgesses while he was a member. Moreover, vestrymen expected unlimited prerogative in return for unlimited service. Few doubted that they were entitled to large commissions on imported goods, or that it was fair for them to grant themselves privileges in church. Moreover, vestrymen were in the habit of inscribing their names or initials on major parish works undertaken under their direction as a mark of their service (Fig. 205).[24]

FIG. 205. Aquia church (1754–57; Mourning Richards, undertaker), Stafford County. West gallery. The panel on the face of the gallery records the names of the minister and vestrymen in 1757. (Photograph, Dell Upton.)

The bonds of mutual obligation extended beyond the vestry to the relationship of the parish with the gentry as a class. Parishioners expected the gentry to demonstrate their right to rule by service; they expected to be taken care of by their leaders. Donation to the parish was an ancient and cherished form of gentry service. Ostensibly the gift was given in the spirit of Captain Henry Creeke's 1681 gift to Christ Church Parish, Middlesex County, extended "out of his pious zeal and love to the Church." To ensure that priorities were not confused, Richard Hooker observed, churches were formally dedicated to saints and holy personages "to surrender up that right which otherwise their founders might have in them, and to make God himself their owner." But in Virginia only the second Bruton Parish church was dedicated. Those that bore the names of saints usually got them from the name of the parish; only a few, like St. Mark's and St. Andrew's churches in Albemarle Parish, received saints' names in the eighteenth century. Most bore the names of their locations, like Lamb's Creek church or Little Fork church, or of the donors or former owners of the land on which they stood, like Payne's church or Williamson's church. Few Virginians donated on a grand scale, but donors were eager to receive full credit for what they did give, and vestries were equally careful to give credit only where it was earned. A recorded gift attested not only to the preeminence of its donor but to the parish's appreciation of a genuine service that relieved it of acquiring some required item through taxation. William Fitzhugh apologized to his friend and London trading partner Nicholas Hayward for his parish's inability to recognize Hayward's gift "by a more lasting continuance than at present our paper built Temples [record books] will admit of." Bruton Parish's vestry obliquely but firmly warded off Governor Francis Nicholson's clumsy attempt to claim credit for more than he had given. The governor gave an altar cloth and cushion and fifty shillings for poor relief, and asked that the money be recorded in the vestry book "as being his Excellency's usual quarterly gift." The vestry thanked him for his generosity and assured him that the gifts would be recorded, "but not knowing it to be his Excellency's Constant Custom, we cannot register it as such without we know att present what his Excellency hath given to the poor [in the past]; but we do promise to examine that matter against the next Vestry, and what appears to us, then shall be registered." [25]

Donations followed relatively clear patterns. With the exception of the building donations recorded in chapter 2, few gifts were architectural. Donors gave land for church building, or, less often, land or money for glebes or poor relief. Otherwise, they gave movables—bells, ornaments, linens, Bibles but not prayer books, hanging altarpieces but not architectural ones, fonts but not pulpits or tables, and most of all plate. No item was donated as often as silver. The value, honorific connotations, and conspicuous role of plate in the central ritual of the church made it the ideal gift; the first bequest of silver to a Virginia parish was made just a decade after colonization. [26]

The preference for expensive, prestigious, and exotic goods showed by the vestries when they built churches was thus manifested by the donors as well. Of the 138 extant and documented vessels whose origins have been identified, 73 were gifts to their parishes. Simply to donate communion pieces, however, was not enough. Pewter, glass, and ceramics were used by many Virginia parishes, but in all but a few recorded instances donated items were made of silver. Silver was invariably obtained from England. It appeared costly, although differences in actual cost varied greatly, according to the weight of the piece. The English scholar Charles Oman has shown that small patens were relatively cheap, and might weigh as little as seven ounces. Flagons weighed a minimum of forty ounces, and so were less frequently given in England or Virginia. In two Virginia instances, the weight of the piece, and by implication its cost, was inscribed right on the vessel. Humphrey Jones's donation to Christ Church Parish, Middlesex County, included a fourteen-ounce silver bowl, but the flagon and plate he gave at the same time were made of pewter. [27]

Jones's gifts were inscribed "For the use of Christ Church Uper Chappell." Most surviving American pewter church vessels were not inscribed, and Jones's were lettered only with the name of the church. Most donors, however, wanted their gifts acknowledged explicitly and conspicuously. The Ball coat of arms was embroidered into the St. Mary's White Chapel church communion cloth; the initials of land donors Anthony and Esther Holladay (he was also a church warden) were inscribed on a brick near the south door of the 1753 Chuckatuck church. Even the bell at Bruton Parish church was labeled "The gift of James Tarpley to Bruton Parish 1761." Silver inscriptions most often recorded the name of the parish. The name, arms, and monograms of donors are recorded on thirty-six of the do-

FIG. 206. Wicomico Parish communion chalice (1711–12; Francis Garthorne, London), Wicomico Episcopal church, Wicomico Church, Virginia. Inscribed on opposite side "Ex Dono/Hancock Lee/to the Parish of Lee/1711." Lee Parish was the official but never used name of Wicomico Parish. (Courtesy of Wicomico church and the Virginia Museum of Fine Arts, Richmond.)

FIG. 207. Chalices, Elizabeth River Parish. The left chalice, made by Thomas Farran in London, 1722–23, is inscribed "The Gift of Mr: Robt: Tucker to the Parish Church of Norfolk Towne Aprill the 3: 1722." The right chalice, made in London by Samuel Smith in 1700–1701, is decorated with the arms of Samuel Boush and is inscribed on the rear "The Gift of Capt: Saml: Boush to the Parish Church of Norfolk Towne March 1700." Early 20th-century photograph. (Photograph, Virginia State Library.)

nated silver pieces (Figs. 206, 207), while the monogram of Christ appears on only seventeen of them. On five both the donor's and Christ's marks appear. The Ten Commandments at St. Mary's White Chapel are labeled "The Gift of David Fox, 1702" (Fig. 208)! Whose house is this?[28]

In return for their gifts, the gentry expected not only recognition, but the kind of treatment they received at other gentlemen's houses. The expectation was particularly evident, and its complexity acutely manifested, in the relationships between the gentry and the minister. In some respects the parish elite treated the clergy like gentlemen. They invited clergymen to social events. Philip Fithian

encountered the rectors of Cople and Lunenburg parishes at a ball he attended in 1774. The ministers' wives danced but, the Presbyterian tutor was relieved to note, neither of the clerics danced or gambled. Some gentlemen allowed their daughters to marry parish clergy. Such social concessions were not merely graceful courtesies, but had practical motivations. Ministers were in notoriously short supply in colonial Virginia. At any given time, a large number of the parishes had no ministers. In 1705, when Robert Beverley wrote, fifteen of forty-nine parishes were vacant. Clergymen were constantly attempting to transfer from Oronoco to "sweet-scented" parishes, that is, to parishes that paid the

FIG. 208. St. Mary's White Chapel church, Lancaster County. Detail of altarpiece (ca. 1702). Gold lettering on black background, probably renewed in 1882 restoration. (Photograph, Dell Upton.)

fixed annual salary of sixteen thousand pounds of tobacco in the more valuable sweet-scented variety. Parishes with good ministers strove to keep them. Christ Church Parish, Middlesex County, raised Bartholomew Yates's salary by four thousand pounds of tobacco in 1720, "In consideration of the Extraordinary Satisfaction he has given to this parish for Seventeene yeares," and to prevent his responding to the "greater Encouragement" that York Hampton parish had offered him. When Yates died, the post was reserved for his son. Proposals were occasionally put forth for attracting good ministers to the colony, and some parishes undertook such projects individually. The *Virginia Gazette* reported in 1771 that extensive renovations were to be made on the glebe farm of Martin's Brandon Parish. "The gentlemen of [the parish] flatter themselves some clergyman of Learning and Distinction will be induced to offer himself" to the parish as a result. Whatever the motives, clergymen were customarily treated as gentlemen, and were accorded sufficient regard that at least two men, one pretending to be the son of a deceased minister and the other the son of the duke of Wirtemberg, posed as clergymen in the late 1750s, gaining access to pulpits and living off the country.[29]

Yet there was ambivalence: clergymen were gentlemen, but of a subordinate sort. A minister who spoke too boldly from the pulpit, despite the shortage of clergy, would soon find himself unemployed. No gentleman would tolerate being insulted in another's house. When the minister of Lunenburg Parish, Isaac William Giberne, was offended at Landon Carter's Sabine Hall, he left, and stayed away for some time. When Carter felt insulted in church, he did the same, and made an explicit connection between the two incidents. The clergyman was in fact a gentleman's gentleman; he was condescended to for the sake of his master. When Carter came into church he bowed to the desk, giving the minister his due as chief servant of the spiritual master of the house.[30]

Travelers in Virginia reported that especially hospitable gentlemen left orders with their stewards that while they were away all comers be entertained as if they were at home. Gentlemen expected no less from the clergy. They thought of a favor to the clergyman as one to the Church, and expected it to be returned by institutional rather than personal gratuities. Again, Landon Carter's conduct illustrates the application of the principle in a particularly vehement, almost fanatical manner. In the early 1750s, he drove the Reverend William Kay from the parish. Kay complained to the bishop of London that Carter "wanted to extort more mean, low, and humble obedience, than I thought consistent with the office of a Clergyman. . . he publicly declared that I preached against him . . . because

I preached against pride." Kay's supporter John Camm reported to the bishop that in the trial in a suit for criminal trespass that Kay brought after being turned out of his glebe, Carter had been the opposing lawyer, accusing Kay of ingratitude. Less than a decade later, Carter attacked another minister, Jacob Townsend, in the press, leading the man to bring suit against Carter for defamation and scandal. Carter's neighbor John Tayloe noted condescendingly that an attorney named Pendleton had taken the case "out of pure compassion as the poor man could get nobody else to do it having applyd to all the Lawyers," Carter's peers. At about the time of Carter's conflict with Townsend, Isaac William Giberne came to Lunenburg Parish. Carter housed him at Sabine Hall for a time. It was an act that haunted Giberne until Carter's death, for the planter's understanding of the reciprocal character of hospitality did not allow him to recognize any claims by the Church or its representative that transcended personal obligation. In 1770 Carter asked Giberne to baptize a Carter grandchild at Sabine Hall, as was the custom of the Virginia gentry. Giberne declined. He had done it before, but was being criticized for it, since strictly speaking home baptisms were against the rules of the Church. Carter was enraged; he attributed Giberne's actions to laziness and personal ingratitude, since "he lies under some obligation for the long time he lived here at free cost." Similarly, as a mere servant of the Church, and not its true master, Giberne should grant the requests of the parishioners who were his master's guests. The minister again infuriated Carter by questioning the need to pray for rain on one occasion. He finally did so, "but introduced it as a particular desire" of one person, rather than accepting Carter as a spokesman for the entire parish, and praying on behalf of the parish. Constantly frustrated in his dealings with Kay, Townsend, and Giberne, Carter thought of his experience in church as an encounter between two masters hindered by the capriciousness of servants, who needed to be restored to a proper subordination to the planter-guests. He observed of Giberne that "Some few have horsewhipped him, and with them he

had [has] grown the most friendly. But I have nobody to do me that favour." [31]

The rubric of hospitality governed gentry interaction in the church. The entire visit was a convivial one, beginning with a churchyard gathering for the purpose of exchanging news and invitations, and continuing, after church, with chat in the pews, followed by dinner at the houses of local planters. William Byrd II regularly invited guests, including the minister, back to Westover for Sunday dinner. The service itself might be an occasion to welcome a newly married couple into parish society. When William Nelson, Jr., Esq., and his new wife first appeared in Stratton Major Parish church on November 25, 1770, they provided the minister, William Dunlap, with the opportunity to celebrate the joys of love, marriage, and family life in a sermon that was delivered "in a new and striking Manner." Gentry might extend hospitality to one another publicly by inviting visitors to sit in their pews, or they might withdraw it equally publicly. Landon Carter would not remain in church when another, objectionable "guest"—his despised son-in-law—was present, because he was not on his own ground and could not deal with the man on his own terms. [32]

The concepts of genteel and Christian hospitality permeated the parish church. They allowed the gentry to see themselves as both masters and guests, their actions as both masterly prerogative and humble service, and the clergy as both hosts and servants. The metaphor of hospitality gave meaning to the Christian world view espoused in church, and it sanctified the secular world of the gentry. It provided a model within which the expectations of parishioners were shaped, and by which they judged gentry activities. The parish church was an indispensable part of this social ritual. In its appearance, it announced that the terms of the transaction were the gentry's. The concreteness of the building made it seem natural and inevitable that this should be so—of course the church should be built in the gentry mode; what else would be proper for the leading gentleman of the universe?

| 8 | Hearers |

The exercise of power through hospitality was particularly evident in the seating of parishioners. The Anglican parish church was fitted with seats so that people's minds might be on the ritual, not their comfort. In that respect, seats, along with the altarpiece and pulpit, can be thought of as part of the presentation of Anglican doctrine. Until late in the Middle Ages ordinary parishioners stood or knelt during the recitation of mass. Some medieval churches had stone ledges built into their perimeter walls at the bases of their piers for the infirm. It was apparently not until the end of the thirteenth century that backless wooden benches began to be installed for seating the majority of the congregation. An increased emphasis on sermons in the late Middle Ages encouraged the growing popularity of benches, but fixed seating became common in most English parish churches only in the second half of the fifteenth century, just before the Reformation (Fig. 209).[1]

All that was really needed to seat the worshipper was a bench. Well into the seventeenth century, many churches were entirely fitted with low, open seats or settles. John Smith's audience would have recognized these in his description of the 1607 awning-church at Jamestown with its "seats unhewed trees till we cut plankes." However, more elaborate accommodations made their appearance in English churches soon after the Reformation, by the conversion to seats of obsolete chantry chapels, small, wooden-screened enclosures, standing in the nave, that originally housed the altars at which specially designated priests offered perpetual masses for the souls of those who had endowed them. With the abolition of chantries during the Reformation, many families retained possession of their ancestral "parcloses," but removed their liturgical fittings and replaced them with seats. The parcloses remind us that *pew* referred to the enclosure of church space, although we use the word now to mean church seating. Within a pew, benches might be affixed to the side walls, or chairs, tables,

FIG. 209. St. Mary's church, Badley, Suffolk, England. Fifteenth-century bench ends. Characteristically attached to a continuous sill, the benches were originally backless, but have been altered. The pulpit and reading desk date from the 17th century. (Photograph, Dell Upton.)

and other loose furniture could be used.[2]

Eighteenth-century Virginians retained this distinction between pews and what they called the seats: pews represented the conversion of a part of the public space to private use. As we will see, the point is an important one, for if seats were provided to promote attention to the ritual, they attained a social significance entirely apart from their utilitarian intention. In the last third of the seventeenth century, a range of seating arrangements was available to Virginia church builders. In 1684, the vestry of Christ Church Parish, Middlesex County, ordered "that there be Benches and Forms provided for all Thre Churches, for Convenience of Seating the people." Forms were simple backless benches, planks supported on wooden pedestals or on legs inserted into the seat. Those installed at St. Peter's Parish church in 1735 were to be "made of saw'd white Oak Plank 2 Inches thick, with good mawld Blocks to support

them, pinnd. down . . . the Benches to be 11 Inches wide." *Form* and *bench* were interchangeable, but the Christ Church Parish vestry intended to distinguish forms from benches with back supports, like the "Benches & back to Each" built in an Augusta Parish chapel in 1774. Benches might be joined—made of stiles, rails, and panels like those that survive in the gallery of Christ church, Lancaster County—but more often they were assembled from planks, not unlike the earliest medieval parish church benches. The benches surviving in the gallery at the former Tillotson Parish church, now Buckingham Baptist church, have simple shaped ends, with two-inch-thick plank seats and ends, inch-plank backs, and stretchers, all joined with wrought nails (Figs. 210, 211). Benches and forms constituted the plainest kind of seating found in Virginia parish churches throughout the colonial period.[3]

More elaborate than open benches and forms were

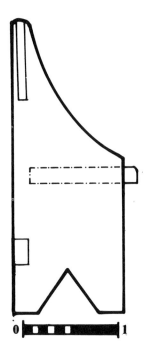

FIG. 210. Tillotson Parish (Buckingham Baptist) church (third quarter 18th century), Buckingham County. Gallery bench (18th century). (Drawing, Dell Upton.)

FIG. 211. Tillotson Parish church benches. Those at the left have been shortened. (Photograph, Dell Upton.)

enclosed, or "close," pews. Like the former chantry parcloses of English churches, close pews were walled-in areas with doors. English parishioners sometimes built extremely high-walled pews, occasionally even with roofs. A seventeenth-century bishop of Norwich was offended by the popularity of "State pews . . . now become tabernacles with rugs and curtains to them. . . . I will not guess what is done within them . . . , but this I dare say they are either to hide some vice, or to proclaim one; to hide disorder or to proclaim pride." Virginia's close pews were rarely so high, although the three early eighteenth-century churches of Christ Church Parish, Middlesex County, were fitted with four-and-one-half-foot-high pews and with "high" pews an unspecified degree more lofty. Most surviving Virginia pews range in height from three to three and one-half feet.[4]

Virginians recognized three classes of pews based on capacity and plan. Single pews had a seat along one side with a walkway in front of it, and were normally oriented so that the occupants faced the pulpit. The 1714 specifications for the lower chapel in Christ Church Parish, Middlesex County, called for single pews three and one-half feet wide, but most surviving examples are two and one-half to three feet wide. Double pews had facing benches along both long sides, with a walkway in the middle and usually a short bench across the inner end. The double pews at the lower chapel in Middlesex County were seven feet wide, but most were five feet wide like those at the upper chapel in the same county or the five-by-nine-foot double pews installed in the addition to the lower church of Suffolk Parish in 1759. Largest of all were the great pews, which were usually large square enclosures seven to ten feet on a side, with benches on three or four sides. Few Virginia pews were built with any fittings other than benches, though the St. Paul's Parish vestry had Harry Gaines add book ledges and kneeling boards to the pews in its church in 1745.[5]

The kinds of seating found in Virginia parish churches varied from building to building. Most churches contained pews, but not all churches were filled with them. Christ church, Lancaster County, and Aquia church, the two churches that survive with most of their original interiors intact, are pewed throughout, and they are misleading in being so (see Figs. 90, 97). Although the height of the pews at Aquia church has been reduced by at least one third—a common nineteenth-century evangelicals' alteration—the church is filled with double pews, except at the east arm, which has been completely altered, and at the crossing. There two corners are occupied by great pews, a third by the pulpit, and the fourth by a pair of double pews that have been opened up by removing part of the wall between them, a modification often made in the eighteenth-century. The church wardens of Christ Church Parish, Middlesex County, were ordered in 1762 "to make all the single Pews in the lower part of the Middle Church into double ones."[6]

In many churches, only a few pews were built. Two chapels were constructed in St. Andrew's Parish in 1735 with "two Close Pughs in Each." Lynnhaven Parish's Pungo chapel of 1740 had two large wainscot pews on the north side of the church and one on the south side. Only three pews were built in a chapel erected by Henrico Parish in 1742, and Antrim Parish's 1753 church on Wynn's Creek was to have just four pews on each side. In these churches, the remainder of the space on each side of the paved "alleys" or aisles was usually equipped with benches or forms. The Sapponey and Nemussens chapels of Bristol Parish, ordered in 1721, were to have "common plain work" on the inside, "the seats to be single benches, Except the two upper pews & them to be double & close with dores."[7]

The differences in seating had several implications. First, as the Bristol Parish order suggests, economy was a consideration. Pews cost more than benches. Second, the choice reflected the degree of importance intended for the church itself. In 1753 the St. Mark's Parish vestry altered the specifications for a chapel, changing the ceiling cladding from split clapboards to more carefully finished sawn plank, "and instead of plain [plank-walled] pews it is ordered [that the undertaker] make wainscot [paneled] Pews in the best manner and that the same be Called when Erected a Church." The architectural improvement accompanied an upgrading of the building's official status.[8]

If elaboration of seating indicated the dignity of a building, it also signified the status of an individual within the church's congregation. Although the entire original building at Christ church, Lancaster County, was furnished with pews from the first, they are subtly differentiated (Fig. 212; see Fig. 90). All are enclosed with paneling; they are "framed," or "wainscot," pews in the language of the vestry books. But the panels on the two great pews in the east arm have raised panels ("quarter Round & rais'd pannel") inside and out, while the double and single pews have raised panels only on the outside and recessed panels ("¼ round pannel'd work") on the inside. In the gallery are straight-

FIG. 212. Christ church (ca. 1732–35), Lancaster County. Interior from south gallery. The pulpit is at the left, and the chancel at the right. (Photograph, Dell Upton.)

backed benches with quarter-round paneled work on their backs (Fig. 213). Thus there are three qualities of seating in the church—the great pews, the other single and double pews on the ground floor, and the added benches in the gallery. The differentiation extends even to the depths of the benches, which are fourteen, thirteen, and eleven inches wide, respectively.[9]

Corresponding distinctions were made in other parishes. In the three early eighteenth-century churches built by Christ Church Parish, Middlesex County, for example, the church was pewed throughout, but four or five were "high" pews located between the pulpit and the chancel, and were larger and higher backed than the rest. Similarly, at the Lynnhaven Parish church of 1691, there was to be "a Row of Pews on Each Side thirty foot" stretching from the west door, then a wainscot pew on each side between there and the chancel, which lay against the east wall between as many "Benches [as are] necessary."[10]

The differentiation of pews in the Virginia church reminds us that if the church was planned and arranged inside to facilitate the practice of a specific ritual, it was also the *parish* church. It served a specific local population, and it embodied not only empire-wide political and theological tenets, but the peculiarities of local society. The nineteenth-century notion that all are one before God inside the parish church, a neutral space designed to accommodate those who come to participate in the worship of a transcendent deity, would have puzzled most eighteenth-century Virginians. In fact, the parish church was a place where social hierarchy was elucidated and affirmed by the assignment to individual parishioners of seats distinguished by size, comfort, and visual elaboration. Pew allocations by the church wardens constituted the parish's official assessment

FIG. 213. Christ church gallery benches (18th century). (Photograph, Dell Upton.)

of the relative standing of its members. The parishioners "replied" by altering their pews, changing seats, or staying home. Although no Virginians that we know of went to the extreme of roofing their pews, as some English did, Virginia vestries did find it necessary to warn pewholders against overelaboration of their pews. St. George's Parish, Spotsylvania County, told Roger Dixon, Gent., "not to Raise the Pew higher than it now stands," a common admonition, while Truro Parish gave George William Fairfax and other occupants of a block of pews at the center of Pohick church permission to raise the floors of their pews to a height above the aisles equal to, but no higher than, those against the walls. At Christ church, Lancaster County, the great pew in the northeast corner of the crossing, traditionally identified as the Carter pew, was reported by a nineteenth-century writer to have had an iron curtain rail that extended its height. No physical evidence of the rail survives, but it is evident that the pew was once entirely upholstered. The tops of the pew walls, where they have not been replaced, and the edges of the partition at the door jambs are scarred by a continuous line of upholstery tack-holes that probably date from the eighteenth century. In Virginia churches, however, the principal indication of social status was the pew's location in the church.[11]

The importance of location was a legacy from English parish churches, where the dominant local family often owned a pew in the chancel itself or one perched atop the chancel screen in the old rood loft, and where social distinctions were observed in the seating of other parishioners as well. Personal social standing and official titles might be taken into account in assigning family pews, seats in clerical or justices' pews, in the corporation pew of a town, or in no pew at all. Similar care was taken in "dignifying" the congregational meeting houses of New England. The allocation of seating was given great thought, even if few towns could boast such a precise system as that of seventeenth-century Beverly, Massachusetts, which used a point system based on age, militia rank, tax burden, and the length of one's family's residence in town.[12]

No single element of the seating of parishioners in Virginia was unique to the colony then. What is of interest is the specific pattern of practices. In eighteenth-century Virginia, the honorific implications of seat assignments were taken as seriously as anywhere else, but the methods of determining precedence were hazy. Rarely was a single individual obviously dominant. Exceptions were Robert

"King" Carter, who could demand a hereditary family pew in the chancel of Christ church, Lancaster County, in return for his contributions to building the church, and Alexander Spotswood, to whom the vestry of St. Mark's Parish sent its church wardens in 1733 to offer him "the prefarance of Chooseing a place in the New Church for a Seate for himself and his family." [13]

Precedence was not easily established in ordinary circumstances. The assignment of seats to the congregation was the responsibility of the vestry, who sometimes delegated it to the church wardens in emulation of English practice. The wardens were instructed "to place the People in Each of the Churches as they think proper." When Falls church was accepted by Fairfax Parish in 1769, the undertaker, James Wren, and the minister, Townshend Dade, as church wardens, were directed to "allott the seats for the parishioners according to dignity." More explicitly, the church wardens of Truro Parish were directed in 1737 to "place the people, that are not already placed, in Pohick and the new Churches, in pews, according to the several ranks and degrees." [14]

Certain principles of seat assignment were taken for granted. Bruton Parish, for example, provided pews for the governor and the royal council in its 1715 church, in part because the legislature had helped to finance the building, but similar accommodations had been made in its earlier church. The parish pointedly ordered "that the Parishioners be seated in the Church, and none others." No pews would be granted to members of the legislature who were not parishioners, and hence not parish taxpayers. In outlying areas, the dignitaries of parish and county were assumed to be entitled to privileged seating. The Henrico Parish vestry ordered that "the Ch[urch] w[ar]dens have proper Seats where Wanting at the churches in this Parish." Others seated according to their official positions were county justices and sometimes vestrymen. Newport Parish vestry set aside the corner pew in the chancel of the parish church for justices' and vestrymen's wives. St. Paul's Parish, Hanover County, gave gallery pews for the justices, vestrymen, and their families, "and The two upper Pews in the Body of the Church for Such of the Above mention'd Family's as cannot have room in the Gallery." Truro Parish set aside one pew "for the Use of the Magistrates and Strangers," and one opposite for the wives of these men, with another pair of pews for the vestrymen and merchants and their wives. Eight other pews were assigned to "the use of the most

respectable Inhabitants and House Keepers of the Parish" in general, and another for the minister's family. [15]

The community could be sorted not only by class and occupation, but by gender and age. Many churches separated men and women. The custom was widely believed to have been practiced among ancient Jews, and therefore among primitive Christians, and it was used by Quaker and Calvinist congregations for that reason. Although Richard Hooker considered it an outmoded Jewish practice that no longer bound Anglicans, the Royal Injunctions of 1547 required that the sexes be segregated at communion, and many Anglican churches extended sex segregation to ordinary seating as well. In Virginia churches, men and women sat in corresponding pews on opposite sides of the aisle. In Bruton Parish and Pohick churches, the men sat on the north and the women on the south. Men and women were also separated in Newport, St. Peter's, Frederick, Stratton Major, and St. George's (Spotsylvania County) parishes. Not all parishes observed the tradition. A surviving list of pew assignments, made for the churches of St. George's Parish, Accomack County, in 1767, mixes men and women in the pew assignments. The vestry of Stratton Major Parish ordered in 1734 "that Mr. John Smith & his wife Sit with his mother," and a year later that Smith and his wife be moved and a Mr. Talliaferro and his wife sit in the right-hand pew by the communion table. The vestry's successors segregated men from women in their new 1768 church. [16]

Vestries also considered age in assigning seats. Newport Parish set aside a pew for young women in 1746. More common was to allocate space to boys in town churches like those of Williamsburg and Norfolk, where there were sizable schools. At Bruton Parish church, Williamsburg, one gallery was reserved for parish boys and another for students of the College of William and Mary, who were allowed to have a lock installed on it to keep out others. There was a "School Boys Gallery" at Elizabeth River Parish church in Norfolk, and the Bristol Parish vestry in 1785 asked its church wardens to rent pews "Reserving two for the use of the Studien's, and four for the use of the poor." [17]

In most pewed churches provision was made for "the public"—"strangers" and unpewed parishioners, including high-status people who had recently come into the parish, and who were often moved to private pews when openings were available. These blocs of public seats might be set in any number of out-of-the-way places. The 1707 plan for the upper church of Christ Church Parish, Middlesex County, had single pews, probably intended for the public, placed under the side-aisle roofs, with private double pews presumably occupying the center of the church. A pair of single pews by the north door of Christ church, Lancaster County, may originally have been for the public. They were supplemented by the benches in the gallery when the latter was built, probably in the third quarter of the eighteenth century. The "Bench or seat Adjoyning the pew next the Front door" of a 1755 church in St. George's Parish, Spotsylvania County, was probably for the public. The same parish in 1770 moved Benjamin Grymes's family to new pews and had his former pews converted to public use as part of a reordering of seats occasioned by the construction of an addition to the Fredericksburg church. Galleries seem to have been favorite places for open seating. At Tillotson Parish church, benches on risers survive, while the gallery supports and wainscoting on the first floor show evidence of removed pew partitions (see Fig. 211). Risers in other churches imply the presence in their galleries of now-vanished benches as well, although this is not always the case. In Fork church, Hanover County, there are risers, even though the gallery rail is scarred by notches that indicate pew partitions were installed originally or that a public gallery had been converted to private use. In the north and south galleries of Abingdon church, the only places where the original seating survives in that building, a pair of private pews occupies the front of each gallery. The pairs of pews are separated by a narrow alley with short benches that probably accommodated slaves of the pewholders (Fig. 214). Across the back of each gallery is a bench that may have been public seating.[18]

The seats most desired by the elite varied from parish to parish and over time. In medieval and postmedieval England the chancel, which was originally reserved for seating and burying clergy, was gradually invaded by the local gentry. The chancel retained its honorific connotation into the early eighteenth century in Virginia. In his 1726 will, Robert "King" Carter claimed for his family a pew in the chancel of Christ church, Lancaster County, and demanded as well that "the Chancel be preserved as a burial place for my family as the present chancel is," in accord with the traditional practice. Other churches less closely tied to a single individual also located the largest and most prominent pews in the chancel or between the chancel and the pulpit. The high pews in the three early

eighteenth-century churches of Christ Church Parish, Middlesex County, were positioned that way. Sometimes the chancel pews served as communicants' pews, seats to which those intending to take communion moved at the call to the altar, and where they remained for the rest of the service. Communicants' pews were common in English churches, but the term is not found in the surviving Virginia records. On the other hand, there is evidence of the assignment of chancel pews to individuals. In the seventeenth century, Colonel John Page was allowed "the privilege to sett a pew for himself and his Family in the Chancell of the new Church" of Bruton Parish, and the joiner Richard Perrott built a pew in the chancel of the upper chapel of Christ Church Parish, Middlesex County, for Henry Corbin, Esq. In the eighteenth century, Richard Booker, Gent., the undertaker of the Flat Creek chapel of Bristol Parish, received permission to build a pew "for his familys conveniency at his own charge on one Side of the communion Table." When space in the chancel ran out, new pews were often built in the passage to the chancel door to accommodate local grandees.[19]

Other elite parishioners were given private pews in galleries. Robert Bolling, William Stark, Theodorick Bland, and Stephen Dewey, vestrymen of Bristol Parish, shared a pew in the gallery of the new Blandford church in 1742. Bland agreed to build three pews in the gallery of the

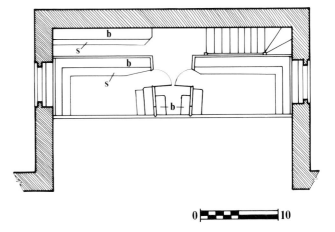

FIG. 214. Abingdon church (ca. 1751–55), Gloucester County. North gallery. Key: b = bench; s = step. (Drawing, Dell Upton.)

addition to the same church in 1751 in order to have one for his own use. Still others were granted the right to build pews for themselves at odd places within the church. The builder Lewis Deloney was allowed to build one "in a vacant place in the Church near his house" in Cumberland Parish in 1746.[20]

It is clear from the varied locations of private pews that the significance of one's place in the church was purely conventional and varied from parish to parish. Although some locations were traditionally preferred, almost any place would do so long as the honor was understood and the pew was private. This was particularly true when the prestige of the chancel faded in the eighteenth century. The Abingdon Parish church gallery pews were juxtaposed to benches for the public. St. George's Parish, Accomack County, assigned its pews to groups of parishioners by lot. The groups had first been formed according to social standing and family ties. The resulting pew assignments were recorded in random order, perhaps in the sequence that the lots were drawn. A reconstruction of the church's plan shows that the vestrymen's and minister's personal seats were scattered throughout the church, rather than concentrated in one part of it, although the vestry retained for themselves as a body the four pews at the east end, and the public was left unassigned pews at the west end (Fig. 215).[21]

If the location of prestigious seating varied, parishioners knew which were the preferred spots in their own churches. William Byrd II gloated in a diary entry of December 18,

1710, that "About 1 o'clock I went to the vestry, who gave me the best pew in church."[22]

The honorific connotations of seating were keenly felt and carefully guarded in Virginia's churches. The form of seating itself made a difference. The Presbyterian planter James Gordon was disappointed in his coreligionists during the construction of a new meeting house in Lancaster County in 1763. He had hoped that the social posturing of Anglican parishioners would be absent there, but he "agreed with Mr. Atkins to have more double seats & less single ones. I understand people are displeased with the single seats, which we thought would be more convenient for the people, as they faced the minister. But as it seems disagreeable to some, especially Mrs. Miller & some other women, & as it is cheaper to have them double, thought it proper to order more to be made. But I have great reason to fear that there is much more pride than piety among us." Gordon does not say why double pews were preferred to single ones, but it is probably because they allowed relatives to assemble en masse in one pew, rather than being distributed throughout the church, and thus raised the possibility of having a traditional "family pew." Although seating by the vestry was by social rank, it was customary in many parishes to divide family members among several pews. Elite parishioners sought to gather their entire families into one pew. George Washington was outraged when a change in the financing of Fairfax Parish's new Alexandria church thwarted his intention to "lay the

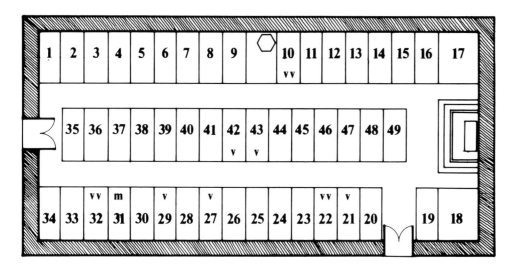

Fig. 215. St. George's Parish church (1763–68; Severn Guttridge, undertaker), Accomack County. Reconstructed plan. Each v represents a vestryman assigned to the pew; m is the minister's pew. (Drawing, Dell Upton.)

foundation of a Family Pew. . . . what matters it," he argued, "whether [a parishioner] assembles his whole Family into one Pew, or, as the Custom is have them dispers'd into two or three?"[23]

It clearly mattered to him and to many of his neighbors, and gentry were willing to pay for the privilege if necessary. Simon Thomas reported to the Northampton County court that when he raised the frame of the new Hungar's Parish church in 1681, John Custis, Jr., offered Thomas a hogshead of tobacco to build him the first pew. Thomas bargained for livestock instead, and Custis gave him his choice of animals. On parting, Custis praised the building's site and workmanship and gave the carpenter a gift of thirty or forty gallons of cider. In the eighteenth century, Custis would have approached the vestry for a private pew. Pew rents were established in some English parishes as early as seating itself, but in Virginia seats were legally free of charge. Nevertheless, Virginians routinely struck bargains with their vestries to obtain choice seats. Captain John Armistead offered to give Blisland Parish the land on which its church already stood "incase the Vestry Wold: Grant him an Order. for a Pew in the: Brick Church of this parish for himself and: his familyes use." Thomas Preeson gave the land on which the 1742 Hungar's Parish church already stood in return for a pew, which was marked "T.P. 1751." William Stith and his relative Buckner Stith, a former vestryman of St. Andrew's Parish, paid £10 each for their pews. In the Upper Parish of Nansemond County, vestryman Lemuel Riddick paid £20 for permission to build a private gallery; while David Mead, Gent., also a vestryman, offered to provide a bell for the parish in exchange for the same privilege. Their actions are characteristic: in keeping with the ethos of hospitality, the privileges were not literally sold, but were traded for a service to the parish.[24]

Having built, or been given, personal pews and galleries, parishioners regarded them as their private possessions, symbols of their independent existence, and vestries usually acknowledged the property right. Two groups of four men in Elizabeth River Parish each obtained permission to build a gallery in the parish church, which the vestry granted "equally betwixt them & their Heirs forever to have & to hold," a standard legal formulation. Augustine Claiborne was given a pew in the 1769 addition to the Nottoway church of Albemarle Parish, for which he was to pay "What Ever Sum Mr. Willie [the minister] Shall Ad Judge the building the Said Pew is worth . . . & the Said Claiborne

is to have an Absulote [*sic*] Right to the Sd Pew to him & his heirs he & they keeping the same in Repair for Ever." Treating the pew as personal property was far more common than treating it as part of the property of one's family estate, as in England, but there were instances of the latter. The pew Richard Perrott built for Henry Corbin, Esq., in Christ Church Parish, Middlesex County, belonged to him "and to those that Shall have Enjoy the house and Land Whereon he now Liveth, on and for ever." An advertiser in the *Virginia Gazette* in 1751 offered for sale a house and land "and a family pew in the Church, belonging to the House in the City of Williamsburg." Wilson Cary bequeathed his house and lot in Elizabeth City Parish as an entity with his pew in the parish church, "willing the said Pew may go and pass forever with the said Messuage, as the same shall descend."[25]

Despite the phrasing of the grants, the right was not really absolute. It depended on the owner's continuing as a member of the community. Parishioners in St. Mary's White Chapel Parish were granted the right to build and own galleries "So Long as theay Shall be Inhabitants of this Parish or most frequently Come to the Said Church." When Alexander McKenzie left the country, the gallery he had built in the north wing of the Elizabeth City Parish church was taken over by the vestry, who decided he had relinquished his title to it.[26]

The Anglican vestry books rarely acknowledged these kinds of aspirations. They were positivistic documents, recording only the results of vestry decisions to act. They blandly registered the granting of "liberty" to build pews and galleries, without mentioning those parishioners who had been denied the privilege, or, of course, those who hadn't had the nerve to ask in the first place. Neither did they consider, except by implication, and largely misleadingly, the larger context in which the seating of the gentry took place. Who attended church? For whom was this display of position intended? To put it another way, who accepted the hospitality of the church and its attendant social order? Colonial accounts report widespread, if theologically uninformed, support for the Church, and evidences of a kind of cultural Anglicanism turn up. At Nomini Hall, for instance, a festive dinner party was marked by the appointment of Philip Lee as pope, and several other diners as

TABLE 6: *Population and Church Attendance, 1724*

Parish	Tithables	Families	Adults	Attendance
Abingdon	. . . .	300	600	200
Accomack	. . . .	400+	800+	. . . .
Blisland	. . . .	136	272	. . . .
Bristol	. . . .	430	860	. . . .
Bruton	. . . .	110	220	. . . .
Christ Church, Lancaster	. . . .	300	600	. . . .
Christ Church, Middlesex	. . . .	260	520	200
Elizabeth City	. . . .	350	700	. . . .
Henrico	1,100	400	800	100–200
Hungar's	. . . .	365+	730+	. . . .
James City	. . . .	78	156	430 T
Lawne's Creek	700	. . . .	642±	. . . .
Newport	. . . .	400	800	500
Overwharton	. . . .	650	1,300	. . . .
Petsworth	. . . .	146	292	300
St. Ann's	. . . .	130	260	100–180
St. Mary's, Essex	. . . .	150	300	150
St. Paul's, Hanover	. . . .	1,200	2,400	200–300
St. Peter's	. . . .	204	408	170–180
St. Stephen's	. . . .	300	600	. . . .
South Farnham	. . . .	200	400	. . . .
Southwark	. . . .	394	788	300
Stratton Major	. . . .	190	380	300
Upper, Isle of Wight	700	. . . .	642	. . . .
Washington	. . . .	200	400	. . . .
Westminster	. . . .	100	200	160
Westover	. . . .	233	466	⅔
Wilmington	. . . .	180	360	. . . .
York Hampton	. . . .	200	400	⅔

Key: T = attendance at all churches in the parish.
Source: Perry 1: 261–318.

friars, "in the play call'd 'break the Popes neck.'" But this general assent has no necessary connection with church-going.[27]

The question of attendance needs to be raised. Church attendance varied from place to place in Virginia. Although presentments for nonattendance were rare, and were often applied selectively, threats were sometimes necessary. Bruton Parish's vestry noted in 1682 that attendance was poor, "tending to the dishonor of God and the contempt of Government," and ordered a warning to be read by the clerks of both parish churches.[28]

Two principal sources of evidence exist for church attendance in the eighteenth century. The first source is the questionnaire sent by the bishop of London in 1724 to the Anglican ministers of the colonies and the twenty-nine Virginia replies that survive. The ministers were asked a variety of questions about the size and population of their parishes, and about attendance and number of communicants. From the responses, it is possible to calculate the expected and reported attendance from many of the parishes (Tabs. 6, 7). It is evident that church attendance varied widely, from about one-eighth to more than one hundred percent of resident adult whites in populous and prosperous Petsworth Parish, and in James City Parish.

TABLE 7: *Expected and Actual Attendance, 1724*

Parish	Expected Attendance (%)	Actual Attendance per Church (+) or Total for all Churches (*)	Churches in Parish
Abingdon	100	33.3*	1
Accomack	65.1	all within 10 miles	3
Blisland	100	the greatest part	2
Bristol	100	pretty strong; more than pews for	2
Bruton	100	a full congregation	1
Christ, Lancaster	50	almost all white persons	1
Christ, Middlesex	100	38.5+	3
Elizabeth City	100	most	1
Henrico	100	12.5+	2
Hungars	50	<33.3*	1
James City	100	64.1+ to 128.1+	3
Lawne's Creek	33	always full	2
Newport	58.9	62.5+	3
Overwharton	68.1	as full as churches can hold; as well as can be expected in thin-seated place	2
Petsworth	90.8	102.7*	1
St. Ann's	100	38.4+	2
St. Mary's, Essex	100	50	?
St. Paul's, Hanover	100	≥8.3+ generally full	4
St. Peter's	100	41.7*	1
St. Stephen's	100	a good congregation	?
South Farnham	100	most	2
Southwark	46.6	38.1+ very large congregation	3
Stratton Major	100	75–79+	2
Upper, Isle of Wight	49.9	small proportion	2
Washington	100	so great a number as to fill 2 60 × 24-foot churches with galleries	2
Westminster	66.7	80	?
Westover	100	67*	3
Wilmington	100	well frequented	3
York Hampton	100	67*	2

Source: Perry 1: 261–318.

Most of the parishes with fifty percent or less attendance were on the fringes of the reporting area. It should be stressed that these figures were for attendance on a single Sunday. The size of Virginia parishes discouraged most Virginians from attending any but the church nearest their houses, and then only on Sundays when the minister was present. Thus St. Paul's Parish had four churches, and its attendance figures should presumably be quadrupled. Petsworth's strong showing on the other hand can be attributed to its being a small parish with only one church, situated in the most populous county in Virginia.[29]

The second source is the Reverend William Willie's lengthy record of attendance or communicants kept in the third quarter of the century in far-flung Albemarle Parish. Willie's numbers ranged from 96 to 297 total for all three of his churches in the early years of the record, around 1750. In 1775, the corresponding figures ranged from 200 to 417. Whether the figures record attendance or communicants is unfortunately not clear. In 1751, there were 2,100 tithables in the parish, or roughly 2,056 white adults. If the figures are for attendance, they represent an attendance rate of 4.7 to 14.4 percent of all white adults in the parish, considerably lower than the attendance rate recorded by Anglican clergy in 1724 (see Tab. 7). Attendance might have been higher had the parish been more compact, or had there been more churches available. In 1750, the vestry denied a petition from the lower part of the parish for another church, "being of Opinion that as there are already four Churches in this Parish they are Sufficient." In 1775, the number of tithables had grown to 2,800 and the white adult population of the parish to about 2,741. Attendance thus ran between 7.3 and 15.2 percent of the white adult population. If Willie's figures record communicants, then the percentages should be increased considerably. The clergy in 1724 reported that on the average attenders outnumbered communicants 4.4 to 1. Willie's earlier attendance should then be adjusted to 20.7 to 63.7 percent, and his later ones to 32.1 to 66.9 percent, numbers more in line with those reported earlier in the century. Willie's parish was a large and widely scattered one, and despite the growth of dissenting churches in southern Virginia in the third quarter of the eighteenth century his parishioners' attendance seems to have improved somewhat later in his career.[30]

On the whole, clergymen were satisfied with attendance. Most of them in 1724 reported full churches—that is, attendance that met or exceeded the vestry's expectations when the buildings were planned. Thomas Baylye of Newport Parish claimed 500 people "constantly attending" his services, while John Bell of Christ Church Parish, Lancaster County, wrote that "almost all white persons in the parish (not necessarily hindered) attend divine Service." William Black of Accomack also claimed that "our churches cannot contain all that come to hear." In Washington Parish, Lawrence DeButts was unable to judge the proportion of his parishioners who attended, "but I have known so great a number of them together that there was not convenient room for them all in the Church, each of my Churches is in length 20 yards, in breadth 8, and has a gallery." Those who ventured to offer numbers estimated attendance at 100 to 300 every Sunday. Emmanuel Jones of Petsworth Parish recorded an attendance of 300 in a parish of 146 families.[31]

Vestries corroborated these estimates in the most concrete ways possible—by enlarging parish churches to accommodate the numbers of parishioners who wanted to attend. New churches, church additions, and the construction of galleries in existing churches were costly projects that needed good reason to be undertaken. Often, it was explicitly recorded, "the Church is much Crowded and . . . their is so large a Congregation Commonly attending the Church that their is not room in the Pews for their reception."[32]

How many people—and whom—did vestries expect to receive? An examination of two surviving pew-assignment rosters from the 1760s offers a basis for some speculation. The first roster recorded seat assignments in the largest parish church ever built in Virginia, the Stratton Major Parish church begun by Harry Gaines in 1760 and completed by his heirs in 1768. In December of that year, the vestry appointed five men to act as a committee to assign pews. Though no plan of the church is given, the pages are laid out in such a way that the plan can easily be reconstructed by comparing the original specifications with the pew roster (Fig. 216). The vestry used one of the new plans of the third quarter of the eighteenth century, which had two east-west aisles that effectively quadrupled the area of the standard rectangular church and resembled two adjacent rectangular churches in its internal arrangement. The pews in the Stratton Major church were numbered in four series, accommodating men and women from the upper and lower precincts in parallel sets of pews along each aisle (Fig. 217). The exact arrangement of the east end of the church is

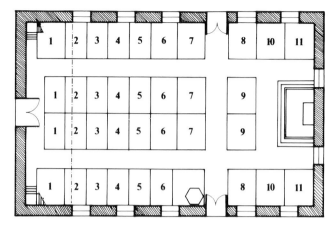

FIG. 216. Stratton Major Parish church (1760–68; Harry Gaines, undertaker), King and Queen County. Reconstructed plan. (Drawing, Dell Upton.)

uncertain, but it is clear that there were eight pews there. The easternmost pew on the north (number 11) was assigned to Richard Corbin, Esq., the donor of the land and a leading gentleman of King and Queen County, and his family. Pew 11 on the south was given to the widow and family of John Robinson, the late Speaker of the House of Burgesses. The scandal that followed Robinson's death had not diminished his family's standing among its neighbors. The pews numbered 10, immediately to the west of these, were reserved for William Meredith and his family (north), and to four leading vestrymen and their families (south). The other four chancel pews were assigned to leading gentry, with the remaining six vestrymen grouped in pew 9 on the south. Like the rest of the pews in the church, but unlike the four pews assigned to parish grandees, these pews were sex segregated, with the men given pews 9 and 9, and their wives 8 and 8. Then intervened the alley connecting the north and south doors. In the remainder of the church, there were four pews of each number. Husbands sat in the interior pews and their wives across the aisle from them against the wall. Pew 7 on the south wall was the pulpit, and pew 6 was the minister's family pew. In this case, the minister was also the commissary of the colony, and only he, Robinson, Corbin, and Meredith were assigned pews to their exclusive use. This church replaced both earlier parish churches, and so had to accommodate everyone who was expected to attend. There were thirty-nine pews on the

floor of the church, and probably five of the same size in the gallery, or forty-four pews. If the vestry had assigned eighteen inches of bench to each person, the pews could have held 16 people, but they never assigned more than 13 people to a pew. Taking 13 as the pew capacity, the building could have held 572 people. In fact, only 250 people—132 men and 118 women—were assigned seats by name. In addition, 8 families were given pews, as well as 5 groups of women identified only by their fathers' names. If we count 5 people per family and 2 women for each group of daughters, the number of people assigned seats in the church was about 300. There were no assignments made for the gallery pews or the four rear pews on the floor of the church, which were certainly the public pews, and could have held 117 people. If these pews were filled, the church's capacity was 487 people. In the year the pews were assigned, there were 973 tithables in the parish, or, according to the formula used above, about 952 white adults in the parish. Just under a third of the parish were assigned seats in the church. Two-thirds of the parish were expected to find seats in the public pews. The building might have held just over one-half of the parish's white adult population in the assigned seats and the gallery, or about sixty percent of them if filled to capacity.[33]

The second, similar roster survives from St. George's

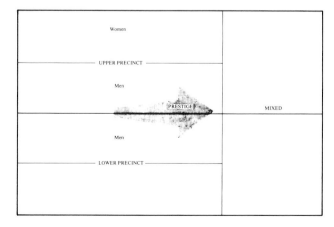

FIG. 217. Stratton Major Parish church. Schematic plan showing allotment of space to parish constituencies. (Drawing, Jocelyn Kwei.)

Parish, Accomack County. It was made just a year before the Stratton Major list, when the parish's new church was received. We have already considered this plan in another context (see Fig. 215). The vestry had ordered "that the Pews in Both Churches be Numbred and the People Divided into Classes," and the groups were matched to the pews by lot. There were forty-seven double pews in the church and two other "Large" or great pews at the east. Altogether, 497 places were assigned in the pews, with 7 to 13 people seated in each pew. Of the 486 different names given pew assignments, only 19 are women's. However, the repetition of names suggests that the places were listed according to the heads of household rather than individuals, as at Stratton Major. In the year that the pew assignment was made, there were 1,948 tithables in St. George's Parish, or, according to our formula, about 1,907 white adults. Pews were assigned to 25.5 percent of the parishioners, or about 48 percent of the males, in the new church. If it was pewed in the customary manner, the parish's other church at Pungoteague probably held about 450 people. Together, the two accounted for slightly over one-half of the parish's white adults.[34]

Although there are great differences between the two churches, there are similarities as well. While the Stratton Major vestry provided for men and women equally, St. George's Parish vestry provided mainly for men, assigning one place in a pew to each household in most instances. Both vestries allotted seats to slightly over one-quarter of the adult population, leaving a relatively small portion of the church unassigned. Stratton Major and St. George's parishes were thus built to accommodate about the proportion of parishioners that our previous estimates indicated were church attenders. This is not to say that no one else could come to the church. It was the practice in England for unpewed attenders to occupy whatever space they could find. Christopher Wren's often-quoted plea that "a church should not be so filled with pews but that the poor may have room enough to stand and sit in the alleys" offers a glimpse of the practice. Less evidence is available for Virginia. Bishop Meade reported that when Henry Skyren preached in King William County, "the Acquinton Church was always so crowded that the people used to bring their seats and fill up the aisle after the pews were full." The right to a seat, unless the pew was owned by a single individual, apparently meant just that. Seat allotments granted the right to a particular place in the church, but not to control of the entire pew. Other people could sit in it if there was room, or if the pew was not occupied by those who had seats in it.[35]

Who attended church? Obviously the hearers included a high proportion of gentry. There is no reason to doubt that the frequent, if restrained, professions of spiritual feeling made by men like Landon and Robert Carter were sincere, yet there were other attractions to church as strong as piety. Philip Fithian and James Reid agreed that the social and commercial attractions of churchgoing made the activity most attractive to gentlemen, who thought it "a matter of convenience, & account[ed] the Church a useful weekly resort to do business." This was in contrast to "All the lower class of People, & the Servants, & the Slaves," for whom Sunday was "a Day of Pleasure & amusement." Alexander MacSparran attributed the social composition of Anglican congregations to the remote locations of the churches. Because the churches required transportation to attend, only gentry in their coaches and middling people on horseback were likely to get there, "so that the Christians here may be, in more Senses than one, called Cavaliers, it being impracticable for the lower Infantry to foot it often to their Parish-Church." The problem of distance was acknowledged by some Virginia clergymen. In his report to the bishop of London in 1724, William Black of Accomack Parish reported that "all within 10 miles that are capable" attended, while Alexander Scott of Overwharton Parish thought that attendance was as full as might be expected in "such a thin seated place."[36]

Naturally, individual gentry varied in their attendance. James Gordon and George Washington were not regular churchgoers. In 1759 and 1760, Gordon attended Anglican parish churches twenty-four times, or about one-quarter of the available Sundays. During the same period, however, he attended thirty Presbyterian meetings, usually held in four- or five-day sequences when a preacher was in the county. By the end of 1760, when Lancaster County's first Presbyterian meeting house was nearing completion, he had stopped going to Anglican churches more than once or twice a year.[37]

Gordon was a dissenter but George Washington was a private scoffer. He wrote to a friend in 1762, merrily scolding him for being at home on a Sunday morning, and reminding him "with what zeal I hye me to Church of every Lords day." In fact, despite his service as a vestryman and his owning pews both in his own parish church at Pohick and in the Fairfax Parish church at Alexandria, Washington rarely attended services. Between 1769 and 1773, his attendance ranged from seven to ten times a year. Often he preferred to remain at home while his family and guests attended. In 1774, he went to church seventeen times, but one of these was a political event—a patriotic fast day. Four of the other sixteen Sundays he attended at Christ church, Philadelphia, and on one he went both to Presbyterian and to Roman Catholic services in that city. It is likely that these were political appearances as well.[38]

Other gentlemen were more scrupulous in their attendance. Landon Carter attended regularly and William Byrd II went to church about fifty percent of the time. Robert "King" Carter attended church every Sunday in 1727 and 1728 when he was not ill, and sometimes even when he was. On December 31, 1727, he "went to Church very Lame recd the Communion." Attendance at church was affected not only by personal outlook and geographical convenience, but by many parishioners' habit of attending only when the minister was officiating at the church nearest them. On several Sundays, Philip Fithian noted that the Carters had stayed home because the sermon was being given at the more distant of the two Cople Parish churches. This habit may account for William Byrd's fifty percent attendance record as well.[39]

If gentry were free to attend or not as they wished, some Virginians were categorically excluded from church attendance as a result of their own choice or that of others. Slaves, for example, rarely went to church. Even if they wanted to attend, most were not allowed to do so by their masters. In the seventeenth century, this refusal by the masters may have been occasioned by the popular belief that baptized people could not be held in bondage, but by the eighteenth century it arose from the slaveowners' assumption that what occurred in church was of no use or interest to blacks. Landon Carter declared that he "never rightly saw into the assertion that negroes are honest only from a religious Principle. Johny is the most constant churchgoer I have; but he is a drunkard, a theif and a rogue." When the bishop of London queried American clergy in 1724, he asked about the efforts made to convert blacks and Indians. Virginia parsons reported that any efforts they made were often opposed by slave owners. George Robertson of Bristol Parish wrote that masters re-fused to send slaves to him to be instructed. Some slave owners attempted to instruct slaves privately—the Presbyterian James Gordon read sermons to his blacks, and Robert Hunter's Essex County host read prayers to his—but even these pious masters saw no reason to send their slaves to church services. When masters encouraged attendance at the parish church, they usually did so in response to less desirable religious enticements. William Lee of Green Spring wrote to his overseer Cary Wilkinson inquiring about a northern evangelical preacher who had "put most of my people Negroes [*sic*] crazy with their new Light." Lee directed Wilkinson to discourage the blacks from associating with the outsider, "& perhaps the best method of doing it effectually is to encourage them all to go every Sunday to their Parish church, by giving those, who are the most constant attendants at church, a larger allowance of food or an additional shirt, more than the rest, whereby you will Make it their interest to do their Duty."[40]

From the point of view of a Virginia gentleman, Lee's fear of the effects of New Light preachers was well founded. Evangelical religion seemed to Virginia's elite to threaten their control over their slaves. Where slaves were excluded by definition from Virginia society, evangelicals and other dissenters excluded themselves, preaching a rejection of gentry values that seemed to the gentry to be tantamount to a repudiation of morality and social order. Lee believed that his slaves would steal for the evangelists, "for I think *that* is generally the consequence of their preaching."[41]

The first Virginia dissenters were the Quakers, who came to Virginia in the 1650s, suffered the same kinds of repression they encountered elsewhere, and eventually found an audience and reluctant toleration at the edges of settlement, particularly in Nansemond, Isle of Wight, and Henrico counties. Increasingly in the eighteenth century, evangelical Christian groups—first the Presbyterians, then the Baptists, and, ultimately, the Methodists—stepped outside the cultural bounds defined by their social superiors and challenged the assumptions that supported the prevailing order. The first evangelicals, the Presbyterians, however, were very moderate, differing from their Anglican neighbors only in preferring a more heartfelt religion. Their chief objection was, in the words of a hostile satirical poem, that "that Vile Beuk, the Common Prayer,/ Transforms the Minister to a Player/ who of praying plays the part,/ freed from the language of the heart." These Virginians sought preaching with a "tendency to lead us to Christ or vital religion." For many of them, the Anglican establishment was socially and doctrinally unobjectionable. The Presbyterian preacher James Waddell wrote that "As a presbyterian I approve the doctrinal articles of the established religion, according to the act of toleration; and as a Minister I preach agreeable to them." The Presbyterian planter James Gordon attended church at Wicomico, St. Mary's White Chapel, and Christ churches, whenever there was no Presbyterian preacher in his area. Moreover, as a gentleman he served on the Anglican vestry of Christ Church Parish, Lancaster County. There were so many dissenters who served on Anglican vestries, in spite of Virginia law requiring that vestrymen subscribe to the doctrine and discipline of the Church and the Anglican vestryman's own oath to "conform to the doctrine & discipline of the Church of England as by law Established," that Commissary William Dawson wrote in 1751 to the bishop of London for advice in dealing with them.[42]

The Establishment's response to dissent seems at first more extreme than this mild challenge warranted. Every time Gordon attended church he heard "the ministers ridiculing the Dissenters . . . ; much against Presbyterians." A newspaper controversy between James Waddell and Lunenburg Parish's Isaac William Giberne was initiated by a Giberne sermon in which Waddell was labeled "a pick-pocket, dark-lantern, moon-light preacher, and enthusiast . . . instigated by folly, natural impudence, and the Devil." Giberne called on his listeners to bring the blind Presbyterian preacher to the public whipping post, foreshadowing Landon Carter's later wish that Giberne himself be lashed into submission. Giberne's intemperate blast was founded in Anglican fears that, in rejecting the Establishment, evangelicals threatened to undermine the very foundations of society.[43]

Later evangelical dissenters actually did attack the foundations of gentry society, just as the Quakers had, repudiating its values and the social rituals that reinforced them. For these more militant evangelicals, Anglican sermons were not only pallid, but dangerous. Parishioners who went to St. Mark's church in Albemarle Parish to hear its minister preach on infant baptism found a note posted on the door urging them instead to go hear an evangelical the following Tuesday: "Reader are you a Sin Sick foul [fool] or Not[?] Ide advise you to Go[.] if the 1st youl hear the Gospell preacht if the 2d youl be well wairnd of your

dainger which this useless tail here [the Anglican sermon] may deseive us of so long that more than Probable if we believe what God has wrote to us some of us before its done may be in hell (if you start at this) Dear fds Depend its the very trick of the Devil to Keep us secure till he lands us there." Unlike moderate, socially respectable dissenters, such as James Gordon or James Waddell, these demanded more than simple heart-felt preaching. They required a reformation of one's entire life, an adherence to a strict code of personal conduct. A visitor to Nomini Hall informed Philip Fithian that the "Anabaptists," or Baptists, of Loudoun County were "quite destroying pleasure in the Country; for they encourage ardent Pray'r; strong & constant faith, & an intire Banishment of *Gaming, Dancing,* & Sabbath-Day Diversions." To genteel commentators these were lunatics, people who had lost their grip on reality. Some outsiders found this laughable, others pitiable. The duke de La Rochefoucault Liancourt passed on the Virginians' claims that most of the inmates at Williamsburg's insane asylum lost their minds through indulgence in "enthusiastical devotion" or alcohol, "and it appears that such as arise from the latter of these causes are less difficult of cure than those which owe their origin to the former." For many Anglicans, however, dissenters were simply dangerous, and imprisonment and violent repression were among the cures attempted for the evangelical insanity.[44]

In fact, while dissenters challenged Anglican spiritual doctrine, most accepted differential social standing in principle. But they denied that such differences mattered, or even existed, in churches, and so they attacked the fusion of holy things and profane on which the Anglican parish church was founded. Whites of every social status and even blacks were treated as spiritual equals, and evangelical churches, like Quaker meeting houses before them, were intended to reflect this. The Quaker meeting houses were small buildings, lacking modish decoration or hierarchically differentiated seating. One built in 1702 on the southern branch of the Nansemond River was a twenty-by-twenty-foot building, "the Inside seled with Planks allso the floor laid with Plank & fitted with formes and seates." The building cost 3,868 pounds of tobacco, a tiny fraction of the cost even of a plain Anglican church. The same group's western branch meeting house of 1702 was twenty-five by twenty feet "fitted in every way with formes & Benches sutable for such A House." This structure cost 3,000 pounds of tobacco. A 1722 meeting house in Henrico

FIG. 218. Providence Presbyterian church (ca. 1750), Louisa County. (Photograph, Dell Upton.)

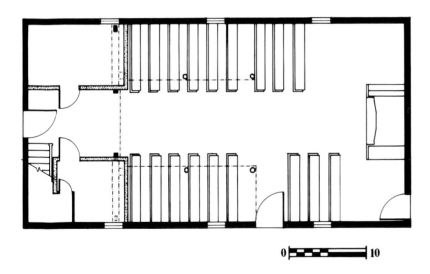

0 ▮▬▬▬▬▬ 10

FIG. 219. Providence Presbyterian church. Plan. The present pulpit dates from the mid-19th century. (Drawing, Dell Upton.)

County was twenty-four by seventeen feet, roofed with shingles, and sealed with pine boards.[45]

In the terms developed in chapter 6, these buildings relied on style, rather than on mode, to establish the context for the rituals that took place in them. This is particularly evident in the only substantially intact dissenting church surviving from the colonial period in Virginia, Providence Presbyterian church, built in Louisa County around 1750

(Figs. 218, 219). It is a weatherboarded frame building, with its main entrance off center on the long south side. At the west end on the interior is an original gallery, which was extended along the north and south walls later in the eighteenth century. The pulpit is at the east, and has been there at least since the galleries were extended. Seating was on benches with backs; those now in the church date from the time the gallery was extended. The interior is presently

FIG. 220. Providence Presbyterian church. Interior. (Photograph, Edward Chappell.)

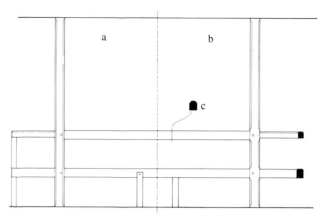

FIG. 221. Providence Presbyterian church. Original decoration of west gallery. Key: a = interior view; b = exterior view; c = section of rail at A-A. (Drawing, Dell Upton.)

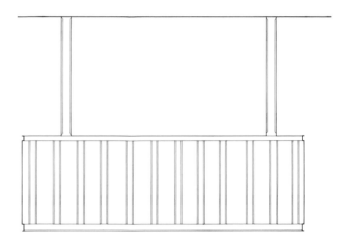

FIG. 222. Providence Presbyterian church. Late 18th-century board-and-batten face of west gallery. (Drawing, Dell Upton.)

sealed with wainscot and plaster on the walls and beaded boards on the ceiling, but this was not the original treatment (Fig. 220). An examination of the fabric shows that originally the church probably had no plaster or other sealing on any interior surface. The original gallery had chamfered and stopped posts and carefully shaped railings (Fig. 221). The newer parts of the gallery were supported on chamfered posts with lambs-tongue stops and were clad with board-and-batten sheating when the new sections were built (Figs. 222, 223). The battens had fine beads on them, and these embellished the edges of the benches as well. Although its gallery did not stand on columns "Fluted & the Capitols of the Dorick Order" as did the gallery at the 1760–68 Stratton Major Parish church, Providence Presbyterian church was a decorated building, whose builders chose to use the vernacular elements common to Virginians of all classes. Its decorative elements could be found at all levels of building, from the outbuilding and the slave house to the plantation house. Providence Presbyterian church was decorated without being filled with the signs of personal and elite dominance that characterized the Anglican parish church. The floor was not divided by pew partitions into private preserves. No distinction in quality differentiated the straight-backed seats. There was no altarpiece, no pulpit or communion table embellished with the modish designs of the upper class. The silver communion cups given to the church in 1767 are tumbler-shaped; they make no reference

to aristocratic standing cups, and they are not embellished with modish designs or with anyone's monogram (Fig. 224). If an Anglican church resembled a great planter's house, not a common planter's, Providence church was the opposite. The combination of decorated structure and unfinished walls and ceilings made it look remarkably like a very large version of John Edwards's house in Isle of Wight County (see Fig. 134), and a myriad of other small planters' houses throughout Virginia. This effect was achieved through careful and deliberate restraint. James Gordon's

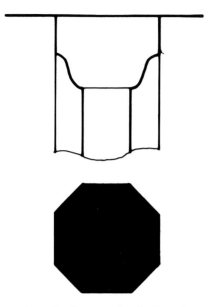

FIG. 223. Providence Presbyterian church. Chamfer and lambs-tongue chamfer stops on post supporting late 18th-century gallery extension. (Drawing, Dell Upton.)

exasperation at the rejection of the practical single pews he desired to have installed in the Presbyterian meeting house in Lancaster County in favor of double pews eloquently demonstrates this.[46]

How serious were the dissenters' inroads into Anglican hegemony? There is no doubt that they siphoned off some potential believers, and that these believers were rarely members of the gentry. Gordon noted that when a Presbyterian minister was available in Lancaster County, services were attended by "a pretty large company of the common people & negroes, but very few gentlemen. The gentlemen that even incline to come are afraid of being laughed at. Mr. Minis (one of the [Anglican] Parsons) endeavors to make it a scandalous thing." Where the population of dissenters was large, they could affect church attendance. In the Upper Parish of Isle of Wight, an early stronghold of Quakerism and later a Baptist area, the minister Alexander Forbes reported in response to a query about church attendance that "often a small proportion of the hearers attend it." William Willie, the Anglican minister who kept attendance records in Albemarle Parish, noted on Christmas

FIG. 224. Providence Presbyterian Church communion cups (ca. 1769–70; JN, London). The legacy of John Williamson, these cups are inscribed "G*S," for Gum Springs, the nearest village, on the bottom. (Courtesy of Providence Presbyterian church and the Virginia Museum of Fine Arts, Richmond.)

Day, 1775, that attendance was down at St. Andrew's church, "many absent at conventicle," or dissenting services. Occasionally dissenters' successes induced Anglicans to give up altogether. The vestry of St. Patrick's Parish ordered its upper church closed because it was "scituate among the Dissenters." [47]

Our assessment of church attendance must be a qualified but positive one. A disproportionate number of gentry attended church. There were conspicuous absences, notably dissenters, who tended despite being lampooned as base ignoramuses to be middling planters, and blacks. But church attendance among the white population ranged from about one-third in dispersed parishes to almost all in more established and densely settled areas. Acceptance of the Church's presence, and of the necessity, if not the desirability, of paying taxes to support it, seems not to have been questioned by many of the people who were not active dissenters. Those who rejected the premise of the church altogether stayed home, as many of MacSparran's "infantry" must have done, or joined an evangelical congregation. [48]

It was for the majority of white Virginians with some loyalty to the Church that the architectural display and social ritual were intended. They helped the parishioners to understand the structure of the local community and to work out contradictions within it. The seating plan was an important tool in these endeavors. It displayed parish society in a physically legible form, in material surroundings that suggested interpretations. It created a spatial framework within which to exercise the hospitable relationships binding the elite and the ordinary parishioners. It created an arena within which the competition for place among upper-class Virginians might take place as well. The seating assignments issued by the vestry might be thought of as the parish leaders' assessment of relative social standing in the parish. Because there was no clear-cut method for determining precedence, however, conflicts invariably resulted. Some ambitious parishioners expressed their disagreement by requesting better seats, or seeking liberty to build their own pews. On extraordinary occasions, the entire congregation rejected the seating plan. These conflicts were noted cryptically in the vestry records. Nevertheless, a few instances of parish uprisings offer the historian a glimpse of the social assumptions and fissures that underlay parish life.

A complaint to the House of Burgesses about the pew assignments in the new Hungar's Parish church of 1742 was rejected by the legislature. The Elizabeth City Parish vestry noted in 1763 that "sundry complaints have been made of many Irregularities in the Church of this Parish" and ordered that the church wardens "do regulate and Place the Parishioners of this Parish and Others, according to their proper Stations in the said Church." The notation implies that attenders were sitting in the wrong places in church, possibly denying seats to the people who were entitled to them. This frequently happened in Bruton Parish church, where "the Parishionrs are very much straightened & often outed of their places & seats, by dispencing with & allowing room for the frequent resort of strangers, & more perticularly at the meetings of the Generall Assemblies: Courts: Councells: & other publick Occasions." [49]

Four conflicts dramatize the use of seating in expressing disagreement over social standing in the parish. In 1671, Richard Price attempted to sit in a seat in St. Mary's White Chapel church reserved for members of the county court. Price was not deliberately causing trouble, but was following the custom allowing people to sit in unoccupied seats in the church. The privilege was circumscribed, however, by a general sense of the social standing appropriate to the occupation of certain seats. Price was evidently not considered qualified to sit with the justices, for one of the pew's occupants, Edward Dale, attempted to keep him out and was pushed back in his seat by Price for his trouble. The county court duly punished Price for behavior "tending to the dishonor of God Almighty and contempt of His Majesty's ministers, offence of the congregation, and scandall to religion." [50]

At the opening of the new Lynnhaven Parish church in 1736, the vestry distributed the seats. The two upper (eastern) great pews were given to the county magistrates and their wives; the next adjoining pew on the north to the Thorowgood family, in return for its gift of the glebe lands; the third great pew on the north to the vestrymen and their wives; and another pew to the Walke family for its gifts and services to the parish over the years. A pew on the south side was allotted to "Such women as the Churchwardens with the approbation of the vestry Shall think fit to place therein." The remainder of the parishioners were scattered among the other benches and pews, "For preserving order peace & Harmony in the New Church." A month later, however, the vestry reported that

Several of the inhabitants of this parish has not thought fit to accept off [*sic*], & others to keep to the Seats & pews the church wardens have assigned to & placed them, in the new Church lately built; to the great disturbance & disorder of the congregation; to prevent which Disorder in the Said Church for the future, we the vestry of the Said parish have meet at the parish Church, & after due consideration, have assigned & Register'd the adjacent persons & family's according to their Several Stations, the most proper Seats or pews; & do hereby publish and declare, that who, or whatsoever person or persons Shall assume to themselves a power: or take the Liberty to place themselves or others in any other Seats or pews in the Said Church: Shall be Esteem'd a Disorderly person & may Expect to be dealt with according to Law: and we Doe further impower and appoint the church wardens for the future to place all persons in the church of the Said parish.

This order constituted an admission of defeat. The vestry repealed their former seating plan and announced their intention to make a new one that would satisfy the objections. They didn't say this directly, of course, and they announced that the new plan would be enforced vigorously. But the congregation had rejected the official interpretation of parish society and successfully forced a new one on their leaders.[51]

Another incident occurred in Bruton Parish church in the early eighteenth century. Vestryman Daniel Parke was a political enemy of the Anglican commissary James Blair. Though Blair lived in Williamsburg, he was minister of James City Parish and his family had no pew in Bruton Parish church. When Blair's wife attended church in Williamsburg, she was in the habit of sitting in the private pew of Philip Ludlow. Daniel Parke was Ludlow's son-in-law, and in Ludlow's absence the "head" of the Ludlow pew. "On a certain Sunday, Mr. Parke, determined to mortify Mr. Blair by insulting his wife, in [Ludlow's] absence . . . came into the church, and, rudely seizing Mrs. Blair by the arm, drew her out of the pew, saying she should not sit there." In the microcosmic community of the parish church, Parke, one of its leading citizens, publicly denied Mrs. Blair the courtesy of hospitality, implying that she stood outside the realm of polite consideration. Parke's act was striking not simply because it was played out in front of a large group of people, but because it was played out in a physical setting that gave the gesture a kind of finality: the parishioners gathered in church stood for the entire community and for the celebration of its fundamental values. Symbolically, Daniel Parke expelled Mrs. Blair from parish society.[52]

A similar, and even more dramatic, incident in late seventeenth-century Christ Church Parish, Middlesex County, suggests the ways that seating precedence was tied not only to abstract concepts of social hierarchy but to specific events in the secular life of the parish. The vestry's account of disturbance in its lower chapel is characteristically brief, and the corresponding court records offer little more. Yet an extraordinarily vivid picture of the conflict emerges from the cryptic notation. The vestry book records an August 25, 1689, order to Matthew Kemp, a church warden, to "make Due prsentment to the next Court of Mrs Jones, housekeeper to the Honorble Xpher Wormeley for haveing bourn Two Children, wch are in this Prish, and may put the Prish to great Charge The Father Unknown." Fatherless children were the responsibility of the parish vestry, who supported them from tax monies. Protecting the parish from the necessity of doing so was part of the vestry's job. The purpose of bringing a formal charge against the mother was not merely to punish her sin but, more important, to extract the father's name so that he could be forced to support his child. However, the order to present Ann Jones was bracketed by two others, which comprised the only other business conducted at this extraordinary vestry meeting. The first order was that "all Prsons shall for the Future Submitt to the Direction of the Church wardens of Each Prcinq for Theire placing & Sitting in the Church during the Time of Divine Service, till Such Time as a full Vestry meeting a larger Order of this Nature be Issued forth and farther Care be Taken &c." Immediately following the complaint against Jones was Kemp's account

of Executing his office as Churchwarden the 21th of July last past, In Peankatanke Church. That he hath Therefore received hard Words, and that this just and honest Action of his in Displaceing of mrs Jones Sitting above her Degree in the Same Church, hath mett with a hard Construction, The Prish after Theire Thanks to the sd mr Kemp for his Dilligence in his Duty, have farther agreed and by this Theire Order do agree That they approve of what was Then and There done by the said mr Kemp, and will Stand by him not onely in this but in all Actions of the like Nature And that none in the least might be Incouraged in Disorder and Rudenesses, It is the Desire of the Vestry that this Theire Order be published in Each Church of this Prish.

The events are certain: Ann Jones gave birth to two bastard children. Ann Jones was sitting in the wrong place in church, and when Matthew Kemp attempted to move her, he was insulted by other members of the congregation. The sequence and specific implications of these events are less clear. Did the church warden attempt to demote Jones from her former pew as a punishment for her unwed motherhood? If so, why did he wait until she had borne two illegitimate children? Was Colonel Wormeley the unacknowledged father of the two children? Was Jones sitting in Wormeley's pew in an attempt to embarrass him or to force a confession or because she felt their relationship gave her the right? It is likely that Wormeley was involved in the incident, and that Jones's behavior had embarrassed him, since, although a member of the vestry, he chose not to attend the meeting called to discuss the incident. Was Jones presented to the court for bearing the illegitimate children or for resisting Kemp in church? What is evident is that Jones, Kemp, and the parishioners all read the incident in Piankatank church in the light of social relations in the secular community of Christ Church Parish. But the parishioners interpreted the situation differently from the church wardens. The congregation attacked the wealthy merchant Matthew Kemp, not the indentured servant Ann Jones, because they thought either Jones had been unjustly condemned or Kemp's kinsman Wormeley deserved to be humiliated. The vestry, as representatives of the parish's ruling order, attempted to override the people's "hard Constructions" by giving Kemp the approbation of "the parish," meaning of his fellow vestrymen.[53]

Underlying all four controversies was the relationship between the secular and religious communities. The juxtaposition of royal and religious emblems in the church announced the official partnership of church and state. The ranked seating of parishioners was not an official policy, but a longstanding tradition that played a vital role in transforming the abstractions of doctrine into the particularities of daily life. It was thus appropriate that the profane details of social division should order the community as it assembled in God's holy house. It was equally appropriate that merits and transgressions outside the realm of religious worship should affect the order inside. And, finally, it was appropriate that the vestry, as both the official local administrators of the state Church and the most meritorious members of the community, should arrange their neighbors in church.[54]

The disturbances illustrated the dynamic quality of the relationship between doctrine and everyday life. At St. Mary's White Chapel we see the process in its ideal form: an individual tried to step out of his place and a member of the parish elite stopped him. For resisting, the offender was punished by the justices in the county court. A clear principle had been violated, and the transgression remedied by the authorities. In the other occurrences we see how conflicts were absorbed by the system. At Lynnhaven Parish church a dispute arose from the official attempt to summarize the structure of the entire community in the new church's seating arrangement and the general rejection of that effort by those affected: the local gentry, and the less elevated, but relatively prosperous slaveholding planters who were assigned seats in the parish church. At Bruton Parish church two gentlemen transposed a private conflict to a public incident by the symbolic denial of hospitality in church. At Piankatank church the congregation repudiated an attempt to shame one person publicly, an attempt that probably grew out of a conflict between individuals of different social classes. In the two individual cases, the architecture of authority and the spatial structure of society, understood by all, formed a setting for the assertion of status. In the two mass revolts, the parish communities rejected their leaders' specific applications of generally accepted rules. But there were differences in the latter two events as well. The Lynnhaven parishioners questioned the overall description of the community as it was proffered, and caused a new one to be drafted. The Christ church parishioners dramatized precinct-wide social divisions in a symbolic setting.

In all four cases, the specific acts carried out in specific settings brought the meaning of the parish church alive for its members. Each of the incidents revolved around the exercise of the gentry's control of the church in their capacity as parish leaders and as leading parishioners. But more important than the incident when the system worked smoothly were the three that involved conflict and disagreement. If the architecture of the parish church was about power, exercised within the particular social metaphor of hospitality, it was also about change.

| III | Dancing |

| 9 | Spaces |

The replacement of the traditional side entry and strongly defined chancel of the English parish church with a west entry and deemphasized chancel in the Virginia church created a conspicuous pathway down the center of the church, but a pathway that had no goal. The act of movement was an end in itself.

The social space of the Virginia church and the landscape of which it was a part was a dynamic one. It was most effective when people moved from one space to another. The continual reassembly of the community and the constant visible construction and destruction of the social order were the deepest experience the Anglican parish church had to offer Virginians. In former chapters we have seen that the church was intended as a self-contained fusion of the divine and social worlds. The artificial insularity of ritual space created by the architecture implied that the world of the church was opposed to the world outside. In fact, the church was part of a network of dynamic spaces, each of which used similar means to create differing, but complementary symbolic environments.

Every church was surrounded by a churchyard. Seventeenth-century law required "That there be a certayne portion of ground appoynted out, and impaled or fenced in (upon the penalty of twenty Marques) to be for the buriall of the dead." A yard was created at the same time as the church itself. The sexton or another member of the parish was employed to "grub" and clean the space around the building, removing most of the trees along with the construction debris, and creating a dirt area surrounding the new building. On exceptionally barren lots sycamores and other trees might be planted for shade. The bounds were then defined. The yards made in 1719 at St. Peter's Parish

church and St. Paul's Parish upper church were 100 feet square, while the one built by John Moore at the upper church of Christ Church Parish, Middlesex County, in 1733 was 134 feet by 110 feet. Most ranged from 100 to 150 feet on a side. The newly designated churchyard was then enclosed. In the wealthiest parishes, 4½- to 5-foot-high English-bond brick walls with ogival or semicircular copings were built (Fig. 225). A good example survives at Blandford church, Petersburg. Although much of the wall has been rebuilt, the 163-by-143-foot enclosure is substantially the one called for as part of Colonel Richard Bland's contract to

FIG. 225. Yeocomico church (1706; enlarged ca. 1740), Westmoreland County, in its 18th-century wall. The distinction between the brickwork of the colonial wall and that of the modern gateposts and repairs is clearly visible. (Photograph, Dell Upton.)

FIG. 226. Blandford church (1734–37, Col. Thomas Ravenscroft, undertaker; addition and wall 1752–70, Col. Richard Bland, undertaker). The yard is still enclosed by Bland's wall. (Photograph, Dell Upton.)

enlarge the church in 1752 (Figs. 226, 227). It has semicircular coping bricks; gates, marked by sandstone finials, aligned with the south and west doors; and a large unrepointed section at the north. Such a wall was handsome but expensive, and might cost as much as sixteen thousand pounds of tobacco, or the equivalent of a year's salary for the minister. Consequently, most parishes, even those that built elaborate churches, elected to build wooden post-and-rail or pale (picket) fences. Truro Parish's vestry reconsidered its order to build a brick wall around the new Pohick church in 1774, "having just finished two expensive Churches, and a Glebe not yet purchased," and settled for a post-and-rail fence instead. Cedar, locust, chestnut, and

white oak were preferred for the posts, with these woods plus yellow pine, poplar, and lightwood employed for pickets and rails. Like other exposed wooden structures, the fence was then tarred. Sometimes a ditch around the outside reinforced the wooden structure. A fence of this sort was much less costly than a brick wall, and might be built for fifteen hundred to fifty-five hundred pounds of tobacco, although the Westover Parish vestry once paid eight thousand for a pale fence.[1]

Whatever the structure of the fence, an elaborate gate, aligned with the doorway of the church building, usually marked the division between the churchyard and the outside. The 1702 Michel drawing of the second Bruton

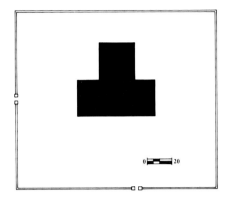

FIG. 227. Blandford church. Site plan. The gates are aligned with the west and south doors of the original structure. (Drawing, Dell Upton.)

FIG. 228. Bruton Parish church (1711–15; James Morris, undertaker), Williamsburg. A mid-19th-century view showing the church with its wall (ca. 1754; Samuel Spurr) and palisaded gate. The door in the east end was cut in the nineteenth century. (From Meade, *Old Churches*, n.p.)

Parish church shows a building enclosed by a brick wall with gabled coping. A north gate consists of a pair of columns of indeterminate order, standing on a sill and connected by a triangular pediment with a spherical finial (see Fig. 15). The fence built in 1719 at St. Peter's Parish church, New Kent County, was to have "Wide Handsom Gates made after the fform of Iron Gates. wth: Handsom Square Peares (or Posts) for the Gates. with a hollow Spire a Top." The brick wall would be "Genteely Rompt [ramped] at each Side of the Gates," and have "a handsome Coopin Brick" on top. The wall and gates were in all other respects to be "as well

Done as the Capitol wall in Williams:Burgh." The post-and-rail fence at Pohick church was similarly provided with "three handsome Palisade Gates" and a palisade gate appears in a nineteenth-century illustration of Bruton Parish church (Fig. 228).[2]

Although Bruton Parish churchyard in the colonial capital contains handsome eighteenth-century monuments, most churchyards were little used as burial places (see Fig. 81). Those members of the gentry who deigned to be interred at church often demanded separate accommodations, giving a similar effect to that created by the private

FIG. 229. Christ church (ca. 1732–35), Lancaster County. A 19th-century view of the church from the north, showing a walled grave enclosure to the right and a fenced enclosure to the left on the site where the Carter tombs stand. (From Meade, *Old Churches*, n.p.)

pew enclosures inside (Fig. 229). Colonel William Poythress, for example, was given permission in 1754 "to Inclose a piece of Ground for a Burying place for his Family tho' the Same should be within the Walls of the Church Yard, provided that he inlarge the same" to make up for the space lost to public use. Even burial inside the church was losing favor among the gentry. Longstanding custom gave burial inside the building an honorific connotation, but it made more impression in the seventeenth and early eighteenth centuries, when parishes established regular fee schedules for burial inside the building. The keepers of the register of Christ Church Parish, Middlesex County, for example, were careful to note which parishioners had been interred inside. As late as the second quarter of the eighteenth century, Robert Carter of Corotoman directed in his will that the chancel of the new Christ church, Lancaster County, "be preserved as a burial place for my family as the

present chancel is." When a grandson of Carter died a few years later, his father brought the corpse to Lancaster County "to be buried at our Church." But Robert and Charles Carter's actions were out of touch with their peers' habits. Increasingly, eighteenth-century commentators noted, planters preferred to hold funerals and to be buried at home, and the churchyards, in which everyone had a right to be interred, were abandoned to the poor. One Sunday at Nomini church, Philip Fithian overheard an "impious expression" uttered by a fellow-tutor employed by the Washington family. The man remarked that "if I was buried here it would grieve me to look up and see *Swine* feeding over me," since the yard was unfenced. Fithian's own employer, Robert Carter, later echoed the tutor's remark in observing that "he dislikes much the Common method of making Burying Yards round Churches, & having them almost open to every Beast." The unease caused Fithian by such comments was soothed when he learned that "only the lower sort of People are buried at the Church; for the Gentlemen have private burying-Yards." Even strangers, if they were members of the elite, were interred in private burying grounds when they died far from home. John Harrower, a tutor in Spotsylvania County, recorded the death of a woman traveling with her daughter and slave. The woman was buried in the graveyard at Snow Creek plantation, and her funeral service was attended by local grandee Mann Page and several other gentlemen.[3]

If the churchyard had little significance as holy ground, it was nevertheless an indispensable part of the church's space and was fitted up for intensive use. In addition to the church, the churchyard might contain a variety of other structures. Most common was a vestry house, a small building used for meetings of the parish's governing body. It was a minimal building, usually wooden, and ranged in size from twelve-by-sixteen to sixteen-by-twenty feet. A door, a window, and a chimney were all the accommodations needed, and some buildings skimped even on those. At the predecessor of the present Pohick church, for example, the Truro Parish vestry constructed a sixteen-foot-square vestry house "framed work & Clapboarded the Covering boards to be Sapt & an Inside wooden Chimney a plank floor & to be lofted with Clapboards & raised on Blocks." When the parish built its brick churches in the 1760s and 1770s, the quality of the vestry houses was improved as well. The new vestry house at Falls church (soon to become part of newly created Fairfax Parish) was a sixteen-by-twenty-foot brick building with a brick or tile floor, shingles, and a "large inside Chimney." Like most such buildings, it was provided with a table and three benches. Those rare churches with towers used the second stories as vestry rooms (Figs. 230, 231). Vestry houses and vestry rooms were used so rarely they were often rented out as schools or residences, and sometimes taken over by squatters between vestry meetings. The Blisland Parish vestry ordered its church wardens to "turn Wm: Broadway & his Family out of the Vestry House" and rent it out for the benefit of the poor relief fund, and the Truro Parish vestry allowed William Weston to use its vestry house at Pohick in return for his covering it.[4]

Of equal importance were the more ephemeral structures that equipped the churchyard as a gathering place for the parishioners before the service commenced. Here each member of the community arrived, some inconspicuously,

FIG. 230. St. Peter's Parish church (1701–3), New Kent County. Tower and vestry room (1739–40; William Walker, undertaker). The dormers were added in 1741 at the vestry's request. The northwest (left) finial houses the flue for the vestry room chimney. The window sash are modern, but the drainspouts above them are original. (Photograph, Dell Upton.)

some with great pomp, to join the assembling congregation. For the gentry, arrival on horseback was an important show of social standing. Hugh Jones claimed to "have known some spend the morning in ranging several miles in the woods to find and catch their horses only to ride two or three miles to church," a tale repeated by many other writers in the eighteenth century. Horseblocks in the

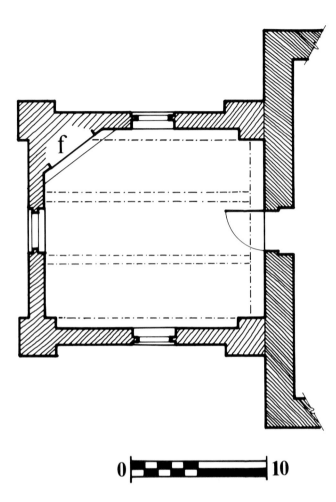

0 |▮▮▮▮▮▮| 10

FIG. 231. St. Peter's Parish church. Plan of vestry room in tower. Key: f = blocked fireplace. (Drawing, Dell Upton.)

not in use, especially when they were located in a town or near a population center. Churchyards retained their customary uses as everyday public gathering places, despite nearly two hundred years of Anglican efforts to extinguish the secular use of churches and a Virginia law forbidding it. On several occasions, William Byrd observed drinking parties in churchyards. When officers of the militia were being feted at the governor's house in Williamsburg, the men were treated with a hogshead set up in Bruton Parish churchyard. In the evening, the officers took a walk about the town and "found a comic freak of a man that was drunk that hung on the pales." [6]

It was on Sunday morning, of course, that the churchyard really came to life. At mid-morning, the parishioners began to gather in groups, standing or sitting on benches scattered under the trees "for the People to sitt on before Divine Service." Notices were tacked to the church door, as they had been on medieval parish churches. Fithian recorded one "dated Sunday Decemr 12th Pork to be sold to-morrow at 20/. per Hundred." Church-door notices were used to "outlaw" slaves, the Virginia term for legal declarations that a slave had run away and that anyone who killed him or her might claim a reward. Gentlemen discussed business, and "rings of Beaux" chatted before and after the service. While they were waiting, the parishioners might witness the punishment of an unruly resident of the parish.

churchyard fixed the ceremony of mounting and dismounting, and helped focus attention on the arrivals and departures of the parish elite. Horses were fastened to a hitching rail, which was sometimes covered, and occasionally a stable was provided. For those few with vehicles, some parishes provided a "Shelter house for the Reception of Chairs & Horses." The church site was chosen for its access to water, and a well head was built or a spring enclosed in palings. A sundial marked the time, and now and then bells futilely summoned the congregation of large rural parishes (Fig. 232).[5]

Colonial church contracts specified that shutters and locks be provided so that churches could be secured when

FIG. 232. Sundial (1717), Yeocomico church, Westmoreland County. The face is inscribed "Philip Smith 1717." (Photograph, Dell Upton.)

St. Peter's Parish ordered the construction of a pair of stocks outside the churchyard wall in 1704. They were rebuilt in 1735 when the vestry ordered "That the Church Wardens cause a good and substantial Pair of Stocks to be forthwith erected near the Church-Yard Wall, for the Restraint of licentious and disorderly Persons several such having lately appeared in the Church, to the great Disturbance of the Minister and Congregation, during divine service."[7]

At Jamestown in the early years of settlement, the governor made a formal processional entry, accompanied by a guard of fifty liveried halberdiers. The tradition of the ranked procession was maintained throughout the colonial period. It marked formal occasions like the 1770 funeral of Lord Botetourt reported in the *Virginia Gazette*. It also was repeated less formally in the entry of the parish gentlemen into the church on a Sunday. At a signal, the parishioners entered the building, but the elite males hung back until the rest of the parish was in place, sometimes until the commencement of the sermon. In churches where men and women sat separately, the absence of the local gentlemen was particularly conspicuous. When they finally entered as a group, moving along the long axial route from the west door, and possibly using the cross aisle at the chancel door, they caught everyone's attention. Aware of the gaze of their inferiors, they did not acknowledge it. Bowing briefly, gravely, almost imperceptibly, to the parson as they passed the desk, they finally made their way to their seats in the chancel, or ascended private stairs to galleries or hanging pews.[8]

The services were often as offhand as the attendance. Landon Carter reported several instances in which the minister did not show up, or came early and rushed through the service before anyone had arrived. However long the service lasted, at the end, the gentlemen waited again, and exited en masse, the group movement and fragmented seating arrangements together demonstrating to all who cared to notice the structure of local society in pre-Revolutionary Virginia.[9]

The religious ritual had spiritual value to some Virginians, but the activity of churchgoing was predominantly secular. The constant assemblings and reassemblings, the array, dissolution, and reformation of the social body as the parishioners moved from home to church yard, into church and back home again, were what attracted Virginians on Sundays. Similar principles of movement, of dissolution and

regrouping, were evident throughout the formal landscape created by the gentry. Two other elements of that landscape will help put the church's role into sharper focus.

The courthouse complemented the church as a place where public rituals reaffirmed and made visible the character of Virginia society. As with the church, its design embodied the principle of movement. The courthouse was an axial building. Most courthouses were rectangles, with jury rooms at one end or in a loft over the courtroom. After 1730, some were T-shaped, with a courtroom stretching the full length of the building, and jury rooms flanking it at the entrance end. The courtroom was entered axially or from the sides at one end of the room. At the far end, under the Royal Arms, sat the county justices, who were often the same men who sat as vestrymen in parish affairs. They occupied a long, raised bench that might be "divided Wainscot fashion above & below into twelve seats," like the one James Jones built for Lancaster County in 1740 (Fig. 233). Among the justices there were distinctions. All had attained their offices by virtue of their rank in the county hierarchy, but some were recognized as wiser and more

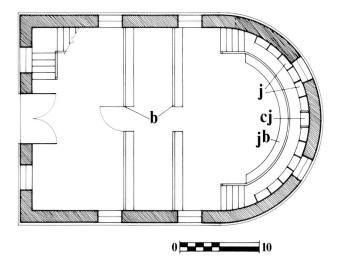

FIG. 233. Lancaster County courthouse (1740; James Jones, undertaker). Reconstructed plan. Key: cj = chief justice's seat; j = justices' benches; jb = jury bench; b = bars, with benches attached. (Drawing, Dell Upton.)

skillful than their peers. The senior magistrates, or justices of the quorum, sat in the center, the most senior of all often provided with a chair. The end of the courthouse was sometimes curved: the compass shape as a marker of importance here makes a rare secular appearance. The specific architectural reference in these courthouses was to the Capitol in Williamsburg, an allusion made more explicit when the courthouse incorporated an oval window in the apse, as did the one built in 1726 in Norfolk County (Fig. 234). The ultimate reference was to the tribunes of Roman basilicas. In addition to their associative value, the apses of county courthouses added a further note of differentiation to the bench, for the senior justices were not only central, they were farther away from the entrance. The judges were raised two or three feet from the floor and beneath them, seated on a lower platform or at floor level, facing the "congregation" (as the King and Queen County records called the audience), were the jury. Between the congregation and the jury were a table for the clerk, a chair for the king's attorney, and chairs or elevated boxes for the sheriff and crier. The participants were separated from the public by a bar, or balustrade. Like the aisles of churches, the public area was frequently paved with brick or stone, but, unlike the churches, the courthouse had no seats. This congregation had to stand. The hierarchy of the court was displayed visually along a longitudinal and gradually ascending axis, and was reinforced by distinctions such as seats for the justices and none for the public. A few

courthouses even had a door near the judges' end corresponding to the south door of the church.[10]

Occasionally the entry of an eighteenth-century courthouse was sheltered by a long, low arcade, which was also paved and was frequently furnished with benches (Fig. 235). In the walled yard enclosing the building the congregation gathered and conducted business much as they did at church, awaiting the signal to enter the courtroom, where they found the justices in place.[11]

The processional use of space extended to the great plantation house. The return of so much of eastern Virginia to woodland disguises the fact that the large planter liked to be dimly visible, but aloof from traffic, when in his house. The greatest planters were seated above the rivers, and visible from them. They were equally visible from the roads. According to Philip Fithian, Nomini Hall could be seen from as far away as six miles. It was linked to the road by a three-hundred-yard poplar avenue (Fig. 236). Its domestic outbuildings defined a court on either side, in the center of which stood the house. One was thus led from the road along an avenue to the house, which was set off in a series of terraced increments and ultimately by a high basement.[12]

A similar route was incorporated into Mount Airy, Richmond County (Fig. 237). The visitor to Mount Airy passed a series of physical barriers that were also social barriers. The house sat on a terraced site above the Rappahannock River, its site a formalized version of the planter's

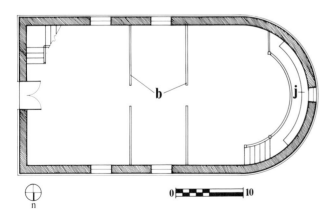

FIG. 234. Norfolk County courthouse (1726; Peter Malbone, undertaker). Reconstructed plan. Key: j = justices' bench; b = bars. (Drawing, Dell Upton.)

FIG. 235. King William County courthouse (ca. 1730). (Photograph, Dell Upton.)

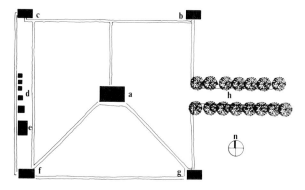

FIG. 236. Nomini Hall (third quarter 18th century), Westmoreland County. Restored site plan. Key: a = main house; b = school house; c = stable; d = dairy, bakehouse, and other domestic outbuildings; e = kitchen; f = coach house; g = work or wash house; h = poplar lane to main road. (Drawing, Dell Upton.)

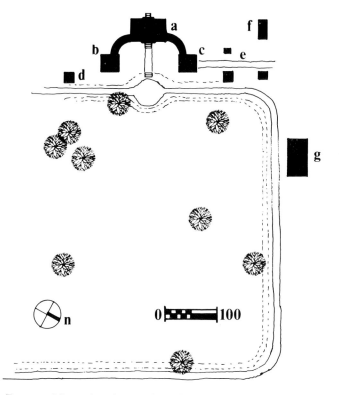

FIG. 237. Mount Airy (ca. 1760), Richmond County. Site plan. Key: a = main house; b = family wing; c = kitchen and working wing; d = schoolhouse; e = domestic outbuildings (18th and 19th centuries) arranged along a street; f = orangerie; g = stable (early 19th century). (Drawing, Dell Upton.)

habit of placing the main house on a hill with its subsidiary buildings around it. Mount Airy was tantalizingly visible from afar, but it disappeared into the hill top as one approached it. To reach the mansion, one traveled around to the rear, then approached along a path that skirted a sunken park. The informal park was in contrast to the formal layout of the house on its terraces, and it also served to make the terraces appear higher than they were. The curved drive showed the visitor the house from a variety of prospects analogous to those experienced when approaching from afar. It ended with the arrival on the lower of two terraces. A low flight of steps led to an upper terrace forming a forecourt defined by two advance buildings. These were originally freestanding, but were connected to the house sometime later in the eighteenth century. The connection served to heighten the constriction of space that accompanied the passing of social barriers and the ascent of terraces and steps, and thus to focus one's gaze in a manner similar to that effected by the apse of the county court-house. Having crossed the upper terrace, one approached the looming house by way of a much higher flight of stairs. This led not into the house, but into a recessed loggia, a shorter version of that in the courthouse (Figs. 238, 239). At last the front door gave entrance to a large reception hall. More exclusive, but still public rooms opened off this. A visitor to the owner, John Tayloe, passed a series of five barriers—two terraces, a flight of steps, a loggia, and an entrance hall—before being admitted to the dining table, the ritual center of the planter's hospitality. Each barrier served to reinforce, architecturally and psychologically, John Tayloe's centrality, affirming the visitor's status as he or she was allowed to pass through it. At the same time, the layout of Mount Airy set Tayloe off from his surroundings. It functioned analogously to the private pews in church, but the complete separation provided by his plantation house would have defeated the purpose of the church gathering.

For the large plantation house, movement is again the key. More important than being in a certain room was the route taken to get there, or how far along the formal route one progressed. George Washington met his neighbors and conversed with them at the land door of Mount Vernon, but he met Benjamin Henry Latrobe, his nephew's friend, in the east river portico and led the architect by stages through several rooms of the house in the course of several days' visit. John Harrower's employer received business visitors, including the tutor and his charges, in the passage

FIG. 238. Mount Airy. North facade. (Photograph, Dell Upton.)

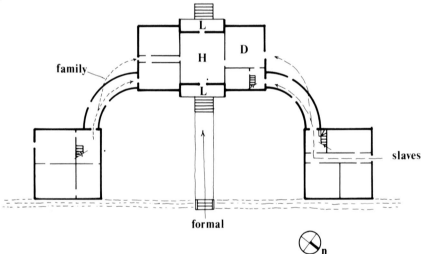

FIG. 239. Mount Airy. Sketch plan showing formal, family, and slaves' routes. Key: H = hall; L = loggias; D = dining room. (Drawing, Dell Upton.)

of his house, and Robert Carter heard a slave's plea for better treatment in his. And while Eliza Custis's family and friends visited in the parlor, the slaves waited in the passage, though they listened to and participated in the merriment taking place inside.[13]

Latrobe's experience at Mount Vernon reminds us that the formal route was not the only way to reach the heart of the house. Just as the clergyman and the justice had separate doors, so did those who were exempt from the intentions of the formal route. Mount Vernon and Mount Airy both had secondary entrances for intimates. At Mount

Airy the east block was a private building. The route from it to the main house was through a doorway marked by an elaborate Palladian opening, into a small side passage (Fig. 240; see Fig. 239). After the hyphens were built, they connected the dependency directly with the northeast room of the main house.

The competitiveness and communal display of church and courthouse were thus given a new form in the great plantation. The single planter argued for his own standing in a setting in which there were no rivals. The architectural devices were the same, however, and as in the church and

FIG. 240. Mount Airy. East end. The hyphen to the right is a later 18th-century addition. The roof of the west dependency can be seen above it. (Photograph, Dell Upton.)

FIG. 241. James house (late 18th century), Surry County. A hall-parlor house with a clapboard roof. The chimneys and piers are 19th-century alterations. (Photograph, Dell Upton.)

FIG. 242. James house. The closet under the stairs is a glazed display cupboard. Key: H = hall; C = chamber or parlor; a = former end door. (Drawing, Dell Upton.)

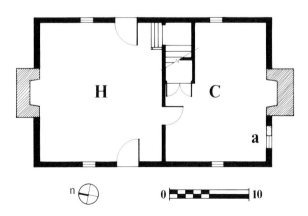

the courthouse, the meaning of the experience was grasped by moving through space. It was a kind of experience, moreover, that was not confined to the great plantation. The lesser county elite used it in their much more modest houses. Houses as small as one and two rooms were tied to their landscapes in similar ways. Front and rear doors in the house provided public access, and access to the farm buildings (Figs. 241, 242), which in some parts of Virginia in the eighteenth century were set in an axial street of two parallel rows stretching from the house to the main road (Fig. 243).[14]

The use of vernacular structures to achieve similar architectural effects to those attained in churches and great

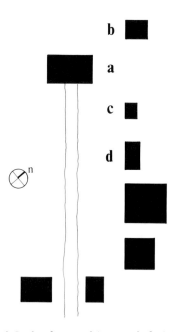

FIG. 243. Joseph Jordan farmstead (1795 and after), Isle of Wight County. Sketch site plan. The original and 19th-century outbuildings that survived in 1975 defined an approach to the house (a). The parlor door and the entrance to the cellar faced the kitchen (b) and smokehouses (c, d). The other buildings were farm structures. All the buildings except the house were demolished in 1979. (Drawing, Dell Upton.)

the auxiliary smokehouse and dairy. Often there was a cellar under the house, accessible from outside at the parlor end, but not from inside the house (Figs. 245, 246). The cellar was another of the outbuildings, but by locating it under the house the planter achieved the same kind of raising that the terraces and high basement accomplished at Mount Airy, and that the magistrates' bench, the chancel, and the pulpit did in other settings.[15]

In the smallest houses the domestic outbuildings were usually set beside or behind the main house, but they were sometimes used to define a ceremonial route for the visitor. The route carried the outsider past the sources of the planter's wealth directly into the hall, or main room, the most elaborately decorated space of the house. In some examples, the stair was moved from its customary position on

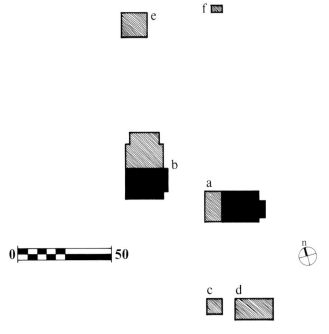

FIG. 244. Edwards-Turner farmstead (late 18th century and after), Isle of Wight County. The kitchen and smokehouses define a drive from the main road to the front of the house. The 19th- and 20th-century structures are hatched to illustrate the growth of the farmstead along the lines defined by the original buildings. Key: a = original house (late 18th century) with 20th-century shed (see fig. 134); b = house (early 19th century) with 19th- and 20th-century leanto; c = and d = mid-19th-century smokehouses; e = late 19th-century log corn crib; f = 19th-century outhouse. (Drawing, Dell Upton.)

plantations is evident. The small house lacked the formalized unity of Mount Airy but was organized along similar principles. Indeed, the high-style exterior at Mount Airy can be thought of as a fashionable new guise for a long-standing Virginia practice. The small house shared with the mansion the tradition of breaking up household functions into a main building and a series of domestic outbuildings. The one- or two-room house typically was furnished with a separate kitchen, a dairy for cool storage of milk and milk products, and a smokehouse for the preservation and storage of meat (Fig. 244). These were integrated with the main house in straightforward ways. The kitchen normally stood near one end of the house and was accessible from a secondary entry, placed, in a two-room house, in the end of the smaller parlor or chamber (see Fig. 242). Near it stood

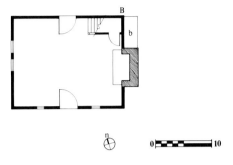

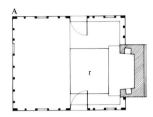

FIG. 245. First and second Edwards houses. The first house was set directly on the ground and had a shallow root cellar under it. It was adapted for use as a kitchen when the second house was built. The latter was raised on a high basement. The buildings were aligned to allow easy access from the kitchen to the basement entry. Key: A = first house; B = second house; b = basement entry; r = root cellar. (Drawing, Dell Upton.)

FIG. 246. Second Edwards house. The ruins of the original house are visible at the right. (Photograph, Dell Upton.)

FIG. 247. King house (late 18th century), Suffolk. Hall. (Photograph, Dell Upton.)

the wall between hall and chamber to the far rear corner, by the fireplace (Figs. 247, 248). This resulted in reduced accessibility of stair to the visitor, terminating the processional route in the hall. At the same time the stair could be a decorative feature, an opportunity that was taken in all the surviving houses with chimney-wall stairs. The hall provided controlled access, through a door, to the semiprivate chamber or parlor. This space normally served both as the main sleeping room, where the head of the household lodged, and as an everyday eating room, as the kitchen access door implies (Fig. 249; see Fig. 242). More formal dining usually took place in the hall.

A house of this type had fewer social barriers than a Mount Airy. There were no terraces, no loggia, to shield the occupants from visitors. One might pass directly from the entrance into the main room; at best a small passage intervened between the two. Yet the elaborate decoration of that room, particularly in the later eighteenth century, showed that it was meant for display, for these were the houses of people at the pinnacle of the social order. They were not members of the stratospheric layer of great planters — the Byrds, the Carters, the Washingtons, the Tayloes — who constituted 0.5 to 3 percent of the colonial population. A vast economic void separated these families

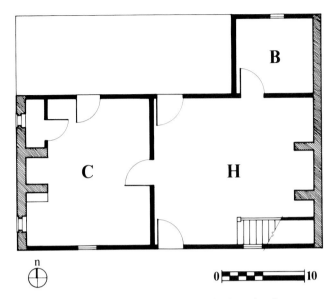

Fig. 248. King house. Plan. Key: H = hall; C = chamber or parlor; B = back room or chamber. (Drawing, Dell Upton.)

incorporated time into the environment in a peculiarly modern manner. It was not time in any of the old senses, where time was defined with reference to external certainties. It was not, for example, sacred time — life versus eternity. Nor was it historical time, defined by a series of discrete, socially shared events that stood in fixed relationships to one another. Rather, it was a purely internal time, in which contingent events were linked only by an individual consciousness that blended each moment into those before and after it. In this kind of time, relationships among events constantly shift according to the position of the observer; there are no fixed bench marks against which to measure them. As Tayloe's visitors moved through Mount Airy, the awareness of where they had been gave significance to where they were. It was a conception that grew out of the investigation of the physical universe undertaken by

from the builders of the smaller houses we have just been examining. Yet those small-house builders, as best we can judge, were sometimes better off than 95 to 98 percent of their neighbors. They shared the outlook if not the great wealth of the grandees, and they used similar architectural devices in similar ways, to create a processional landscape that was meant to impress as one moved through it.[16]

The principles of movement and visual linking that organized individual buildings governed the entire landscape. The rows of trees at Nomini Hall and the row of farm buildings in the small planter's house tied the houses to the network of roads and public ways linking plantation, church, and courthouse. These public roads, Thomas Anburey noted, were altered at will by planters to suit their convenience. Particularly powerful Virginians connected their houses directly with churches and other public buildings by avenues of trees. The remains of the cedar lane from Robert Carter's Corotoman to Christ church, Lancaster County, can still be seen. A similar oak avenue connected Thomas Walker's house Belvoir to Walker's church in Albemarle County.[17]

Movement and position were the subjects of the landscape of the eighteenth-century Virginia elite. They

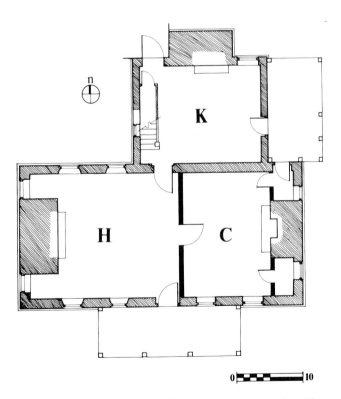

Fig. 249. Sweet Hall (ca. 1720), King William County. Plan. The porches were added in the 19th century. Key: H = hall; C = chamber or parlor; K = kitchen. (Drawing, Dell Upton.)

post-Reformation Euro-Americans. These investigations replaced the fixed hierarchies of an older world view with shifting networks of relationships. In many respects, the orrery, a mechanical model of the solar system in which the planets move about the sun when a crank is turned, is the characteristic embodiment of the new idea of the world. The orrery is a machine that attempts to account for the evanescent character of planetary relations. It admits that no single image can sum up the solar system. Similarly, no fixed image could embody the dynamic character of local society as Virginians perceived it. Only in moving about among the related settings of parish church, courthouse, and greater and lesser planters' houses could Virginia be understood.[18]

This explains the relatively plain exterior appearance of church, courthouse, and plantation house. Though the best of the exteriors were elegantly made, none were elaborate, except Mount Airy. Their careful exterior ordering and meticulous workmanship testified to gentry control over labor and environment. But they lacked facades in the conventional sense of the term (see Figs. 5, 199). Architectural energy was concentrated on the doorway, which in the church marked the transition from churchyard to church. Correspondent to the doorway were the gates that led to the plain dirt yard from the road. Similarly, courthouses literally had no facades. Plain fronts were most common; in some instances arcaded fronts created dynamic voids that visually drew one inside. Architectural devices in the gentry landscape lead us on. Except in the ultimate repose of the planter's hall, or the momentary pauses of the magistrate's bench and the gentleman's pew — the goals of all processions — Virginians valued movement over stasis, and marked comings and goings rather than providing sets for posing. Thus the large plantation house, courthouse, and church in most cases evidence an indifference to facade and elevation.

While the gentry landscape was a processional one, it was also an articulated one. If evanescence was one great discovery of early modern thought, another was that the network of relations comprising the natural and social worlds was flexible and could be manipulated from many points within it. There was no single peak or center. For Virginians, this amounted to a realization that the hierarchical social relations of their landscapes were not fixed. At the church, white society arrayed itself in an image of communal wholeness. At the courthouse, another image of communal wholeness, or of its maintenance and rectifica-

tion, was offered. At the plantation house, yet another image, somewhat subversive of the other two, was offered, for the plantation itself took on the image of self-contained communal wholeness.

The image was credible because the plantation did in fact perform many public functions. It was a commercial center, where the common planters' crops were gathered and shipped with the great planters' produce to Europe. From the grandee's store the ordinary planter could purchase imported European goods. It was an educational center. The planter often kept a school, where men like Philip Fithian and John Harrower tutored his own and others' children. It was a center of sociability, where formal entertainments — balls and house parties — were held, and where friends were invited for meals and extended stays. Most of all, it was a kind of governmental center for the residents of the plantation. On large holdings like those of Landon and Robert Carter, John Tayloe, or George Washington, where there were many outlying subordinate farms called quarters, the plantation was a kind of county seat, an administrative center that affected the lives of those slaves farming them, who might come to the home house very seldom. Socially, then, the private plantation usurped many functions of the town, and the planter appropriated to himself the prerogatives and the good of the community. In effect, the planter's house was the town hall. But the social and economic activities of this community were intended, so far as it was possible to control them, to enrich a single individual. The analogy was not lost on eighteenth-century observers. Philip Fithian recounted an incident on a stormy March night at Nomini Hall when "Before night it grew fair when on a Sudden all are out, so that we seem like a Town; but most of the Inhabitants are black." Repeatedly in the seventeenth and eighteenth centuries, travelers characterized the appearance of plantations as resembling villages. Durand de Dauphiné, a visitor in the 1680s, thought that "when you come to the home of a person of some means, you think you are entering a fairly large village." William Hugh Grove in 1732 described the York River as lined with "pleasant Seats on the Bank which Shew Like little villages, for having Kitchins, Dayry houses, Barns, Stables, Store houses, and some of them 2 or 3 Negro Quarters all Seperate from Each other but near the mansion houses which make a shew to the river of 7 or 8 distinct Tenements, tho all belong to one family." A century after Durand's initial use of the metaphor, the German traveler

Johann David Schoepf noted that a Virginia plantation "has often more the appearance of a small village." [19]

Schoepf's village was meant to be seen and to command the surrounding landscape. Whether rising above its surroundings on terraces, as at Mount Airy, or on a basement, as in the smaller plantation houses, or simply by its siting at the top of a small rise, as in the home of Captain B. H., whom Schoepf visited, the planter's house "stood out well by contrast" with the slave houses and outbuildings around it. Benjamin Latrobe noted that Mount Vernon could be seen from a mile away, and Luigi Castiglioni offered the complementary observation that the view it commanded was equally pleasing. "The view of the Potomac River and of the boats that go up and down it to Alexandria, the spectacle of a broad expanse of cultivated terrain contrasting with the adjacent hills still clad in ancient oaks and lofty pines, contribute to render the site varied and charming." Philip Fithian caught the spirit when he wrote in his *Journal* in August 1774, of a family walk from Nomini Hall. "Then we stroll'd down the Pasture quite to the River, admiring the Pleasantness of the evening, & the delightsome Prospect of the River, Hills, Huts on the Summits, low Bottoms, Trees of various Kinds, and Sizes, Cattle & Sheep feeding some near us, & others at a great distance on the green sides of the Hills, People, some fishing, others working, & others in the Pasture among the Horses;—The Country emphatically in her goodly Variety! I love to walk on these high Hills where I can see the Tops of tall Trees lower than my Feet, at not half a miles Distance—Where I can have a long View of many Miles & see on the Summits of the Hills Clusters of Savin Trees, through these often a little Farm-House, or Quarter for Negroes; these airy Situations seem to me to be the Habitations of Health, and Vigor." [20]

The culmination of this kind of planning, and of the intentions behind it, was Thomas Jefferson's Monticello. Situated on the flank of its little mountain, Monticello, like Mount Airy, was approached by a circuitous route that concealed it until one was very near (Fig. 250). Though Monticello could not be seen, its builder commanded a prospect of a vast territory around it (Fig. 251). The "Blue Mountains," the lowlands, other planters' houses—all were part of a prospect Isaac Weld thought stretched forty miles in each direction. Weld noted approvingly that "The mists and vapours arising from the low grounds give a continual variety to the scene." Although the mountain rose above

Monticello, it, too, was turned to visual advantage. Gardens, vineyards, and orchards lined it, picturesque garden walks were threaded through it, and Jefferson originally intended to place striking pavilions on it that could be seen from his house. [21]

The entire landscape of Piedmont Virginia was thus focused on Thomas Jefferson at Monticello. The house was filled with revolving desks, dumb waiters, two-faced clocks, devices to open doors in unison. It was the articulated landscape in its most hopeful form—the natural and human world refashioned to converge on the individual at its center. The architectural techniques were the same as those found in the pre-Revolutionary church, courthouse, and plantation. Emphasis by height and distance was there, on a grander scale than any attempted before the Revolution. Yet there was a critical difference—a dislocation, a disengagement at Monticello. Jefferson could see, but not be seen. The relationship was one-sided. The complementary quality of the older landscape was gone. The processional aspect is also missing from Jefferson's landscape; everything can be absorbed from a single point by the central actor. The dome, which might provide the focal point, leading the visitor to the building and providing a vantage point for its occupants, is at the rear of the house. It might be a centralizing dome of heaven, but it is not visible from the state rooms of the building. Its presence must be imagined, rather than perceived, at the heart of the scheme. [22]

At Jefferson's Monticello, the landscape of the plantation was entirely disengaged from the landscapes of the courthouse and church. The collapse of the Anglican parish and the diminution of court day's importance during the Revolution were complemented by the ascendancy of the plantation. The centrality of the individual planter was established. For pre-Revolutionary Virginians, however, this reorganization was not clear. The gentry used the church, the courthouse, the plantation complexes, and the connective tissue of the landscape all equally as important tools of social assertion.

However, the landscape was not exclusively the gentry's. It incorporated elements created by slaves and dispossessed whites, whose contradiction of the gentry's social vison became more evident as the eighteenth century passed. But while the landscape asserted the gentry's aims imperfectly, it worked *well enough* during most of the eighteenth century. Moreover, there are signs that the gentry system was beginning to accommodate the social

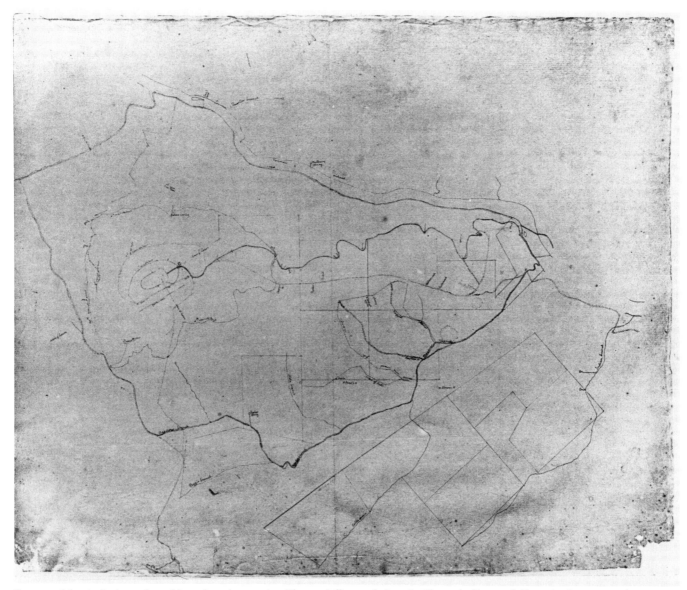

FIG. 250. Monticello (1770; late 18th, early 19th centuries; Thomas Jefferson, designer), Albemarle County. Jefferson's 1803 survey, showing outbuildings and "roundabouts." (Photograph, Virginia State Library.)

changes of the eighteenth century, and might have made the transition to the nineteenth century without serious disruption in many areas. The disintegration recorded in Samuel Mordecai's letter and enshrined at Jefferson's Monticello was not inevitable. Nevertheless, the gentry synthesis of church, courthouse, and plantation house was an unstable one.

The power of the gentry landscape was undermined by inconsistencies within it and by systematic exclusions from it. Just as family members and other intimates were exempted from the formal route through the plantation house, so were slaves. At Mount Airy their route began in the street of outbuildings that stretched west from the west dependency, passed through that dependency, which con-

FIG. 251. The view from Monticello. (Photograph, Marlene Heck.)

FIG. 252. Mount Airy. West end. The pediment marks a former entrance into the dining room. Entrance through the later eighteenth-century hyphen to the left superseded it. (Photograph, Dell Upton.)

tained the kitchen and other work rooms, and into the main house through a small pedimented doorway in the dining room (Fig. 252). Like the east wing, this was later connected directly to the house by the hyphen. The slave's route thus mirrored the private routes that led from the east wing (see Fig. 239). But the slave was exempted for a different reason. Eighteenth-century Virginians did not imagine that their slaves would be susceptible to the same kinds of displays at church, home, or court that were intended to bind the white community together, and to rationalize its hierarchical form. Rather, they assumed only force could bind slaves.

Because the planters did not expect slaves to be drawn into assenting to Virginia's social structure through public ceremonies, they exempted slaves from their formalities. In the planter's landscape, blacks could pass almost at will, even to places where whites from outside were forbidden. The traveler Alexander Macaulay was annoyed to be reminded of this in 1783 when he visited Christiana Campbell's house in Williamsburg, thinking that it was still a tavern. In "a large cold room on the left hand," the parlor, Macaulay observed several slaves lounging about. Macaulay, however, was left in the passage, until he marched indignantly into the parlor. This remarkable absence of clear barriers also characterized the slave's sojourn in public, once he or she had passed the all-important barrier of obtaining permission to leave the master's property. Slaves mixed with court-day crowds. At church, if they went, there was no definite seating arrangement reserved to them. The "slave gallery" of the nineteenth century was a rarity in the eighteenth century. Slaves might share a section set aside for them, but as often as not they would sit in, or adjacent to, their masters' pews.[23]

In the end, the gentry landscape was meant to have an integrating function, to make a place for everyone. While it incorporated new conceptions about the nature of the world, about time and memory, its explicit intention was to manifest old hierarchical and patriarchal values, to demonstrate the planter's superior claims. It served equally importantly as a device to help the gentry understand and adjust to the changes that were transforming eighteenth-century Virginia.

10 | Dancing

Europeans were astounded at the Virginians' attachment to the dance. Joseph Hadfield and Andrew Burnaby described the colony's residents as "immoderately fond" of dancing. Ebenezer Hazard found it "a Proof of the Luxury & Extravagance" of tiny Fredericksburg that the townsfolk had subscribed to build a house "which is entirely devoted to Dissipation," with one room for dancing and two for cards. Dancing was more than mere pleasure; it was a necessary requirement of good breeding. Philip Fithian regretted that his Presbyterian upbringing barred him from it, for in Virginia dancing was "a necessary qualification for a person to appear even decent in Company!" To James Reid, it was "the principle characteristic of a fine gentleman" to know "how to skip and caper when ever he hears a few horse hairs rubbed with rozin, scrapped across the gutts of a Cat." Dancing was the active part of hospitality: Fithian was taught that a ball and a supper were equal components of the Virginia housewarming, and he later observed that they were major components of the good fellowship of Christmas. At the same time, this genteel accomplishment allowed for the orderly violation of social constraints. Robert Hunter, Jr., discovered at a ball at Blandfield that "you dance with anybody you please, by which means you have an opportunity of making love to any lady you please." The most popular dances in Virginia were jigs, "a practice originally borrowed . . . from the Negroes." In other words, the very dances that elegant ladies and gentlemen engaged in were borrowed from their slaves, an impropriety that shocked their visitors. To Nicholas Cresswell, it looked "more like a Bacchanalian dance than one in a polite assembly." In their dances Virginia's gentry transformed chaotic and antisocial forces into social graces. The lesson was clear to Philip Fithian. Watching his young pupils perform for their dancing master one December day, Fithian found it "beautiful to admiration, to see such a number of young persons, set off by dress to the best Advantage, moving easily, to the sound of well performed Music, and with perfect regularity, tho' apparently in the utmost Disorder." [1]

In addition to its social advantages, dancing was calculated to appeal to the Virginia mind in other ways. The articulated movement of the Virginia landscape was strikingly visible in the dance: individuals did not matter, but existed only in their movements in relation to one another. Yet each man and woman had individual roles that contributed to the larger pattern. No single force controlled them. Dancing differed in this respect from the mechanism of the orrery mentioned in the last chapter, since the result was not predetermined. Things could go wrong, and it was cause for pleasure when they went right. The contrast of chance and pattern—or the pattern apparently created by chance—that Fithian caught in the dance addressed another facet of eighteenth-century Virginia's life— significant changes in its social values. During the fifty years before the American Revolution, elite Virginians redefined their relationships with their neighbors in accord with a more agriculturally diversified, economically active society whose political structure was altered from outside by the reorientation of imperial policy. Dancing was a symbolic act of reassurance. Through it, Virginians created an image of order emerging from movement and change. [2]

The dance metaphor is appropriate for understanding the eighteenth-century Virginia parish church as well. The consensus that had bound white Virginians and allowed vestrymen to rank parishioners with only occasional protests was abandoned by the gentry themselves, as they turned their attentions and aspirations outward. Beginning in the 1720s in the more prosperous parts of eastern Virginia, such as Princess Anne and Middlesex counties, and taking hold in the 1750s in commercially active northern Virginia, the move to redefine the nature of the parish community spread throughout the colony in the quarter-century before the Revolution. Traditional architectural forms and customary patterns of movement and spatial use within the church were retained, however. In casting new social relationships in old appearances, the same coincidence of pattern and change, of movement and resolution that Fithian noted in the dance might be found in the Virginia parish on the eve of the war.

The principle of precedence governed seventeenth- and eighteenth-century Virginia, and was the basis on which vestries attempted to assign seating in the parish church. The socially meritorious parishioner was entitled to a private seat that was more prominent, more comfortable, or larger than others, or simply reserved. A corollary to the idea of precedence was the understanding of gentry obligations embodied in the concept of hospitality: the exchange of unlimited and unspecified service in return for unlimited and unspecified prerogative. The distinction was recognized by both rich and poor Virginians. Devereux Jarratt recorded in an autobiographical account of his childhood in St. Peter's Parish that "We were accustomed to look upon, what were called *gentle folks*, as being of a superior order. For my part, I was quite shy of *them*, and kept off at a humble distance. A *periwig*, in those days, was a distinguishing badge of *gentle folk*—and when I saw a man riding the road, near our house, with a wig on, it would so alarm my fears, and give me such a disagreeable feeling, that, I dare say, I would run off, as for my life. Such ideas of the difference between *gentle* and *simple*, were, I believe, universal among all of my rank and age." Another Virginian, St. George Tucker, reminiscing about the era immediately before the Revolution and writing from a gentry rather than a common planter's point of view, avowed that the gentry on their horses or seated in their carriages "never failed to pull off their hats to a poor man when they met, & generally, appear'd to me to shake hands with every man in a Court yard, or a Churchyard, and as fair as I could judge the planter who own'd half a dozen negroes, felt himself perfectly upon a level with his rich neighbor that own'd a hundred." The evidence suggests that Jarratt's observation was closer to the truth than Tucker's. Beginning in the 1720s, the concepts of precedence and service underwent a gradual and piecemeal transformation. The links implied in precedence were dissolved. Elite parishioners strove to drive a wedge between themselves and their neighbors, not merely to maintain distinctions but to amplify and clarify them. James Reid noted the extreme

localism of social status in Virginia when he professed to be "surprised how a man, who was reckoned a wise and learned Being in one County, should be esteemed a fool and an ignoramus in another neighboring County." Consequently, it was at the local level that social differentiation was most critical, and in the principal local institution, the Anglican parish, that differentiation was enforced. The local definition of importance was transformed in the half-century before the Revolution.[3]

The enforcement of status was a two-part process, with legal regulation of those at the bottom and unofficial aggrandizement allowed those at the top. If the periwig was the rich man's insignia, beginning in the 1750s a cloth badge with the parish's initials on it was the poor man's or woman's. The "Act for employing and better maintaining the Poor" of May 1755 noted that "the number of poor people hath of late years much increased throughout this colony," and proposed to provide more efficiently for their maintenance, and "for the prevention of great mischiefs arising from such numbers of unemployed poor." One clause of the act required that anyone who received poor relief from the parish must "upon the shoulder of the right sleeve of his or her uppermost garment, in an open and visible manner, wear a badge, with the name of the parish to which either he or she belongs, cut either in blue, red, or green cloth, as the vestry or churchwardens shall direct." Accordingly, Suffolk Parish's vestry "Ordered that the Church wardens provide Badges for the poor of the Parrish and that they wear them," and in Accomack County the newly formed St. George's Parish vestry, as one of its first acts, required "that the Churchwardens agree that Nothing be paid for Keeping Parishioners Unless they Wear on there Brests SGP in Red or Blue Letters on thare Upper Garments."

Traditionally, parishes were responsible only for those poor people who were legal residents by virtue of birth or other circumstances. As in Anglican parishes in England and Puritan townships in New England, the Virginia church wardens were authorized to remove forcibly any poor person who had no legal claim to parish relief. On one level, the use of the badges was a response to the growing size of the population, where a vestry might not be expected to know all its parish poor by sight. But on another, the intention to stigmatize and set aside went beyond mere administrative convenience, and some poor people objected. The foresighted burgesses had provided for the denial or

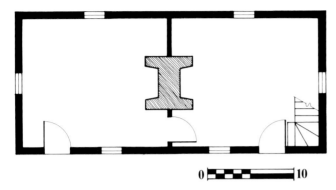

FIG. 253. Poor house (1762), Frederick Parish. Reconstructed plan. (Drawing, Dell Upton.)

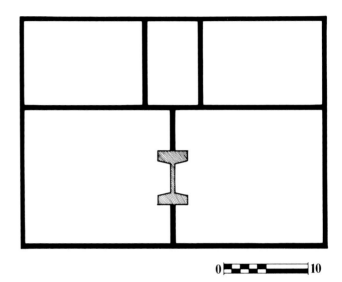

FIG. 254. Poor house (1767), Stratton Major Parish. Reconstructed plan. The number and location of doors and windows were not specified in the vestry's order. (Drawing, Dell Upton.)

reduction of support and the administration of five lashes to those who refused to wear their badges, as did James Nail and William Hole, "a Blind Man," in Suffolk Parish.[4]

Moreover, poor relief had formerly taken the form of a monetary supplement that allowed paupers to subsist in their own manner. Sick or aged people were occasionally placed in the homes of other parishioners to be cared for, as the joiner Richard Perrott was in Christ Church Parish, Middlesex County. An exceptionally destitute person might receive even more. The Blisland Parish vestry paid John Collier fifty shillings in 1732 to build a twelve-by-sixteen-foot house on his own land for Alice Daniell to live in for the remainder of her life. But the 1755 act now provided that vestries could build houses in their parishes to which the poor could be forced to move. Most poorhouses took the two-room, central-chimney form commonly used for slave houses, kitchen-laundries, and other agricultural outbuildings. Frederick Parish constructed a sixteen-by-thirty-six-foot log house on this plan (Fig. 253); and a similar one, with a shed on the back, was built in Stratton Major Parish (Fig. 254). In Elizabeth City, St. George's (Accomack), and Elizabeth River (Fig. 255) parishes the two-room plan was enlarged by doubling it to the rear. The superintendents of these buildings were authorized "to employ all such persons, in such works as shall be directed by the said vestry, or churchwardens; and to take and apply the benefit of their labor, for and toward their maintenance and support." Those who refused to move to the houses could be denied relief, and extralocal beggars were liable to

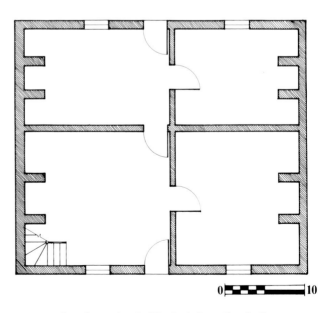

FIG. 255. Poor house (1756), Elizabeth River Parish. Reconstructed plan. (Drawing, Dell Upton.)

incarceration in them for up to twenty days. Uncooperative residents of the houses risked up to ten lashes per offense.[5]

At the same time that Virginia's parish leaders sought to make poverty visibly humiliating, they devised ways to make the signs of their own honor in church more conspicuous. As we have seen, the assignment of pews by rank was standard from the seventeenth century in Virginia parish churches. The proprietary interest in these private pews was keen in the seventeenth century, but by the second quarter of the eighteenth century assignment to the front, or largest, or most elaborate pew was no longer sufficient. The leading gentlemen must be set off more decisively from the mass of parishioners. A pew in the chancel adequately acknowledged precedence in the churches of Christ Church Parish, Middlesex County, built in the second decade of the eighteenth century, and still satisfied the Carters in Christ church, Lancaster County, in the mid-1730s, but private galleries became the favorite mode of seating in the second and third quarters of the century. The shift is evident in a 1745 order in St. Paul's Parish designating the "upper" chancel pews in its parish church to receive the overflow from the magistrates' gallery. Some private galleries were additions, built on the excuse that the church was crowded; others were constructed as the church was going up. This happened in St. Mary's White Chapel church in 1740, when three Balls, all vestrymen, built a gallery in one arm of the new church. Another gallery was built in the church at the same time by members of the Fox, Burges, and Ball families, and a third was erected for the use of the parish. The minister of St. Mark's Parish was given liberty to build a private gallery in the lower church "for the Use of his family and friends," and private galleries were built routinely in most Virginia parishes in the decades before the Revolution.[6]

The advantages of a private gallery were exclusivity and isolation. While the assignment of pews by status created a visible social stratigraphy, from the humble to the most exalted members of the parish, the construction of a gallery created a radical discontinuity in the seating pattern. It was a privilege that was limited physically by the nature of the building and economically by the cost of the undertaking. Private galleries were built at their owners' expense, and they were costly. Daniel DeGernett built a gallery for a small wooden church in Cumberland Parish in 1774 for sixteen pounds plus the salvage of the old church. More in line with prices in the settled areas was the organ gallery,

"Winscoted, painted hansom & Substantially Well Built," installed in 1737 in the Poplar Springs church of Petsworth Parish. William Rand received forty pounds current money for it. The vestry of Dettingen Parish, exercising its option to buy a gallery the undertaker had built at his own expense in the new Cedar Run church, paid one hundred pounds for it in 1760. By contrast, an ordinary slaveholding planter might expect an income of fifteen to twenty pounds per year, and those without slaves less than ten pounds per year. The construction and occupation of private galleries thus had exclusive connotations, and the physical character of the church further limited construction and occupation to a select few families who proudly maintained their property long after its contextual significance had vanished.[7]

During the second and third quarters of the eighteenth century, the desire for separation and assertion in many parishes extended beyond the construction of private galleries to the use of even more secluded accommodations. In these cases, the privatization of the public space frequently required the alteration of the church fabric and even of the space itself. "Hanging pews" were built adjacent to existing ones and even hanging free of other pews and galleries (Fig. 256). Not really galleries, which occupied the end of the church or a wing of it, hanging and other isolated pews were devices known to Virginians from English parish churches (Fig. 257). But where in England they were assigned to the preeminent person in the parish, in Virginia their use by several prominent people in a given community promoted the competition characteristic of other aspects of gentry life. Hanging pews embodied the spatial ideal of gentry self-expression in mid-eighteenth-century Virginia. They made their occupants at once conspicuous and not clearly visible, placing them in the context of their fellow parishioners but absolutely distinct from them, foreshadowing the strategy employed at Monticello in the late eighteenth century. Hanging pews were literally on a different spatial plane from the remainder of the church, and there was no access from any other part of the building except by a private stair. Occasionally there was a separate exterior door leading to the stairs, or the stairs themselves might rise outside the walls (Fig. 258). The first recorded hanging pew, "the stairs to goe up behind the Said Chancel Doore," was granted by the Lynnhaven Parish vestry to Captain Hillary Moseley in 1724. The exclusive and competitive nature of the privilege was made clear when the parish's new church was built in 1736.

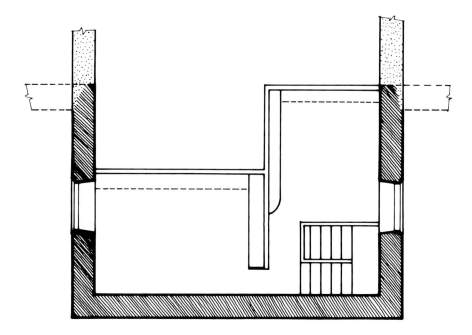

FIG. 256. St. Mary's White Chapel Parish church (1739–41; James Jones, undertaker). South gallery plan. At the right is the gallery granted to members of the Ball and Burges families "on the East Side of the South Wing of the new Church to reach from the South Door til it comes for[th] flush with the Main [east-west] Wall of the Church and ten feet in Width . . . & to have Six feet in Breadth" (Christ, Lancaster VB, p. 10). There is no record of ownership of the other section, which is contemporary with the Ball-Burges gallery. The dashes suggest the original, cruciform shape of the church and indicate the locations of missing benches. The east and west wings were demolished in the 19th century to create the present north-south rectilinear building. (Drawing, Dell Upton.)

0 ▭ 10

FIG. 257. St. Mary's church, Warbleton, East Sussex, England. Hanging pew (1722). (Photograph, Edward Chappell.)

Fig. 258. Bruton Parish church (1711–15; James Morris, undertaker), Williamsburg. Nineteenth-century view showing private stairs. (Photograph, Colonial Williamsburg Foundation.)

William Robinson was granted the right to build a hanging pew contingent on the failure of the Moseleys, "who have the first liberty," to build one. Their right had carried over from the old church. It is in this context of striving for distinction that the other parishioners' revolt against the churchwardens' seating plan (see chapter 8) must be understood. In the 1760s, the next generation of Lynnhaven parishioners made the same requests. In 1765, Edward Moseley, Jr., was allowed to build a gallery along the south side of the church (the old hanging pew in the 1736 church

was on the north side). In the same year, Captain William Keeling was allowed to build a hanging pew in the parish's Eastern Shore chapel, adjoining the gallery but with private stairs.[8]

The sense of separation from the common order is conveyed in all these instances by the vestry's reminding the grantees of the public good. Hillary Moseley's private pew was to take up as little room as possible; William Robinson's was not to obstruct the light of the windows; and Edward Moseley, Jr.'s, hanging pew was "not [to] Effect the pulpitt." These strictures give a striking, though exaggerated, sense of a kind of Piranesian space, with pews and private accommodations dangling at all levels from all parts of the church. Similar cautions were issued by other vestries, who directed hanging-pew and gallery builders not to "discommode the light of the said Church," its other pews, or its headroom, and not to inconvenience in any way the other parishioners. Southam Parish even warned Alexander Trent, John Mayo, and Nicholas Davies on separate occasions not to endanger the structural stability of the building![9]

The centrifugal tendency could not be contained. Gentry pewholders obtained permission not only for building hanging pews and private stairs and entries, but for cutting their own windows in the church. In 1769, Captain James Kempe, Walter Lyon, and Thumar Hoggard were all granted permission to cut windows into the Lynnhaven Parish churches to light their hanging pews. The exterior order of uniformly sized and spaced compass windows was rudely interrupted by other smaller, miscellaneous shapes (Figs. 259, 260). The north side of Lynnhaven Parish church collapsed and was rebuilt in the present century, but the south side survives, with the old windows remaining. A small rectangular opening and a slightly larger compass opening were inserted above and between the original windows of the church. In 1785, other windows were cut in Lynnhaven churches to serve the pews of Charles Sayer and Thomas Walker. The windows lighting the latter's pew

FIG. 259. Lynnhaven Parish (Old Donation) church (1733–36; Peter Malbone, undertaker). South side, showing private windows. The size and shape of the small rectangular window have been altered somewhat by a reduction in the wall's height. All the sash are modern. (Photograph, Dell Upton.)

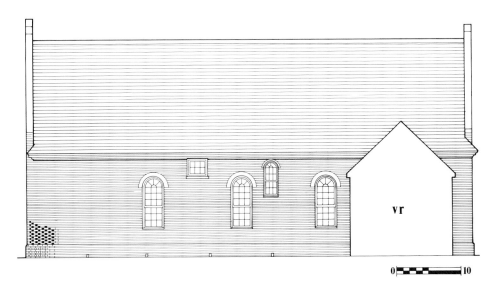

FIG. 260. Lynnhaven Parish church. Elevation drawing of south side. Key: vr = 1916 vestry room. (Drawing, Dell Upton.)

interrupted the traditional fenestration pattern at the east end of Eastern Shore chapel. Private windows appeared in other parishes much earlier. They are recorded from the Upper Parish of Isle of Wight County in 1725, St. Patrick's Parish in 1763, and Bristol Parish, at Blandford church, in 1773. Only the last of these three churches survives, and it shows no trace of the windows, if they were ever made.[10]

If private windows were the most visually striking physical evidence of the gentry's effort to separate themselves in the eighteenth century, the most extreme expression of this effort was reached in Christ Church Parish, Middlesex County, where the dominant local families proposed not merely to establish distinctive locations in the church space, but to attach their own private spaces to the body of the church. They wished to exclude themselves from the public space constructed by and for the parish, and to append wings to two of the parish churches, allowing them to be present at the service, but absolutely separate from their neighbors. In 1733, the families of Colonel John Grymes, Colonel Armistead Churchill, Major Edmund Berkeley, and Mr. Ralph Wormeley were given permission "to Build an Addition of Twenty foot Squar. to the Middle Church, and they are to have a property in the Same keeping it in repair at their Own Charge provided they do no Damage to the present Building." They were granted the same privilege at the lower chapel, which was an added expression of their prominence in the parish, since few gentry bothered to attend or to maintain pews at any but the churches nearest to their homes. The same permission was granted to Nicholas Davies and Carter Henry Harrison in Southam Parish in 1760, when the two were allowed to build a north wing at Ham chapel "for the Use of thier Familys Provided the same do not hurt or Pregudice the said Chappel."[11]

As the parish social network unraveled, parishes sought less consensual methods of establishing rank. The acquisition of exclusive seating became more urgent for individuals, and the seating order thus more difficult for the vestrymen to establish and maintain. The old habit of making a gift of goods or service in gratitude for pew privileges gave way to the sale of pews and privileges. Prestigious pews were now available on an ability-to-pay basis. This critical change in emphasis first occurred in northern Virginia in the 1750s. When a new church was built, the best pews were sold at auction. In practice, the choicest pews still went to the county elite as intended, but the vestry no longer had to

make fine status distinctions, and hierarchy was established purely by economics.[12]

The first open attempt to sell the right to high-status seating is recorded in the Dettingen Parish vestry book for 1755, where William Waite, the undertaker of the new Quantico church, was authorized "to Agree with any Person or Persons to build a Gallary at the Lower End of the Church . . . & the Property of the said Gallary to be Vested in the Persons Concerned in the Building thereof." A similar scheme was effected in Fairfax parish in 1767. Several parishioners requested that the church already contracted to be built at Alexandria (the present Christ church) be made ten feet longer than the contract specified (Fig. 261). Rather than pay the builder, James Parsons, more money, the vestry directed that he "build the said church and lay of[f] the pews, by a plan produced and Numbered 4.5.15.18.29.14.19.28.13 and 20 which said pews to be sold by the said James Parsons, for his benefit."[13]

When Truro Parish finished Pohick church in 1772, it auctioned the choicest pews for its own benefit. The vestry first sold six pews in the center of the two-aisle church, nearest the east end, at prices ranging from £16 for "one of the six Center Pews adjoining to the South Isle and next to the Communion Table," sold to the Honorable George William Fairfax, Esq., and the corresponding pew on the north aisle, sold to Colonel George Washington, down to a minimum of £13 10s. for each of two pews next to the cross aisle, sold to an unnamed purchaser. One pew was reserved for the rector, the Reverend Lee Massey, who was given a legal title to it, as were the successful bidders to their pews. The result was similar to that which would have eventuated had the vestry assigned the pews. George William Fairfax, a relative of the proprietor of the Northern Neck land grant in which Truro Parish lay, and George Washington, the other great man of the parish, acquired the most prestigious pews. The difference is that the vestry were able to avoid disputes over the lesser rankings. The significance of the ranking remained the same, and pew owners were as sensitive as ever to its nuances. At its next meeting after the auction, the vestry approved a request by Fairfax and Alexander Henderson, Gent., speaking on behalf of all the purchasers of central pews east of the north-south aisle, "to take up the stone in the Isles and to raise the said six Pews at their own private Expence to the same height above the Isles and exactly in the same manner with the Pews next to the Walls, they making good any

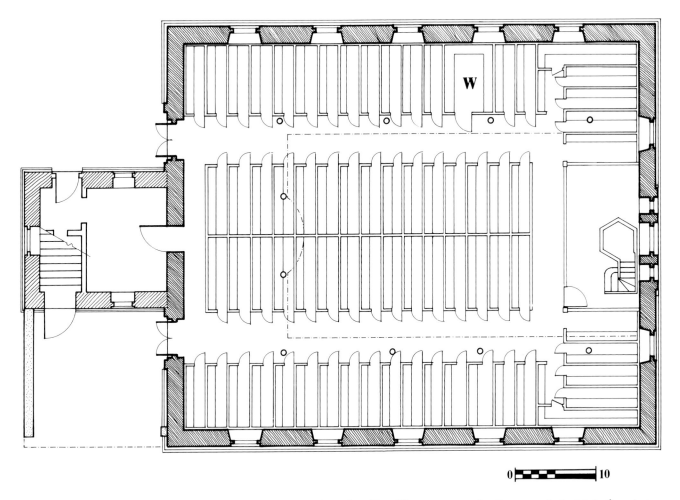

FIG. 261. Christ church (1767–73; James Parsons, undertaker), Alexandria. Plan. The tower serves in effect as a private stair to the private gallery installed in 1785. The pews shown in the plan date from the early 19th century. The Washington double pew (W) is supposed to be original, but dates from the same time as the other pews. (Drawing, Dell Upton.)

Damage that may happen in doing the same; and it is also ordered that the eight inside pews below the Cross Isle be raised in the same manner at the expense of the Parish." [14]

The gentry sought to use the articulated landscape to deny the traditional social order. For example, the right to build galleries and private pews had formerly been granted by vestrymen to themselves and other gentlemen as a prerogative of service, but in the third quarter of the

eighteenth century privileges were demanded by men who refused to serve on vestries. These new-style gentlemen desired a limited and carefully defined relationship to the parish. In place of the old ideal of unlimited service in return for unlimited prerogative, they offered a specific service in return for a specific prerogative. In 1783, six gentlemen proposed to the Fairfax Parish vestry that they build a gallery in the Alexandria church, financing it by private subscription (see Fig. 261). The surplus funds from the subscription would remain in the hands of the pew-holders to be used for the maintenance of the gallery, and what was left from these funds might from time to time "be applyed to the repairs and uses of the sd. Church in Other Instances," at the discretion of the subscribers, "when ever applied to for that purpose." Seats were to be divided into three classes and distributed by a lottery to the subscribers in each class. A group of well-to-do parishioners, in other words, had disengaged themselves from the general and nonspecific obligations of the individual in the traditional parish, and proposed to deal with the church on a contractually limited, economic basis as a corporate entity. The six men who proposed the plan were the minister and five of eight vestrymen. It is not surprising, therefore, that "it was Unanimously agreed that the design is Laudable," or that such a scheme should be undertaken at a time when the Establishment was unable to collect parish levies. It is telling that the proponents could separate their roles as private parishioners and as vestrymen so clearly in their minds.[15]

Though these transactions were reported in the traditional language of the vestry books, they represented a new kind of association within the parish, in which prerogative and service were reduced to commodities mediated by price. This change has been widely noted in studies of eighteenth-century America and is sometimes discussed in terms of the sociological theory of modernization. The evangelical temper, with its focus on individual conduct and individual merit, is seen as modern, in contrast to the elite concern with inherited merit and the good of the group, which is seen as traditional. But the auctioning of pews in late colonial parishes and the demand for hanging pews and private wings forty years earlier were as much a statement of a "modern" outlook as evangelical religion. Both evangelicalism and gentry separatism sprang from a desire for a new relationship to the local community. The striking thing is that it was the gentlemen who made the initial move: the first hanging pews and private windows date from the 1720s. Evangelicalism arose in the Great Awakening of the 1730s and 1740s. Thus the rise of evangelicalism was perhaps less a modernizing reaction to traditionalism, as Rhys Isaac and others have suggested, than a response to the elite's dismantling of tradition. Isaac has shown that although the evangelicals denied the social basis of religious bonding, they sought to recover the benefits of the tradi-

tional community the parish promised but failed to provide, forging new bonds from the very individualism that was destroying the old ones. In the parish church, the gentry attempted to maintain the old hierarchies and the old symbols, while replacing the premises that supported them.[16]

Although the changes in Virginia parish life represent variations on a familiar story, they have architectural interest in the ways architecture mediated the transformation, "explaining" it symbolically, as dancing did in other arenas. Until the end of the colonial period, Virginia's gentry clung to the architectural forms and spatial patterns invented in the late seventeenth and early eighteenth centuries. But the church buildings did change. In an earlier chapter I distinguished style from mode. A third way of using forms began to affect Virginia's churches in the mid-eighteenth century: I call it *fashion*.

The church before 1750 depended for its visual impact on the manipulation of formal modes customarily associated with and controlled by the upper classes. The use of artifacts to assert or maintain social standing is, of course, a very old practice. Access to costly artifacts, and those that accorded with elite tastes, was a sign of social status to which Anglo-Americans were traditionally sensitive. Sumptuary laws were sometimes used in early Virginia to enforce social boundaries of possession, and the violation of these boundaries was viewed as a sign of severe social disorder. "Our Cowe-keeper here of James Citty on Sundayes goes acowterd all in fresh flaming silkes and a wife of one that in England had professed the black arte not of a scholler but of a collier of Croydon, weares her rough bever hatt with a faire perle hattband, and a silken suite therto correspondent." By applying classical detailing to their houses, and, as vestrymen, having it installed in the churches, gentry demonstrated their economic power to command surplus labor to their own ends. More important, they showed their familiarity with the aesthetic preferences of an international elite with whom they were connected through trade. This was most apparent in the furnishings of the church, which, though readily obtainable from highly skilled local craftsmen, were "sent for" by merchant vestrymen, usually at a substantial commission to themselves. The gentry thus obtained goods for the parish that were inaccessible to most of their neighbors. Modish forms served to define social power.[17]

Modish design continued to characterize the churches of many parishes after 1750, but sometimes the conscious pursuit of fashion came to dominate architectural decisions. Modish forms were fashionable, of course, in that they indicated current access to certain social and economic circles. But *fashion* is reserved here for a more specific phenomenon that arose from the greatly expanded availability of consumer goods in Anglo-American society after the mid-eighteenth century. Merely to have desirable goods was no longer as distinctive an achievement after the middle of the century as it had been before. The manufacture of vast quantities of new goods brought to middling consumers items that had previously been restricted to upper-class purchasers. This was accompanied by the invention of marketing strategies that goaded individual consumers not simply to maintain acceptable standards within social groups but to keep pace with the rapidly and capriciously changing forms created by designers and manufacturers. Fashionable late eighteenth-century consumers learned to adapt rapidly. Status was no longer a stable condition, but had to be maintained constantly by a quick grasp and speedy adoption of the newest material goods. The commercial exploitation of fashion differed from the marketing of elite modes in several respects. Elite modes depended for their appeal in large part on their inaccessibility. New-style entrepreneurs played on this tradition by charging artificially high prices for their new goods and releasing them initially to a restricted, prestigious audience, thereby whipping up demand for them when they were available for general sale. Old-style modes revolved around the tastes of the ruling class — around patronage. In the new order, the elite were as much the tools of fashion as its guides; they were often manipulated by merchants and manufacturers to enhance the salability of new goods. The patron-producer relationship was replaced by a merchant-customer relationship, although the latter was still described in the language of the former. The change was not simple or sudden, and once fashion was established it went beyond the manipulation of a handful of manufacturers such as, for example, the potter Josiah Wedgwood. The important point is that producers now emphasized the quick acquisition of generally available goods and ideas over the exclusive possession of scarce commodities.[18]

The notion of fashion came to Virginia almost as soon as it had developed in England. It affected the material world of the Virginia parish church in various ways, depending on the class of artifact. Small objects like fonts and hangings that were imported directly from England remained unmediated by Virginia taste. Large objects like buildings and architectural fittings were produced locally; their fashionability, though less pure than that of the imported objects, is nonetheless unmistakable. Virginia's church builders were content to use a generalized classical vocabulary before mid-century, but after 1750 some of them found it necessary to refer to specific buildings, and even to reproduce specific fashionable forms from recent architectural publications. Many northern Virginia churches have exterior fenestration that is derived from Gibbsian precedent and that recalls the urban Anglican churches of Philadelphia, Boston, and New York. Their doorways, pulpits, altarpieces, canopies, and desks, as we have seen, were specified to be in particular classical orders. In several cases, details were copied directly from the architectural books of Batty Langley (Figs. 262, 263; see Figs. 150, 155, 166).

As in their relations with their fellow parishioners, the leaders of Fairfax, Truro, and other parishes were beginning to look beyond parish borders for an architecture unmixed with local and traditional forms. The values of fashion drained older forms of their meanings. For example, compass ceilings declined in popularity in Virginia after 1750, and while they never stopped being built, flat or "square" ceilings became increasingly common, even in elaborate brick churches and in additions to churches with compass ceilings. St. John's church, King William County, built around 1730 with a compass ceiling, had a square ceiling in its north wing of the 1750s. A similar ell was built onto the brick, compass-ceilinged Blandford church beginning in 1752. The vestry specified the addition's square ceiling in its original minute. At the same time, the domestic visual reference was intensified in some of the most fashionable churches. Pohick and Falls churches and Christ church, Alexandria, as it was originally planned, all *look* much more like gentry houses than any of their earlier and more southern neighbors. These churches occasion a final comment on the qualities of movement in the Anglican parish church.[19]

The material and ritual displays of the parish church had as their intended audience the gentry and middling Virginians. The latter were likely to become Presbyterian, Baptist, and Methodist dissenters, as they saw the gentry leaders presuming to rule while increasingly unwilling to serve. The mixture of holy things and profane was a deception. The Anglican elite, unable to relinquish their own centrality, adapted to change more subtly. For them,

FIG. 262. Aquia church (1754–57; Mourning Richards, undertaker), Stafford County. South door. The tablet in the tympanum, cut by William Copein, is inscribed "Built/AD 1751 Destroyed/By Fire 1754 & Rebuilt AD 1757/By Mourning Richards Undertaker William Copein Mason." (Photograph, Dell Upton.)

FIG. 263. Pohick church (1769–74; Daniel French, undertaker), Fairfax County. South door. The Ionic capitals of the Aquia-stone doorway have been destroyed by exposure and vandalism. (Photograph, Dell Upton.)

the social and architectural metaphor of hospitality retained its symbolic utility, and so they began to fashion a new world from the materials of the old. In the new parish church, as with Philip Fithian's dancers, things might come out right — not much changed — even if no one appeared to take responsibility for them. Hence the fascination with the dance.

The movement in the landscape, the dance of society, served as a mediating structure for making this change: it assured Virginians that beneath apparent anarchy and self-serving behavior there was a pattern of shared beliefs or impulses that kept everyone on the same track. The French analyst of New World culture Médéric-Louis-Élie Moreau de Saint-Méry summed up this point of view as he depicted the origins of dance in a manner strikingly similar to Fithian's description of his pupils' dancing. "Anyone who feels an emotion strongly," he wrote, "will express it by movements very similar to dance; and, if this joyful emotion is felt by several individuals, it is natural that hands and arms come together almost involuntarily in a manner which links one to the other, and the movements mingle and are shared." The augmented domestic imagery and the retention of ranked seating in the Virginia parish church were the Anglican equivalent of the dance: they assured the Virginia gentleman that things were really not any different, that his own withdrawal from communal responsibility and his flirtations with atomism would result not in chaos but in some ultimate pattern as yet invisible. During the third quarter of the century, the Anglican Church was embroiled in Virginian and colonial political controversies that undermined the hegemonic authority of the Church. The Parsons' Cause in Virginia and the controversy over a bishop for the American colonies seemed to locate the Church on the wrong side of larger political battles. Yet its hegemony was already being undermined in Virginia by the gentry's redefinition of their role in the institution. The Church was increasingly dispensable for elite dominance; many of the gentry found it inconvenient even to give token service to the vestry. Over and over in the vestry books men invited to serve in the third quarter of the century refused to do so; occasionally two or three invitations had to be issued to fill a single post. But the parish church continued to perform a function: it helped elite Virginians to imagine a new Church. At the time of the Revolution, the process of reconception was most advanced in urban parishes, particularly those in northern Virginia. The new model parish, one that relinquished its claims to social universality, was already in place by 1776, and Anglican churches survived the conflict. Christ church, Alexandria, for example, was never without a congregation. These parishes were able to accomplish the transition from state Church to denomination that has interested historians of American religion for decades. Unlike other strong Establishments, such as the Congregational Church in New England, northern Virginia's Anglican Church was transformed smoothly. By dressing new ways in old images, the parish church acted as the mediator of the transformation. The shift from Church to denomination in northern Virginia was less a theological or institutional process than a symbolic one.[20]

In rural and southern Virginia parishes, where the process of redefinition was much less advanced, entire parishes collapsed. In those parishes, the delicate interrelationships of the parish church were forgotten in the Revolution. Without the animating mixture of holy things with profane, the church was meaningless, even to the gentry who formerly supported it. The transition from vital institution to antiquity was sudden. As Anglicanism contracted in all parts of Virginia, small and great sacrileges affronted the parish church. In Alexandria, a glazier named Patrick Riley was jailed for "an unparalleled Species of Robbery, viz. Stealing the Glass from the Windows of the Protestant Espicopal Church." More shocking was the 1798 attack by gentry sons on Bruton Parish church. "The Communion Table was broken into a thousand pieces," Isaac A. Coles reported, "all the prayer Books and Bibles scattered about the Church Yard, one winder entirely destroyed, and the pulpit itself bedaubed from one end to the other, with human excrement." The perpetrators, he noted, were too many and too respectable to be punished.[21]

Less spectacular but more insidious was the early republican notion that what had been owned communally in undivided shares was now owned divisibly in common, that what had belonged to the community could be appropriated by the individual. Bishop William Meade denounced the attitude, but it was fully in keeping with the highly articulated and individualized relationship to the Church the gentry themselves had defined before the Revolutionary War. The Wicomico Parish vestry book was closed in 1840 with this note:

The Church having become useless both on account of its dilapidation — for want of Members to repair it — and the people in the neighbourhood thinking they had a right to use the materials as suited their convenience after every particle of the woodwork had been torn away the Revd. William Meade assistant Bishop of the Diocese (with my consent and advice) sold the site and ruins of the Church to Captain Hiram Ingram for five hundred dollars on a credit of six & twelve months this 17th day of July 1840. . . .

Jos. Ball
Ditchley 1840

Ingram never paid.[22]

Appendix

Agreement for Spring Swamp Chapel, Albemarle Parish, 1747

The Vestry haveing covenanted & agreed with James Anderson of Amelia County for the building of a Church or Chapel at or near where the Chapel at Spring Swamp now stands, for which he is to have £290. Currt. Money of Virginia, according to the Demensions & Manner following Vizt. 69 feet in Length & 26 feet in Bredth in the Clear: 16 feet Pitch under pin'd 2 feet high vizt. a foot below & 1 foot above the surface of the Ground with good well burnt Bricks & air Holes at proper Distance, a strong substantial Girt Floor laid with sound well season'd quarter'd Pine Plank in bredth not above 10 Inches, all the Pews to be 6 feet wide & 10 feet long, except two Vizt. one on each side of the Communion Table, which are to be 9 by 7 the Ally to be 6 feet wide: The church to have two Doors in the South Side & one in the West end 4 feet wide and 9 feet high, all to be folding, and the work quarter Round & Rais'd pannel; the two Doors in the South Side to be made fast with Bars & Iron Hooks, that in the West End with two spring Bolts & a neat & strong Lock: all to be hung with suitable HL Hinges: the Pews to be 4 feet high & close the Front to be quarter Round & raised Pannel, the Partitions plain Wainscot, all the Pews to be neatly cap'd Plank Seats on three Sides, the Doors to be of size according to the Plan & hung with Substantial H Hinges, the Communion Table to be rais'd two steps above the Floor of the Church, and inclos'd with Rails & neatly turn'd Ballusters, the Door there to [be] hung with neat substantial Hinges, a Pulpit with a neat & suitable Canopy & Door hung with H Hinges & both that & the two Reading Desks Vizt. for the Minister & Clerk to be the sort of Work with the Front of the Pews & of Demension according to the Plan, Rails & Ballusters from the Minister's reading Pew to the Pulpit: The length & width of the space for the Comunion Table & Number of steps to ascend to the Reading Pews & Pulpit to be determined & directed by the Minister. The space of two Pews on the North Side at the West end of the Church to be set apart for a Baptistry with Seats all round: A neat turn'd Post erected in the Area with handsom Mouldings round the Top, whereon to place the font or Bason, & a Desk adjoining to it to lay the Book on: two Plank Seats to be Put up in the Westmost front Door way & one in that of the Eastermost. the Church to have 6 Windows in the South Side 7 in the North side of Scituation & size in the clear according to the Plan, a large Window in the East End 6 feet wide in the Clear & of a Proportional highth divided by a Post in the Middle a Window in the West End above the Plate of a Demension suitable to the Place: all the Windows to be glaz'd with good Crown Glass, the runing sashes to be supported when up with Iron Pins made fast to the Frame with a Leather thong the Church to be done up the heighth of the Pews with Feather Edge Plank plain'd & beaded, to have a comon Substantial Roof with a Compass Cieling the Walls & Roof to be strengthen'd with great Beams across in a Number & size suitable, the Walls above the Pews & Cieling to be well Plaister'd & whitewash'd: The Window Frames on the inside & Door Cases on both sides to be architrav'd: a small Window in the back of the Pulpit of size suitable to the Place, Shutters for all the Windows of Plain Wainscot, to be hung with substantial H Hinges & made fast when open with Iron Hooks & Staples & when shut with an Iron Spring Bolt, the Walls & Gable Ends to be done with Feather Edg Plank Plain'd & beaded to show not above 6 Inches, with Cornish Eaves the Roof to be coverd on saw'd Laths with good Cypress Heart Shingles in length 20 Inches in thickness 1 Inch & in Bredth not above 4 Inches & nail'd with 6d. Nails the Roof to be hip'd from the Coller Beams, the Side & Gabel End Walls to be well tar'd: the Window Shutters on both sides the out side of the Doors & Door Cases, the out side of the Window Frames & Sashes the Cornish the Corner &

Barge Boards all to be well painted with White Lead & Oil: a Fronton or Pediment over each Door Shingled &C. as the Roof: White Oak or Light wood Steps at each Door mitred at the Corners. A Gallery in the West End of the Church of Pitch, Demention & Form according to the Plan with a Proper Stair Case & close Breast or Front of Wainscot quarter'd round & rais'd Pannel with Architrave frese & Cornish & proper Base, one Pew in the fore Part on the North side 6 feet by 11½ feet by 11½ a Passage from the stairs of 3 feet wide, a Passage to the back side of 3 feet wide, 8 Seats on each side, four 2 by 11½ feet to rise above one another 9 Inches, a Partition betwixt each Seat 2 feet high above each respective Floor of Plain Wainscot, The Gallery Plastered underneath the whole to be compleated & finished at the Proper Cost & Charges of the sd. James Anderson and that in a neat & workmanlike Manner; by the 15th. of June which shall Happen in the Year 1750. For the Performance thereof the sd. James Anderson is to give Bon with Sufficient Security as soon as may be, to the Church wardens of the sd. Parish for the Time being.*

* Albemarle VB, pp. 42–43.

| Notes |

Introduction

1. Samuel Mordecai to Rachel Mordecai, Sept. 11, 1814, in Alexander Wilbourne Weddell, "Samuel Mordecai, Chronicler of Old Richmond, 1786–1865," *VMHB* 53, no. 4 (October 1945): 283–84.

2. Weddell, "Mordecai," p. 284; George Washington, *The Diaries of George Washington, 1748–1799*, ed. John C. Fitzpatrick (Boston: Houghton, Mifflin, 1925), 4: 195; David Klingaman, "The Significance of Grain in the Development of the Tobacco Colonies," *Journal of Economic History* 29, no. 2 (June 1969): 268–78; Cary Carson, Norman F. Barka, William M. Kelso, Garry Wheeler Stone, and Dell Upton, "Impermanent Architecture in the Southern American Colonies," *WP* 16, nos. 2–3 (summer–autumn 1981): 162; Carville Earle and Ronald Hoffman, "Staple Crops and Urban Development in the Eighteenth-Century South," *Perspectives in American History* 10 (1976): 19–58. In Isle of Wight County, 19.7% of the landholders listed in the 1782 Land Tax Books held less than 100 acres of land. The proportion increased to 28.5% by 1796, and to 36.4% by 1809. Similar changes occurred in adjacent Surry County, where the corresponding figures were 15.5% in 1782, 25.6% in 1795, and 33.2% in 1810. (Dell Upton, "The Virginia Parlor, National Museum of American History, Smithsonian Institution: A Report on the Henry Saunders House and Its Occupants," MS., Smithsonian Institution, 1981, pp. 20–26; Surry County Land Tax Books, 1782, 1795, 1810, VSL.)

3. A.G. Roeber, "Authority, Law and Custom: The Rituals of Court Day in Tidewater Virginia, 1720–1750," *WMQ* 3d ser., 37, no. 1 (January 1980): 29–30, 52n.; Rhys Isaac, "Dramatizing the Ideology of Revolution: Popular Mobilization in Virginia, 1774 to 1776," *WMQ* 3d ser. 33, no. 3 (July 1976): 364; Latrobe, p. 183.

4. Henry Hartwell, James Blair, and Edward Chilton, *The Present State of Virginia, and the College* (1697), ed. Hunter Dickinson Farish (Williamsburg: Colonial Williamsburg, 1940), p. 65; Robert Beverley, *The History and Present State of Virginia* (1705), ed. Louis B. Wright (Chapel Hill: University of North Carolina Press, 1947), p. 253; Brydon, p. 241; G. MacLaren Brydon and Mary Goodwin, *The Colonial Churches of Virginia* (Richmond: Virginia State Chamber of Commerce, 1937), p. 1; George Carrington Mason, "The Colonial Churches of Spotsylvania and Caroline Counties," *VMHB* 58, no. 4 (October 1950): 442. For the history of county divisions in Virginia, see *A Hornbook of Virginia History* (Richmond: VSL, 1965), pp. 12–30; for the complex history of the parish divisions, see Charles Francis Cocke, *Parish Lines, Diocese of Southern Virginia* (Richmond: VSL, 1964), and Charles Francis Cocke, *Parish Lines, Diocese of Virginia* (Richmond: VSL, 1967). Throughout the book, I will use Church to refer to the institution, and church to refer to the building or church services (as in "going to church").

5. David L. Holmes, "The Decline and Revival of the Church of Virginia," in *Up from Independence: The Episcopal Church in Virginia*, ed. the Interdiocesan Bicentennial Committee of the Virginias (Orange, Va.: Interdiocesan Bicentennial Committee of the Virginias, 1976), pp. 60–66; Rhys Isaac, "Evangelical Revolt: The Nature of the Baptists' Challenge to the Traditional Order in Virginia, 1765 to 1775," *WMQ* 3d ser. 31, no. 3 (July 1974): 345–68; Rhys Isaac, "Preachers and Patriots: Popular Culture and the Revolution in Virginia," in *The American Revolution: Explorations in the History of American Radicalism*, ed. Alfred F. Young (De Kalb: Northern Illinois University Press, 1976), pp. 137–40; Rhys Isaac, *The Transformation of Virginia, 1740 to 1790* (Chapel Hill: University of North Carolina Press, 1982), pp. 161–77, 260–87. Among the extant parish churches that were taken over by other Protestant denominations in the half-century after the Revolution were the upper church of Stratton Major Parish (Baptists and Methodists), Mangohick church (Baptists), Mattaponi church (Baptists), and St. Peter's Parish church (Presbyterians). The last returned to Episcopal hands in the mid-19th century.

6. Holmes, "Decline and Revival," pp. 53–55, 75–78, 86–89; Meade, 1: 404.

7. Meade, 1: 399–400.

8. Meade, 1: 331–32.

9. Meade, 2: 22. Though not compensated for their services, those vestrymen who were merchants were often paid a commission on goods ordered from England on behalf of the parish. (See below, chapter 7.) In addition, certain domestic parish offices, notably that of collector (of taxes), carried a commission as well.

10. For a recent reassessment of the issue of clerical quality, see Joan R. Gunderson, "The Search for Good Men: Recruiting

Ministers in Colonial Virginia," *HMPEC* 48, no. 4 (December 1979): 455–72.

11. Horton Davies, *Worship and Theology in England*, 3, *From Watts and Wesley to Maurice, 1690–1850* (Princeton: Princeton University Press, 1961), p. 61; Carter, pp. 376–77, 536, 743–44.

12. St. Peter's VB, p. 182; Carter, p. 752; Horton Davies, *Worship and Theology in England*, 2, *From Andrewes to Baxter and Fox, 1603–1690*, pp. 133–42; VG (Purdie and Dixon), January 17, 1771; Fithian, p. 100; *St. Peter's Parish, New Kent County, Virginia* (n.p.: St. Peter's Parish, 1979), unpaginated; Devereux Jarratt, "The Autobiography of the Reverend Devereux Jarratt, 1732–63," ed. Douglass Adair, *WMQ* 3d ser., 9, no. 3 (July 1952): 364.

13. Fiske Kimball, *Domestic Architecture of the American Colonies and of the Early Republic* (1922; reprint ed., New York: Dover Publications, 1966); Thomas T. Waterman, *The Mansions of Virginia, 1706–1776* (Chapel Hill: University of North Carolina Press, 1944); Wallace B. Gusler, *Furniture of Williamsburg and Eastern Virginia, 1710–1790* (Richmond: Virginia Museum, 1979).

Chapter 1

1. George Percy, *Observations Gathered Out of 'A Discourse of the Plantation of the Southern Colony in Virginia by the English, 1606,'* ed. David B. Quinn (Charlottesville: University Press of Virginia, 1967), p. 10; John Smith, *Travels and Works of Captain John Smith*, ed. Edward Arber and A.G. Bradley (Edinburgh: John Grant, 1910), p. 957.

2. Bernard Sheehan, *Savagism and Civility: Indians and Englishmen in Colonial Virginia* (New York: Cambridge University Press, 1980), p. 2; William Strachey, comp., *Lawes Divine, Morall and Martiall, etc.*, ed. David H. Flaherty (Charlottesville: University Press of Virginia, 1969), pp. 10–12.

3. *Records of the Virginia Company of London*, ed. Susan M. Kingsbury (Washington: Government Printing Office, 1906–1935), 3: 17; Ralph Hamor, *A True Discourse of the Present State of Virginia* (1615; reprint ed., Richmond: VSL, 1957), pp. 30–31. The Henrico church would have contained 5,000 square feet. The two largest parish churches known to have been built in 18th-century Virginia were the Stratton Major Parish church of 1768, and Bruton Parish church, built 1711–15 and enlarged in 1752. The former contained 4,800 square feet and the latter 4,403 square feet after it was expanded. I have discussed the role of the landscape in a civil society in "Early Vernacular Architecture in Southeastern Virginia" (Ph.D. diss., Brown University, 1980), chapter 1.

4. *Journal of the House of Burgesses, 1619–1658/59*, ed. H.R. McIlwaine (Richmond: n.p., 1915), pp. 21, 32–33, 35; Brydon, 1:

85; John C. McCabe, "Colonial Churches in Virginia, VI, Church at Jamestown," *Church Review* 8, no. 1 (April 1855): 131–33; Hening, 1: 160–61.

5. The earliest surviving Virginia vestry books, in order of their age, are those for Christ Church Parish, Middlesex County; Petsworth Parish; Kingston Parish; and St. Peter's Parish.

6. Henry Hartwell, James Blair, and Edward Chilton, *The Present State of Virginia, and the College* (1697), ed. Hunter Dickinson Farish (Williamsburg: Colonial Williamsburg, 1940), p. 65; Hugh Jones, *The Present State of Virginia*, ed. Richard L. Morton (1724; reprint ed., Chapel Hill: University of North Carolina Press, 1956), pp. 95, 257 n. 286; Brydon, 1: 67; William H. Seiler, "The Anglican Parish in Virginia," in *Seventeenth-Century America: Essays in Colonial History*, ed. James Morton Smith (Chapel Hill: University of North Carolina Press, 1959), pp. 125–27; Elizabeth City VB, pp. 27–28. Many of Virginia's resident chief executives were legally lieutenant governors serving in the place of absentee governors. Henceforth no distinction of title will be made between lieutenant governors and governors.

7. *Cal. State Pap.*, p. 122.

8. Brydon, 1: 464–66; Hening, 6: 259; Carter, pp. 120–21.

9. Jones, *Present State*, pp. 96, 225 n. 184; Wallace Notestein, *The English People on the Eve of Colonization, 1603–1630* (New York: Harper Torchbooks, 1962), p. 241; Seiler, "Anglican Parish," pp. 127–41; Arthur Pierce Middleton, "The Colonial Virginia Parish," *HMPEC* 40, no. 4 (December 1971): 433–34; Strachey, *Lawes Divine*, p. 12; Hartwell, Blair, and Chilton, *Present State*, pp. 66, 68; Robert Beverley, *The History and Present State of Virginia* (1705), ed. Louis B. Wright (Chapel Hill: University of North Carolina Press, 1947), pp. 262–63; Brydon, 1: 90–93. The analogy to congregationalism was first made by Hugh Jones, who described the Anglican clergyman as "a kind of independent in his own parish" (Jones, *Present State*, p. 98).

10. Jones, *Present State*, p. 259 n. 290; Middleton, "Colonial Virginia Parish," pp. 439–40.

11. Brydon, 1: 448.

12. Beverley, *History*, p. 263; Jones, *Present State*, p. 96; *Certain Sermons or Homilies . . . to Which Are Added, The Constitution and Canons of the Church of England, Set Forth A.D. 1603* (3d American ed.; Philadelphia: George and Wayne, 1844), p. 566; Robert Carter, "Rules for the Conduct of churchwardens," ca. 1775, Carter Family Papers, 1651–1861, sec. 30, MS., VHS, fols. 6–17.

13. Alexander Forbes, "Mr. Forbes' Account of the State of the Church in Virginia" (1724), in Perry, p. 327; Christ, Middlesex VB, pp. 22, 61–62; "The Church in Lower Norfolk County," *Lower Norfolk County Virginia Antiquary* 4, no. 1 (1897):

32–33; *VG*, December 11, 1766. Examples of women sextons include Alice Mazy, who tended the upper chapel of Christ Church Parish, and Anne Clear and Grace Soward of Stratton Major Parish (Christ, Middlesex VB, p. 169; Stratton Major VB, p. 7).

14. J. Charles Cox and Charles Bradley Ford, *The Parish Churches of England* (London: B. T. Batsford, 1935), p. 2; W. G. Hoskins, *The Making of the English Landscape* (1955; reprint ed., Harmondsworth: Penguin, 1970), pp. 108–10; Colin Platt, *The Parish Churches of Medieval England* (London: Secker & Warburg, 1981), pp. 1–9; Brydon, 1: 94–97, 370–73; Charles Francis Cocke, *Parish Lines, Diocese of Southern Virginia* (Richmond: VSL, 1964), pp. 195–98; Charles Francis Cocke, *Parish Lines, Diocese of Virginia* (Richmond: VSL, 1967), pp. 263–68; Jones, *Present State*, p. 100; Perry, pp. 260–318.

15. Perry, pp. 260–318; Wicomico VB, fols. 10, 31, 65, 86; Christ, Lancaster VB, pp. 2, 64, 92; Elizabeth City VB, pp. 13, 127; Albemarle VB, pp. 27, 279; Frederick VB, p. 43; Augusta VB, pp. 12, 463. For a discussion of parish size in remote Cumberland Parish, see Richard R. Beeman, "Social Change and Cultural Conflict in Virginia: Lunenburg County, 1746 to 1774," *WMQ* 3d ser. 35, no. 3 (July 1978): 463.

16. Hening, 2: 44; Perry, pp. 335–36.

17. *Certain Sermons*, p. 560.

18. Horton Davies, *Worship and Theology in England*, 1, *From Cranmer to Hooker, 1534–1603* (Princeton: Princeton University Press, 1970), pp. 34–39, 176–78, 228–31; Marion J. Hatchett, *The Making of the First American Book of Common Prayer, 1776–1789* (New York: Seabury Press, 1982), p. 3.

19. Brydon, 1: 459; Davies, *Worship and Theology*, 1: 213, 219–26; Meade, 1: 27–28, 45–46.

Chapter 2

1. Cumberland VB, pp. 324, 330, 333. For the use of a house as a church: Christ, Middlesex VB, p. 3; Shelburne VB, p. 18; for the use of a tobacco barn: Truro VB, pp. 88, 90.

2. Truro VB, p. 58; Christ, Middlesex VB, pp. 106–7, 120–22; Upper VB, p. 47. In 17th- and 18th-century Virginia, "lower" referred to the earliest or most densely settled portion of a county or parish, and "upper" referred to the newest or most sparsely settled portion.

3. For the vernacular threshold, see R.W. Brunskill, *Illustrated Handbook of Vernacular Architecture* (2d ed.; London: Faber & Faber, 1978), pp. 26–28.

4. Fredericksville VB, pp. 18, 24; Newport VB, p. 27; St. Andrew's VB, fol. 38.

5. Shelburne VB, pp. 15–17, 21.

6. Petition of Elizabeth City parishioners, June 26, 1726, Virginia General Assembly, House of Burgesses, Committee on Propositions and Grievances, Papers, 1711–1730, sec. 8, MS., VHS; Mason, pp. 107–8; St. George's, Spots. VB, 1: 30–31; *Executive Journals of the Council of Colonial Virginia*, 4, *1721–1739*, ed. H.R. McIlwaine (Richmond: VSL, 1930), p. 468; George Carrington Mason, "The Colonial Churches of Spotsylvania and Caroline Counties," *VMHB* 58, no. 4 (October 1950): 449; *Cal. State Pap.*, pp. 208–9; E. Lee Shepard, "'The Ease and Convenience of the People': Courthouse Location in Spotsylvania County, 1720–1740," *VMHB* 87, no. 3 (July 1979): 279–99.

7. *The Correspondence of the Three William Byrds of Westover, Virginia, 1684–1776*, ed. Marion Tinling (Charlottesville: University Press of Virginia, 1977), p. 567; St. Peter's VB, pp. 74–75, 80, 82, 90. The gift of land could bring honorific rewards as well. See below, chapter 7.

8. Truro VB, p. 88; St. Paul's VB, p. 514; *VG*, April 18, 1751; *VG* (Rind), July 18, 1766. Distance from Williamsburg did not affect the decision to advertise in the *Virginia Gazette*, as advertisements placed by the remote Cumberland Parish vestry show (*VG* [Purdie and Dixon], May 9, 1771).

9. St. Paul's VB, p. 514; St. George's, Acc. VB, fol. 2; Lynnhaven VB, p. 50; Christ, Middlesex VB, p. 235; Truro VB, p. 132. For examples of detailed bonds and contracts, see "Church Building in Colonial Virginia," *VMHB* 3, no. 4 (April 1896): 421–22; Blisland VB, pp. 55–56; Albemarle VB, pp. 5–6, 42–43; Truro VB, pp. 96–97, 115–17.

10. Bruton Recs., pp. 12–14, 31–33, 38; *Cal. State Pap.*, pp. 145–46; Mason, p. 232; "Carter Papers," *VMHB* 6, no. 1 (July 1898): 3; Petsworth VB, p. 157; Louise Belote Dawe, *Christ Church, Lancaster County, 1732, and the Life Around It* (Irvington, Va.: Foundation for Historic Christ Church, 1970), p. 9; Wicomico VB, fol. 58; John, Landon, and Charles Carter Letter Book, 1732–1781, microfilm, Colonial Williamsburg Foundation, pp. 21, 32; Robert Lidderdale to Charles Carter, December 12, 1734, Genealogical Material on Carter Family, Box 8, Minor Collection—Carter Family, Papers from the James Monroe Law Office Museum, Reel 7, Trinkle Library, Mary Washington College (courtesy of Mark R. Wenger). Currency exchange rates from John J. McCusker, *Money and Exchange in Europe and America, 1600–1775: A Handbook* (Chapel Hill: University of North Carolina Press, 1978), pp. 210–11; tobacco exchange rates from Paul G.E. Clemens, *The Atlantic Economy and Colonial Maryland's Eastern Shore: From Tobacco to Grain* (Ithaca: Cornell University Press, 1980), p. 226; and Lewis Cecil Gray, *History of Agriculture in the Southern United States* (1933; reprint ed., Gloucester, Mass.: Peter Smith, 1958), 1: 272.

11. Darrett B. Rutman and Anita H. Rutman, *A Place in Time: Middlesex County, Virginia, 1650–1750* (New York: Norton, 1984), p. 198; Wicomico VB, fol. 65–80; Christ, Lancaster VB, pp. 2–54.

12. Mason, p. 347; St. Andrew's VB, fol. 40; Albemarle VB, pp. 65, 270; Dettingen VB, 1: 104; Fairfax VB, p. 13; *The Writings of George Washington, from the Original Manuscript Sources, 1745–1799*, ed. John C. Fitzpatrick (Washington: Government Printing Office, 1931), 3: 112–14.

13. VG (Purdie and Dixon), February 19, 1767; Christ, Middlesex VB, p. 277. Sometimes there was no advance payment at all. The Cumberland Parish vestry constructed a church in 1759 for which it offered one half of the fee when the building was enclosed, and the remainder at completion (Cumberland VB, p. 373).

14. Albemarle VB, p. 270; Bristol VB, p. 78. Rare instances of the one-job stipulation are found in Simon Thomas's 1679 contract for building the first Hungar's Parish church, and in the 1703 plasterer's contract for St. Peter's Parish church, where James Knott agreed "not to doe any other worke till it be Complete and Finished" (Mason, p. 338; St. Peter's VB, p. 88). Bristol Parish's suspicion of Ravenscroft may have been justified. The Cypress church that Ravenscroft built for Southwark Parish in 1743–45 needed repairs to a cracked wall before the building was accepted. The vestrymen questioned "the ability and goodness of the Brick work" (Mason, p. 37).

15. VG, June 6, 1751, March 21, 1754, May 16, 1754; Christ, Middlesex VB, pp. 279, 290; Dettingen VB, 1: 35; Hening, 7: 151; Middlesex County Deeds, etc., 1687–1750, p. 186; King George County Order Book, 1751–65, pp. 870, 903 (last two references courtesy of Carl Lounsbury). A similar case to Richards's occurred in St. Patrick's Parish, where Thomas Wood was reimbursed for a burned church, also with legislative permission. It was rebuilt at a different site by someone else. (St. Patrick's VB, p. 17; Hening, 6: 611.)

16. Wicomico VB, fol. 92; VG (Purdie and Dixon), May 25, 1769; Dettingen VB, 1: 56.

17. VG (Purdie and Dixon), December 11, 1766, February 19, 1767, March 5, 1767; "Election for Vestrymen, Norfolk County, 1761," *Lower Norfolk County Virginia Antiquary* 1, no. 1 (1895): 19.

18. Dettingen VB, 1: 67; Albemarle VB, p. 66; Truro VB, p. 110.

19. Fairfax VB, p. 49; St. Peter's VB, p. 333; Bristol VB, p. 165; Albemarle VB, pp. 284, 302, 377.

20. Cocke, *Parish Lines, Diocese of Virginia*, pp. 152–53; Brydon, 1: 479 n. 10; *Journals of the House of Burgesses, 1712–1714, 1715, 1718, 1720–22, 1723–1726*, ed. H.R. McIlwaine (Richmond: VSL, 1912), pp. 11, 19–20, 23; Christ, Middlesex

VB, pp. 3–5, 48, 52, 57–58, 106–8, 118–23, 161, 163, 172, 178, 181. Clark's fee for this small wooden church was the same as that paid Mourning Richards for the enormous brick church at Aquia forty years later.

21. Christ, Middlesex VB, pp. 126–30, 136, 161–63, 165, 169–73, 175.

22. Christ, Middlesex VB, pp. 139–41, 144–47, 158, 161, 175.

23. Rutman and Rutman, *A Place in Time*, pp. 202, 215–19.

Chapter 3

1. Bruton Recs., p. 39.

2. St. George's, Acc. VB, fols. 7, 11; Accomack County Order Book, 1744–1753, p. 455; Accomack County Order Book, 1753–1763, p. 72; Accomack Deed Book, 1777–1783, p. 16; Dettingen VB, 1: 29. I am indebted to Carl Lounsbury for sharing with me information about Guttridge and several other builders discussed in this chapter.

3. Hipkins: Robert L. Montague, "Report on a Building at Urbanna, Virginia, for the APVA," MS., VHLC, 1958, p. 5; Middlesex County Order Book, 1705–10, p. 23; Darrett B. Rutman and Anita H. Rutman, *A Place in Time: Middlesex County, Virginia, 1650–1750* (New York: Norton, 1984), pp. 202, 215–19; Christ, Middlesex VB, pp. 128–30; Christ Reg., p. 191; Jones: Christ, Lancaster VB, pp. 1, 10; Lancaster County Orders No. 8, 1729–1743, MS., VSL, pp. 286–87; Legrand: St. Patrick's VB, pp. 7, 13, 15, 18, 33, 38; Mrs. W.S. Morton, "The Dwelling House on the Glebe Land in the Parish of St. Patrick in Prince Edward County," *WMQ* 2d ser. 17, no. 3 (July 1937): 409–10. Legrand also made alterations to the glebe house of Bristol Parish in 1765 (Bristol VB, p. 173).

4. VG (Purdie and Dixon), January 10, 1771; Cary: St. Paul's VB, p. 123; Rawlings, p. 106; Rand: Petsworth VB, p. 242; Kingston VB, pp. 25, 27, 31–32; Upper VB, pp. 46–47; Newport VB, pp. 71–72, 82; VG, December 10, 1736; Moore: Petsworth VB, p. 208; Christ, Middlesex VB, p. 234; Blisland VB, pp. 55–56; Kingston VB, pp. 25, 31–32; Fredericksville VB, p. 76; Walker: St. Paul's VB, pp. 157–58; St. Peter's VB, pp. 262–63, 338–39; Richmond County Account Book, 1724–1783, p. 153; Westmoreland County Order Book, 1747–1750, p. 102a; Marcus Whiffen, *The Public Buildings of Williamsburg, Colonial Capital of Virginia: An Architectural History* (Williamsburg: Colonial Williamsburg, 1958), p. 134; VG, October 17, 1751; Smith: Fredericksville VB, pp. 17–18; St. Paul's VB, p. 334; Augusta VB, pp. 319, 323.

5. Petsworth VB, p. 69; Beverley Fleet, ed., *Colonial Virginia Abstracts*, 14, *King and Queen County: Records Concerning 18th Century Persons*, 5th coll. (Richmond: privately printed, 1942), pp. 6–8; George Carrington Mason, "The Colonial Churches of Spotsylvania and Caroline Counties, Virginia," *VMHB* 58, no. 4 (October 1950): 442; *Cal. State Pap.*, pp.

208–9; E. Lee Shepard, " 'The Ease and Convenience of the People': Courthouse Location in Spotsylvania County, 1720–1840," *VMHB* 87, no. 3 (July 1979): 281–82; Richard L. Morton, *Colonial Virginia* (Chapel Hill: University of North Carolina Press, 1960), pp. 541–42; VG (Rind), October 18, 1770. Chew's land grant was forestalled by Lord Fairfax's competing claim to the same tract. (Morton, *Colonial Virginia*, pp. 541–42.)

6. Whiffen, *Public Buildings*, pp. 79, 137; Blisland VB, pp. 55–56, 66; Albemarle VB, p. 31; St. Andrew's VB, fol. 6; Cumberland VB, p. 325; VG, May 9, 1751. Other Virginia craftsmen prospered as Deloney did, and some abandoned their trades on the way up. Larkin Chew, Jr., apparently left carpentry for the tavern business just as Williamsburg cabinetmaker Anthony Hay did. Severn Guttridge and William Rand both obtained ordinary licenses, but continued to build. (Wallace B. Gusler, *Furniture of Williamsburg and Eastern Virginia, 1710–1790* [Richmond: Virginia Museum, 1979], p. 62; Accomack County Order Book, 1753–1763, p. 140; Isle of Wight County Order Book, 1755–1757, p. 74.)

7. Stratton Major VB, pp. 11–12, 131–33, 141–42, 173; Christ, Middlesex VB, pp. 234–35; St. Paul's VB, p. 182; VG, March 27, 1752; Morton, *Colonial Virginia*, pp. 749–50; VG (Purdie and Dixon), July 16, 1767, November 12, 1767. Westover has long been thought to have been built by William Byrd II in the 1730s, but recent evidence suggests to me that it may have been built by Byrd's widow and his son William Byrd III. Byrd II had been talking to John Ravenscroft, a well-known Prince George County contractor who built several churches south of the James River, about "building our house" in 1740, but Byrd died in 1744. In 1752 Gaines advertised in the *Virginia Gazette* for the return of two house carpenters who had run away from him while working at Westover. They may have been working on the main house, which was reported to have burned in 1748, and which contains several architectural elements, notably the plaster ceilings and several of the marble mantels on the first floor, which, as Mark Wenger has noted, accord more with a third-quarter date than a second-quarter one. (William Byrd, *Another Secret Diary of William Byrd of Westover, 1739–1741*, ed. Maude H. Woodfin [Richmond: Dietz Press, 1942], p. 104; VG, March 27, 1752; [Dell Upton], architectural description, Historic American Buildings Survey, Westover Project, HABS No. VA-402, MS., VHLC; Mark R. Wenger, "Westover, William Byrd's Mansion Reconsidered," M. Arch. Hist. thesis, University of Virginia, 1981, pp. 24–25, 42–60.)

8. VG (Purdie and Dixon), November 12, 1767. For a representative career of one of the workmen who appeared only once for a minor repair (in Dettingen Parish), see Luke Beckerdite, "A Virginia Cabinetmaker: The Eventon Shop and Related Work," *Journal of Early Southern Decorative Arts* 10, no. 2 (November 1984): 1–33.

9. VG, May 16, 1766; VG (Purdie and Dixon), August 16, 1770, March 27, 1752, December 17, 1736, February 25, 1737; St. Paul's VB, p. 163; Petsworth VB, pp. 247–48, 253; Truro VB, pp. 129, 135.

10. Rosamond Randall Beirne and John H. Scarff, *William Buckland, 1734–1774: Architect of Virginia and Maryland* (n.p.: Board of Regents, Gunston Hall and Hammond-Harwood House Association, 1958), pp. 1, 4, 9, 11, 37, 147; Luke Beckerdite, "William Buckland and William Bernard Sears, the Designer and the Carver," *Journal of Early Southern Decorative Arts* 8, no. 2 (November 1982): 9, 26–27, 29–35, 38 n. 10; VG (Rind), January 10, 1771, August 8, 1771; William Buckland to Robert Carter of Nomini Hall, March 25, 1771, Carter Family Papers, 1561–1861, VHS; Truro VB, pp. 134–35. For useful observations on the organization of 18th-century Virginia craft workshops, see Gusler, *Furniture of Williamsburg*, pp. 59–67 and passim.

11. Richmond County Order Book No. 12, 1746–1752, microfilm, VSL, p. 159; Blisland VB, pp. 85, 122. The Reverend Alexander Forbes, in a 1724 letter to the bishop of London, noted that builders were expensive, but did not say they were hard to find: "The hiring of Workmen being very chargeable here and other things relating to building, this hath greatly augmented the difficulty of my own circumstances; yet for it all I could not hitherto supply my own necessity in this, so as not be greatly incommoded with regard to my calling" (Perry, p. 330).

12. Peter C. Marzio, "Carpentry in the Southern Colonies during the Eighteenth Century with Emphasis on Maryland and Virginia," *WP* 7 (1972): 230–32, 236–39. For a glimpse of the varied activities of a 19th-century Virginia builder, see Jerry Donovan, "John Jordan, Virginia Builder," *JSAH* 9, no. 3 (October 1950): 17–19; and L. Moody Simms, Jr., "John Jordan, Builder and Entrepreneur," *Virginia Cavalcade* 23, no. 1 (summer 1973): 18–29.

13. Fiske Kimball, *Domestic Architecture of the American Colonies and of the Early Republic* (1922; reprint ed., New York: Dover Publications, 1966), pp. 61, 66. For a discussion of the relationship between 18th-century building and the early history of the architectural profession in America, see Dell Upton, "Pattern Books and Professionalism: Aspects of the Transformation of Domestic Architecture in America, 1800–1860," *WP* 19, nos. 2–3 (summer–autumn 1984): 107–50.

14. Marcus Whiffen and Frederick Koeper, *American Architecture, 1607–1976* (Cambridge: MIT Press, 1981), pp. 3, 53, 76; John Clive and Bernard Bailyn, "England's Cultural Provinces: Scotland and America," *WMQ* 3d ser. 11, no. 2 (April 1954): 211; Alan Gowans, *Images of American Living: Four Centuries of Architecture and Furniture as Cultural Expres-

sion (Philadelphia: Lippincott, 1964), pp. 226–38; Thomas T. Waterman, *The Mansions of Virginia, 1706–1776* (Chapel Hill: University of North Carolina Press, 1944), pp. 103, 107, 243–53.

15. Clive and Bailyn, "England's Cultural Provinces," pp. 212–13; Bernard Bailyn, *The Origins of American Politics* (New York: Vintage Books, 1967), pp. 124–61 and passim; Gordon S. Wood, *The Creation of the American Republic, 1776–1787* (Chapel Hill: University of North Carolina Press, 1969), pp. 28–36, 46–70 and passim; Whiffen and Koeper, *American Architecture*, p. 76; Gowans, *Images*, p. 15; William H. Pierson, *American Buildings and Their Architects: The Colonial and Neo-Classical Styles* (Garden City, N.Y.: Anchor Books, 1976), p. 141.

16. Pierson, *American Buildings*, p. 141; Dell Upton, "Toward a Performance Theory of Vernacular Architecture in Tidewater Virginia," *Folklore Forum* 12, nos. 2–3 (1979): 173–96; Eric Mercer, *Furniture, 700–1700* (New York: Meredith Press, 1969), p. 120.

17. For another discussion of the idea of design responsibility in 18th-century American architecture, see Gowans, *Images*, p. 226. I have analyzed shared local architectural forms using a sociolinguistic model in "Toward a Performance Theory," pp. 173–96.

18. St. Peter's VB, p. 68; Albemarle VB, pp. 42–43; Bristol VB, p. 117; Dettingen VB, 1: 23, 33. The St. Peter's minute refers to the extant St. Peter's Parish church, New Kent County. For an instance of workmen's correcting a vestry error in drafting a glebe house plan, see Dell Upton, "Vernacular Domestic Architecture in Eighteenth-Century Virginia," *WP* 17, nos. 2–3 (summer–autumn 1982): 107.

19. Alan Gowans, *King Carter's Church, Being a study in Depth of Christ Church, Lancaster County, Virginia* (Victoria, B.C.: University of Victoria Maltwood Museum, 1969), p. 25; Wicomico VB, fols. 58, 60–61, 75–76; Lynnhaven VB, p. 28; Christ, Middlesex VB, p. 107; Petsworth VB, p. 17; VG (Purdie and Dixon), February 15, 1770. On changing concepts of copying buildings, I have been stimulated by Richard Krautheimer, "Introduction to 'An Iconography of Medieval Architecture,'" *Journal of the Warburg and Courtauld Institutes* 5 (1942): 1–33.

20. Whiffen, *Public Buildings*, pp. 80–82, 157–60; Dell Upton, "Traditional Timber Framing," in *Material Culture of the Wooden Age*, ed. Brooke Hindle (Tarrytown, N.Y.: Sleepy Hollow Press, 1981), pp. 51–68; Bristol VB*, p. 89; Upper VB, p. 89. The exception to my statement about framing is roof framing. See chapter 4.

21. Upper VB, p. 28; Christ, Middlesex VB, p. 3; Cunningham Recs., p. 16.

22. Christ, Middlesex VB, pp. 6, 12; Lynnhaven VB, p. 50; St. Andrew's VB, fol. 6; Truro VB, p. 46; Henrico VB, fol. 17; Bristol VB, p. 67. Patterns of copying in New England are discussed in Peter Benes, "The Templeton 'Run' and the Pomfret 'Cluster': Patterns of Diffusion in Rural New England Meetinghouse Architecture, 1647–1822," *Old-Time New England* 68, no. 3–4 (winter–spring 1978): 1–21. The practice of modeling extends beyond the design of churches, and beyond 18th-century America. See, for example, the contract printed in Peter Smith, *Houses of the Welsh Countryside* (London: Her Majesty's Stationery Office, 1975), pp. 334–35, for a house to be "in such sort manner and fashion and in as good plight as the pile of buildings [that] was lately built & wrought for Evan Edwards Esquire."

23. Dettingen VB, 1: 6, 49, 64; Fredericksville VB, p. 24; Lynnhaven VB, pp. 94–95; St. Mark's VB, p. 20; Christ, Middlesex VB, p. 136; Wicomico VB, fol. 82; Upper VB, pp. 54–55; Suffolk VB, p. 23.

24. Truro VB, p. 116. Marcus Whiffen illustrates two 18th-century architectural detail drawings, one scribed on a board, in *The Eighteenth-Century Houses of Williamsburg: A Study of Architecture and Building in the Colonial Capital of Virginia* (rev. ed.; Williamsburg: Colonial Williamsburg Foundation, 1984), pp. 42–43.

25. St. Peter's VB, pp. 68, 76.

26. Albemarle VB, p. 94; St. George's, Acc. VB, fol. 11; Suffolk VB, p. 8.

27. St. Peter's VB, p. 262; St. Paul's VB, p. 157; Albemarle VB, p. 288; Truro VB, pp. 87–88; Cunningham Recs., pp. 49–50; Bruton Recs, pp. 34–35; Whiffen, *Public Buildings*, pp. 77–82. Ariss was credited by Thomas Tileston Waterman with having designed many of the large northern Virginia mansions of the third quarter of the 18th century, largely on circumstantial evidence. (Waterman, *Mansions of Virginia*, pp. 243–53.) There is no evidence that his activities were markedly different from those of any of the other major undertakers discussed here, however.

28. Truro VB, p. 94; Fairfax VB, p. 11.

Chapter 4

1. Cary Carson, Norman F. Barka, William M. Kelso, Garry Wheeler Stone, and Dell Upton, "Impermanent Architecture in the Southern American Colonies," *WP* 16, nos. 2–3 (summer–autumn 1981): 135–96; Dell Upton, "Traditional Timber Framing," in *Material Culture of the Wooden Age*, ed. Brooke Hindle (Tarrytown, N.Y.: Sleepy Hollow Press, 1981), pp. 51–52, 54–59; St. Peter's VB, p. 17; Petsworth VB, pp. 3–4, 7, 11, 27, 37, 41.

2. Christ, Middlesex VB, p. 37. Cedar Park, a house built in 1702 in Anne Arundel County, Md., is just such a holeset post building with interrupted sills. Under the old rear wall, now protected by a leanto, the sills are held a few inches above the ground by the posts. (Carson, et al., "Impermanent Architecture," pp. 187–89.)

3. St. Peter's VB, pp. 60–61, 103; Newport VB, pp. 51–52; Bristol VB, p. 4; Southam VB, p. 2; Upper VB, p. 127.

4. Frederick VB, p. 27; Camden VB, p. 7.

5. St. Paul's VB, p. 123; Henrico VB, fols. 23, 85.

6. John C. McCabe, "Colonial Churches in Virginia, VII, Sketches of Bruton Parish Church, Williamsburg," *Church Review* 8, no. 4 (January 1856): 587–616; Bruton Recs., pp. 13–16; Lyon G. Tyler, "Bruton Church," *WMQ* 1st ser. 3, no. 3 (January 1895): 172–76.

7. For a more extensive treatment of the origin and form of Virginia framing, see Dell Upton, "Early Vernacular Architecture in Southeastern Virginia," Ph.D. diss., Brown University, 1980, pp. 65–78, 93–96; and Upton, "Traditional Timber Framing," pp. 51–61.

8. St. George's, Spots. VB, 1: 23–24; Christ, Middlesex VB, pp. 120, 122; Fredericksville VB, p. 17.

9. *The Builder's Dictionary: or, Gentleman and Architect's Companion* (1734; reprint ed., Washington, D.C.: Association for Preservation Technology, 1981), 2: n.p. ("Walls"); *Cal. State Pap.*, pp. 174–75; Lynnhaven VB, pp. 91, 94–95.

10. Upton, "Traditional Timber Framing," pp. 63–65; St. George's, Spots. VB, 1: 24; Fredericksville VB, p. 17. Clasped purlin roofs survive in common-rafter form in Virginia at Pear Valley (18th century), Northampton County, and in principal-rafter form on the kitchen (early 18th century?) at Westover, Charles City County.

11. Fairfax VB, p. 12; Upton, "Traditional Timber Framing," pp. 61–64; Carson, et al., "Impermanent Architecture," pp. 187–89; Philip Slaughter, "St. Luke's Church, Isle of Wight County, Virginia," date and source unidentified (ca. 1900), pp. 124–25, St. Luke's church file, item no. 9438, Picture Collection, VSL; Chapman, Evans, and Delehanty, Architects, Drawings 8 ("Perspective from Photo E showing roof ca. 1880"), 9 ("Projection of roof members to elevation"), 1955, St. Luke's Church Restoration Committee Papers, Research Department, Colonial Williamsburg Foundation; Petsworth VB, p. 7; Christ, Middlesex VB pp. 120, 126, 140; Southam VB, p. 2.

12. Stratton Major VB, pp. 132, 150.

13. Barry Harrison and Barbara Hutton, *Vernacular Houses in North Yorkshire and Cleveland* (Edinburgh: John Donald Publishers, 1984), pp. 170, 172, 175; Joseph Moxon, *Mechanick Exercises, or the Doctrine of Handy–Works* (3d ed.; reprint Scarsdale, N.Y.: Early American Industries Association, 1975), p. 145 pl. 11; *Builder's Dictionary*, 2: pls. 24–26; Petsworth VB, p. 39; Augusta VB, p. 323; Truro VB, p. 116; Rawlings, p. 28; Charles Francis Cocke, *Parish Lines, Diocese of Virginia* (Richmond: Virginia State Library, 1964), pp. 90–91. For examples of king-post trusses in other colonies, see Harley J. McKee, "St. Michael's Church, Charleston, 1752–1762," *JSAH* 23, no. 1 (March 1964): 41; and Antoinette F. Downing and Vincent J. Scully, Jr., *The Architectural Heritage of Newport, Rhode Island, 1640–1915* (2d ed.; New York: Bramhall House, 1967), pl. 52. The earliest section of the Old Ship church (1681), Hingham, Mass., has a king-post roof of an older form, with braces running down from the post to the tie beam, but the earliest strutted king-post roof in New England is that on the Lynnfield, Mass., church. (Marian Card Donnelly, *The New England Meeting Houses of the Seventeenth Century* [Middletown, Conn.: Wesleyan University Press, 1968], p. 74; cf. Harrison and Hutton, *Vernacular Houses in North Yorkshire and Cleveland*, pp. 170–75; Abbott Lowell Cummings, personal communication, May 6, 1983.) The earliest Virginia house with a king-post roof that I know of is Stratford Hall, built ca. 1730–35, or about the same time as Christ church, Lancaster County. See the Historic American Buildings Survey drawings published in Connie H. Wyrick, "Stratford and the Lees," *JSAH* 30, no. 1 (March 1971): 71–90.

14. "Church Building in Colonial Virginia," *VMHB* 3, no. 4 (April 1896): 421–22; Albemarle VB, pp. 5, 25.

15. Style is discussed at greater length in chapter 6. The definition used in this paragraph is derived from Meyer Schapiro, "Style," in *Anthropology Today: An Encyclopedic Inventory*, ed. A.L. Kroeber (Chicago: University of Chicago Press, 1953), p. 287.

Chapter 5

1. Richard Hooker, *Of the Laws of Ecclesiastical Polity* (1597; reprint ed., London: Dent, Everyman's Library, 1907), 2: 37, 442; Horton Davies, *Worship and Theology in England*, 1, *From Cranmer to Hooker, 1534–1603* (Princeton: Princeton University Press, 1970), pp. 177, 219–54; Charles Wheatly, *A Rational Illustration of the Book of Common Prayer of the Church of England* (4th ed.; London: for the Author, 1722), p. 35.

2. A.G. Dickens, *The English Reformation* (New York: Schocken Books, 1964), pp. 112–22, 139–41, 167–74, 179–82, 186–89, 231–40, 287–89, 294–311, 325–26; Davies, *Worship and Theology*, 1: 11–15, 25–30; Hooker, *Laws*, esp. 2: book 5.

3. Dickens, *English Reformation*, pp. 232–33; Davies, *Worship and Theology*, 1: 173–201.

4. Addleshaw and Etchells, pp. 15, 22–23, 31, 40–43, 45; Hooker, *Laws*, 2: 47; Wheatly, *Rational Illustration*, pp. 348–50.

5. Addleshaw and Etchells, pp. 30–31, 37–51; Francis Bond, *Screens and Galleries in English Churches* (London: Oxford University Press, 1908), pp. 98–99; Hooker, *Laws*, 2: 47.

6. Addleshaw and Etchells, pp. 24, 27–28, 33–34, 117–32; Dickens, *English Reformation*, pp. 247–48; John Campbell, "The Quarrel Over the Table," *HMPEC* 40, no. 2 (June 1971): 173–84; Horton Davies, *Worship and Theology in England*, 2, *From Andrewes to Baxter, 1603–1690* (Princeton: Princeton University Press, 1975), pp. 13–14.

7. J. Charles Cox, *Pulpits, Lecterns and Organs in English Churches* (London: Oxford University Press, 1915), p. 147; Addleshaw and Etchells, p. 69; *Certain Sermons or Homilies . . . to Which Are Added, The Constitutions and Canons of the Church of England, Set Forth A.D. 1603* (3d American ed.; Philadelphia: George and Wayne, 1844), p. 564.

8. Addleshaw and Etchells, pp. 64–68; J. G. Davies, *The Architectural Setting of Baptism* (London: Barrie and Rockliff, 1962), pp. 91–100; *Certain Sermons*, p. 564.

9. John Phillips, *The Reformation of Images: Destruction of Art in England, 1535–1660* (Berkeley: University of California Press, 1973), pp. 41–63, 82–97; Davies, *Worship and Theology*, 1: 21–22; Horton Davies, *Worship and Theology in England*, 3, *From Watts and Wesley to Maurice, 1690–1850* (Princeton: Princeton University Press, 1961), pp. 39–40; Addleshaw and Etchells, pp. 35, 101–7, 158–65; Marcus Whiffen, *Stuart and Georgian Churches: The Architecture of the Church of England Outside London, 1603–1837* (London: B. T. Batsford, 1948), pp. 5–6.

10. Addleshaw and Etchells, pp. 52–62; Davies, 2: 44, 3: 31.

11. William Strachey, "A True Reportory of the Wreck and Redemption of Sir Thomas Gates, Knight," in *A Voyage to Virginia in 1609*, ed. Louis B. Wright (Charlottesville: University Press of Virginia, 1964), p. 80; Addleshaw and Etchells, p. 111; St. Andrew's VB, pp. 39–40.

12. Lewis P. Clover, "Colonial Churches in Virginia. The Old Smithfield Church," *Church Review* 5, no. 4 (January 1853): 572. The name "St. Luke's" was given to Newport Parish church in 1828 (Mason, p. 197).

13. Rawlings, pp. 31–33; Clover, "Smithfield Church," p. 572; Robert I. Powell and Worth Bailey, "Memorandum and Report of Visit to St. Luke's Church, Smithfield, Va., of April 18, 19, and 20, 1955," MS., St. Luke's Church Restoration Committee Papers, Research Department, Colonial Williamsburg Foundation, Section A, p. 3; James Grote Van Derpool, "The Restoration of St. Luke's, Smithfield, Virginia," *JSAH* 17, no. 1 (March 1958): 12–18; Marcus Whiffen, *The Public Buildings of Williamsburg, Colonial Capital of Virginia* (Williamsburg: Colonial Williamsburg, 1958), pp. 75–77; Nikolaus Pevsner, *The Buildings of England: Suffolk* (2d ed.,

Harmondsworth: Penguin, 1974), p. 415; Whiffen, *Stuart and Georgian Churches*, p. 26; Alfred Clapham, "The Survival of Gothic in Seventeenth-Century England," *Archaeological Journal* 106 (supplement, 1949): 4–9; Mason, pp. 8, 196; Thomas T. Waterman, "The Bruton Church of 1683 and Two Contemporaries," *JSAH* 4, nos. 3–4 (July–October 1944): 43–46, 54; Samuel H. Yonge, *The Site of Old "James Towne", 1607–1698* (1907; reprint ed., Richmond: L. H. Jenkins, 1930), pp. 65–66; Cary Carson, Norman F. Barka, William M. Kelso, Garry Wheeler Stone, and Dell Upton, "Impermanent Architecture in the Southern American Colonies," *WP* 16, nos. 2–3 (summer–autumn 1981): 135–96. St. Luke's church was restored in 1955–57 by Chapman, Evans, Delehanty, Architects, of New York, under the guidance of a committee of architectural historians. Two examples will illustrate the ways the restorers let the assumed date of St. Luke's shape their assessment of the physical evidence. First, they dismissed the former principal-rafter roof as a 19th-century alteration because they could find nothing like it in published photographs of Elizabethan and Jacobean churches (Powell and Bailey, "Memorandum and Report," Section B, pp. 1–5; "Review and Recommendations," MS., n.d., St. Luke's Church Restoration Committee Papers, Research Department, Colonial Williamsburg Foundation, p. 2). Second, they installed the reproduced balusters upside down, having perceived the original they found as "country Jacobean, but rather delightfully and expressively detailed with an early inverted form to the baluster shaft" (James Grote Van Derpool to J.C. Harrington, December 12, 1956, St. Luke's Church Restoration Committee Papers, Research Department, Colonial Williamsburg Foundation).

14. Waterman, "Bruton Church," pp. 43–46; Whiffen, *Public Buildings*, pp. 75–77; Bruton Recs., pp. 13–16; Lyon G. Tyler, "Bruton Church," *WMQ* 1st ser. 3, no. 3 (January 1895): 172–76; John C. McCabe, "Colonial Churches in Virginia, VI, Church at Jamestown," *Church Review* 8, no. 1 (April 1855): 138–39; Yonge, *Site of Old "James Towne,"* pp. 65–66; John L. Cotter, *Archaeological Excavations at Jamestown Colonial National Historical Park and Jamestown National Historic Site, Virginia* (Washington: National Park Service, 1958), pp. 17–21; Nancy Halverson Schless, "The Province House: English and Netherlandish Forms in Gables and Chimneys," *Old-Time New England* 62, no. 2 (April–June 1972): 115–23.

15. St. Peter's VB, pp. 68, 76, 119; Rawlings, pp. 41–49; *St. Peter's Parish, New Kent County, Virginia* (n.p., St. Peter's Parish, 1979), n.p. (woodcut, 19th-century photograph); Robert A. Lancaster, *Historic Virginia Homes and Churches* (Philadelphia: Lippincott, 1915), p. 258 (early 20th-century photograph); Francis Marion Wigmore, *The Old Parish Churches of Virginia: A Pictorial-Historic Exhibition* (Washington: Government Printing Office, 1929), pp. 26–27

(early 20th-century photographs). James Scott Rawlings was the principal and most recent restoration architect at St. Peter's, and he continues to work on it.

16. Rawlings, p. 31; Mason, p. 196. It was at the same time that the character of Virginia's domestic forms was crystallized. (Dell Upton, "The Origins of Chesapeake Architecture," in *Three Centuries of Maryland Architecture* [Annapolis: Maryland Historical Trust, 1982], pp. 44–57.)

17. George Carrington Mason, "The Colonial Churches of Westmoreland and King George Counties, Virginia," *VMHB* 56, no. 2 (April 1948): 157; YCM, pp. 30, 36, 40, 44, 46, and passim; Meade, 2: 155.

18. Christ, Middlesex VB pp. 126–28, 139–41.

19. Petsworth VB, p. 166; Albemarle VB, pp. 42–43; Truro VB, pp. 96–97; Wicomico VB, fol. 97; Fairfax VB, p. 12.

20. M.D. Anderson, *History and Imagery in British Churches* (London: John Murray, 1971), pp. 71–74; Hugh Braun, *Parish Churches: Their Architectural Development* (London: Faber and Faber, 1970), p. 16; Edwin Smith, Graham Hutton, and Olive Cook, *English Parish Churches* (London: Thames and Hudson, 1976), pp. 16–17, 38–39, 68–69; J. Charles Cox, *The Parish Churches of England*, ed. Charles Bradley Ford (London: Batsford, 1935), pp. 41–43; Petsworth VB, pp. 16–17; Wicomico VB, fol. 33; William Byrd, *The Secret Diary of William Byrd of Westover, 1709–1712*, ed. Louis B. Wright and Marion Tinling (Richmond: Dietz Press, 1941), p. 188; St. Peter's VB, pp. 262–63, 338–39.

21. Fairfax VB, p. 3; St. James VB, p. 78.

22. Mason, pp. 313–15; Albemarle VB, p. 25.

23. Davies, *Worship and Theology*, 2: 9; Hooker, *Laws*, 2: 47; Bruton Recs., pp. 42–43.

24. James Grote Van Derpool, *Historic St. Luke's, Its History and Restoration* (Smithfield, Va.: Historic St. Luke's Restoration Committee, n.d.), p. 10; Petsworth VB, p. 3; Christ, Middlesex VB pp. 57–58; Médéric-Louis-Élie Moreau de Saint-Méry, *Voyage aux États-Unis de l'Amérique, 1793–1798*, ed. Stewart L. Mims (New Haven: Yale University Press, 1913), p. 73. Moreau's word *jubé* is usually translated "rood loft," but there were certainly no roods in Virginia's churches, and Moreau was probably using the nearest equivalent for the division between church and chancel. (Médéric-Louis-Élie Moreau de Saint-Méry, *Moreau de St. Méry's American Journey [1793–1798]*, trans. and ed. Kenneth and Anna M. Roberts [Garden City, N.Y.: Doubleday, 1947], p. 64.)

25. Aymer Vallance, *English Church Screens, Being Great Roods, Screenwork and Rood-Lofts of Parish Churches in England and Wales* (London: B. T. Batsford, 1936), pp. 86–94; Christ, Middlesex VB, pp. 121, 127, 140, 146, supplemented with MS.

original in VSL. An existing screen similar to the description of those in the Poplar Spring and Christ Church Parish churches is the screen of ca. 1719 in Devonshire church, Bermuda. (Bryden Bordley Hyde, *Bermuda's Antique Furniture and Silver* [Hamilton: for the Bermuda National Trust, 1971], pp. 10–11.)

26. Christ, Middlesex VB, pp. 107–8.

27. Christ, Middlesex VB, pp. 120–22.

28. Christ, Middlesex VB, pp. 126–28.

29. Christ, Middlesex VB, pp. 139–41, 144–47.

30. John E. Booty, ed., *The Book of Common Prayer, 1559: The Elizabethan Prayer Book* (Charlottesville: University Press of Virginia, 1976), p. 53; Addleshaw and Etchells, pp. 52–58; Davies, *Worship and Theology*, 3: 41.

31. Southam VB, p. 121; Bristol VB, p. 34. The exception was Bruton Parish church, enlarged in 1752 to a 100-foot length. As the following paragraphs in the text will make clear, the preferable mode of enlargement—perpendicular wings—had already been used at Bruton when the church was built. Property rights in the church space, proximity of the church's south wall to Duke of Gloucester Street, heavy use of the burying ground to the north, and demands for space at the east end inside made by government functions and government officials probably combined to make an eastern addition seem most suitable in this case.

32. Stratton Major VB, pp. 131–33, 165–71; Rawlings, p. 172; St. George's, Acc. VB, fol. 2; *Colonial Churches in the Original Colony of Virginia* (2d ed.; Richmond: Southern Churchman, 1908), p. 194.

33. Petsworth VB, p. 68; George Hay, *The Architecture of Scottish Post-Reformation Churches, 1560–1843* (Oxford: Clarendon Press, 1957), pp. 23, 29, 42, 52–53, 86, 120; Joan R. Gunderson, "The Search for Good Men: Recruiting Ministers in Colonial Virginia," *HMPEC* 48, no. 4 (December 1979): 455, 457; Alan Gowans, *King Carter's Church: Being a Study in Depth of Christ Church, Lancaster County, Virginia* (Victoria, B.C.: University of Victoria Maltwood Museum 1969), pp. 14–17; Orlando Ridout V, "An Architectural History of Third Haven Meetinghouse," in *Three Hundred Years and More of Third Haven Quakerism*, by Kenneth L. Carroll (Easton, Md.: Queen Anne Press, 1984), pp. 69–71; Carson, et al., "Impermanent Architecture," pp. 152, 156, 180; Fraser D. Neiman, *The "Manner House" Before Stratford (Discovering The Clifts Plantation)* (Stratford, Va.: Robert E. Lee Memorial Association, 1980), pp. 8–9 and passim. The disposition of interior spaces in Virginia Anglican churches was different from that in Scots Presbyterian kirks, where there was no chancel. The east-west orientation of the medieval church was retained in the Scots kirks, but the pulpit was usually in the middle of the south wall, the north wall of the church was

blank if there was no aisle, galleries were often built at both east and west ends, and an entrance was sometimes made in the east as well as the west end. To whatever extent the Virginia T can be credited to Scotland, then, the idea was grafted onto an English-derived Anglican plan.

34. Walter H. Godfrey, "The Unitarian Chapels of Ipswich and Bury St. Edmunds," *Archaeological Journal* 108 (1951): 122, 125, and plate facing p. 121. There was a double or M roof on the Robert Carter house, Williamsburg.

35. St. Paul's VB, p. 81.

36. George Carrington Mason, "The Colonial Churches of Essex and Richmond Counties," *VMHB* 53, no. 1 (January 1945): 15; Rawlings, pp. 89–95; Christ, Middlesex VB, pp. 233–35; Suffolk VB, fol. 22.

37. Upper VB, pp. 46–47, 54–55; Mason, pp. 348–49.

38. Bruton Recs., pp. 33–35; A. Lawrence Kocher, "Architectural Report—Bruton Parish Church (A Restoration), Block 21, Building 1," MS., Architectural Research Department, Colonial Williamsburg Foundation, n.d. (ca. 1950), p. 1; Whiffen, *Public Buildings*, pp. 77–82; Rawlings, pp. 64–66.

39. Whiffen, *Public Buildings*, p. 84; Mason, pp. 107–8, 165, 304–5; Rawlings, p. 113; Elizabeth City VB, pp. 55–56; VG (Purdie and Dixon), December 8, 1768. The builders of Scots kirks also used cruciform plans for very large aisled churches (Hay, *Architecture of Scottish Post-Reformation Churches*, pp. 42, 63–65, 90–94).

40. Gowans, *King Carter's Church*, pp. 14–30.

41. Alan Gowans has argued that the use of the cruciform plan at Christ church was a manifestation of the tradition of cruciform memorial churches in late seventeenth- and early eighteenth-century England, a function the cruciform Scots churches sometimes fulfilled as well. This may be true for Christ church, where one would want to understand it as an adaptation to the memorial-church tradition of the auditory plan with perpendicular arms represented by the other cruciform and T-plan churches, and of the general English tradition of burying the elite in the chancel. Virginia churches from Jamestown on contained chancel burials; there were ten under the chancel of Ware Parish church, for example. Like the T-plan churches themselves, the use of Christ church as a memorial church must thus be thought of as a syncretic creation peculiar to Virginia. Moreover, it was the striking visual image for a vernacular church plan rather than the memorial idea that attracted Virginians in other parishes to use Christ church as a model. In these parishes, there was no single figure as dominant as Carter was in Christ Church Parish, Lancaster County. (Gowans, *King Carter's Church*, pp. 23–32; "Carter Papers," *VMHB* 6, no. 1 [July 1898]: 3;

Cotter, *Archaeological Excavations at Jamestown*, p. 22; *Colonial Churches in the Original Colony of Virginia*, p. 194.)

42. Meade, 2: 172–80; Rawlings, pp. 145–47; Mason, "Colonial Churches of Essex and Richmond," p. 19.

43. Christ, Lancaster VB, pp. 5, 10 and passim; George Carrington Mason, "The Colonial Churches of Northumberland and Lancaster Counties, Virginia," *VMHB* 54, no. 2 (April 1946): 236–37; Rawlings, pp. 162–65; Cocke, *Parish Lines, Diocese of Virginia*, pp. 153–54.

44. Wicomico VB, fols. 58, 60–61, 75, 82; Mason, "Colonial Churches of Northumberland and Lancaster," pp. 141–51; Meade, 2: 133–35.

45. VG (Purdie and Dixon), May 7, 1772; St. Paul's VB, p. 514; VG, February 14, 1751; Mason, pp. 255–57.

46. VG, February 12, 1762; VG (Rind), July 18, 1766.

47. Fairfax VB, p. 12; Shelburne VB, p. 30. A 19th-century illustration shows that Trinity church, Norborne Parish, Jefferson County (now in West Virginia), was a member of this group as well ("American Ecclesiastical History. Colonial Churches in Virginia. No. III—Trinity Church, Norborne Parish, Jefferson County," *Church Review* 6, no. 2 [July 1853]: 272).

48. St. Mark's VB, pp. 415, 417, 419, 421; W.B. McGroarty, "Lamb's Creek Church," *VMHB* 45, no. 1 (January 1937): 98–99; G. MacLaren Brydon, "Date of Erection of Lamb's Creek Church," *VMHB* 45, no. 2 (April 1937): 193–94; Truro VB, pp. 94, 96–97, 110–11.

49. Marian Card Donnelly, *The New England Meeting Houses of the Seventeenth Century* (Middletown: Wesleyan University Press, 1968), pp. 44–108; Philip B. Wallace, *Colonial Churches and Meeting Houses: Pennsylvania, New Jersey, Delaware* (New York: Architectural Book Publishing Co., 1930), pls. 2, 12, 79, 129, 177, 254–64; George Fletcher Bennett, *Early Architecture of Delaware* (1932; reprint ed., New York: Bonanza, n.d.), pp. 28–32, 36–37; Henry Chandlee Forman, *Maryland Architecture: A Short History from 1634 through the Civil War* (Cambridge, Md.: Tidewater Publishers, 1968), pp. 45, 48.

50. Henry Chandlee Forman, *Old Buildings, Gardens and Furniture of Tidewater Maryland* (Cambridge, Md.: Tidewater Publishers, 1967), pp. 101–2; Henry H. Hutchinson, "Collected Notes on Christ Church, Broad Creek, and Her Neighbors," *The Archeolog: Publication of the Sussex Society of Archeology and History* 23, no. 1 (summer 1971): 1–38; Paul G.E. Clemens, *The Atlantic Economy and Colonial Maryland's Eastern Shore: From Tobacco to Grain* (Ithaca: Cornell University Press, 1980), pp. 176–78 and passim; Edward C. Papenfuse, Jr., "Planter Behavior and Economic

Opportunity in a Stable Economy," *Agricultural History* 46, no. 2 (April 1972): 297–311.

51. Addleshaw and Etchells, pp. 52–56; Davies, *Worship and Theology*, 2: 8, 3: 31; Carter, p. 377.

52. Addleshaw and Etchells, pp. 56–57; Hening, 1: 180; Hooker, *Laws*, 2: 41.

53. Foulke Robarts, *Gods Holy House and Service* (1639), quoted in Davies, *Worship and Theology*, 2: 15 n. 26; Whiffen, *Stuart and Georgian Churches*, pp. 5–6.

Chapter 6

1. Meyer Schapiro, "Style," in *Anthropology Today: An Encyclopedic Inventory*, ed. A.L. Kroeber (Chicago: University of Chicago Press, 1953), p. 287; James R. Sackett, "The Meaning of Style in Archaeology: A General Model," *American Antiquity* 42, no. 3 (July 1977): 370 and passim. My thoughts about style have been clarified by these essays in particular, as well as by Robert C. Dunnell, "Style and Function: A Fundamental Dichotomy," *American Antiquity* 43, no. 2 (April 1978): 192–202; David J. Meltzer, "A Study of Style and Function in a Class of Tools," *Journal of Field Archaeology* 8, no. 3 (fall 1981): 313–26; and Carroll L.V. Meeks, *The Railroad Station: An Architectural History* (1956; reprint ed., New York: Castle Books, 1978), pp. 2–25. I am indebted to Fraser D. Neiman for an introduction to the archaeological literature of style.

2. Sackett, "Meaning of Style," p. 370. For a brief discussion of convention as the elimination of the necessity to rethink architectural problems, see Thomas Hubka, "Just Folks Designing: Vernacular Designers and the Generation of Form," *Journal of Architectural Education* 32, no. 3 (1979): 27–29. The importance of convention in communication is a commonplace in linguistics (John Lyons, *Introduction to Theoretical Linguistics* [Cambridge: Cambridge University Press, 1968], pp. 53–54). For marking or contrasting, see Lyons, *Introduction*, pp. 79–80. For applications of the idea to the artifactual world, see Mary C. Beaudry, "Worth Its Weight in Iron: Categories of Material Culture in Early Virginia Probate Inventories," *Quarterly Bulletin of the Archaeological Society of Virginia* 23, no. 1 (March 1978): 19–26.

3. Dunnell, "Style and Function," p. 194; Dell Upton, "Toward a Performance Theory of Vernacular Architecture in Tidewater Virginia," *Folklore Forum* 12, nos. 2–3 (1979): 173–96.

4. For a treatment of mode as a means of self-differentiation within a society, see Dick Hebdige, *Subculture: The Meaning of Style* (London: Methuen, 1979). I use *mode* rather than *fashion* because I am reserving the latter word for a more specific context (see below, chapter 10).

5. Horton Davies, *Worship and Theology in England*, 1, *From Cranmer to Hooker, 1534–1603* (Princeton: Princeton University Press, 1970), pp. 177–78, 225.

6. For colored exterior painting, see Christ, Middlesex VB, pp. 121, 127, 140; Truro VB, p. 116; for a painted roof: Elizabeth City VB, p. 66 ("of a Lead Colour"). For a discussion of clapboard roofing, see Dell Upton, "Board Roofing in Tidewater Virginia," *APT Bulletin* 8, no. 4 (1976): 22–43. Descriptions of cladding conventions in 18th-century Virginia can be found in Marcus Whiffen, *The Eighteenth-Century Houses of Williamsburg: A Study of Architecture and Building in the Colonial Capital of Virginia* (rev. ed.; Williamsburg: Colonial Williamsburg Foundation, 1984), pp. 98–102; Paul E. Buchanan, "The Eighteenth-Century Framed Houses of Tidewater Virginia," in *Building Early America: Contributions to the History of a Great Industry*, ed. Charles E. Peterson (Radnor, Pa.: Chilton Book Co., 1976), pp. 54–56, 67–72; and Dell Upton, "Early Vernacular Architecture in Southeastern Virginia," Ph.D. diss., Brown University, 1980, chapters 3, 6.

7. For discussions of brick building in colonial Virginia, see Herbert A. Claiborne, *Comments on Virginia Brickwork Before 1800* (Boston: Walpole Society, 1957); Calder Loth, "Notes on the Evolution of Virginia Brickwork from the Seventeenth Century to the Late Nineteenth Century," *APT Bulletin* 6, no. 2 (1974): 82–120; and Whiffen, *Eighteenth-Century Houses*, pp. 102–7. For an overview of brick construction in the colonies, see Harley J. McKee, *Introduction to Early American Masonry: Stone, Brick, Mortar and Plaster* (Washington, D.C.: National Trust for Historic Preservation and Columbia University, 1973), pp. 41–54.

8. Bricks were fired in kilns built of "clamps" of unfired bricks themselves. In this method of manufacture, the bricks closest to the fire will always be glazed through the interaction of excessive heat with the impurities of the clay. Brick masons in the 18th century chose to use these bricks for decorative effect. Before the early 18th century and after the Revolution in Virginia, glazed bricks were not discarded, but most masons hid the glazed surfaces inside the wall to achieve a uniform surface color.

9. Bristol stone: Bristol VB, pp. 54, 128; Blisland VB, p. 55; plain walls: Frederick VB, p. 27; interior weatherboards: Albemarle VB, p. 43. The two definitions of ceiling can be found in William Salmon, *Palladio Londinensis: or, The London Art of Building* (3d ed.; London: For S. Birt, 1748), p. 56 and dictionary section, "Ceiling," n.p. For interior finish of Virginia houses, see Whiffen, *Eighteenth-Century Houses*, pp. 112–23; Buchanan, "Eighteenth-Century Framed Houses," pp. 70–72; Upton, "Early Vernacular Architecture," chapter 6; and Edward Chappell, "Acculturation in the Shenandoah Valley: Rhenish Houses of the Massanutten Settlement," *Proceedings*

of the American Philosophical Society 124, no. 1 (February 1980): 57–58 and passim.

10. David Pye, *The Nature and Art of Workmanship* (New York: Van Nostrand Reinhold, 1971), pp. 7–10; *The Builder's Dictionary: or, Gentleman and Architect's Companion* (1734; reprint ed., Washington, D.C.: Association for Preservation Technology, 1981), "Balusters," 1: n.p. *The Builder's Dictionary* was consulted by Virginians as a source for pricing guidelines, although there was disagreement over the applicability of its English advice to the colony. John Carter and Charles Carter both cited it in a dispute over the charges for painting Rosewell. (John, Landon, and Charles Carter Letter Book, 1732–1781, microfilm, Colonial Williamsburg Foundation, pp. 193–94.) For descriptions of the turner's methods of working, see Joseph Moxon, *Mechanick Exercises, or the Doctrine of Handy-Works* (3d ed.; reprint ed., Scarsdale, N.Y.: Early American Industries Association, 1975), pp. 167–236; and Robert F. Trent, *Hearts and Crowns: Folk Chairs of the Connecticut Coast, 1720–1840* (New Haven: New Haven Colony Historical Society, 1977), p. 27.

11. Andrea Palladio, *The Four Books of Andrea Palladio's Architecture* (1738 ed.; reprint ed., New York: Dover Publications, 1965), p. 82; Charles Wheatly, *A Rational Illustration of the Book of Common Prayer of the Church of England* (4th ed.; London: for the Author, 1722), p. 104; John Fowler and John Cornforth, *English Decoration in the Eighteenth Century* (Princeton: Pyne Press, 1974), p. 202; Salmon, *Palladio Londinensis*, p. 63. Brown paint: Wicomico VB, fol. 75; wainscot color: Petsworth VB, p. 253; Stratton Major VB, p. 132; sky color: Lynnhaven VB, p. 50; light blue: Wicomico VB, fol. 92. For 18th-century Virginia domestic painting, see Whiffen, *Eighteenth-Century Houses*, pp. 115, 117.

12. Paul Davies and David Hemsoll, "Renaissance balusters and the antique," *Architectural History* 26 (1983): 1–23; Wheatly, *Rational Illustration*, p. 91; Chappell, "Acculturation," pp. 57–58; Wicomico VB, fol. 91.

13. Dunnell, "Style and Function," pp. 197–98. For a discussion of accidental change in the shape of turned chair parts, see Trent, *Hearts and Crowns*, pp. 41–42, 46 and passim.

14. Isle of Wight County, Record of Wills, Deeds, etc., vol. 1, 1662–1715, MS., Isle of Wight County Courthouse, p. 577; Edmund Pendleton, *The Letters and Papers of Edmund Pendleton, 1734–1803*, ed. David John Mays (Charlottesville: University Press of Virginia, 1967), p. 306.

15. Upton, "Board Roofing," p. 40; St. Mark's VB, p. 97; St. George's, Spots. VB, 2: August 6, 1755; Truro VB, p. 121. The preference for uniformity of surface is related to the general preference for uniformity of appearance that grew in Anglo-America from the late 17th century, and was manifested in such phenomena as the demand for matched sets of ceramics, tableware, and furniture. (Fowler and Cornforth, *English Decoration*, pp. 199–200; Irving W. Lyon, *The Colonial Furniture of New England: A Study of the Domestic Furniture in Use in the Seventeenth and Eighteenth Centuries* [1891; reprint ed., New York: E. P. Dutton, 1977], pp. 153–55; James Deetz, *In Small Things Forgotten: The Archaeology of Early American Life* [Garden City, N.Y.: Anchor Books, 1977], pp. 39–40, 59–60, 136.)

16. Upton, "Board Roofing," pp. 39–40; Upton, "Early Vernacular Architecture," pp. 313–14, 327–28.

17. Bristol VB, pp. 70, 128; St. Patrick's VB, p. 16.

18. John Ferdinand Dalziel Smyth, *A Tour in the United States of America* (1784; reprint ed., New York: Arno Press, 1968), 1: 49; George Washington, *The Diaries of George Washington, 1748–1799*, ed. John C. Fitzpatrick (Boston: Houghton, Mifflin, 1925), 4: 195; Harry Toulmin, *The Western Country in 1793: Reports on Kentucky and Virginia*, ed. Marion Tinling and Godfrey Davies (San Marino, Cal.: Huntington Library, 1948), p. 17.

19. Upton, "Early Vernacular Architecture," pp. 347–49, 399–400; Edward C. Papenfuse, "Planter Behavior and Economic Opportunity in a Stable Economy," *Agricultural History* 46, no. 2 (April 1972): 310.

20. Upton, "Early Vernacular Architecture," pp. 347, 517, 519–20, 555, 557–58; Jeffrey M. O'Dell, *Chesterfield County: Early Architecture and Historic Sites* (Chesterfield: Chesterfield County, 1983): pp. 99, 105, 107–8.

21. Isle of Wight County Land Tax Books, 1782–1800, MS., Isle of Wight Courthouse, Isle of Wight, Va.

22. Chesterfield County Land Tax Book, 1791, microfilm, VSL; Dell Upton, "The Virginia Parlor, National Museum of American History, Smithsonian Institution: A Report on the Henry Saunders House and Its Occupants," MS., National Museum of American History, Smithsonian Institution, 1981, p. 23. For discussions of the housing of poor white and black Virginians in the 18th century, see Upton, "Virginia Parlor," pp. 41–80; Dell Upton, "Slave Housing in Eighteenth-Century Virginia," MS., National Museum of American History, Smithsonian Institution, 1982, pp. 5–35.

23. Samuel Kercheval, *A History of the Valley of Virginia* (2d ed.; Woodstock, Va.: John Gatewood, 1850), p. 219.

24. Most unglazed arcades were used on colonial courthouses, but they could be found on the Capitol, the College of William and Mary, and one book-derived house, Mount Airy, as well.

25. Karl Lehmann, "The Dome of Heaven," *Art Bulletin* 27, no. 1 (March 1945): 1–27; E. Baldwin Smith, *The Dome: A Study*

in the History of Ideas (1950; reprint, Princeton: Princeton University Press, 1956), pp. 3–9, 61–94; E. Baldwin Smith, *Architectural Symbolism in Imperial Rome and the Middle Ages* (Princeton: Princeton University Press, 1956), p. 30.

26. Petsworth VB, p. 7; Robert I. Powell and Worth Bailey, "Memorandum and Report of Visit to St. Luke's Church, April 18, 19, and 20, 1955," MS., St. Luke's Church Restoration Committee Papers, Research Department, Colonial Williamsburg Foundation, Section B, p. 5; Mason, p. 338; "Church Building in Colonial Virginia," *VMHB* 3, no. 4 (April 1896): 421; Meade, 1: 323n; Lynnhaven VB, p. 50. The literal representation of the sky could also be found in some New England Puritan meeting houses. (Peter Benes, "Sky Colors and Scattered Clouds: The Decorative and Architectural Painting of New England Meeting Houses, 1738–1834," in *New England Meeting House and Church*, ed. Benes and Benes, pp. 67–69.)

27. Petsworth VB, p. 11; Smith, *Dome*, pp. 71–72. The equation of vault with dome was an old one, and it was accepted as a matter of course in 18th-century Virginia. Benjamin Latrobe reported an amusing story about a member of the Amelia County gentry who was embarrassed when the sound of his own reciprocal sneezing and farting echoed in the "high dome" of the parish church. (Latrobe, p. 110.) Alan Gowans has interpreted the vaulted Christ church, Lancaster County, as a domed funereal monument to the Carter family. (*King Carter's Church: Being a Study in Depth of Christ Church, Lancaster County, Virginia* [Victoria, B.C.: University of Victoria Maltwood Museum, 1969], pp. 26–27.)

28. Smith, *Dome*, pp. 3–9; Smith, *Architectural Symbolism*, pp. 19–51; Petsworth VB, p. 166; Albemarle VB, p. 43. I have no idea why the French synonym *fronton* was used by the Albemarle Parish vestry.

29. *Builder's Dictionary*, "Pediment," 2: n.p.

30. For an example of the addition of pediments as an afterthought, see Wicomico VB, fol. 82; for a similar example for compass windows, see Upper VB, p. 55.

31. Charles Oman, *English Church Plate, 597–1830* (London: Oxford University Press, 1957), p. 246; Horton Davies, *Worship and Theology in England*, 2, *From Andrewes to Baxter and Fox, 1603–1690* (Princeton: Princeton University Press, 1975), p. 36; John Phillips, *The Reformation of Images: Destruction of Art in England, 1535–1660* (Berkeley: University of California Press, 1973), pp. 41–139, 157–210; Petsworth VB, pp. 11, 253; Meade, 1: 323 n. An idea of the appearance of the Poplar Spring painting is conveyed by photographs of similar paintings executed by John Gibbs, Jr., on the chancel arch of Christ church, Boston, Mass., the exact contemporary of the Poplar Spring church. (Bettina A. Norton, "Anglican

Embellishments: The Contributions of John Gibbs, Junior, and William Price to the Church of England in Eighteenth-Century Boston," in *New England Meeting House and Church*, ed. Benes and Benes, pp. 70–85.)

32. Davies, *Worship and Theology*, 2: 11–22; George Carrington Mason, "The Colonial Churches of Westmoreland and King George Counties, Virginia," *VMHB* 56, no. 2 (April 1948): 292.

33. M.D. Anderson, *History and Imagery in British Churches* (London: John Murray, 1971), p. 87; Colin Platt, *Medieval England: A Social History and Archaeology from the Conquest to 1600 A. D.* (New York: Charles Scribner's Sons, 1978), p. 147; Aymer Vallance, *English Church Screens: Being Great Roods, Screenwork and Rood–Lofts of Parish Churches in England and Wales* (London: B. T. Batsford, 1936), pp. 16–26; Gabriel Williamson Galt to Elizabeth J. Galt, January 10, 1840, transcript in Bruton Parish church file, Architectural Research Department, Colonial Williamsburg Foundation; Edwin Dethlefsen and James Deetz, "Death's Heads, Cherubs and Willow Trees: Experimental Archaeology in Colonial Cemeteries," *American Antiquity* 31, no. 4 (April 1966): 502–10; Deetz, *In Small Things Forgotten*, pp. 69–72.

34. Marcus Whiffen, *Stuart and Georgian Churches: The Architecture of the Church of England Outside London, 1603–1837* (London: B. T. Batsford, 1947), p. 5; Rhys Isaac, "Dramatizing the Ideology of Revolution: Popular Mobilization in Virginia, 1774 to 1776," *WMQ* 3d ser. 33, no. 3 (July 1976): 372; Petsworth VB, pp. 54–55; "Will of Mrs. Elizabeth Stith," *WMQ* 1st ser. 5, no. 2 (October 1896): 115; Lewis P. Clover, "Colonial Churches in Virginia. The Old Smithfield Church," *Church Review* 5, no. 4 (January 1853): 575. For an example of special payments to letter an altarpiece, see Fairfax VB, pp. 32–33 (£8 "for writeing the commandments &c."). The ruins of Lower Southwark church show no evidence of the altarpiece or the painting.

35. Mason, p. 330; Christ, Middlesex VB, pp. 159, 171; *Colonial Churches in the Original Colony of Virginia*, p. 309; "Extracts from Virginia County Records," *VMHB* 12, no. 3 (January 1905): 291.

36. Meade, 2: 149. It is possible that the Mattaponi tablets were once part of an architectural altarpiece like those discussed in the following text paragraphs.

37. *Builder's Dictionary*, "Ionick Order," 2: n.p.; Batty Langley, *The City and Country Builder's and Workman's Treasury of Designs* (3d ed., 1750; reprint, New York: Benjamin Blom, 1967), pls. CVIII, CIX, CX, CXI; Fairfax VB, p. 12; Truro VB, pp. 97, 116, 135. An altarpiece nearly identical to Langley's plate CX was published in 1758 in William Pain, *The Builder's Companion and Workman's General Assistant* (1762 ed.; reprint ed., Westmead, Hants.: Gregg International,

1972), p. 61. I attribute the Falls church altarpiece to the Langley book because the *Designs* was mentioned in the Truro Parish records, because details like the frames of the side tablets are closer to Langley, and because surviving details elsewhere in northern Virginia point to Langley rather than to Pain. Still, the evidence is circumstantial, and 18th-century pattern-book writers lifted designs from one another routinely. Pain's designs for the altarpiece and for pulpits are close enough to Langley's for either to have been a source for James Wren's workmen. Cf. Pain's p. 62 and Langley's pl. CXIII.

38. Petsworth VB, pp. 247, 253. My attribution of the Rosewell painting to Richard Cooke is circumstantial. It rests on the proximity of Cooke's work at Poplar Spring to a dispute between Charles and John Carter over the charges Charles Carter assessed his brother-in-law Mann Page's estate for painting Rosewell. Cooke was obviously known in Gloucester County. After Samuel Peacock failed to do the Poplar Spring painting, the vestry asked one of its number to "Write to Mr Charles Carter for his painter." (John, Landon, and Charles Carter Letter Book, 1732–1781, microfilm, Colonial Williamsburg Foundation, pp. 139–40; Petsworth VB, pp. 247–48, 252.)

39. Petsworth VB, p. 3; Addleshaw and Etchells, pp. 179–80. For a good 18th-century description of a three-level pulpit, see Frederick VB, pp. 6–7. Pulpits standing on columns include the ones formerly at St. John's church, King William County, and, according to physical evidence, at Abingdon church (Meade, 1: 38). A pulpit arrangement like that at Christ church, Alexandria, and contemporary with it, was originally used for the 1770 pulpit in Christ church, Philadelphia (*The Story of Christ Church in Philadelphia* [rev. ed.; Philadelphia: Christ Church in Philadelphia, 1969], pp. 23–24).

40. Henry Havard, *Dictionnaire de l'ameublement et de la décoration depuis le XIIIe siècle jusqu'à nos jours* (Paris: Maison Quantin, 1887–90), "Dais," 2: 7–11; Eric Mercer, *Furniture, 700–1700* (New York: Meredith Press, 1969), pp. 81–83; Peter Thornton, *Seventeenth-Century Interior Decoration in England, France and Holland* (New Haven: Yale University Press, 1978), p. 172; Fowler and Cornforth, *English Decoration*, pp. 57–58; Wallace B. Gusler, *Furniture of Williamsburg and Eastern Virginia, 1710–1790* (Richmond: Virginia Museum, 1979), pp. 13–16; "Journal of Ebenezer Hazard's Journey to the South, 1777," excerpted in Bruton Parish church file, Architectural Research Department, Colonial Williamsburg Foundation; George Ferguson, *Signs and Symbols in Christian Art* (London: Oxford University Press, 1954), p. 54; Fairfax VB, p. 12; Truro VB, pp. 97, 116; Antrim VB, p. 114. For a use of *canopy*: Fredericksville VB, p. 34; for *type*: Bristol VB, p. 54; for *top*: Wicomico VB, fol. 20. There is one instance of the use of *sounding board*, in the 1752 specifications for a chapel in Frederick Parish, which was to have "a sounding Board Over the Pulpit." (Frederick VB, p. 27.) This is early evidence of a change in the perception of the canopy, but the source and traditional meaning of the element are as I have outlined them.

41. Truro VB, pp. 97, 116; Benson J. Lossing, *Mount Vernon, The Home of Washington* (Cincinnati: John C. Yorston, 1882), p. 93; Langley, *Designs*, pls. CXII, CXIII, CXIV, CXVII; Luke Beckerdite, "William Buckland and William Bernard Sears: The Architect and the Carver," *Journal of Early Southern Decorative Arts* 8, no. 2 (November 1982): 29. The likelihood that Pohick's pulpit was derived from Langley is reinforced by the 1770 pulpit at Christ church, Philadelphia, which resembles Lossing's drawing and the 18th- and 19th-century accounts of Pohick church, and which can be shown to have been derived from five Langley plates (*Story of Christ Church*, pp. 23–24; Clarence Wilson Brazer, "Jonathan Gostelowe, Philadelphia Cabinet and Chair Maker," in *Philadelphia Furniture and Its Makers*, ed. John J. Snyder, Jr. [New York: Main Street/Universe, 1975], pp. 54–55).

42. Hening, 2: 30, 52; *Certain Sermons or Homilies . . . to Which Are Added, The Constitutions and Canons of the Church of England, Set Forth A.D. 1603* (3d American ed.; Philadelphia: George and Wayne, 1844), pp. 560, 564–65; Robert Carter, "Rules for the Conduct of churchwardens," ca. 1775, Carter Family Papers, 1651–1861, VHS, sec. 30, fol. 6; Perry, p. 213.

43. Mason, p. 326; Meade, 1: 372; Christ, Middlesex VB, p. 26; Christ Reg., p. 33 (checked against the manuscript, p. 36). For a brief account of Perrott's life, see Darrett B. Rutman and Anita H. Rutman, *A Place in Time: Middlesex County, Virginia, 1650–1750* (New York: Norton, 1984), pp. 86, 99, 148–49, 152.

44. Robert Blair St. George, "Style and Structure in the Joinery of Dedham and Medfield, Massachusetts, 1635–1685," WP 13 (1979): 9, 11, 26; Christ, Middlesex VB, p. 320.

45. For comparable domestic chests, see St. George, "Style and Structure," p. 6; Robert Blair St. George, *The Wrought Covenant: Source Material for the Study of Craftsmen and Community in Southeastern New England, 1620–1700* (Brockton, Mass.: Brockton Art Center/Fuller Memorial, 1979), p. 39; Jonathan L. Fairbanks and Robert F. Trent, eds., *New England Begins: The Seventeenth Century* (Boston: Museum of Fine Arts, 1982), 2: 211; 3: 515–17; and Patricia E. Kane, *Furniture of the New Haven Colony: The Seventeenth-Century Style* (New Haven: New Haven Colony Historical Society, 1973), pp. 12–19.

46. *Certain Sermons*, p. 560.

47. Some parishes found it safer to keep their valuables in the homes of parishioners. The surplice in one of Albemarle Parish's churches was damaged by rats, and a Bible given to Bruton Parish was found "in danger of spoiling by lying in the chest." In the third quarter of the 18th century, several parish

churches were the targets of thieves who stole their valuable ornaments. Between 1746 and 1772, Nottoway, Ware, Charles, and Southwark parishes all advertised in the *Virginia Gazette* for the return of stolen goods of the sort that might have been kept in chests (Albemarle VB, p. 61; Bruton Recs., p. 36; VG June 26, 1746, May 15, 1752; VG [Purdie and Dixon] December 16, 1768; VG [Rind] October 29, 1772).

48. Shelburne VB, p. 29; Cunningham Recs., p. 47; Christ, Middlesex VB, p. 320; Petsworth VB, p. 285.

49. *Certain Sermons*, p. 564; Perry, pp. 261–318; Margaret Davis, "Tidewater Churches," *South Atlantic Quarterly* 35, no. 1 (January 1936): 86–97; St. James VB, p. 190.

50. Thomas K. Ford, *The Bookbinder in Eighteenth-Century Williamsburg, An Account of his Life & Times, & of his Craft* (Williamsburg: Colonial Williamsburg, 1978), pp. 13, 21; Truro VB, p. 134.

51. Addleshaw and Etchells, pp. 24, 64–68; J. G. Davies, *The Architectural Setting of Baptism* (London: Barrie and Rockliff, 1962), pp. 94–100; Antrim VB, p. 50; Perry, p. 271; *Church Silver of Colonial Virginia* (Richmond: Virginia Museum, 1970), pp. 41, 68–71. The Antrim basin may also have been intended as an alms basin.

52. William A.R. Goodwin, *Bruton Parish Church Restored and Its Historic Environment* (Petersburg, Va.: Franklin Press, 1907), n.p.; Rawlings, p. 77. A font base similar to that at St. Mary's White Chapel existed at St. Peter's Parish church in the 1920s. Its present location is unknown (1927 photograph labeled "purchased from Charles Carter in 1736," St. Peter's, New Kent County, file, item no. 64433, Picture Collection, VSL).

53. Langley, *Designs*, pl. CL; Wat Tayler Mayo, Walter Randolph Crabbe, and S. Downing Cox, *A Sketch of Yeocomico Church (Built 1706) in Cople Parish, Westmoreland County, Va.* (n.p., 1906), n.p.; Meade, 2: 155, 157.

54. Albemarle VB, p. 43.

55. *Colonial Churches in the Original Colony of Virginia*, p. 55; Truro VB, p. 129.

56. Blisland VB, p. 56; Christ, Middlesex VB, p. 19.

57. Addleshaw and Etchells, pp. 24–33; Edward Welchman, *The Thirty-Nine Articles of the Church of England* (6th ed.; London: For John and Francis Rivington, 1774), pp. 66, 71–72; Wheatly, *Rational Illustration*, pp. 273–76.

58. Addleshaw and Etchells, pp. 117–19; J.H. Overton, *Life in the English Church (1660–1714)* (London: Longmans, Green and Co., 1885), pp. 182, 198; Davies, *Worship and Theology*, 2: 308–9.

59. Petsworth VB, p. 3; Christ, Middlesex VB, p. 127; Hugh Jones, *The Present State of Virginia*, ed. Richard L. Morton (1724; reprint ed., Chapel Hill: University of North Carolina Press, 1956), p. 98. The issue of kneeling was a hotly disputed one in the 17th and 18th centuries.

60. William Strachey, "A True Reportory of the Wreck and Redemption of Sir Thomas Gates, Knight" (1625), in *A Voyage to Virginia in 1609*, ed. Louis B. Wright (Charlottesville: University Press of Virginia, 1964), p. 80; Antrim VB, p. 114; Christ, Middlesex VB, pp. 121, 127, 140; Lanto Synge, *Chairs* (Poole, Dorset: Blandford Press, 1978), p. 25; Lyon, *Colonial Furniture*, pp. 193–94; Rawlings, pp. 55, 124; *Colonial Churches in the Original Colony of Virginia*, p. 241; Gusler, *Furniture*, p. 18. One Virginia joined table, traditionally dated 1710, is illustrated in Gusler, *Furniture*, pp. 22–23. A good selection of joined tables made in Bermuda, a colony with close historic, commercial, architectural, and personal ties to 17th- and 18th-century Virginia, can be found in Bryden Bordley Hyde, *Bermuda's Antique Furniture and Silver* (Hamilton: Bermuda National Trust, 1971), pp. 10–12, 78–91. Many are Anglican communion tables. For earlier English joined communion tables, see Christopher Gilbert, Anthony Wells-Cole, and Richard Fawcett, *Oak Furniture from Yorkshire Churches* (Leeds: Temple Newsam House, 1971), pp. 42–43.

61. Addleshaw and Etchells, pp. 24–26.

62. Mercer, *Furniture*, pp. 27–29, 137; Strachey, "True Reportory," p. 80; Susan Prendergast Schoelwer, "Form, Function, and Meaning in the Use of Fabric Furnishings: A Philadelphia Case Study, 1700–1775," *WP* 14, no. 1 (spring 1979): 26–39; Thornton, *Seventeenth-Century Interior Decoration*, pp. 105, 180, 239, 243, 353n.; Addleshaw and Etchells, p. 33; John E. Booty, ed., *The Book of Common Prayer, 1559: The Elizabethan Prayer Book* (Charlottesville: University Press of Virginia, 1976), p. 248; Wheatly, *Rational Illustration*, pp. 276–77.

63. Petsworth VB, pp. 284–85, 289; St. George's, Spots. VB, 1: 31–32; Wicomico VB, fol. 89; *Colonial Churches in the Original Colony of Virginia*, p. 310; Thornton, *Seventeenth-Century Interior Decoration*, p. 112; Christ, Middlesex VB, pp. 15, 59, 163, 237, 267, 280. Broadcloth was a fine and durable woolen cloth most commonly used for men's garments. (John S. Moore, ed., *The Goods and Chattels of Our Forefathers: Frampton Cotterell and District Probate Inventories, 1539–1804* [London: Phillimore, 1976], p. 295.) To get a sense of the Petsworth Parish vestry's extravagance, we can note that in 1751 St. Mark's Parish paid the equivalent of only £99 Virginia currency (9,900 pounds of tobacco) for its new 44-by-20-foot frame Little Fork chapel, and in 1754 Lynnhaven Parish paid £324 10s., just over twice the Petsworth expenditure, for its 50-by-25-foot brick Eastern Shore chapel. (St. Mark's VB, p. 88; Lynnhaven VB, p. 50; tobacco prices from Lewis Cecil Gray, *History of Agriculture in the Southern*

United States To 1860 [1933; reprint ed., Gloucester, Mass.: Peter Smith, 1958], 1: 272; exchange rate from John J. McCusker, *Money and Exchange in Europe and America, 1600–1775: A Handbook* [Chapel Hill: University of North Carolina Press, 1978], p. 211.)

64. Thornton, *Seventeenth-Century Interior Decoration*, pp. 113, 117; Christ, Middlesex VB, p. 35. Henry Creeke's wife, Alice, was Henry Corbin's widow (Rutman and Rutman, A *Place in Time*, pp. 51, 107).

65. VG, June 26, 1746, May 15, 1752; VG (Purdie and Dixon), December 16, 1768; VG (Rind), October 29, 1772; George Carrington Mason, "The Colonial Churches of Westmoreland and King George Counties, Virginia," *VMHB* 56, no. 2 (April 1948): 159–60.

66. Graham Hood, *American Silver: A History of Style, 1650–1900* (New York: Praeger, 1971), p. 12; Barbara McLean Ward and Gerald W.R. Ward, eds., *Silver in American Life* (New York: American Federation of Arts, 1979), pp. 3, 15, 34; William Fitzhugh, *William Fitzhugh and His Chesapeake World, 1676–1701: The Fitzhugh Letters and Documents*, ed. Richard Beale Davis (Chapel Hill: University of North Carolina Press, 1963), p. 246; Mark Girouard, *Life in the English Country House: A Social and Architectural History* (New Haven: Yale University Press, 1977), p. 47.

67. Oman, *English Church Plate*, pp. 129, 152; Bennet, *Paraphrase*, p. 167; Christ, Middlesex VB, p. 163; St. George's, Spots. VB, 1: 6.

68. Mrs. G.E.P. How, "Seventeenth-Century English Silver and Its American Derivatives," in *Arts of the Anglo-American Community in the Seventeenth Century*, ed. Ian M.G. Quimby (Charlottesville: University Press of Virginia, 1975), p. 200; *Church Silver of Colonial Virginia*, pp. 22–23, 38–39; Charles F. Montgomery, A *History of American Pewter* (New York: Praeger, 1973), pp. 60, 79; Kathryn C. Buhler, *American Silver, 1655–1825, in the Museum of Fine Arts, Boston* (Greenwich, Conn.: New York Graphic Society, 1972), 1: 25.

69. Oman, *English Church Plate*, p. 152; *Church Silver of Colonial Virginia*, pp. 38–39.

70. St. Patrick's VB, p. 19; Southam VB, p. 45; Davis, "Tidewater Churches," p. 92.

71. Buhler, *American Silver*, 1: 87; Davis, "Tidewater Churches," p. 92.

72. Hood, *American Silver*, pp. 11, 13, 22, and passim; Anthony N.B. Garvan, with Arlene Kringold, Philip Stone, and Robert Jones, "American Church Silver: A Statistical Study," in *Spanish, French, and English Traditions in the Colonial Silver of North America*, ed. John D. Morse (Winterthur, Del.: Winterthur Museum, 1969), pp. 83–85, 98, 101–2; Thomas

K. Ford, *The Silversmith in Eighteenth-Century Williamsburg: An Account of his Life & Times, & of his Craft* (Williamsburg: Colonial Williamsburg Foundation, 1980), pp. 1, 4, 10, 35–36; *Church Silver of Colonial Virginia*, pp. 26–27, 56–61, 68–69, 76–77; John D. Davis, *English Silver at Williamsburg* (Williamsburg: Colonial Williamsburg Foundation, 1976), pp. 127–28. My remarks about the universality of importation are based on a survey of all pieces included in *Church Silver of Colonial Virginia* and all pieces mentioned in the documents. Of 120 items whose origin can be identified, 116 are certainly English, and 3 are probably so. One late 17th-century basin or paten donated to Hungar's Parish by Governor Francis Nicholson has been tentatively attributed to the Boston silversmith John Coney. (*Church Silver of Colonial Virginia*, pp. 34–35.) My figures differ from those of Anthony N.B. Garvan, who attributed 85% of Virginia church silver to England, because Garvan was limited in his resources to E. Alfred Jones's early 20th-century attributions, and because his survey included vessels made after the American Revolution (Garvan, et al., "American Church Silver," p. 83).

73. *Church Silver of Colonial Virginia*, pp. 38–39 (compare the salver illustrated in Buhler, *American Silver*, p. 24); Hood, *American Silver*, p. 14; Christ, Middlesex VB, p. 163.
  Three categories of church furnishings have been omitted from this chapter, largely for lack of evidence about them. Among the church linens were the *surplices* worn by ministers. Surplices were required by the Church of England and by its successor Virginia Episcopal Church in the canons enacted in 1787. There is evidence that many churches had them, but the lack of surplices was among the complaints voiced at a meeting of Virginia clergy in 1719, and Hugh Jones claimed in 1724 that surplices "were disused . . . for a long time in most churches, by bad examples, carelessness and indulgence, [but] are now beginning to be brought in fashion, not without difficulty." (St. James VB, p. 198; Perry, p. 213; Jones, *Present State*, p. 98.) *Organs* were owned in a few wealthy churches. Bruton Parish attempted to beg one from the king in 1729, and succeeded in 1752 in obtaining a legislative appropriation for an organ that was installed in 1755. As usual, Petsworth Parish was a leader; it installed "A Good Substantial Gallery at the west End of the Church at Popler Springs for the Use of placing an Organ" in 1737. By the end of the colonial period organs were more common. Stratton Major Parish had one on loan from a parishioner who, on leaving the colony in 1772, advertised for sale at £200 current money "vastly under the prime cost, a Church Organ, which for sweetness of tone and elegance is inferior to none on the continent. The case is polished mahogany, the pipes gilt, and the imagery that adorns it striking. It is loud enough for any church in Virginia." The Fredericksburg congregation of St. George's Parish financed one by lottery in 1768, and by 1773 even rural St. Mary's Parish, Caroline County, advertised for

an organist. ("The Organ of Bruton Parish Church," MS., February 14, 1939, Architectural Research Department, Colonial Williamsburg Foundation; Hening, 6: 230–31; Bruton Recs., p. 44; Petsworth VB, p. 242; VG [Rind], December 31, 1772, July 28, 1768; VG [Purdie and Dixon], March 11, 1773.) *Bells* were among the items Robert Carter included in his list of furnishings that church wardens were obliged to obtain, but as we have seen few churches had belfries or bells unless they were donated. (Carter, "Rules for the conduct of churchwardens," fol. 6.)

74. Bruton Recs., p. 36; Wicomico VB, fol. 19; George Carrington Mason, "The Colonial Churches of Northumberland and Lancaster Counties, Virginia," *VMHB* 54, no. 2 (April 1946): 147–48.

75. Augusta VB, p. 323; Truro VB, p. 121.

76. Hood, *American Silver*, p. 12; Schoelwer, "Fabric Furnishings," pp. 29, 31–34.

Chapter 7

1. Horton Davies, *Worship and Theology in England*, 2, *From Andrewes to Baxter and Fox, 1603–1690* (Princeton: Princeton University Press, 1975), pp. 22–29.

2. The following discussion of symbolism and ideology is based on: Janet L. Dolgin, David S. Kemnitzer, and David M. Schneider, " 'As People Express Their Lives, So They Are . . . ,' " in *Symbolic Anthropology: A Reader in the Study of Symbols and Meanings* (New York: Columbia University Press, 1977), pp. 3–44; Dan Sperber, *Rethinking Symbolism*, trans. Alice L. Morton (Cambridge: Cambridge University Press, 1977); Victor W. Turner, *Dramas, Fields and Metaphors: Symbolic Action in Human Society* (Ithaca: Cornell University Press, 1974); John Skorupski, *Symbol and Theory: A Philosophical Study of the Theories of Religion in Social Anthropology* (Cambridge: Cambridge University Press, 1976); Clifford Geertz, *The Interpretation of Cultures* (New York: Basic Books, 1973); Richard Krautheimer, "Introduction to 'An Iconography of Medieval Architecture,' " *Journal of the Warburg and Courtauld Institutes* 5 (1942): 1–33; E. Baldwin Smith, *The Dome: A Study in the History of Ideas* (1950; reprint ed., Princeton: Princeton University Press, 1971); E. Baldwin Smith, *Architectural Symbolism of Imperial Rome and the Middle Ages* (Princeton: Princeton University Press, 1956); Antonio Gramsci, *Selections from the Prison Notebooks of Antonio Gramsci*, ed. Quintin Hoare and Geoffrey Nowell Smith (New York: International Publishers, 1971); Carl Boggs, *Gramsci's Marxism* (London: Pluto Press, 1976), esp. chapter 2; Anne Showstack Sassoon, ed., *Approaches to Gramsci* (London: Writers and Readers, 1982); and Steve Barnett and Martin G. Silverman, *Ideology and Everyday Life: Anthropology, Neomarxist Thought, and the Problem of Ideology and the Social Whole* (Ann Arbor: University of Michigan Press, 1979).

3. Turner, *Dramas, Fields and Metaphors*, pp. 13, 24–26, 36, 64.

4. Geertz, *Interpretation of Cultures*, pp. 89–90.

5. Emile Mâle, *The Gothic Image: Religious Art in France of the Thirteenth Century*, trans. Dora Nussey (New York: Icon Editions, Harper and Row, 1972), pp. 5–22; Otto von Simson, *The Gothic Cathedral: Origins of Gothic Architecture and the Medieval Concept of Order* (New York: Harper Torchbooks, 1964), pp. 21–58; Davies, *Worship and Theology*, 2: 5, 9, 11, 14, 17, 38–41.

6. "One of the commonest totems is the belief about everything that exists, that it is 'natural' that it should exist, that it could not do otherwise than exist." (Gramsci, *Selections*, p. 157.)

7. Richard Hooker, *Of the Laws of Ecclesiastical Polity* (London: J. M. Dent, 1907), 2:43; Carter, pp. 616–17; James Reid, "The Religion of the Bible and Religion of K[ing] W[illiam] County Compared," *Transactions*, American Philosophical Society, 57, pt. 1 (1967): 62.

8. Thomas Bennet, *A Paraphrase with Annotations upon the Book of Common Prayer* (2d ed.; London: James Knapton, 1709), p. 303.

9. Mark Girouard, *Life in the English Country House: A Social and Architectural History* (New Haven: Yale University Press, 1977), p. 23; Edward Kimber, "Observations in Several Voyages and Travels in America in the Year 1736," *WMQ* 1st ser. 15, no. 3 (January 1907): 146; Robert Beverley, *The History and Present State of Virginia*, ed. Louis B. Wright (Chapel Hill: University of North Carolina Press, 1947), p. 308; George Washington, *The Diaries of George Washington*, ed. Donald Jackson and Dorothy Twohig (Charlottesville: University Press of Virginia, 1976), 1: 90; Thomas Anburey, *Travels Through the Interior Parts of America* (Boston: Houghton, Mifflin, 1923), 2: 200; Latrobe, p. 141; Luigi Castiglioni, *Luigi Castiglioni's Viaggio: Travels in the United States of North America, 1785–87*, trans. and ed. Antonio Pace (Syracuse University Press, 1983), p. 196; Johann David Schoepf, *Travels in the Confederation [1783–1784]*, trans. and ed. Alfred J. Morrison (Philadelphia: William J. Campbell, 1911), 2: 93; "Journal of Alexander Macaulay," *WMQ* 1st ser. 11, no. 3 (January 1903): 182.

10. "Some Colonial Virginia Records," *VMHB* 11, no. 2 (October 1903): 157–58; Kimber, "Observations," p. 22; Beverley, *History*, p. 313; Anburey, *Travels*, 2: 201–10.

11. Hugh Jones, *The Present State of Virginia*, ed. Richard L. Morton (Chapel Hill: University of North Carolina Press, 1956), p. 84; Gregory A. Stiverson and Patrick H. Butler III, eds., "Virginia in 1732: The Travel Journal of William Hugh Grove," *VMHB* 85, no. 1 (January 1977): 30.

12. Beverley, *History*, pp. 313, 308; "Charges Against Governor

Nicholson," *VMHB* 3, no. 4 (April 1896): 381; J.P. Brissot de Warville, *New Travels in the United States of America, 1788*, trans. Mara Soceanu Vamos and Durand Echeverria, ed. Durand Echeverria (Cambridge: Harvard University Press, 1964), p. 348; Anburey, *Travels*, 2: 208. Tuckahoe still stands in Goochland County. It was built in at least two sections. The two-story, single-pile, central-passage north block was probably built around 1730 and may have been enlarged from a single-story house. This was Anburey's guest wing. The identically planned south wing and the connecting saloon were probably built in the third quarter of the century. For a plan and an extensive discussion of Tuckahoe, see Jessie Thompson Krusen, "Tuckahoe Plantation," *Winterthur Portfolio* 11 (1976): 103–22.

13. "Extracts from the County Records," *VMHB* 8, no. 2 (October 1900): 171–72. Another 17th-century banqueting hall was built by the Middlesex County planter Henry Corbin and two of his neighbors (Darrett B. Rutman and Anita H. Rutman, *A Place in Time: Middlesex County, Virginia, 1650–1750* [New York: Norton, 1984], p. 50).

14. Kimber, "Observations," p. 146; Robert Hunter, Jr., *Quebec to Carolina in 1785–1786*, ed. Louis B. Wright and Marion Tinling (San Marino, Cal.: Huntington Library, 1943), p. 197; Brissot de Warville, *New Travels*, p. 343.

15. Edward Welchman, *The Thirty-Nine Articles of the Church of England, Illustrated with Notes* (6th ed.; London: John and Francis Rivington, 1774), pp. 86, 31, 66; Howard Mackey, "Social Welfare in Colonial Virginia: The Impact of the English Old Poor Law," *HMPEC* 36 (1967): 357–82; Fithian, p. 43.

16. Fithian, pp. 58, 70; Schoepf, *Travels*, 2: 93; Joseph Hadfield, *An Englishman in America 1785*, ed. Douglas S. Robertson (Toronto: Hunter-Rose Co., 1933), pp. 5–6; Castiglioni, *Viaggio*, p. 114; Reid, "Religion," p. 48. Part I of Rhys Isaac's *The Transformation of Virginia, 1740–1790* (Chapel Hill: University of North Carolina Press, 1982) is an extended analysis of the concept of the gentry; see esp. pp. 70–73, 115–38.

17. J.F.D. Smyth, *A Tour in the United States of America* (1784; reprint, New York: Arno Press, 1968), 1: 65; Anburey, *Travels*, 2: 215.

18. Michael Zuckerman, "William Byrd's Family," *Perspectives in American History* 12 (1979): 253–312; T.H. Breen, "Horses and Gentlemen: The Cultural Significance of Gambling Among the Gentry of Virginia," *WMQ* 3d ser. 34, no. 2 (April 1977): 244; Fithian, p. 129; Andrew Burnaby, *Travels Through the Middle Settlements of North-America in the Years 1759 and 1760* (2d ed.; Ithaca: Cornell University Press, 1960), p. 22; Reid, "Religion," p. 56.

19. Reid, "Religion," pp. 68, 48.

20. Burnaby, *Travels*, p. 24; Reid, "Religion," p. 68; Schoepf, *Travels*, 2: 44; Breen, "Horses and Gentlemen," pp. 239–57; Isaac, *Transformation*, pp. 98–101; Jones, *Present State*, p. 84; Kimber, "Observations," p. 158; Smyth, *Tour*, 1: 23.

21. Schoepf, *Travels*, 2: 33; Hadfield, *Englishman in America*, pp. 8–9; Breen, "Horses and Gentlemen," pp. 242–48; Isaac, *Transformation*, pp. 98–104; VG, March 20, 1752, supplement; Castiglioni, *Viaggio*, pp. 196, 305 n. 51; Duke de La Rochefoucault Liancourt, *Travels Through the United States of North America . . . in the Years 1795, 1796, and 1797* (London: T. Davison for R. Phillips, 1799), 2: 39–40.

22. Burnaby, *Travels*, p. 23; Schoepf, *Travels*, 2: 38; Latrobe, p. 138; Reid, "Religion," p. 54; William Byrd, *The Secret Diary of William Byrd of Westover, 1709–1712*, ed. Louis B. Wright and Marion Tinling (Richmond: Dietz Press, 1941), p. 233; Charles S. Sydnor, *American Revolutionaries in the Making: Political Practices in Washington's Virginia* (New York: The Free Press, 1952), pp. 44–59.

23. Reid, "Religion," p. 54.

24. Carter, pp. 120–21.

25. Christ, Middlesex VB, p. 35; Hooker, *Laws*, 2: 42; William Fitzhugh, *William Fitzhugh and His Chesapeake World, 1676–1701: The Fitzhugh Letters and Documents*, ed. Richard Beale Davis (Chapel Hill: University of North Carolina Press, 1963), p. 167; Bruton Recs., pp. 25–26.

26. *Church Silver of Colonial Virginia* (Richmond: Virginia Museum, 1970), pp. 20–21.

27. Charles Oman, *English Church Plate, 597–1830* (London: Oxford University Press, 1957), p. 152; Christ, Middlesex VB, p. 25; *Church Silver of Colonial Virginia*, pp. 32–33, 90–91.

28. Christ, Middlesex VB, p. 25; Charles F. Montgomery, *A History of American Pewter* (New York: Praeger, 1973), p. 58; *Colonial Churches in the Original Colony of Virginia* (2d ed.; Richmond: Southern Churchman, 1908), p. 310; Hugh De Samper, *Bruton Parish Church Yesterday and Today* (Williamsburg: Walter H. Miller and Co., 1972), n.p.

29. Fithian, p. 57; Joan R. Gunderson, "The Search for Good Men: Recruiting Ministers in Colonial Virginia," *HMPEC* 48, no. 4 (December 1979): 465–72; Beverley, *History*, pp. 253, 262; Christ, Middlesex VB, pp. 177, 342; VG (Purdie and Dixon), January 10, 1771; VG June 5, 1752; February 28, 1755.

30. Henry Hartwell, James Blair, and Edward Chilton, *The Present State of Virginia, and the College* (1697), ed. Hunter Dickinson Farish (Charlottesville: Dominion Books, 1964), pp. 66–67; Beverley, *History*, p. 264; Jones, *Present State*, p. 65; Perry, 1: 325; Carter, pp. 819–21, 617, 744.

31. Beverley, *History*, p. 313; Perry, pp. 386–93; John Tayloe to Landon Carter, October 16, 1762, Carter Family Papers, reel 1,

microfilm, Colonial Williamsburg Foundation; Carter, pp. 376–77, 809, 616–17, 820.

32. Zuckerman, "William Byrd's Family," pp. 290–91; Fithian, pp. 29, 100, 137; Meade, 2: 45; 1: 180–81; Reid, "Religion," pp. 49–50; VG (Purdie and Dixon), January 17, 1771; Carter, p. 807.

Chapter 8

1. J.H. Bettey, *Church and Community: The Parish Church in English Life* (New York: Barnes and Noble, 1979), pp. 24, 44; Hugh Braun, *Parish Churches: Their Architectural Development in England* (London: Faber and Faber, 1970), pp. 208–9; Christopher Howkins, *Discovering Church Furniture* (2d ed.; Aylesbury, Bucks.: Shire Publications, 1980), pp. 27–32.

2. Addleshaw and Etchells, pp. 87–88; John Smith, *Travels and Works of Captain John Smith, President of Virginia, and Admiral of New England, 1580–1631*, ed. Edward Arber and A.G. Bradley (Edinburgh: John Grant, 1910), p. 957; J. Charles Cox and Alfred Harvey, *English Church Furniture* (2d ed.; London: Methuen, 1908), p. 285; Braun, *Parish Churches*, p. 209.

3. Christ, Middlesex VB, p. 43; Jonathan L. Fairbanks and Robert F. Trent, eds., *New England Begins: The Seventeenth Century* (Boston: Museum of Fine Arts, 1982), 2: 218–19; St. Peter's VB, p. 44; Augusta VB, p. 493.

4. Cox and Harvey, *English Church Furniture*, p. 284; St. Andrew's VB, fol. 4; Christ, Middlesex VB, p. 127.

5. Christ, Middlesex VB, p. 145; Suffolk VB, fol. 22; St. Paul's VB, p. 187.

6. Christ, Middlesex VB, p. 319.

7. St. Andrew's VB, fol. 5; Lynnhaven VB, p. 28; Henrico VB, fol. 30; Antrim VB, p. 5; Bristol VB, p. 4.

8. St. Mark's VB, p. 97.

9. Blisland VB, p. 56; Fredericksville VB, p. 17. There is double-sided raised paneling on the great pew at the northwest corner of the crossing of Christ church, as well, but this pew has been completely rebuilt. James Scott Rawlings believes that the gallery benches at Christ church are not original, but my own examination indicates that they are original to the gallery, although the gallery is an 18th-century alteration to the church (Rawlings, pp. 124–26).

10. Christ, Middlesex VB, pp. 121, 127, 140; "Church Building in Colonial Virginia," *VMHB* 3, no. 4 (April 1896): 421.

11. St. George's, Spots. VB, 2: April 6, 1762; Truro VB, p. 129; Joseph Ball to St. Leger, Landon Carter, February 3, 1835, Genealogical material on the Carter family, Box 8, Minor Collection, Carter Family Papers from James Monroe Law Office Museum, microfilm reel 7, Trinkle Library, Mary Washington College (courtesy of Mark R. Wenger). Ball's letter informed

Carter that "This Church is yet standing, pews pulpit & all, unchanged even to the iron railing which supported the curtains around Mr. Carter's pew." Bishop Meade published oral reports that the railing was brass (Meade, 2: 118).

12. Bettey, *Church and Community*, pp. 78, 107; Addleshaw and Etchells, pp. 90–94; William Root Bliss, *Side Glimpses from the Colonial Meeting-House* (Boston: Houghton Mifflin, 1896), pp. 86–87; Peter Benes and Phillip D. Zimmerman, *New England Meeting House and Church: 1630–1850* (Boston: Boston University and the Currier Gallery of Art for the Dublin Seminar for New England Folklife, 1979), pp. 55–56.

13. "Carter Papers," *VMHB* 6, no. 1 (July 1898): 3; St. Mark's VB, p. 15.

14. Christ, Lancaster VB, p. 83; Fairfax VB, p. 320; Truro VB, p. 18.

15. Bruton Recs., pp. 31–32, 42–43; *Cal. State Pap.*, p. 145; Henrico VB, fol. 68; "Isle of Wight County Records," *WMQ* 1st ser. 7, no. 4 (April 1899): 269; St. Paul's VB, p. 187; Truro VB, pp. 129, 133.

16. Benes and Zimmerman, *New England Meeting House*, p. 55; Hooker, *Laws*, 2: 47; Addleshaw and Etchells, pp. 24, 90; Bettey, *Church and Community*, p. 46; Bruton Recs., p. 43; Truro VB, pp. 57, 65, 133; "Isle of Wight County Records," p. 269; St. Peter's VB, p. 224; Cunningham Recs., p. 12; Stratton Major VB, pp. 166–71, 17–21; St. George's, Spots. VB, 2: August 6, 1775; St. George's, Acc. VB, fol. 7–9.

17. "Isle of Wight County Records," p. 269; Bruton Recs., pp. 43–44; Elizabeth River VB, p. 5; Bristol VB, p. 240.

18. Christ, Middlesex VB, p. 107; St. George's, Spots. VB, 2: August 6, 1755; June 26, 1770; December 16, 1772.

19. Braun, *Parish Churches*, p. 203; "Carter Papers," p. 3; Alan Gowans, *King Carter's Church: Being a Study in Depth of Christ Church, Lancaster County, Virginia* (Victoria, B.C.: University of Victoria Maltwood Museum, 1969), pp. 39–40, pl. 1a; Addleshaw and Etchells, pp. 58, 113–15; Bruton Recs., pp. 41–42; Christ Reg., p. 33; Bristol VB, p. 47; Wicomico VB, fol. 33; St. George's, Spots. VB, 2: May 12, 1755.

20. Bristol VB, pp. 93, 122; Cumberland VB, p. 325.

21. St. George's, Acc. VB, fols. 7–9. The plan of St. George's was reconstructed by comparing standard Virginia church plans and pew dimensions with the plans of Anglican churches built nearby on the Delmarva peninsula at the same time: Christ church, Broad Creek, Delaware, and St. Paul's church, Wicomico County, Maryland, both built as churches of Stepney Parish, Maryland, and with pew plans from colonial churches in other American colonies. I assumed, in accord with all those sources, that pew number one was located adjacent to the entry, that the pews moved in sequence, that

the unassigned pews numbered 16 to 19 were the east end pews later assigned to the vestry, and that the others were public pews. I also assumed, in accord with the plans of the Delaware and Maryland churches and the deep churches of northern Virginia, all double-aisled churches, that the pulpit was located in the middle of the north wall. (Henry H. Hutchinson, "Collected Notes on Christ Church, Broad Creek, and Her Neighbors," *The Archeolog* 23, no. 1 [summer 1971]: 36; Wilkins Updike, *A History of the Episcopal Church in Narragansett, Rhode Island, Including a History of Other Episcopal Churches in the State*, ed. Daniel Goodwin [2d ed.; Boston: Merrymount Press, 1907], 1: 614; 2: 214; Heard Robertson, "The Reverend James Seymour, Frontier Parson, 1771–1783," *HMPEC* 45, no. 2 [June 1976]: 144; Benes and Zimmerman, *New England Meeting House*, p. 144.) For a New England Congregationalist pew plan, with pewholders ranked by economic standing, see Patricia J. Tracy, *Jonathan Edwards, Pastor: Religion and Society in 18th-Century Northampton* (New York: Hill and Wang, 1980), p. 127.

22. William Byrd, *The Secret Diary of William Byrd of Westover, 1709–1712*, ed. Louis B. Wright and Marion Tinling (Richmond: Dietz Press, 1941), p. 273.

23. James Gordon, "The Journal of Colonel James Gordon of Lancaster County, Va.," *WMQ* 1st ser. 12, no. 1 (July 1903): 3; George Washington, *The Writings of George Washington from the Original Manuscript Sources, 1745–1799*, ed. John C. Fitzpatrick (Washington: Government Printing Office, 1931–44), 3: 113–14.

24. Mason, pp. 339–40; Bettey, *Church and Community*, p. 46; Blisland VB, pp. 24–25; St. Andrew's VB, fol. 58; Upper VB, pp. 46–47.

25. Elizabeth River VB, p. 5; Albemarle VB, p. 241; Christ Reg., p. 33; "Virginia Gazette," *WMQ* 1st ser. 12, no. 2 (October 1903): 79; "Will of Wilson Cary," *VMHB* 10, no. 2 (October 1902): 190. For a sense of the attachment of pews to estates in England, see Richard Gough, *The History of Myddle*, ed. David Hey (Harmondsworth: Penguin Books, 1981), an account of 1700 in which Gough uses the pew plan of the parish church as an organizing device for recounting a genealogically based history of his neighborhood.

26. Christ, Lancaster VB, pp. 5, 10; Elizabeth City VB, p. 72.

27. Beverley, *History*, pp. 261–62; Fithian, p. 34.

28. Bruton Recs., p. 41.

29. Perry, pp. 261–318. Expected attendance was calculated as follows: Throughout the 18th century, pastors seemed to agree that a 10-mile radius was the greatest distance from which people could be expected to come to church. The number of churches in a parish was, therefore, compared with the reported parish size. If a parish was 30 miles long and there

were two churches, each expecting to draw people from 10 miles on either side, for example, coverage was complete and the expected attendance was assumed to be 100%. If the parish was wider than 20 miles, or was longer than the equivalent of 20 times the number of churches, a catchment area was calculated, and a prorated percentage of the parish population expected to attend was determined. For an assessment of church attendance in 18th-century America, see Patricia U. Bonomi and Peter R. Eisenstadt, "Church Adherence in the Eighteenth-Century British American Colonies," *WMQ* 3d ser. 39, no. 2 (April 1982), esp. pp. 254–59.

30. Albemarle Reg., pp. 1–7; Albemarle VB, pp. 27, 65, 279. The population of Albemarle Parish was calculated by compiling and comparing figures from several sources. A 1773 list of tithables gave the total for Virginia (less a couple of thinly settled frontier parishes) as 155,278. The population of Virginia at that time has been estimated at half a million, and the white population at 60% of that. United States government estimates of Virginia's population at the time of the first census in 1790 place the proportion of the population over 14 years of age at 51%. I have therefore calculated the number of adult whites in the parishes at the number of tithables × 3.2 × .6 × .51. I stress that these figures are only rough approximations to aid in assessing levels of attendance very generally. The population figures prepared by Darrett and Anita Rutman for Middlesex County in 1724 and 1740 suggest that the ratio of population to tithables might have been as low as 2.28 : 1 or 2.34 : 1, respectively. If these figures are accurate, then attendance was better than I have suggested. ("List of Tithables in Va. Taken 1773," *VMHB* 28, no. 1 [January 1920]: 81–82; Rhys Isaac, *The Transformation of Virginia, 1740–1790* [Chapel Hill: University of North Carolina Press, 1982], p. 12; Gerald W. Mullin, *Flight and Rebellion: Slave Resistance in Eighteenth-Century Virginia* [New York: Oxford University Press, 1972], p. 6; U.S. Bureau of the Census, *Historical Statistics of the United States: Colonial Times to 1970* [Bicentennial ed.; Washington, D.C.: Government Printing Office, 1975], 1: 36; Darrett B. Rutman and Anita H. Rutman, *A Place in Time: Middlesex County, Virginia, 1650–1750. Explicatus* [New York: Norton, 1984], pp. 25–34.)

31. Perry, pp. 273–74, 284, 301, 292, 304; Bonomi and Eisenstadt, "Church Adherence," pp. 255, 275.

32. Suffolk VB, fol. 63.

33. Stratton Major VB, pp. 131–33, 164–71.

34. St. George's, Acc. VB, fols. 7–9. The percentage of white males (51.3) is taken from the Census Bureau estimate for 1790. (U.S. Census Bureau, *Historical Statistics*, 1: 36.)

35. J.H. Overton, *Life in the English Church (1660–1714)* (London: Longmans, Green and Co., 1885), p. 202; Addleshaw and

Etchells, p. 92; Meade, 1: 382; Lynnhaven VB, p. 28; Cunningham Recs., p. 16; Elizabeth Combs Peirce, "History of St. Mary's White Chapel," *WMQ* 2d ser. 16, no. 4 (October 1936): 526.

36. Fithian, pp. 137, 122; James Reid, "The Religion of the Bible and Religion of K W County Compared," *Transactions*, American Philosophical Society n.s. 57, pt. 1 (1967): 50; Alexander MacSparran, *America Dissected* (1752), reprinted in Updike, *History*, 3: 12; Perry, pp. 301, 312.

37. Gordon, "Journal," passim.

38. Washington, *Writings*, 37: 484; George Washington, *The Diaries of George Washington*, ed. Donald Jackson and Dorothy Twohig (Charlottesville: University Press of Virginia, 1976–78), 3: 254 and passim.

39. Bonomi and Eisenstadt, "Church Adherence," pp. 258–59 n. 46; Robert Carter, Diary, 1722–1727, Microfilm, Colonial Williamsburg, entry for December 31, 1727, and passim; Fithian, pp. 114, 122. Robert Carter could attend church every Sunday in part because the only church in the parish was near his house.

40. Winthrop D. Jordan, *White Over Black: American Attitudes Toward the Negro, 1550–1812* (Chapel Hill: University of North Carolina Press, 1968), pp. 180–86; Albert J. Raboteau, *Slave Religion: The "Invisible Institution" in the Antebellum South* (New York: Oxford University Press, 1978), pp. 97–128; Carter, p. 292; Perry, 1: 267; Robert Hunter, Jr., *Quebec to Carolinas in 1785–1786*, ed. Louis B. Wright and Marion Tinling (San Marino, Calif.: Huntington Library, 1943), p. 206; William Lee to Cary Wilkinson, May 22, 1771, William Lee Letter Book, 1769–1771, MS., VHS, pp. 24–25.

41. Lee to Wilkinson, Lee Letter Book, p. 25.

42. Brydon, 1: 191–98; 2: 43, 59, 71–72; Rhys Isaac, "Evangelical Revolt: The Nature of the Baptists' Challenge to the Traditional Order in Virginia, 1765 to 1775," *WMQ* 3d ser. 31, no. 3 (July 1974): 345–68; "O Dinwiddianae," in *Colonial Virginia Satirist*, ed. Davis, p. 22; James Waddell, "To the Rev. Mr. W------ G------, Rector of Lunenburg parish, in Richmond" county, VG, July 21, 1768; Gordon, "Journal," pp. 110, 200; Stratton Major VB, p. 7; Perry, p. 380. The use of set prayers had divided Anglicans and Puritans since the 16th century, and much Anglican ink was devoted to defending the practice (Horton Davies, *Worship and Theology in England*, 1, *From Cranmer to Hooker, 1534–1603* [Princeton: Princeton University Press, 1970], pp. 264–65, 268–73). The dissenters of 18th-century Virginia have been analyzed in Wesley M. Gewehr, *The Great Awakening in Virginia, 1740–1790* (Durham: Duke University Press, 1930), and most extensively and perceptively by Rhys Isaac in "Evangelical Revolt"; in "Religion and Authority: Problems of the Anglican Establishment in Virginia in the Era of the Great Awakening and the Parsons' Cause," in *Colonial America: Essays in Politics and Social Development*, ed. Stanley N. Katz (2d ed.; Boston: Little, Brown, 1976), pp. 305–33; and especially in *Transformation of Virginia*. I have relied heavily on Isaac's account.

43. Gordon, "Journal," pp. 108–9; Waddell, "To the Rev. Mr. W------ G------."

44. VG (Purdie and Dixon) December 3, 1772; Fithian, p. 72; Luigi Castiglioni, *Luigi Castiglioni's Viaggio: Travels in the United States of North America*, trans. and ed. Antonio Pace (Syracuse: Syracuse University Press, 1983), p. 183; Duke de La Rochefoucault Liancourt, *Travels Through the United States of North America . . . in the Years 1795, 1796, and 1797* (London: T. Davison for R. Phillips, 1799), 2: 26; Isaac, "Evangelical Revolt," pp. 346–47; J. Stephen Kroll-Smith, "Tobacco and Belief: Baptist Ideology and the Yeoman Planter in Eighteenth-Century Virginia," *Southern Studies* 21, no. 4 (winter 1982): 353–68.

45. Miles White, Jr., comp., "Early Quaker Records in Virginia," *Publications of the Southern History Association* 6, no. 3 (May 1902): 223–24; 6, no. 5 (September 1902): 408; George Carrington Mason, "The Colonial Churches of Henrico and Chesterfield Counties, Virginia," *VMHB* 55, no. 1 (January 1947): 57.

46. Stratton Major VB, p. 132; *Church Silver of Colonial Virginia* (Richmond: Virginia Museum, 1970), p. 97; Isaac, "Evangelical Revolt," pp. 345–68; Isaac, *Transformation*, pp. 161–77; Gordon, "Journal," p. 3. The date of Providence church is based on the traditional belief that the church was constructed when Presbyterian meetings that began at Samuel Morris's house in the early 1740s outgrew the house. The earliest surviving Providence church records date from 1822; the first entry notes that no records had been kept until then. Architecturally, the mid-century date seems reasonable. The church was old enough to have been remodeled in the 18th century. (Rawlings, pp. 161–77; William Henry Foote, *Sketches of Virginia, Historical and Biographical* [Philadelphia: William S. Martien, 1850], p. 121; Providence Church [Presbyterian] Session Book, 1822–1893, Photostat, VSL, p. 5.) One other dissenting church, Mauck's meeting house in Page County, is thought to be pre-Revolutionary, but the architectural evidence makes it difficult to assign it a date much before 1800.

47. Gordon, "Journal," p. 199; Richard R. Beeman, "Social Change and Cultural Conflict in Virginia: Lunenburg County, 1746 to 1774," *WMQ* 3d ser. 35, no. 3 (July 1978): 455–76; Perry, pp. 295, 333; Bonomi and Eisenstadt, "Church Adherence," p. 255; Albemarle Reg., p. 7; St. Patrick's VB, p. 12.

48. Kroll-Smith, "Tobacco and Belief," pp. 353–68.

49. Mason, p. 340; Elizabeth City VB, p. 71; *Cal. State Pap.*, p. 145.

50. Lancaster County Order Book 1: 185, quoted in Peirce, "History of St. Mary's White Chapel," p. 526.

51. Lynnhaven VB, pp. 21–22.

52. Meade, 1: 180–81; Lothrop Withington, "Virginia Gleanings in London," *VMHB* 20, no. 4 (October 1912): 373–74; Louis B. Wright, *The First Gentlemen of Virginia: Intellectual Qualities of the Early Colonial Ruling Class* (Charlottesville: Dominion Books, 1964), pp. 79–81.

53. Christ, Middlesex VB, pp. 62–63. Ann Jones's presentment on September 2, 1689, "for haueing a base begotten Childe" is in Middlesex County Order Book, 1680–1694, MS., VSL, p. 418. There is no further explanation of the original incident, nor did Jones ever appear in court to answer the charge as she was ordered to do. At the same time, in response to several suits, including one from the parish minister, John Vause, Matthew Kemp himself confessed that in his capacity as county sheriff and tax collector he had countenanced "concealed levies," that is, he had allowed some planters to evade their full head-tax burden. His excuse was that everyone did it. (Middlesex OB, 1680–1694, pp. 445–46, 449, 459.) For an English conflict over sitting in a seat inappropriate to one's station, see Gough, *History of Myddle*, pp. 117–20.

54. Addleshaw and Etchells, pp. 90–96.

Chapter 9

1. Hening, 1: 160–61; Petsworth VB, pp. 167, 120; Kingston VB, p. 2; St. Andrew's VB, fol. 63; Cumberland VB, p. 433; Upper VB, p. 220; Blisland VB, pp. 69, 85; St. Peter's VB, pp. 174–75, 56; St. Paul's VB, p. 86; Christ, Middlesex VB, pp. 234, 37, 161, 165; Bristol VB, p. 128; Truro VB, pp. 135–36, 127; Lynnhaven VB, p. 45; William Byrd, *The Secret Diary of William Byrd of Westover, 1709–1712*, ed. Louis B. Wright and Marion Tinling (Richmond: Dietz Press, 1941), p. 138. A set of specifications in the St. George's, Spots., vestry book gives a good idea of the appearance and construction of one of these fences. The vestry agreed "to Rail in the Churches at Rappahannock and Mattapony [with] Ten feet pannels five Rails to each to be done with white oak Posts and Poplar rails without any Sap the Posts to be burnt all under ground and six Inches above . . . , the Tenents of rails to be Tar'd before fixed in the Mortice." (St. George's, Spots. VB, 1: 55.)

2. St. Peter's VB, p. 174; VG (Purdie and Dixon) March 31, 1774.

3. Bristol VB, p. 136; Christ, Middlesex VB, pp. 18–19; Bruton Recs., pp. 42–43; "Carter Papers," *VMHB* 6, no. 1 (July 1898): 3; John Carter to William Dawkins, September 11, 1733, John, Landon, and Charles Carter Letter Book, 1732–1781, microfilm, Colonial Williamsburg Foundation, p. 18; Hugh

Jones, *The Present State of Virginia*, ed. Richard L. Morton (1724; reprint ed., Chapel Hill: University of North Carolina Press, 1956), p. 97; Fraser D. Neiman, *The "Manner House" Before Stratford (Discovering the Clifts Plantation)* (Stratford, Va.: Robert E. Lee Memorial Association, 1980), pp. 28–29; Médéric-Louis-Élie Moreau de Saint-Mèry, *Moreau de St. Mèry's American Journey [1793–1798]*, trans. and ed. Kenneth Roberts and Anna M. Roberts (Garden City, N.Y.: Doubleday, 1947), p. 53; Fithian, pp. 41, 61; *The Journal of John Harrower, An Indentured Servant in the Colony of Virginia, 1775–1776*, ed. Edward Miles Riley (Williamsburg: Colonial Williamsburg Foundation, 1963), pp. 87–88. Most of the elaborate 18th-century tombs now standing in colonial churchyards, it might be mentioned, were moved there in the 20th century from their original plantation locations.

4. St. Paul's VB, p. 196; Christ, Lancaster VB, p. 16; Truro VB, pp. 58, 102–3; Blisland VB, p. 175.

5. Jones, *Present State*, p. 84; Alexander MacSparran, *America Dissected* (1752), reprint in Wilkins Updike, *A History of the Episcopal Church in Narragansett Rhode Island*, ed. Daniel Goodwin (2d ed.; Boston: Merrymount Press, 1907), 3: 12; T.H. Breen, "Horses and Gentlemen: The Cultural Significance of Gambling Among the Gentry of Virginia," *WMQ* 3d ser. 34, no. 2 (April 1977): 248–49; St. Mark's VB, pp. 26, 65; Petsworth VB, p. 89; Elizabeth City VB, pp. 67, 85, 126, 55–56, 88; Christ, Middlesex VB, pp. 18, 78, 81, 321; Truro VB, p. 48; Upper VB, pp. 19–20, 220; St. Peter's VB, p. 217, 108, 224; Wicomico VB, fols. 47, 10, 36, 96; Byrd, *Diary*, p. 470.

6. Wicomico VB, fols. 60–61, 75, 91; Bristol VB, p. 51; Truro VB, pp. 88, 91; Byrd, *Diary*, pp. 174, 233. In an attempt to eliminate the nonliturgical uses of parish churches that were common in the Middle Ages, Anglican authorities between 1550 and 1640 issued 200 separate articles and injunctions prohibiting them. (Marcus Binney and Peter Burman, *Chapels and Churches: Who Cares?* [London: British Tourist Authority, 1979], p. 111.)

7. Albemarle VB, p. 44; Wicomico VB, fol. 53; Newport VB, p. 84; Bristol VB, p. 184; Truro VB, p. 132; Gerald Randall, *Church Furnishing and Decoration in England and Wales* (London: B. T. Batsford, 1980), p. 31; Fithian, p. 29; Gerald W. Mullin, *Flight and Rebellion: Slave Resistance in Eighteenth-Century Virginia* (New York: Oxford University Press, 1972), pp. 56–58; Carter, p. 289; St. Peter's VB, pp. 104, 240–41.

8. William Strachey, *A True Repertory of the Wreck and Redemption of Sir Thomas Gates, Knight* (1625), in *A Voyage to Virginia in 1609*, ed. Louis B. Wright (Charlottesville: University Press of Virginia, 1964), pp. 80–81; Rhys Isaac, *The Transformation of Virginia, 1740–1790* (Chapel Hill: University of North Carolina Press, 1982), pp. 326–28; Fithian, pp. 29, 100, 137; Carter, p. 536.

9. Carter, p. 743.

10. A. G. Roeber, "Authority, Law and Custom: The Rituals of Court Day in Tidewater Virginia, 1720 to 1750," *WMQ* 3d ser. 37, no. 1 (January 1980): 29–33, 36–37; Wesley Frank Craven, *The Southern Colonies in the Seventeenth Century, 1607–1689* (Baton Rouge: Louisiana State University Press, 1949), p. 274; William H. Seiler, "The Anglican Parish in Virginia," in *Seventeenth-Century America: Essays on Colonial History*, ed. James Morton Smith (Chapel Hill: University of North Carolina Press, 1959), pp. 139, 141–42; Richard R. Beeman, "Social Change and Cultural Conflict in Virginia: Lunenburg County, 1746 to 1774," *WMQ* 3d ser. 35, no. 3 (July 1978): 467; Lancaster County Order Book No. 8, 1729–1743, MS., VSL, pp. 286–87; Norfolk County Orders, 1724–1734, MS., VSL, p. 60; Essex County Wills and Deeds No. 10, MS., VSL, fol. 109; A.G. Roeber, *Faithful Magistrates and Republican Lawyers: Creators of Virginia Legal Culture, 1680–1810* (Chapel Hill: University of North Carolina Press, 1981), pp. 78–80; Marcus Whiffen, "The Early County Courthouses of Virginia," *JSAH* 18, no. 1 (March 1959): 2–10. James Jones, builder of the Lancaster County courthouse, also built St. Mary's White Chapel Parish church at the same time, while Peter Malbone, who undertook the 1726 Norfolk County courthouse, was also responsible for the 1734–36 Lynnhaven Parish church. This discussion of courthouses and the reconstructed plans that accompanied it has benefited from a careful criticism by Carl Lounsbury, who is preparing a book on Virginia courthouses.

11. Roeber, "Authority, Law and Custom," pp. 48, 35. It is unlikely that the use of benches in the arcade had anything to do with concern for the common people as Roeber suggests.

12. Harrower, *Journal*, p. 37; Fithian, pp. 79–82, 95, 178; Latrobe, p. 163; Dell Upton, "The Origins of Chesapeake Architecture," in *Three Centuries of Maryland Architecture* (Annapolis: Maryland Historical Trust, 1982), pp. 44–57; Dell Upton, "White and Black Landscapes in Eighteenth-Century Virginia," *Places* 2, no. 2 (winter 1985): 59–72.

13. Latrobe, pp. 163–70; Harrower, *Journal*, p. 104; Fithian, pp. 129–30; Daniel Blake Smith, *Inside the Great House: Planter Family Life in Eighteenth-Century Chesapeake Society* (Ithaca: Cornell University Press, 1980), p. 43.

14. The following discussion of small houses is derived from Dell Upton, "Vernacular Domestic Architecture in Eighteenth-Century Virginia," *WP* 17, nos. 2–3 (summer-autumn 1982): 95–119; and Dell Upton, "The Virginia Parlor, National Museum of American History, Smithsonian Institution: A Report on the Henry Saunders House and Its Occupants," MS., National Museum of American History, 1981.

15. Upton, "Origins," pp. 44–57.

16. Aubrey C. Land, "Economic Base and Social Structure: The Northern Chesapeake in the Eighteenth Century," *Journal of Economic History* 25, no. 4 (December 1965): 639–54; Upton, "Virginia Parlor," pp. 20–34.

17. Thomas Anburey, *Travels Through the Interior Parts of North America* (1789; reprint ed., Boston: Houghton, Mifflin, 1923), 2: 196; Meade, 2: 45.

18. For discussions of changing concepts of time, see E.P. Thompson, "Time, Work Discipline, and Industrial Capitalism," *Past and Present* no. 38 (December 1967): 56–97; on the orrery and its place in 18th-century thought, see Daniel J. Boorstin, *The Lost World of Thomas Jefferson* (Boston: Beacon Press, 1948), p. 13 and passim.

19. Land, "Economic Base," p. 649; Edmund S. Morgan, *Virginians at Home: Family Life in the Eighteenth Century* (Williamsburg: Colonial Williamsburg, 1952), chapters 1, 4; Harrower, *Journal*, p. 83; Isaac, *Transformation*, pp. 70–79; Upton, "Origins," pp. 48–57; Upton, "Vernacular Domestic Architecture," p. 102; Joseph A. Ernst and H. Roy Merrens, "'Camden's Turrets Pierce the Skies!': The Urban Process in the Southern Colonies During the Eighteenth Century," *WMQ* 3d ser. 30, no. 4 (October 1973): 554, 568–73; John C. Rainbolt, "The Absence of Towns in Seventeenth-Century Virginia," *Journal of Southern History*, 35, no. 3 (August 1969): 343–60; Carville Earle and Ronald Hoffman, "Staple Crops and Urban Development in the Eighteenth-Century South," *Perspectives in American History* 10 (1976): 7–78; Fithian, p. 73; Durand de Dauphiné, *A Huguenot Exile in Virginia, or Voyages of a Frenchman Exiled for his Religion*, trans. and ed. Gilbert Chinard (New York: Press of the Pioneers, 1934), p. 120; "Virginia in 1732: The Travel Journal of William Hugh Grove," ed. Gregory A. Stiverson and Patrick H. Butler III, *VMHB* 85, no. 1 (January 1977): 26; Johann David Schoepf, *Travels in the Confederation [1783–1784]*, trans. and ed. Alfred J. Morrison (Cleveland: Arthur H. Clark Co., 1911), 2: 32.

20. Latrobe, p. 163; Luigi Castiglioni, *Luigi Castiglioni's Viaggio: Travels in the United States of North America, 1785–87*, trans. and ed. Antonio Pace (Syracuse: Syracuse University Press, 1983), p. 112; Fithian, p. 178.

21. Frederick Doveton Nichols and Ralph E. Griswold, *Thomas Jefferson, Landscape Architect* (Charlottesville: University Press of Virginia, 1978), pp. 90–116; Castiglioni, *Viaggio*, pp. 185–86; Isaac Weld, Jr., *Travels Through the States of North America . . . During the Years 1795, 1796, and 1797* (London: John Stockdale, 1799), p. 119.

22. For a description of Monticello and some of its contents, see Frederick D. Nichols and James A. Bear, Jr., *Monticello: A Guidebook* (Monticello: Thomas Jefferson Memorial Foundation, 1967).

23. "Journal of Alexander Macaulay," *WMQ* 1st ser. 11, no. 3 (January 1903): 187; Duke de La Rochefoucault Liancourt, *Travels Through the United States of North America, the Country of the Iroquois, and Upper Canada, in the Years 1795, 1796, and 1797* (London: T. Davison for R. Phillips, 1799), 2: 5; *Colonial Churches in the Original Colony of Virginia* (2d ed.; Richmond: Southern Churchman, 1908), p. 183; Moreau de Saint-Mèry, *American Journey*, p. 64.

Chapter 10

1. Joseph Hadfield, *An Englishman in America 1785*, ed. Douglas S. Robertson (Toronto: Hunter-Rose Co., 1933), p. 10; Andrew Burnaby, *Travels Through the Middle Settlements in North-America in the Years 1759 and 1760* (2d ed.; Ithaca: Cornell University Press, 1960), p. 26; "The Journal of Ebenezer Hazard in Virginia, 1777," ed. Fred Shelley, *VMHB* 62, no. 4 (October 1954): 403; Fithian, pp. 43, 34, 33; James Reid, "The Religion of the Bible and Religion of K W County Compared," *Transactions*, American Philosophical Society, n.s. 57, pt. 1 (1967): 56–57; Robert Hunter, Jr., *Quebec to Carolinas in 1785–1786*, ed. Louis B. Wright and Marion Tinling (San Marino, Calif.: Huntington Library, 1943), p. 208; Nicholas Cresswell, *The Journal of Nicholas Cresswell, 1774–1777* (New York: Dial Press, 1924), p. 53; Anya Peterson Royce, *The Anthropology of Dance* (Bloomington: Indiana University Press, 1977), pp. 154–74, 192–211.

2. Carville Earle and Ronald Hoffman, "Staple Crops and Urban Development in the Eighteenth-Century South," *Perspectives in American History* 10 (1976): 19–50; Charles M. Andrews, *The Colonial Period of American History, 4, England's Commercial and Colonial Policy* (New Haven: Yale University Press, 1938), pp. 368–428 and passim.

3. Devereux Jarratt, "The Autobiography of the Reverend Devereux Jarratt, 1732–1763," ed. Douglass Adair, *WMQ* 3d ser. 9, no. 3 (July 1952): 361; "Notes of Judge St. George Tucker to William Wirt's Life of Patrick Henry" (1815), *WMQ* 1st ser. 22, no. 4 (April 1914): 252–57; Reid, "Religion," p. 67.

4. Howard Mackey, "Social Welfare in Colonial Virginia: The Impact of the English Old Poor Law," *HMPEC* 36 (1967): 357–82; Hening, 6: 475–78; Suffolk VB, fols. 34, 36; St. George's, Acc. VB, fol. 1; Robert Carter, "Rules for the Conduct of churchwardens," ca. 1775, MS., Carter Family Papers, 1651–1861, VHS, fols. 16–17.

5. Christ, Middlesex VB, p. 223; Blisland VB, p. 11; Cunningham Recs., pp. 13–14; Stratton Major VB, p. 159; Elizabeth City VB, p. 104; St. George's, Acc. VB, fol. 11; Elizabeth River VB, p. 23; Hening, 6: 476–77.

6. St. Paul's VB, p. 187; Truro VB, pp. 33–34; Christ, Lancaster VB, pp. 5, 10; St. Mark's VB, pp. 382, 406; Upper VB, pp. 46–47; Bristol VB, p. 129; Wicomico VB, fol. 44; Suffolk VB, fols. 23, 60; Dettingen VB, 1: 7, 23, 49.

7. Cumberland VB, p. 431; Petsworth VB, p. 242; Dettingen VB, 1: 62, 74; Paul G.E. Clemens, *The Atlantic Economy and Colonial Maryland's Eastern Shore: From Tobacco to Grain* (Ithaca: Cornell University Press, 1980), p. 161; T.H. Breen, "Horses and Gentlemen: The Cultural Significance of Gambling Among the Gentry of Virginia," *WMQ* 3d ser. 34, no. 2 (April 1977): 252–53, 257; Meade, 2: 21–22.

8. Lynnhaven VB, pp. 21, 75–76.

9. Lynnhaven VB, pp. 3, 21, 75–76; Suffolk VB, fol. 23; Dettingen VB, 1: 49, 7; Truro VB, p. 34; Wicomico VB, fol. 44; St. Mark's VB, p. 382; Southam VB, pp. 118, 139, 142.

10. Lynnhaven VB, pp. 85, 121; Newport VB, p. 11; St. Patrick's VB, p. 17; Bristol VB, p. 207.

11. Christ, Middlesex VB, pp. 234–35; Southam VB, p. 134. The construction of a private addition is similar in effect to, but different in intent from, the construction of a memorial wing as discussed by Alan Gowans in connection with Christ church, Lancaster County. (Alan Gowans, *King Carter's Church: Being a Study in Depth of Christ Church, Lancaster County, Virginia* [Victoria, B. C.: University of Victoria Maltwood Museum, 1969], pp. 22–32.) In the memorial wing, a private mausoleum was annexed to the church body (an example is the 18th-century family mausoleum of the dukes of Chandos at St. James church, Little Stanmore, Middlesex, England). In the Virginia examples, the living members of the family were housed in the addition, aloof from the public spaces in the body of the church. Both traditions were combined in Scots churches where a laird's or heritor's "aisle" or wing often contained a mausoleum on the ground-floor level and a loft or gallery for seating above. Opening off the loft was usually a small private retiring room, where its occupants could spend the time between morning and afternoon services. (George Hay, *The Architecture of Scottish Post-Reformation Churches, 1560–1843* [Oxford: Clarendon Press, 1957], pp. 52–53, 190, 192.) The structural evidence of the two Middlesex County churches indicates that the wings were never constructed.

12. Christ, Middlesex VB, p. 107.

13. Dettingen VB, 1: 49; Fairfax VB, p. 13. Even when pews were auctioned, the welfare of the parish was considered. The Fairfax Parish pews could not be sold to anyone who was not a resident or a taxpayer of the parish. (Fairfax VB, pp. 13, 54.)

14. Truro VB, pp. 127–28. George Washington was also the highest bidder for a pew in Christ church, Alexandria, a year later. He paid £36 10s. (Fairfax VB, p. 54.)

15. Fairfax VB, pp. 101–2, 107–8.

16. The standard historical discussion of modernization is Richard D. Brown, *Modernization: The Transformation of American Life, 1600–1865* (New York: Hill and Wang, 1976), esp. chapter 3; Rhys Isaac, *The Transformation of Virginia, 1740–1790* (Chapel Hill: University of North Carolina Press, 1982), esp. pp. 310–11; J. Stephen Kroll-Smith, "Tobacco and Belief: Baptist Ideology and the Yeoman Planter in Eighteenth Century Virginia," *Southern Studies* 21, no. 4 (winter 1982): 353–68; J. Stephen Kroll-Smith, "Transmitting a Revival Culture: the Organizational Dynamic of the Baptist Movement in Colonial Virginia, 1760–1777," *Journal of Southern History* 50, no. 4 (November 1984): 551–68. For a discussion of the modernizationist aspects of Isaac's work, see Gary Kulik's review of *The Transformation of Virginia* in the *Vernacular Architecture Newsletter*, no. 16 (summer 1983), pp. 2–3.

17. Edmund S. Morgan, *American Slavery, American Freedom — The Ordeal of Colonial Virginia* (New York: Norton, 1975), p. 111.

18. Neil McKendrick, John Brewer, and J.H. Plumb, *The Birth of a Consumer Society: The Commercialization of Eighteenth-Century England* (London: Europa, 1982), pp. 1–99 and passim.

19. Bristol VB, p. 128.

20. Médéric-Louis-Élie Moreau de Saint-Méry, *Dance*, trans. by Lily and Baird Hastings (1796; reprint ed., Brooklyn: Dance Horizons, 1976), p. 2; Rhys Isaac, "Religion and Authority: Problems of the Anglican Establishment in Virginia in the Era of the Great Awakening and the Parsons' Cause," in *Colonial America: Essays in Politics and Social Development*, ed. Stanley N. Katz (2d ed.; Boston: Little, Borwn, 1973), pp. 305–33; Carl Bridenbaugh, *Mitre and Sceptre: Transatlantic Faiths, Ideas, Personalities, and Politics, 1689–1775* (New York: Oxford University Press, 1962), pp. 230–59.

21. *The Virginia Journal and Alexandria Advertiser*, November 16, 1786 (reference courtesy of Edward Chappell); "Letters from William and Mary, 1795–1799," *VMHB* 30, no. 3 (July 1922): 241.

22. Wicomico VB, fol. 115; Meade, 2: 134–35.

Glossary

Alley. Aisle of a church.

Altarpiece. Altarpieces in Anglican churches comprised wall tablets, sometimes mounted in an architectural framework, that contained the Ten Commandments, and often the Apostles' Creed and the Lord's Prayer. Altarpieces were legally required fittings in all Anglican churches.

American bond. Brick bond in which three or more courses, or rows, of stretchers alternate with one course of headers. Also called common bond.

Bay. In timber framing, the interval between major structural members. Also used colloquially to describe the width of a building according to the number of openings on the facade; e.g., a church six windows and a door wide would be a seven-bay church.

Bolection. Molding that covers the joint between two surfaces and projects beyond both. The molding is usually heavy, with a complex profile.

Bond. Bricks interlocked inside a wall to create a unified structure. Brick bonds are named after the surface pattern of headers and stretchers created by the bonding.

Brown coat. Rough undercoat of plaster to which the finishing layer is applied.

Cabriole. In furniture, a leg with a double-, or S-, curved shape.

Cavetto. Concave quarter-round molding.

Chancel. The part of a church containing the altar. In Anglican churches, the chancel was traditionally set apart from the rest of the church in a separate, adjoining structure or distinguished visually by a screen or a low rail.

Church warden. Lay official responsible for day-to-day supervision of Anglican parish life. Each parish had two church wardens at a time.

Clapboard. Riven wall, ceiling, or roof cladding board, four to five feet long, usually applied by lapping the lower edge of each horizontal course over the upper edge of the course below it.

Clipped gable. A gable roof hipped near the apex.

Collar. Horizontal timber connecting a pair of rafters at a point between the feet and the apex.

Common bond. See *American bond.*

Compass. Colonial term for the curved part of an architectural element, as in compass ceiling, compass railing, compass-headed windows and doors.

Cross bond. Brick bond in which alternating rows of headers and stretchers are arranged so that the joints form regular, stepped diagonal patterns across the surface of the wall.

Cyma. Double-, or S-, curved molding.

Cyphered boards. Wall or roof-covering boards with beveled edges, which are laid flush.

English bond. Brick bond in which rows of headers alternate with rows of stretchers.

Entablature. In classical architecture, the horizontal group of moldings above the columns.

Flagon. In Anglican usage, a large vessel for holding communion wine. Flagons have handles, hinged covers, and often spouts.

Flemish bond. Brick bond in which alternating rows of headers and stretchers are staggered to produce a checkerboard pattern.

Font. Basin of stone, wood, or metal containing the water used in baptism.

Form. Backless bench.

Frontispiece. Technically the main entrance bay of a building, but used by 18th-century architectural writers to refer to an elaborately decorated, often pedimented doorway.

Gable roof. Roof in which two opposed planes meet at a ridge. The term *gable* also refers to the triangular or irregularly shaped portion of vertical wall bounded by the rafters of a gable roof.

Gadroon. Decoration used on buildings, furniture, and decorative objects consisting of a series of billowing convex lobes, or a two-dimensional representation of such curves.

Gallery. Church seating raised above the ground floor of the building; a balcony.

Girder. Major horizontal structural timber in a frame.

Girt. Traditional form of girder.

Glebe. The land set aside for the support of an Anglican minister. Most ministers lived on their glebes and farmed them, but some chose to rent the land out and collect the income. The term is also used colloquially to refer to the glebe house, the ministerial residence on the glebe.

Half-hip. See *Clipped gable.*

Header. In brickwork, the short end surface of a brick.

Hip roof. Roof in which at least two sloping planes are adjacent to one another. Most hip roofs have four sloping sides. The term *hip* is also employed as the name for the projecting edge where two planes of a hip roof meet.

Interlace. Carved or painted decoration on the surface of a molding depicting bands woven together. Also called *guilloche.*

Japanning. An Anglo-American decorative technique, imitative of Asian lacquer work, in which a base of several coats of varnish tinted dark red, black, or tortoise shell is embellished with painted, sometimes raised, pseudo-Asian designs.

Joist. Horizontal timbers to which floor or ceiling surfaces are attached.

King post. Vertical post in the center of a roof truss. It runs from the tie beam to the ridge of the roof, and the ends of the principal rafters are tenoned into it.

Lap joint. Simple joint in which one timber is set into a shallow recess in the face of another, and the two are fastened by a nail.

Mensa. Top stone slab of an altar.

Mortise and tenon joint. Joint in which a narrow tongue, or tenon, on one timber is fitted into a matching rectangular slot in another. Usually the two are secured with a pin, nail, or, in furniture, glue.

Mullion. Vertical bar dividing the lights, or openings, of a window. Usually the term *mullion* is reserved for the heavy wood or masonry stones of a multipart window, while *muntin* is used for the light wooden bars separating the lights of individual sashes.

Ogee. English alternate name for cyma, especially when applied to the profile of a roof or other three-dimensional architectural element.

Ovolo. Convex quarter-round molding.

Paten. In Anglican usage, a shallow circular plate, often footed, used to serve communion bread; sometimes also made to fit on the top of the chalice as a cover.

Pediment. Gable treated with moldings along all three sides; also a similar shape applied to a wall, usually over a door, window, or other architectural feature, as a decoration. Decorative pediments might be of many shapes, but Virginia church builders used only triangular and segmental pediments.

Pilaster. Shallow pier or square column, attached to a wall.

Plate. Horizontal timber at the top of a wall on which the rafters sit.

Post. Major vertical structural timber in a framed building.

Pulvinated. Convex: of swollen or cushion-like profile. The term is usually applied to a convex frieze.

Purlin. Horizontal roof timber, running parallel to the ground, in or just behind the plane of the roof's surface. The purlin is supported by the principal rafters and in turn supports the common rafters.

Queen post. Vertical post that connects the tie beam and the rafters in a roof truss and is located to one side or the other of the ridge.

Quoin. Stone or brick block set at the outer corner of an exterior masonry wall to reinforce it. Usually overscaled and treated as a decorative feature.

Rafter. Diagonal timbers running from the eave to the ridge of a roof. May be a *principal rafter*, serving a structural function similar to that of a post in a wall, or a *common rafter*, acting primarily as a nailing surface, in a manner analogous to a wall stud.

Rail. In wainscot work, the horizontal part of the frame enclosing a panel.

Raked/raking. Inclined, usually following the slope of a roof.

Ramped. A curve in a rail or a wall that increases its slope as it approaches a newel or a gate post.

Riven. Split, rather than sawn.

Saddle notching. In log construction, a form of corner notching, or joining, in which the ends of a log are hollowed out to accommodate the shapes of logs above or below it.

Salver. A flat tray or platter, often with a raised edge, placed under another vessel to catch spilled contents. In Anglican usage, a large paten.

Sheathing. Continuous covering of flush boards. On exterior walls or roofs, sheathing may serve as the base for an outer layer of shingles or boards; on interior walls, it is often exposed to view and treated decoratively.

Sill. Lower horizontal portion of a window frame or, in a building's frame, the horizontal supporting timber at the base of a wall.

Soffit. Horizontal undersurface of a molding; by extension, any exposed undersurface other than a ceiling.

Spandrel. The vertical surface on the side of a flight of stairs.

Stile. In joined work, the vertical parts of the frame enclosing a panel.

Stretcher. In brickwork, the long side of a brick. In furniture, a horizontal piece connecting the legs and serving to stiffen the frame.

Stud. Vertical, nonstructural member of a timber frame to which the interior and exterior cladding are nailed.

Throating. In brickwork, a course of beveled bricks immediately under the wooden sill of a window.

Tie beam. Timber connecting the feet of a pair of rafters.

Truss. Frame constructed entirely of members in tension and compression, designed to support a weight. Although walls and floors can be trussed, the builders of Virginia churches used trusses only in roof framing.

Type. The canopy over a pulpit; colloquially called a sounding board.

Undertaker. An individual who contracted, or undertook, to build a church, using his own or others' labor.

Vestry. The board of laymen who governed the affairs of an Anglican parish.

Wainscoting. In colonial Virginia terms, the construction of furniture or architectural decoration by means of panels held in mortised and tenoned frames. By extension, a wall covering of wainscot work.

Water table. The ledge in a masonry wall created by a reduction in thickness from the lowest portion of the wall to the portions above it. In Virginia churches, the water table might be located from six inches to four feet above the surface of the earth. It was normally decorated with specially shaped bricks, and the name *water table* is applied to this course of bricks.

Weatherboard. A sawn board, six to ten inches wide and ten to twenty feet long, applied to a wall in horizontal lapped courses.

Wind brace. A diagonal timber connecting a principal rafter and a purlin or several common rafters, used to stiffen a roof frame.

| Index |

Virginia Anglican churches are indexed by parish, other Virginia buildings by county or city, and all other buildings by state or country. Figure numbers are given in italics following page numbers.

Abingdon Parish, 3
  church, 81, 86, 88, 127; *1, 93, 94, 95, 124, 125, 137, 138*
    altarpiece, 122; *144, 147*
    font, 147; *183*
    pews, 181, 182; *214*
    pulpit, 248
Accomack Parish, 81, 186, 189; *3*
Acquinton church. *See* St. John's Parish
Addleshaw, G.W.O., 47
Afro-Americans. *See* Blacks
Albemarle County, *2*
  Belvoir, 213
  Monticello, 215–16, 222; *250, 251*
Albemarle Parish, 16, 19, 24, 34, 72, 105, 145, 193–94, 248; *3*
  church attendance in, 186
  Nottoway (St. Mark's) church, 16, 46, 170, 183, 190
  population of, 8, 254
  Spring Swamp (St. Andrew's) church, 170, 194, 233–34
Alexandria, 232
Allerton, Isaac, 166
Alms, 166. *See also* Charity; Poor
Altarpieces, 16, 98, 120–33, 159
  English, 55, 120
Altars, 50, 147. *See also* Chancel; Tables
Amelia County, 247; *2*
Anburey, Thomas, 165, 166, 167, 213, 252
Anderson, James, 19
Anglican Church
  changing position in Virginia, 231–32
  disestablishment, in Virginia, xviii
  establishment of, 4–5
  in England and Virginia, 5
  parishes, number of in Virginia, xiv
  political role, 4–5, 96–97
  services/liturgy in Virginia, xx, 9–10
  social services, 9, 220–22
Antrim Parish, 137, 142, 177; *3*
Apostles Creed: as wall text or altarpiece, 55, 97, 120
Aquia church. *See* Overwharton Parish
Architects. *See* Churches: design and designers
Architectural Setting of Anglican Worship (Addleshaw and Etchells), 47

Ariss, John, 34, 240
Arlington County, *2*
  Ball-Sellers house, 111–12; *129, 130*
Armistead, John, 183
Armstead, Henry, 22
Attendance, church, xx–xxi, 183–91, 193–94, 254; *tab. 6, tab. 7*
  dissenters', 189–90, 193–94
  gentry's, 188–89
  slaves', 189
Augusta County, 24; *2*
Augusta Parish, 159, 176; *3*
  population, 8
  Staunton church, 24, 43
Ayres, John. *See* Ariss, John

Bailey, Samuel, 27
Bailyn, Bernard, 27
Ball family, 153, 170, 222
Ball, John, 111
Ball, Joseph, 232
Balls (dances), 166, 219. *See also* Dancing
Balusters, 107–8, 242; *126, 127, 128*
Banqueting houses, 166, 252
Baptism, 50, 173, 190
Baptists, xviii, 189, 190, 193, 229
  use of Anglican churches, 235
  See also Dissenters; Evangelicalism
Baylye, Thomas, 186
Bell, John, 186
Bells, church, 21, 170, 183, 204, 251
Benches. *See* Seating, church
Bennet, Thomas, 162, 164
Berkeley, Edmond, 22, 226
Bermuda: Devonshire, church, 243
Beverley, Robert, 165, 171
Bibles, 138, 141–42, 248
Black, William, 186, 189
Blacks, and dance in Virginia, 219. *See also* Slaves
Blackstone, Argall, 110
Blair, James, 195
Bland, Theodorick, 181–82

Blandford church. *See* Bristol Parish

Blethyn, William, 25

Blisland Parish, 24, 147, 183, 221; 3
  Hickory Neck (lower) church, vii
  upper church, xiii
  vestry house, 203

Bolling, Robert, 181

Book of Common Prayer, 47, 102, 138, 141, 189

Booker, Richard, 181

Books, church, 141–42

Botetourt, Lord, 205

Braine, Sarah, 142, 154, 157

Brent, James, 26

Brick construction, 11, 38–39, 41

Bricklayers, 25

Brick making, 245

Brickwork, 103–4; *119, 120, 121*
  decorative, 104, 158–59
  English bond, 103–4
  Flemish bond, 104
  glazed, 104, 245
  water tables, 104; *122*

Brissot de Warville, Jean Pierre, 166

Bristol Parish, 16, 29, 36, 110, 177, 180, 181–82, 189, 238; 3
  Blandford church, 110, 229; *1, 75, 226*
    churchyard, 199–200; *227*
    private windows, 226
    seating, 181–82
  Flat Creek chapel, 181
  Nemussen's chapel, 177
  Sapponey chapel, 177

Broadcloth. *See* Textiles

Broadway, William, 203

Brookes, William, 120

Brunswick Parish: Lamb's Creek church, 91–92, 119, 170; *1, 107, 108*

Bruton Parish, 8, 180, 184, 194, 204, 248; 3
  first church, 31, 32
  second (1681–83) church, 15, 38–39, 61, 62–63, 73, 158, 170, 181; *15, 49*
    churchyard, 200–201
  third (1711–15) church, 24, 39, 41, 72, 77, 81–82, 84, 85, 96, 109, 142, 180, 232, 236, 243; *1, 81, 82, 228, 258*
    altarpiece, 128; *152*
    bell, 170
    churchyard, 201
    cost, 15
    design, 34
    governor's pew, 135
    organ, 250
    paintings in, 119–20
    proportional system, 31
    roof structure, 42; *19*

    tower, 29, 31, 72, 168
    seating dispute in, 195, 196

Brydon, George MacLaren, xiv

Buckingham Baptist church. *See* Tillotson Parish

Buckland, William, 26; workmen of, 26

Builders, 25. *See also* Bricklayers; Carpenters; Glaziers; Joiners; Undertakers; Workmen; and individuals' names

Builder's Dictionary, 43, 108, 117, 128
  use in Virginia, 246

Burges family, 222

Burial in church, 73, 181, 202, 244

Burnaby, Andrew, 167, 219

Byrd, William II, 14, 71, 167, 168, 173, 182, 204, 239
  church attendance, 189

Byrd, William III, 239

Callis, John Ariss, 26

Camden Parish, 36; 3

Camm, John, 6, 173

Caroline County, xiv; 2

Carpenters, 25

Carter family, 179, 189, 222, 247

Carter, Ben, 166

Carter, Charles, 26, 119, 182, 248, 249

Carter, John, 14, 246, 248

Carter, Landon, xx, 6, 26, 96, 164, 169, 172–73, 188, 205
  and Isaac William Giberne, 172, 173, 190
  and William Kay, 172–73
  and Jacob Townsend, 173

Carter, Robert "King," of Corotoman, 15, 151, 180, 181, 202, 213, 244
  church attendance, 188, 189

Carter, Robert, of Nomini Hall, 7, 202, 207, 214, 251

Cary, Henry, Sr., 23, 81

Cary, Henry, Jr., 23, 79, 82

Cary, Wilson, 183

Castiglioni, Luigi, 165, 215

Chalices, communion. *See* Plate

Chambers, Edward, Jr., 36

Chancel, 48, 50, 73, 76–77, 150, 202
  seating in, 181
  use, 48, 50, 73

Chancel rails, 50, 150

Chancel screens. *See* Screens

Chantry chapels, 48, 72, 175, 176

Chapman, Evans, Delehanty, Architects, 242

Charity, 166, 168. *See also* Alms; Poor

Charles City County, 2
  Kittiewan, 202
  Westover, 25, 173, 239, 241; *200, 201*

Charles Parish, 6, 249; 3

Chesterfield County, 112, 114; 2
  Perkinsons, 112; *131, 132*

Chesterfield County (continued)
    Wilson farm, 112; 133
Chests, 139–41, 249
    canonical regulations regarding, 140
    domestic, 140
    English, 139
Chew, Larkin, 25, 78
    career of, 24
Chew, Larkin, Jr., 239
Christ church, Alexandria. See Fairfax Parish
Christ church, Middlesex. See Christ Church Parish, Middlesex
        County
Christ Church Parish, Lancaster County, 186, 190; 3
    church, xxi, 29, 31, 46, 84, 88, 96, 213, 244, 247, 258; 1, 5, 90,
        123, 124, 229
        altarpiece, 122; 145, 146
        Carter pew, 179, 180, 181, 222, 253
        churchyard, 202
        cost, 15
        font, 143; 177
        as model for other churches, 29, 31, 84–86, 96
        pulpit, 133, 134, 137; 159, 164
        roof structure, 44, 241
        seating, 176, 177–78, 181, 253; 212, 213
        table, 151; 190
    plate, 193
    population, 8
Christ Church Parish, Middlesex County, 6, 11, 16, 19–22, 24, 31,
        42, 141, 150, 159, 170, 172, 176, 177, 178, 181, 183, 202, 221,
        222, 243; 3
    building process in, 19, 21–22; tab. 4
    first middle (mother, great) church, 19, 31, 32, 35
    second middle church, 16, 17, 21, 23, 69, 70, 72; 1, 60, 61, 70
        altarpiece, 120
        evolution of design, 21, 23, 75–76; tab. 4
        pews, 177
        private wing, 226
        screen, 74
    first lower (Piankatank) chapel, 19, 139
        chest, 139–40; 168, 169, 170
        seating dispute in, 195–96
    second lower chapel, 21–22, 69, 91, 139; 1, 62
        evolution of design, 21–22, 76–77; 71, tab. 4
        pews, 177
        private wing, 226
    first upper chapel, 19, 140, 181, 183
        plate, 170
        screen, 74
    second upper chapel, 19, 21, 24, 40, 69, 181; 69, tab. 4
        addition, 80
        altarpiece, 120
        churchyard wall, 199

        evolution of design, 24, 74–75
        screen, 74
    third upper chapel, 86
    plate, 154, 157, 170
    private wings in, 226, 258
    seating dispute in, 195–96
    textiles, 153
Chuckatuck church. See Suffolk Parish
Church building
    completing and receiving, 17–19
    contracts and specifications, 14, 26, 32
    costs, 15–16, 32, 249
    cycles, 11, 13; 4
    disputes, 13–14
    drawings, 32–34
    financing, 15–17, 238
    frequency, 11
    legislation regarding, 5
    siting, 13–14
    time to build, 16
Church of England. See Anglican Church
Church wardens
    duties, 7, 169, 179, 180, 195, 220, 251
    origins, 7
Churches, Virginia
    additions and enlargements, 8
    attendance. See Attendance
    decoration, 35, 86, 114, 119, 142, 158
        and domestic decoration, 180, 214
        in England, 50
        exterior, 158, 214
        interior, 159
    decorative painting, 26, 114, 119–20
    dedications, 170
    design and designers, 27–29
        gentlemen architects, 27, 34
        relation to European ideas, 27–28
    exterior covering, 103
    finish, exterior, 103–5, 110
    finish, interior, 105–10, 177, 191–92
    furnishings, legal requirements for, 139
    as houses, 164, 192, 229, 231
    materials, 11, 35–39, 103, 105
    naming practices, 170
    paint colors, 103, 108
    paint, exterior, 103
    paint, interior, 108
    plans, English, 47–50, 56
        auditory, or room, 56, 77
        evolution, 47–50
        medieval, 47–48
        nave and chancel, 56, 72

Churches, Virginia (continued)
    parts, 48–50
    Wren plans, 56–57
  plans, Virginia, 56–96; 117
    cruciform, 80–89; 80, 117
    deep, 91–94; 117
    double-aisle, 94–95, 254; 114, 117
    enlarging, 78–89
    evolution of, 65–70, 96, 199, 243
    meaning, 96–97
    nave-and-chancel, 57
    room, 57
    south-entry, 91–93; 106, 117
    T, 78–80; 117
    use, 77, 96–97
  proportional systems, 31
  shutters, 204
  use by other denominations, 235
  useful life, 11, 35
Churchill, Armistead, 226
Churchyards, 199–205, 214, 220
  burial in, 201–3, 256
  as gathering places, 204–5
  legal requirements for, 199
  secular uses, 204, 256
  size, 199
  walls, 199–201
City and Country Builder's and Workman's Treasury of Designs
    (Langley), 130, 132, 133, 145, 147, 248; 154, 155, 166, 179, 180
Civility, religion and, 4–5
Claiborne, Augustine, 183
Clapboards, 103, 105, 110, 112
  on ceilings, 105, 110; 25
  on floors, 110
  on roofs, 103, 111
Clark, John, 21, 238
Classicism, 108–9, 229. *See also* Orders, classical
Clergy
  appointment of, 5
  and gentry, 171–73
  impostors, 172
  position of, in Anglican theology, 47
  quality of, xix
  salaries, 171–72
  social position of, 171–73
Clerks, parish, 7
Clive, John, 27
Coles, Isaac A., 232
Collier, John, 221
Colonial Williamsburg Foundation, xxi
Communion (service), 166; 192
  as meal, 153, 164

  attendance at, 186
  meaning, 164
Compass elements, 62, 110, 117–18
  ceilings, 110, 114, 229
    structure of, 44, 46; 25
  doorways, 114
  meaning, 114, 117–18
  windows, 62, 114, 117
Coney, John, 250
Contractors. *See* Undertakers
Cooke, Richard, 26, 119, 120, 133, 248
Cooper, Appollis, 34
Copein, William, 26, 147
Cople Parish, 6, 169, 171, 189; 3
  Nomini church, 202
  Yeocomico church, 46, 65, 69, 70, 72, 122, 158; 1, 25, 57, 58,
    127, 225
    font, 145, 147; 178
    porch, 71, 158; 59
    sundial, 232
    table, 150–51; 188
Corbin, Henry, 153, 181, 183, 250, 252
Corbin, Richard, 187
County court: power in Church, 6
Courthouses, 205–6, 214, 220
  plans, 205
Creeke, Alice Corbin, 250
Creeke, Henry, 153, 170, 250
Cresswell, Nicholas, 219
Crosses (crucifixes), 118–19
Cumberland Parish, 11, 24, 182, 222, 237, 238; 3
Cupboards: in churches, 140
Cups, communion. *See* Plate
Curtis, James, 23
Cushions, 152
Custis, John, Jr., 183

Dade, Townshend, 180
Daingerfield, Edward, 26
Dale, Edward, 194
Dancing, 219, 231
  African origins, 219
Daniell, Alice, 221
Davies, Horton, xx, 102, 119, 163
Davies, Nicholas, 225, 226
Davis, Vernon Perdue, xx
Dawson, Thomas, 6, 190
DeButts, Lawrence, 186
DeGernett, Daniel, 222
Delaware
  Broad Creek, Christ church, 94, 253
  Middletown, St. Anne's church, 94; 113

Delaware (*continued*)
Odessa, Old Drawers church, 93–94; *112*
Designs (Langley). See *City and Country Builder's and Work-man's Treasury of Designs*
Deskin, John, 23
Dettingen Parish, 16, 17, 18, 23; *3*
Broadrun chapel, 32
Cedar Run church, 222
Quantico church, 18–19, 32
gallery, 226
Dewey, Stephen, 181
Dining as a social ritual, 164, 166, 173
Dissenters, 189–94, 228, 229
Anglican attitudes toward, 189–90
effect on Anglican attendance, 193–94
social views of, 190–91, 228
See also Baptists; Methodists; Presbyterians; Quakers
Dixon, Roger, 179
Donation, 170–71, 183, 250
Doom paintings, 119
Doorways, 70–71, 159
compass, 114
evolution of, 61
location of, 71–72, 96; *106*
Drawings, architectural. *See* Church building: drawings
Drysdale, Hugh, 24
Duning, Samuel, 35
Dunlap, William, xx, 173
Durand de Dauphiné, 214

Eastern Shore chapel. *See* Lynnhaven Parish
Edwards, Isham, 113
Edwards, John, 113, 114, 192
Egalitarianism, 167
Elizabeth City Parish, 6, 13, 183, 194; *3*
church, 23, 82, 84, 183; *1, 83, 84, 85*
poorhouse, 221
population of, 8
Elizabeth River Parish, 183; *3*
plate, *106*
poorhouse, 221; *255*
St. Paul's church, 82, 128, 180; *1, 86, 87*
England
Badley, Suffolk, St. Mary's church, 29, 209
Cerne Abbas, Dorset, St. Mary the Virgin church, *31, 32*
Chesterton, Hunts., St. Michael's church, 145
Croscombe, Somerset, St. Mary the Virgin church, 74; *27, 35, 163*
Foremark, Derbys., church, 39
Greensted-juxta-Ongar, Essex, St. Andrew's church, 56
London
Christ church, Spitalfields, 42

St. Martin's in the Fields, *41*
March, Cambs., St. Wendreda church, 114; *135*
North Runcton, Norfolk, All Saints church, 52, 60, 114, 140, 145; *37, 173, 181*
Puddletown, Dorset, St. Mary's church, 28, 33
Rye, Sussex, church, 26
Shelland Green, Suffolk, King Charles the Martyr church, 56, 60, 114; *38*
Shropshire, Langley chapel, *40*
Terrington St. Clement, Norfolk, church, 34, 36
Warbleton, East Sussex, St. Mary's church, 257
Winterborne Tomson, Dorset, St. Andrew's church, 74; *30*
Essex County, 189; *2*
Blandfield, 219
courthouse, 24
Elmwood, xviii
Etchells, Frederick, 47
Eucharist. *See* Communion
Evangelicalism, xviii, 189–94, 228
appeal to slaves, 189
See also Dissenters
Ewen, John, 26

Fairfax County, 93; *2*
Gunston Hall, 26
Mount Vernon, 26, 166, 207–8, 215
Fairfax, George William, 179, 226
Fairfax Parish, 16, 42, 131–32, 159, 203, 229, 258; *3*
Alexandria (Christ) church, 16, 19, 34, 71, 89, 94, 189, 229, 231, 232, 258; *1, 158, 261*
altarpiece, 128, 130, 132; *153*
doorway, 132; *157*
gallery, 227–28
pulpit, 133–34, 137, 248; *165*
seating, 182–83, 226
Falls church, 34, 71, 133, 180, 229; *1, 104, 105*
altarpiece, 128, 132, 248; *150*
doorway, 132; *156*
vestry house, 203
Farnham church. *See* North Farnham Parish
Fashion, 228–29, 245
defined, 229
See also Mode; Style
Fences, 200–201, 256
Fenestration, evolution of, 71
Field, Thomas, 25
Fithian, Philip, xx, 166, 167, 171, 188, 189, 202, 204, 206, 214, 219, 231
Fitzhugh, William, 153, 170
Floors, 105
Fonts, 50, 142–47, 159; *179*
canonical regulations, 50
English, 142–43

Fonts (continued)
  location, 48, 142
  replaced by bowls, 142
Forbes, Alexander, xx, 193, 239
Fork church. See St. Martin's Parish
Forms. See Seating, church
Fox family, 222
Fox, David, 121, 171
Fox, William, 121, 143
Frame construction, 11, 35–38, 40, 41–46; 8
  Virginia system, 40; 8, 16
  See also Post construction; Roof structures
Frazer, William, 25
Frederick Parish, 6, 31, 34, 36, 105, 141, 180, 248; 3
  poorhouse, 221; 253
  population, 8
Fredericksburg, 219
Fredericksville Parish, 13, 32, 40, 41; 3
French, Daniel, 14–15, 26

Gables, shaped, 62, 63, 64, 158
Gaines, Harry, 177, 186, 239
  career, 24–25
Gaines, Henry, 24, 80
Galleries, xix, 72, 183, 222, 226
  organ, 222, 250
  private, 183, 222, 224
Galt, Gabriel Williamson, 119
Gambling, 168
Garvan, Anthony N. B., 250
Gates, Thomas, 152
General Assembly, 15
  interventions in parishes, 13, 19, 169
  role in Virginia Church, 6
Gentleman, concept of, 167–68
Gentlemen architects. See Churches: design and designers
Gentry, 229–30
  and Church, xviii–xix
  duties to parish, 170, 227–28
  lower-class deference toward, 220
  relations with one another, 167–68, 172–73, 195
Gerrard, Thomas, 166
Gibbs, James, 56, 229
Gibbs, John, Jr., 247
Giberne, Isaac William, 96, 172, 173, 190
Gifts. See Donation
Glaziers, 25
Glebe church. See Suffolk Parish
Glebe houses, 24, 26, 34, 35, 172
Gloucester County, 3
  Rosewell, xix, 133, 246, 248
Gooch, William, 6, 14

Goochland County, 3
  Tuckahoe, 165, 166, 167, 252
Good neighborhood, 165. See also Hospitality
Gordon, James, 182, 188, 190, 192–93
Governor, 236
  intervention in parishes, 13–14
  power in Virginia Church, 5–6
Gowans, Alan, 29, 244, 247, 258
Grave markers, 119; 142
Graves, Alexander, 21, 32
Great Awakening, 228
Grove, William Hugh, 165, 214
Grubhill church. See Raleigh Parish
Grymes, Benjamin, 181
Grymes, John, 21, 120, 157, 226
Guttridge, Severn, 23, 34, 239

Hadfield, Joseph, 219
Hamor, Ralph, 5, 57
Hampton Roads, 111
Handbooks, architectural. See Pattern books
Hanover County, 24; 2
Hardy, George, 110
Harrison, Carter Henry, 226
Harrower, John, 203, 207, 214
Harvey, John, 60
Hay, Anthony, 239
Hayward, Nicholas, 170
Hazard, Ebenezer, 219
Hegemony, 163
Henderson, Alexander, 226
Henrico County, 180, 190–91; 2
Henrico Parish, 168, 177, 180; 3
  church siting, 14
  Curl's church, 32
  population, 8
  St. John's church, 14, 36, 38, 117; 1, 13, 14
    pulpit, 133, 134, 137; 161
    roof structure, 22
  Williamson's church, 170
Henrico Town: church in, 5, 57, 236
Henry, Patrick (minister), 34
Hickory Neck church. See Blisland Parish
Hipkins, John, Sr., 21, 23, 26, 76
Hoggard, Thomas, 225
Holladay, Anthony and Esther, 170
Holme, Randle, 108
Holy Communion. See Communion
Hooker, Richard, 47, 48, 164, 170, 180
Horseblocks, 203–4
Horses: importance to gentry, 203
Hospitality, 162, 165–73, 183, 196

Hospitality (*continued*)
  and church, 166–73
  domestic, 165–68, 169, 173
  and salvation, 166
House, Lawrence, 19
House of God, 164
Houses, 110–14, 205–18
  decoration, 160, 191, 214
  interior finish, 111–14
  outbuildings, 210–11, 214
  owners' economic standing, 212–13
  plantation: in landscape, 206–11, 213, 215
    processional arrangement, 206–8, 214
    room use, 207–8
    social and economic functions, 214
    as villages, 214–15
  size, 111–13
  spatial use, 206–12, 218
Howel, Sam, 25
Hughes, Will, 32–33
Hungar's Parish, 183, 250; 3
  Bible, 141–42; 173
  1681 church, 183
  1742 church, vii, 77, 183, 194
Hunter, Richard, 189, 219
Hunter, William, 141

Ideology, 163, 164
  and symbolism, 163–64
Ingraham, James, 25
Ingram, Hiram, 232
Isaac, Rhys, 120, 228
Isle of Wight County, 166, 189, 192; 2
  Edwards house, 113–14, 192; 134, 244, 245, 246
  Joseph Jordan farmstead, 243
  landholding in, 235

Jackson, Thomas, 14, 29
James City County, 24; 2
  Green Spring, 189
James City Parish, 3
  church attendance in, 184
  font, 142–43, 147; 175
  plate, 160, 162; 203, 204
  population, 8
  1610 church, 57, 59
  1639 church, 60, 62
  1680 church, xiii, 62; 1, 50
    date, 62
    tower, 72; 66
Jamestown, 152, 169, 205, 228, 244
  first settlers' church, 4, 175

Jamestown church. *See* James City Parish
Jarratt, Devereux, xx, 220
Jefferson, Thomas, 215–16
Jennings, Edmund, 81
Johnson, Jacob, 44
Joiners, 25
Jones, Ann, 195–96, 256
Jones, E. Alfred, 250
Jones, Emmanuel, 186
Jones, Hugh, 165, 203, 236, 250
Jones, Humphrey, 170
Jones, James, 23, 205, 257
Jones, John, 34

Kay, William, 172–73
Keeling, William, 224
Keller, Abraham, 36
Kemp, Matthew, 6, 195–96, 256
Kempe, James, 225
Kercheval, Samuel, 114
Kimball, Fiske, xxi, xxii, 27
Kimber, Edward, 165, 166
King and Queen County, 187, 206; 2
  courthouse, 24
King William County, 167, 188; 2
  courthouse, 235
  Sweet Hall, 44
Kinked, David, 32
Kirks, Scots, 78–79, 243, 258
Knott, James, 238
Kocher, A. Lawrence, 81

Lamb's Creek church. *See* Brunswick Parish
Lancaster County, 166, 182, 193; 2
  Corotoman, 213
  courthouse, 23, 205, 257; 233
Landscape, xiii, xix
  appreciation of, 215
  articulated, 214, 227
  and civility, 5
  dynamic quality, 199, 205–18, 219–20, 222, 231–32
  poor whites', 215
  processional, 214
  slaves', 215
  social function, 214–18, 227
  and time, 213
  vistas, 215
Langfier, Gawan, 26
Langley, Batty, 130, 137, 229, 248
Latrobe, Benjamin Henry, xiii, xiv, 165, 207, 208, 215, 247
Laud, William, 50, 75
Lawne's Creek Parish, 8; 3

Laws of Ecclesiastical Polity, Of the (Hooker), 47
Lee, John, 166
Lee, Thomas, 6
Lee, William, 189
Lee Parish. *See* Wicomico Parish
Legrand, Peter, 23, 26
Levy, parish. *See* Taxation
Lightfoot, Phillip, 35
Linens. *See* Textiles
Little Fork church. *See* St. Mark's Parish
Log construction, 36
Lord's Prayer, as wall decoration or altarpiece, 55, 97, 120; *33, 34*
Lord's Supper. *See* Communion
Loudoun County, 190; *2*
Louisa County, 24, 191; *2*
    Providence Presbyterian church, 40, 41, 191–92, 255; *1, 17, 218,*
        219, 220, 221, 222, 223
      plate, 192; *224*
Lower United Methodist church. *See* Christ Church Parish,
    Middlesex County: second lower chapel
Ludlow, Philip, 195
Lunenburg Parish, 84, 171, 172, 173, 190; *3*
Lynnhaven Parish, 141, 169, 225; *3*
    Eastern Shore chapel, 31, 114, 157
      cost, 249
      hanging pews, 224
      private windows, 226
    Old Donation church, 104, 122, 157, 257; *1*
      font, 147; *185*
      hanging pews, 222, 224
      private windows, 225; *259, 260*
      seating dispute, 194, 196, 224
    1691 parish church, 42, 44
      hanging pews, 222
      pews, 178
    plate, 156, 157; *196*
    Pungo chapel, 32, 41, 157, 177
    seating dispute in, 194–95, 196, 224
Lyon, Walter, 225

Macaulay, Alexander, 165, 218
McKenzie, Alexander, 183
MacSparran, Alexander, 188, 194
Madison, James (bishop), xiii, xviii, 9
Malbone, Peter, 157
Mangohick church. *See* St. Margaret's Parish
Martin's Brandon Parish, 3
    glebe, 172
    Merchant's Hope church, 71, 109, 117; *1, 64, 121, 123, 125, 140*
      roof structure, 43–44, 46; *24*

Maryland
    Anne Arundel County
      Cedar Park, 42, 241
      St. James's church, 94
    Easton, Third Haven Friends' meeting house, 79; *77*
    Quantico, Wicomico County, St. Paul's church, 94, 253; *115, 116*
      chest, 140; *171*
    Queen Anne's County, Cloverfields, 44
    Stepney Parish, 94, 253
Maryland Gazette, 14
Mason, George, 14, 26
Mason, George Carrington, xx
Massachusetts
    Boston, Christ church, 247
    Hingham, Old Ship church, 241
    Lynnfield, church, 241
Massey, Lee, 226
Master builders. *See* Churches: design and designers
Mattaponi Baptist church. *See* St. Stephen's Parish
Mayo, John, 225
Mead, David, 183
Meade, William, xviii–xx, 9, 85, 119, 188, 232, 253
Mechanick Exercises (Moxon), 43; *23*
Mercer, Eric, 27
Merchant's Hope church. *See* Martin's Brandon Parish
Meredith, William, 187
Methodists, xviii, 189, 229
    use of Anglican churches, 235
    See also Dissenters; Evangelicalism
Methodology, xxi
Michel, Franz Ludwig, 62, 200
Middlesex County, 24, 219, 252; *2*
    courthouses, 23
Mode, 102, 109, 142, 147, 157, 158, 159, 160, 163, 173, 191–93,
    228–29, 245
    defined, 102
    See also Fashion; Style
Modernization, 228
Moldings, 107; *123, 124, 125*
Monticello. *See* Albemarle County
Moore, John, 24, 147, 199
Mordecai, Samuel, xii, xiv, xviii, xix–xx, 216
Moreau de St. Mèry, Médéric-Louis-Élie, 74, 231, 243
Morris, James, 25
Morris, Samuel, 255
Morrison, Francis, 162
Moseley, Edward, Jr., 224
Moseley, Hilary, 222, 224
Mossom, David, xx, 141
Mount Vernon. *See* Fairfax County
Moxon, Joseph, 43

Muir, William, 25
Murfee, Samuel, 34

Nansemond County, 25, 189; 2. *See also* Suffolk
Nave, 48, 73
Nelson, William, Jr., 173
Netherland, John, 26
Netherland, Wade, 25, 26
New Kent County, xiii; 2
Newport Parish, 36, 61, 110, 180, 186; 3
    St. Luke's church, vii, 44, 59–62, 64–65, 70, 72, 104, 117, 158,
        180; *1, 43, 44, 45, 127, 136*
        date, 60–62, 64–65
        pulpit, 137
        restoration, 242
        roof structure, 42
        screen, 74
        wall painting, 120
Nicholson, Francis, 165, 166, 170, 250
Nomini Hall. *See* Westmoreland County
Norfolk, 180
Norfolk County, 2
    courthouse, 206, 257; *234*
North Farnham Parish, 3
    church, 84–85, *1, 91, 92*
Northampton County, 183, 2
    Pear Valley, 241
Nottoway Parish, 249; 3

Ohern, Lawrence, 26
Old Church United Methodist church. *See* Stratton Major parish:
        upper church
Old Donation church. *See* Lynnhaven Parish
Oman, Charles, 170
Orders, classical, 128, 137, 159, 192, 229. *See also* Classicism
Organs, 222, 250
Ornaments of the church
    definition, 139
    legal requirements for, 138
Overwharton Parish, 3
    Aquia church, 88–89, 107–8, 159, 238; *1, 96, 97, 98, 123, 124,
        125, 126, 262*
        altarpiece, 122; *149*
        burns, 17
        cost, 17
        gallery, 205
        pulpit, 133, 137; *160*
        seating, 177
    size, 8

Page County: Mauck's meeting house, 255
Page, Mann, 203, 248
Pain, William, 248
Parishes
    budget, 15–16, 22
    building cycles, 11–13; *4, tab. 2, tab. 3*
    establishment of, 8–9
    geographical size, 8
    population, 8–9
Parke, Daniel, 195
Parker, Clement, 34
Parker, Matthew, 55
Parsons, James, 19, 226
Pattern books, use in Virginia, 130, 132–33, 137, 147, 229, 248. See
        also *City and Country Builder's and Workman's Treasury
        of Designs*; Langley, Batty; Pain, William
Payne, Edward, 19, 92
Peacock, Samuel, 25, 133, 248
Pediments, 117, 118
Pendleton, Edmund, 110
Pennsylvania: Philadelphia, Christ church, 159, 189, 248; *199*
Perrott, Richard, Jr., 139–40, 181, 183, 221
Perry, Micajah, 15
Petersburg, xiii, 111
Petsworth Parish, 43, 141, 152–53; 3
    church attendance in, 184, 186
    1677 Poplar Spring church
        addition, 24, 78, 80
        decoration, 119
        porch, 71
        pulpit, 133
        screen, 74, 243
        structure, 35, 42
    1721 Poplar Spring church, 70, 117
        altarpiece, 133
        cost, 15
        organ gallery, 222, 250
        painting, 26, 114, 119–20, 247, 248
Pevsner, Nikolaus, 60
Pews, 175–83
    communicants', 181
    defined, 176
    hanging, 222–24, 228
    private, 181–83, 195, 222
    tied to houses, 183
    types, 177
    See also Seating, church
Pewter. *See* Plate
Piankatank church. *See* Christ Church Parish, Middlesex County:
        first lower chapel
Pinchback, Thomas, 36

Plate, 143, 153–58, 160, 162, 170–72, 192
    alms basins, 154
    bowls, 170
    chalices, 153
    cups, 153, 157, 192
    defined, 153, 156
    domestic, 156
    flagons, 154, 156, 170
    gifts, 157, 170–72
    inscriptions, 162, 170
    patens, 154, 156, 157, 170, 250
    plates, 154, 156
    salvers, 156
    significance, 153
    sources, 157, 250
    tankards, 156
    tumblers, 192
Pohick church. *See* Truro Parish
Poor
    badges for, 220
    legal control of, 220
    relations with gentry, 220
    relief, 220–22
Poorhouses, 34, 221–22
Porches, 71–72
Portsmouth Parish, 16; 3
    church, 41
        screen, 74
    scandal in, 18
Post construction, 19, 35–36; 8
    block, 35–36
    earthfast, 35
    interrupted-sill, 35, 241
    See also Frame construction
Powell, Benjamin, 29
Powell, Thomas, 119, 120
Poythress, William, 202
Preaching, xx
Preeson, Thomas, 183
Presbyterians, 189–90, 219, 229, 255
    in Lancaster County, 182, 193
    Scots, 79
    use of Anglican churches, 235
    See also Dissenters; Evangelicalism
Price, Richard, 194
Prince Edward County, 23; 2
Prince George County, 239; 2
Prince William County, 93; 2
Princess Anne County, 219; 2
Processioning, 7
Pryer, Robert, 35
Pulpits, xviii, 50, 120, 133–38, 159, 163

    canonical regulations, 50
    placement, 133, 248, 254
    types (sounding boards), 134–35, 137, 163, 248
Pungoteague church. *See* St. George's Parish, Accomack County
Pye, David, 107

Quakers, 189, 190, 193
    meeting houses, 190–91
    See also Dissenters

Raleigh Parish: Grubhill church, xix
Rand, William, 23–24, 25, 222, 239
Randall, John, 26
Randolph family, 166, 167
Ravenscroft, John, 16–17, 238, 239
Rawlings, James Scott, vii, xx, 243, 253
Readers, parish, 7
Reformation, English, 47, 175
Reid, James, 164, 167, 168, 188, 219, 220
Richards, Mourning, 17, 88, 238
Richmond County, 24; 3
    courthouse, 26
    Mount Airy, 206, 208, 210, 213, 214, 215, 216–18, 246; 237, 238, 239, 240, 252
    Sabine Hall, 172, 173
Riddick, Lemuel, 183
Ridley, Nicholas, 147
Riley, Patrick, 232
Robertson, George, 189
Robinson, Christopher, 35
Robinson, John, 157
Robinson, John (Speaker), 25, 187
Robinson, William, 224
Rochefoucault Liancourt, duke de La, 168, 190
Roof structures, 41–44
    clasped-purlin, 41, 241; 18
    common rafter, 41; 17
    king-post, 42–44, 241; 20, 21, 22, 23
    principal-rafter, 41–42, 242
Royal Arms, 55, 74, 163
    in courthouses, 205
    legal requirements for, 56
    rationale, 55–56, 97–98
Rutman, Darrett and Anita, 22

Sabine Hall. *See* Richmond County
Sackett, James M., 101
St. Andrew's Parish, 13, 16, 24, 57–58, 177, 183; 3
St. Anne's Parish, Albemarle County, xiv; 3
    Walker's church, 213
St. Anne's Parish, Essex County, xx; 3
    Vauter's church, xviii, 80, 117; 1, 73, 74

St. Asaph's Parish, 3
   church, xiv, 110
St. David's Parish, 3
   Cattail church, vii
St. George's Parish, Accomack County, 23, 220; 3
   church attendance in, 187–88
   parish church, 77, 253; 215
      seating, 182
   poorhouse, 34, 221
   seating plans, 180, 182
   Pungoteague church, vii, 81
St. George's Parish, Spotsylvania County, 13–14, 40, 110, 153, 179,
      180, 181; 3
   Fredericksburg (Rappahannock) church, 41, 181
      fence, 256
      organ, 250
   Mattapony church, 24, 41
      fence, 256
St. James-Northam Parish, 141; 3
St. John's church, Chuckatuck. See Suffolk Parish
St. John's church, Hampton. See Elizabeth City Parish
St. John's church, Richmond. See Henrico Parish
St. John's Parish, 3
   lower (St. John's) church, 229; 1, 48, 139
      altarpiece, 128, 130; 144, 151
      font base, 145; 182
      pulpit, 248
   upper (Acquinton) church, 188
St. Luke's church. See Newport Parish
St. Margaret's Parish, 3
   Mangohick church, 72; 1, 67, 68, 128
St. Mark's Parish, 32, 110, 117, 180, 222; 3
   Germanna church, burned, 14
   Little Fork chapel, 249
   Little Fork church, 92, 170; 1, 109, 110, 123
      altarpiece, 122; 148
St. Martin's Parish, 3
   Fork church, 1, 123, 127
      font, 147; 187
      roof structure, 20
      seating, 181
      table, 150–51; 189
St. Mary's Parish, 250; 3
St. Mary's White Chapel Parish, 15, 85–86, 153, 183, 196; 3
   church, 23, 190, 257; 1
      altarpiece, 120–21, 122, 171; 143, 144, 208
      communion cloth, 170
      font, 143, 249; 176
      private galleries, 222; 256
   population, 8
   seating dispute in, 194, 196
St. Patrick's Parish, 23, 34, 156, 194, 226, 238; 3

St. Paul's church, Norfolk. See Elizabeth River Parish
St. Paul's Parish, Hanover County, 25, 177, 180, 186, 199, 222; 3
   glebe house, 24, 26, 34
   Hanover Town church, 86, 88
   lower church, 79, 82
   population, 8
   upper (Slash) church, 36, 38; 1, 9, 10, 125, 127
St. Paul's Parish, Stafford (King George) County, 3
   church, 80, 88–89; 1, 99, 100
      advertisement for, 14
St. Peter's Parish, xx, 141, 180, 204–5; 3
   first lower church, 36
   font base, 249
   glebe houses, 35
   second lower (St. Peter's) church, 63–65, 158, 238, 243; 1, 51,
      52, 53, 54, 55, 56
      churchyard, 199, 201, 204–5
      design, 29
      drawings, 32–33
      seating, 176
      site, 14
      tower, 24, 34, 72, 168; 230, 231
   upper church, 36
St. Stephen's Parish, 3
   lower (Mattaponi) church, 84; 1, 63, 88, 89
      altarpiece, 121; 144
      font, 147; 186
Salmon, William, 108
Salvation, 166
   and hospitality, 166
Sayer, Charles, 225
Schapiro, Meyer, 101
Schoepf, Johann David, 165, 166, 215
Scotland: Moray, Drainie kirk, 76
Scott, James, 8
Screens, 35, 73, 74, 76, 243
   English, 48, 50, 74, 179
Sears, William Bernard, 26, 133
Seating, church, 175–83, 191
   by age, 180
   assignments, 179–82, 187–88
   benches, 176, 178
   competition for, 222–28
   disputes, 194–96
   forms, 176
   location, 179, 181, 182, 222
   medieval, 175
   for public, 180
   purchase of, 226–28, 258
   by sex, 180
   social implications, 179–80, 182, 187–94, 196, 220
   by status, 179–80

Selden, John, 6
Sermon books, 141
Sermons, xx
Sextons, 7
Shelburne Parish, 34, 89, 141; 3
  building dispute, 13
  glebe house, 34
Shingles, 103
Sign, and symbol, 163
Silver, church. See Plate
Skelton, James, 71
Skyren, Henry, 188
Slash church. See St. Paul's Parish, Hanover County
Slaves, 167, 188, 208, 218
  attendance at Anglican churches, 189, 194
  as builders, 25, 26
  and evangelicals, 189, 193
  landscape of, 215, 217–18
  seating in church, 181, 218
  social standing among dissenters, 190
  See also Blacks
Smith, Augustine, 152
Smith, Charles, 31
Smith, Francis, 24, 159
Smith, Captain John, 4, 175
Smith, John, 180
Smyth, J.F.D., 111, 167
Society of Friends. See Quakers
Socker (sermon writer), 141
Southam Parish, 36, 42, 156; 3
  Ham chapel, private wing at, 226
Southwark Parish, 8, 139, 249; 3
  Cypress church, 41, 238
  lower church, 117, 247; 1, 65
    wall painting, 120, 247
Spotswood, Alexander, 14, 15, 24, 180
  and Bruton Parish church, 34, 81
Spotsylvania County, xiv, 24, 203; 2
  Snow Creek plantation, 203
Stables, 204
Stark, William, 181
State furniture, 135
Statues, in churches, 50
Stith, Buckner, 183
Stith, Elizabeth, 120, 139
Stith, William, 168, 183
Stone, 104, 105
Strachey, William, 57, 59
Stratton Major Parish, 24, 180, 188; 3
  1760–67 parish church, 25, 42, 77, 94, 173, 186–87, 192, 236; 216
    seating pattern, 186–87; 217
  church attendance in, 186–87

organ, 250
poorhouse, 221; 254
upper (Old Church United Methodist) church, 1, 120
Stringer, John, 120
Style, 101–14, 142, 158, 159, 191–93, 228
  change in, 109
  defined, 101
  function, 101, 110
  preferences, 109–10
  See also Fashion; Mode
Suffolk: King house, 147, 148. See also Nansemond County
Suffolk Parish, 32, 220, 221; 3
  lower (Glebe) church, 177; 1, 78, 80
    addition, 80, 177
  upper (St. John's, Chuckatuck) church, 34, 44–45, 170; 1
Surplices. See Vestments
Surry County, 42; 2
  Bacon's Castle, 42, 63
  James house, 241, 242
  landholding in, 235
Symbol, and sign, 163
Symbolism, 163–64, 228, 229, 231–32
  and artifacts, 164, 229, 231
  domestic, 164, 229, 231
  and ideology, 163
  and meaning, 163
  and metaphor, 163

Tables, 147–51, 152
  English, 50; 28
  joined, 150–51
  legal requirements for, 150
  materials, 150
Tankards. See Plate
Tar, 103
Tarpley, James, 170
Taxation, 6, 7, 15–16
  size of levy, 15–16
Tayloe, John, 173, 207, 213, 214
Ten Commandments, as wall text or altarpiece, 55, 97, 120, 171
  legal requirements for, 55
  rationale, 97
Terry, Joseph, 137
Textiles, 141, 151–53, 157, 249
  cost, 152–53, 249
  domestic, 152, 160; 191
  linens, 152
  thefts of, 153, 249
  velvet, 152, 153
Thilman, Paul, 86
Thirty-Nine Articles, 166
Thomas, Simon, 183

Thorowgood family, 194
Tillett, John, 81
Tillotson, John, 141
Tillotson Parish, 3
    parish (Buckingham Baptist) church, vii, 36; *1, 11, 12, 125, 127*
    roof structure, 20
    seating, 176, 181, 210, 211
Timber framing. *See* Frame construction; Roof structures
Tithables: defined, 7. *See also* Taxation
Toulmin, Harry, 111
Towers, bell, 72
Townsend, Jacob, 173
Trent, Alexander, 225
Truro Parish, 11, 34, 159, 179, 180, 200, 226, 229; *3*
    glebe house, 26
    Payne's church, 19, 92, 132, 137, 170; *111*
    first Pohick church, 36
        vestry house at, 203
    second Pohick church, 14–15, 26, 32–33, 36, 43, 89, 94, 110,
        180, 189, 229; *1, 6, 101, 102, 103, 263*
        altarpiece, 132–33, 159
        churchyard, 200
        fonts, 147; *184, 187*
        pulpit, 137, 248; *166*
        sale of pews, 226–27
Tucker, St. George, 220
Turner, Victor, 163

Undertakers, 14, 23–29, 32
    as businessmen, 26–27
    as designers, 29
    identity, 23, 26
    social status, 26
    trades, 25
    typical careers, 24–25
    vestrymen as, 23
Upper Parish, Isle of Wight County, 193, 226; *3*
Upper Parish, Nansemond County, 11, 31, 36, 81, 183; *3*
    Suffolk church, 32

Vause, John, 256
Vauter's church. *See* St. Anne's Parish, Essex County
Veale, George, 18
Velvet. *See* Textiles
Vernacular threshold, 11
Vestments, 139, 153, 248, 250
Vestry, 168–70
    composition of, 6
    dissenters serve on, 190
    duties of, 6, 168–69
    evolution of, 6–7
    prerogatives, 235

prosecution of, 6
Vestry houses, 25, 168, 203
Virginia Gazette, 29, 153, 172, 205
    advertisements in, 14, 17, 18, 25, 183, 237, 239, 249

Waddell, James, 190
Waite, William, 18–19, 32, 226
Walke family, 194
Walker, Thomas, 213, 225
Walker, William, 24, 25, 34
Wall, John, 46, 72
Wall paintings, 35
    English, 50
Wall texts, 120, 163
    English, 50, 55, 56, 120
Waller, Hardress, 32
Ware Parish, 249; *3*
    church, 77, 94, 244; *1, 72, 124*
Warrington, Thomas, 6
Washington family, 202
Washington, George, xiii, 15, 111, 141, 165, 166, 182–83, 207, 214,
        226, 258
    church attendance, 188–89
Washington Parish, 186; *3*
    Lower Mattox church, 153
Waterman, Thomas Tileston, xxi, 34, 240
Weatherboards, 103; *118*
Wedgwood, Josiah, 229
Wells, 204
Wenger, Mark, 239
Westmoreland County, 24; *2*
    Nomini Hall, 166, 167, 183, 190, 206, 213, 214; *236*
    Stratford Hall, 241
Weston, William, 203
Westover Parish, 71, 200; *3*
    plate, 142, 154, 156; *174, 195*
    Westover church, *1*
Wheatly, Charles, 47
Whiffen, Marcus, 31
Whitewash, 108
Wicomico (Lee) Parish, 232; *3*
    first church, 71, 159, 190
    second church, 15, 17–18, 29, 31, 32, 72, 86, 109, 232
        cost, 15
        1753 project for, 15, 17, 86
    levy size, 16
    plate, 206
    population, 8
    textiles, 153
Wilkinson, Cary, 189
Wilkinson, Thomas, 165

Williamsburg, xxi, 141, 157, 168, 169, 180, 183, 190, 195, 204, 218
    Capitol, 23, 24, 206, 246
    College of William and Mary, xviii, 180
       college chapel, vii, 23
       main building ("Wren Building"), 246
    Governor's Palace, 23
Willie, William, 183, 186, 193–94
Wily, John, 17–18, 19, 32
Windows, private, 225–26, 228
Wings, private, 226, 258
Women
    attendance at church, 188
    seating in church, 186, 188, 194
    as sextons, 7
Wood, Thomas, 238

Woodward, John, 19
Workmen, 25–26
    cost, 239
Wormeley, Christopher, 195–96
Wormeley, Ralph, 226
Wren, Christopher, 56–57, 101, 188
Wren, James, 34, 132, 180, 248

Yates, Bartholomew, 172
Yeocomico church. *See* Cople Parish
York, George, 165
York (Yorkhampton) Parish, 110, 172; 3
    Grace church, vii
    plate, 154; *194*
Yorktown, 165